Harry Smith's Last Throw

Harry Smith's Last Throw

THE EIGHTH FRONTIER WAR
1850–1853

Keith Smith

Foreword by Ian Knight

FRONTLINE BOOKS, LONDON

FRONTLINE BOOKS, LONDON

Harry Smith's Last Throw: The Eighth Frontier War, 1850–1853

This edition published in 2012 by Frontline Books, an imprint of
Pen & Sword Books Limited, 47 Church Street, Barnsley, S. Yorkshire, S70 2AS
www.frontline-books.com

ISBN: 978-1-84832-646-0

CIP data records for this title are available from the British Library
and the Library of Congress

For more information on our books, please visit
www.frontline-books.com,
email info@frontline-books.com
or write to us at the above address.

Typeset by JCS Publishing Services Ltd, www.jcs-publishing.co.uk
Printed in Great Britain by CPI Group (UK) Ltd, Croydon, CR0 4YY

Contents

Maps and Illustrations

Map 1 was specially commissioned, and was created by Ken Thompson of North Plymton, South Australia. Maps 3, 7 and 27 are taken from Sir George Cathcart, *Correspondence*. The remaining maps were prepared by Ken Thompson, based on maps created by Neville Mapham.

Plates

Plates 1–11 and 13–16, courtesy of Ian Knight
Plates 12 and 17, courtesy of Africana Museum, Johannesburg
Plates 18–32, author's collection

Genealogical Tables

The tables on the following pages illustrate the various families of the Xhosa people. Readers will readily perceive the split between, first, Rharhabe and Gcaleka and, second, that of the Rharhabe between the Ngqika and the Ndlambe.

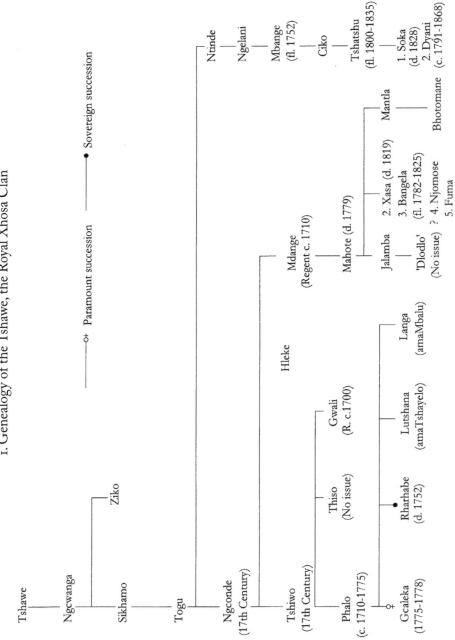

1. Genealogy of the Tshawe, the Royal Xhosa Clan

—o+ Paramount succession

—● Sovereign succession

2. Genealogy of the Rharhabe

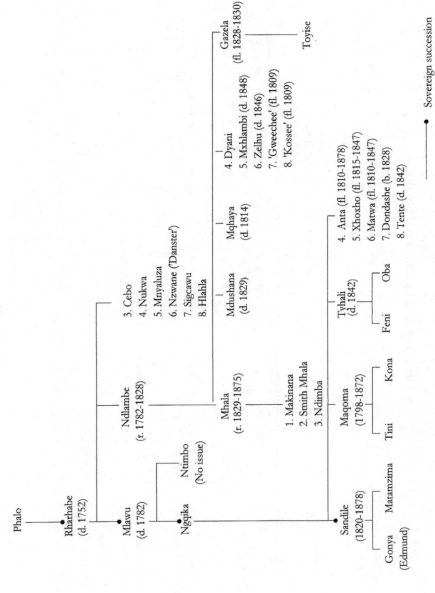

Phalo

Rharhabe (d. 1752)

Mlawu (d. 1782)

Ndlambe (r. 1782-1828)

3. Cebo
4. Nukwa
5. Mnyaluza
6. Nzwane ('Danster')
7. Sigcawu
8. Hlahla

Mdushana (d. 1829)

Mqhaya (d. 1814)

4. Dyani
5. Mxhlambi (d. 1848)
6. Zelhu (d. 1846)
7. 'Gweechee' (fl. 1809)
8. 'Kossee' (fl. 1809)

Gazela (fl. 1828-1830)

Toyise

Ngqika

Ntimbo (No issue)

Mhala (r. 1829-1875)

1. Makinana
2. Smith Mhala
3. Ndimba

Tyhali (d. 1842)

Feni   Oba

4. Anta (fl. 1810-1878)
5. Xhoxho (fl. 1815-1847)
6. Matwa (fl. 1810-1847)
7. Dondashe (b. 1828)
8. Tente (d. 1842)

Maqoma (1798-1872)

Tini   Kona

Sandile (1820-1878)

Gonya (Edmund)   Matamzima

● Sovereign succession

3. Genealogy of the Gcaleka and Gwali

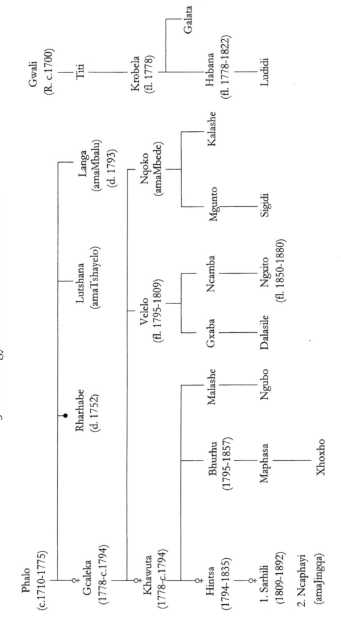

Phalo
(c.1710-1775)

Gcaleka
(1778-c.1794)

Khawuta
(1778-c.1794)

Hintsa
(1794-1835)

1. Sarhili
(1809-1892)

2. Ncaphayi
(amaJingqa)

Rharhabe
(d. 1752)

Lutshana
(amaTshayelo)

Langa
(amaMbalu)
(d. 1793)

Bhurhu
(1795-1857)

Maphasa

Xhoxho

Malashe

Ngubo

Velelo
(fl. 1795-1809)

Gxaba

Dalasile

Ncamba

Ngxito
(fl. 1850-1880)

Nqoko
(amaMbede)

Mgunto

Sigidi

Kalashe

Gwali
(R. c.1700)

Titi

Krobela
(fl. 1778)

Habana
(fl. 1778-1822)

Galata

Ludidi

⚬+ Paramount succession

━━━━ Sovereign succession

4. Genealogy of the Tshayelo and Mbalu

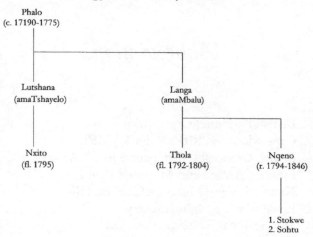

Phalo
(c. 17190-1775)

Lutshana
(amaTshayelo)

Langa
(amaMbalu)

Nxito
(fl. 1795)

Thola
(fl. 1792-1804)

Nqeno
(r. 1794-1846)

1. Stokwe
2. Sohtu

5. Genealogy of the Gqunukhwebe

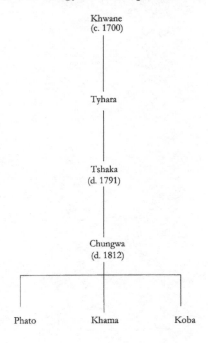

Khwane
(c. 1700)

Tyhara

Tshaka
(d. 1791)

Chungwa
(d. 1812)

Phato

Khama

Koba

Abbreviations

BPP	British Parliamentary Papers.
CMR	Cape Mounted Rifles (later FAMP).
CO	British Colonial Office papers in TNA.
FAMP	Frontier Armed and Mounted Police.
NAM	National Army Museum, Chelsea, UK.
RMLI	Royal Marine Light Infantry.
TNA	The National Archives, Kew, UK.
WO	War Office papers in TNA.

Foreword

'The Land is Dead'

The human habitation of the southern tip of Africa is almost unimaginably ancient.

In 1995, on the edge of the Langebaan Lagoon about sixty miles north of Cape Town, three human footprints were found fossilised in a block of sandstone. They are among a scant handful of remains dating to the emergence of modern Homo sapiens, an intensely personal fragment from the life of a woman – inevitably nick-named Eve – who had once scurried down a steep sand dune in a heavy rainstorm some 117,000 years ago. Whether or not modern man had first evolved in Africa – and some palaeontologists argue on the strength of recent genetic evidence that he may have done so in southern Africa specifically – he certainly lived in the shadow of Table Mountain, and walked the rugged shores of the rocky coves where the Indian and Pacific oceans meet, in the very dawn of his youth. More widespread evidence scattered in caves and rock-shelters across the region, dating back as far as 100,000 years, suggests connections with hunter-gatherer societies who still lived in the same area just a few hundred years ago. The stories of those people, their daily routines, their quarrels and fights, their prominent individuals, heroes and villains, are lost to recorded history, but the pattern of their lives seems to have continued, largely unaltered, cut off by the crashing seas on one side and the great spread of Africa on the other and unnoticed by the wider world beyond, for millennia.

It is tempting to put a precise date – 7 April 1652 – to the moment when that all changed, when Europe first established the beach-head and forced a gateway into the southern African hinterland. Tempting, but not entirely true, since Europe had already been aware of the Cape for more than a century and a half before it made that opening gambit for possession. The great Portuguese explorer, Bartholome Diaz, had first edged his way tentatively past the *Cabo das Tormentas*, the 'Cape of Tempests', from west to east as early as 1488, before, intimidated by the sheer expanse of the world opening up beyond, his crew had forced him to return. Yet it was Diaz who would subsequently pioneer the long and hazardous maritime highway which passed right around Africa and then onwards to India. At the same time he secured a Portuguese mercantile advantage while stimulating an intense competition among Portugal's emerging rivals in the European race for empire. Yet the Portuguese found the Cape itself too hostile – in more ways than one – for them to attempt to establish a settlement there, and for centuries Europe continued to pass by, evidenced to those watching quizzically from the shore by no more than a smudge of white sails on the horizon or the occasional shipwrecked sailor, washed up on the beaches like some bedraggled sea creature from the depths.

In April 1652, however, that outside world arrived to stay – bringing with it all of Europe's restless quest for wealth and knowledge, its voracious strategic and economic demands, and buoyed up with all its overwhelming cultural arrogance and self-righteousness. When one Jan van Riebeeck – an employee of the Verenigde Oostindische Compagnie (VOC, Dutch East India Company) – waded ashore in the shadow of Table Mountain at the head of fewer than a hundred men and a handful of women, he was the spearhead of a historical process that would irrevocably reshape the human landscape of southern Africa.

Yet van Riebeeck initially had no interest in conquest. His mission was to give his corporate employer a commercial edge by establishing a way-station to provision and repair their ships on their long haul to the Dutch colonies in Malaysia. Indeed, his commission specifically prohibited him from attacking any indigenous societies he might encounter, or seizing land or allowing anyone in his party to claim ownership over foreign territory – largely because the VOC feared the cost of any such entanglements. Yet Van Riebeeck's arrival was still to bring to an end the age-old dominance of the Cape by African societies. He found there a semi-nomadic pastoral people, the Khoikhoi – whom the Dutch dismissively called Hottentots – and, further off among the distant mountain ranges, a hunter-gatherer society, the San or Bushmen. The European intrusion inevitably brought with it a competition for land and resources, for which neither local society was militarily equipped, and despite the VOC strictures it took less than a decade before sporadic outbreaks of violence had seen the Khoikhoi driven away from the Dutch enclave. And over subsequent decades, as the VOC's boundaries expanded in proportion to its need for grazing and agricultural land, the Khoikhoi were largely dispossessed, pressed into servitude or simply eliminated.

Those first encounters established a pattern of interaction between Europeans and Africans that would last for nearly two and a half centuries. As the

Dutch interests in Batavia (Jakarta, Indonesia) expanded so did the demand on the resources produced by the Cape and the settlement assumed an expansionist dynamic of its own. To bolster the European population the original indentured VOC employees were augmented over the years by Dutch 'free burghers', by slaves imported from Malaysia to carry the burden of heavy manual labour – these were the origin of the Cape's large community of mixed descent, categorised in the race-conscious past as 'Coloureds' – and later by French religious refugees from Europe, and even by a smattering of Germans. On the fringes of the colonial borders settler society developed a distinct character: a rugged, individualistic self-reliance born out of the solitudes and hardships of daily life. Many frontier farmers turned away from Europe, seeking refuge against the new and challenging philosophies emerging there in the more conservative beliefs that they had brought with them, and turned their faces instead towards Africa. Many, indeed, chafed at the constraints imposed by the VOC and restlessly wandered beyond the borders in search of the 'greener grasses' beyond, dragging authority reluctantly in their wake as they trickled slowly into the great swathe of rolling, fertile down-land that the African coast offered eastwards. For the Khoikhoi already living there the settlers' progress was marked by violence, with a succession of small skirmishes, ambushes and massacres in which the Khoikhoi were invariably the losers.

At the beginning of the eighteenth century, in a patch of ground known as the Zuurveld – the 'sour land', from the type of grasses that grew there – the frontier farmers were brought up short by a collision with a more robust African society moving in the opposite direction.

The Xhosa were the vanguard of an age-old shift of black African peoples southwards, although they had already been in possession of the eastern hills for at least a century, perhaps much longer. They were organised not into one centralised kingdom but into scores of smaller groups, and they were a pastoral people whose lives revolved around their cattle. As such they were in direct competition for the same resource – land – as the newcomers, a point made clear early in the contact between them: as early as 1702 a party of Dutch scouts had blundered into a band of Xhosa and fighting had broken out between them. For the next seventy years, however, as both sides infiltrated the Zuurveld, the relationship between them had relied largely upon trade, and had been tense but pragmatic. By the 1770s, however, the settlers were occupying the Zuurveld in such large numbers that they petitioned the VOC to annex it formally to deny the Xhosa any title – an action that was not lost upon the Xhosa. Over the next few years both sides complained of mistreatment by the other, of stock-theft and rough handling. In 1799 the

VOC decided to resort to force simply to drive the Xhosa out of the Zuurveld, and the first in a wearing series of 'Cape Frontier Wars' began. With only a small regular garrison at the Cape the Dutch forces consisted largely of a settler militia raised on the frontier under the 'commando' system, in which every farmer was required to serve in defence of his own district when called upon to do so, whilst the Xhosa – who lacked the strong centralised military system which would later characterise the emergence of the Zulu kingdom further north – fought under their traditional leaders. The fighting quickly assumed a pattern which would typify almost all the subsequent campaigns, as the Xhosa, giving way in the face of superior Dutch firepower, retired to mountain strongholds or wooded thickets, challenging the Dutch to drive them out. As it would later, it was also characterised on occasion by sudden bouts of ruthlessness: in one incident, during a parley, a Dutch commandant threw sticks of tobacco among the gathered Xhosa and, as they scrabbled to pick them up, ordered his men to open fire and gun them down.

Two subsequent wars pushed the Dutch boundaries further forward without in any way resolving the fundamental points of conflict. Then, at the beginning of the nineteenth century, history introduced two new twists that ratcheted up the tension still further. The various Xhosa groups acknowledged a hierarchy based on the lineage of their leaders but a series of rifts among the senior royal house led to a bitter succession dispute which resulted in some groups fleeing the conflict and moving into land claimed by the colony. When the dust finally settled, the senior group, the amaGcaleka, still lived in independent territory east of the colony's borders, but a junior branch, the amaNgqika, were now living west of them – within the colony's boundaries yet unwilling to acknowledge Dutch authority. In most subsequent conflicts with Europeans it would be the amaNgqika who were destined to find themselves most painfully exposed.

Even as the frontier was convulsed by local rifts, the Dutch lost their international claim to possession of the Cape Colony. In Europe the established political order had been shattered by the wars which followed the French Revolution and the rise of Napoleon Bonaparte; as the Netherlands fell prey to Napoleon's ambitions France's rivals sought to shore up their own strategic imperatives. Worried that a pro-French regime in Holland might use the Cape to cut British lines of communication to India, the British had intervened to seize the Cape in 1795, only to give it back under a peace treaty a few years later. When war with Napoleon flared up again, however, they returned in force and in 1806, after a bizarre European-style land-battle fought out on the sand dunes close to Cape Town, they took it once more, this time permanently.

Their arrival did little to resolve existing hostilities and actually fostered new ones, adding fresh layers to an already complex mesh of resentments. Many of the established frontier farmers had considered the VOC's government alien and unsympathetic – the seat in Cape Town was a long way from the scattered frontier villages –and they found the advent of a new metropolitan authority even more so. Touring the frontier British officials noted the simmering hostility between the farmers and the remaining Khoikhoi in their employ as well as the widespread hostility towards the Xhosa. The British resorted to the VOC's preferred policy – they proclaimed a new border and set about driving the Xhosa beyond it. In 1811 British redcoats were deployed on the frontier for the first time, adopting methods which, as their commander Sir John Cradock said, were intended to 'impress on the minds of these savages a proper degree of terror and respect'. Cradock was neither the first nor the last commander on the frontier to overestimate the salutary effect of the violence at their disposal, or to underestimate the determination of the Xhosa to remain in a land they considered their own, and in 1819 the Xhosa mounted a counter-attack which lapped against the very walls of the strongest settler villages.

Once they had been repulsed – again – the British Government tried a new tactic: weighting the frontier population in their favour by encouraging a programme of immigration from the UK. These '1820 settlers' arrived in Africa to find that not only had the attractions of their new properties been distinctly over-sold but that they were exposed in some of the most volatile and bitterly contested areas. When fresh fighting broke out in 1834 it was these settlers who bore the brunt of the attacks, prompting one exasperated British commander, Colonel Harry Smith, to carry the war beyond the colony's boundaries and into the heart of the independent amaGcaleka territory. Smith arranged a meeting with the amaGcaleka paramount, King Hintsa, but when Hintsa arrived Smith arrested him; when Hintsa tried to escape, Smith's escort opened fire on him, blowing out his brains.

The death of Hintsa marked a new escalation in the levels of violence and ruthlessness prevailing on the frontier, and it would have a profound effect on subsequent events. British vacillation after that Sixth Frontier War – territory was annexed beyond the colonial borders as a buffer zone by the governor at the Cape, but then repudiated by the administration in London – encouraged a further inconclusive outbreak in 1846. By 1850, however – nearly 150 years after that first skirmish between the Dutch and Xhosa vanguards – tensions on the frontier were again steadily rising. Dutch, British, Khoikhoi and Xhosa jostled abrasively against one another, each with their own agenda and entrenched resentments, fuelled by then with generations of bitterness, a festering sense of injustice, and by 'a great deal of blood to avenge'.

In Xhosa society, when a chief committed himself to war, he sent a messenger among his followers, with a leopard's tail mounted on a stick as a sign of his authority, and summoned the men to fight with words which spoke of the end of all peaceful hopes of a resolution. '*Ilizwe ilfile*', the messenger cried, 'The land is dead', and all the fighting men who heard him gathered up their spears and wrapped their hide cloaks about them and set off to war.

By 1850 the land of the Eastern Cape was indeed in many ways dead – but the worst was yet to come.

Ian Knight

Acknowledgements

This book is really the work of two authors and not one, as the title might suggest. Let me explain.

Quite by chance, in September 2009, I had the good fortune to be introduced to Mr Derek Painter and his wife Anne. Derek owns two farms which lie in the shadow of the Kroome escarpment, both of great historical significance: 'Endwell', a part of which was known in the 1850s as 'Andrew's', and 'Longnor Park', then known as 'Blakeway's'.

Whilst visiting Endwell to meet Anne and Derek, I was shown a document which was completely unknown to me at that point. It was a copy of a typescript called *The War of Mlangeni* [sic] *in the Waterkloof*, written by someone named N.C. Mapham in 1977/78. I had a quick look through this document and was excited to find that it contained, in great detail and in thrilling prose, a narrative of the engagements in an area within what the author called 'The Waterkloof Triangle' – that is, the area having Post Retief at its apex, and Adelaide and Fort Beaufort as the left and right lower corners respectively. The narrative began with the action in the Boma Pass in December 1850, which precipitated the Eighth Frontier War, and ended with the last attack in the Kroome Heights on 15 September 1852.

I asked Derek if he would kindly photocopy the document for me (no mean feat at some 280 pages) and send it to me in Australia, which he subsequently did. I have since studied this document at great length, and have obtained almost every source document that the author mentions, which have proved to be a mine of valuable information. I am delighted to acknowledge the contribution that the Painter family has made towards this work, even though it was by chance.

A little detective work enabled me to track down relatives of the mysterious author. Sadly Neville Mapham passed away in 1992; he was an electrical engineer until his retirement, and an enthusiastic amateur historian. After exhausting local South African sources, he was sufficiently dedicated to travel to the United Kingdom in search of further documentary material for his magnum opus.

I could, of course, have used Mapham's work as the basis for parts of my own, using the same source material. However, it seemed to me that Mapham's words, and his thorough scholarship, demanded acknowledgement in their own right. The difficulty was that his work did not provide a sufficiently full treatment of the war, which I was anxious to provide.

In collaboration with his family, therefore, it was agreed that I should include as much of Mapham's work in my own as was relevant, and identify it as such. This commitment I have been happy, and proud, to honour.

Mapham's contribution, and it is a very substantial one, is identified in the Contents pages by sub-headings with a superscript M (M). I have corrected some of the spelling (which shows a manuscript typed in haste), improved the punctuation and clarified some matters. Where possible, I have also provided the source of Mapham's information by means of endnotes.

Neville Mapham was born in 1919 and thus lived through the early days of the Union and the 'apartheid' era in South Africa. As a result, he uses some words that are no longer acceptable, such as 'Native', 'Hottentot' and 'Kaffir'. 'Hottentot' was a word that had been used since the settlement of the Cape in the seventeenth century to identify the Khoikhoi people and, subsequently, the mixed-race coloured people who descended from them. 'Kaffir' was generally used to describe the Xhosa people, and, less often, the Mfengu.

While the term 'Kaffir' can be readily replaced by 'Xhosa' or 'Thembu', the word 'Hottentot' presents more difficulties. I am encouraged to note that I am not alone in this matter:

> The term 'Hottentot' was used in the early nineteenth-century Cape as . . . an ethnic . . . category. . . . it was used loosely to refer to the descendants of the indigenous Khoikhoi pastoralists who were distinguished in colonial parlance from the [Bushmen] living on the peripheries of the Colony and from the Xhosa on the eastern frontier. This usage was necessarily imprecise, for the distinctions between Khoikhoi and San ('Bushmen') had been blurred even in pre-colonial times and were no less confused in the early nineteenth century. Furthermore, the process of colonisation was accompanied by racial admixture and by far-reaching cultural change which still awaits research. The racial heterogeneity of the 'Hottentots' was sometimes recognised in colonial discourse. Thus the off-spring of Khoisan and slaves (and of Khoisan and Xhosa) were sometimes known as 'Bastard Hottentots' and the offspring of whites and Khoisan were sometimes known as 'Colonial Bastards'. Yet 'Hottentot' remained a portmanteau term.[1]

In the case of 'Hottentot', I have, like Ms Newton-King, retained the word 'Khoikhoi', even though in the two hundred years since the first Dutch settlement, the pure-blood people had been largely replaced by one of a very mixed race.

In a similar fashion, Mapham sometimes betrays some of the attitudes towards the non-white population in South Africa commonly held by men of his age in the 1970s. It has been my task to revise some of these expressed attitudes to provide a more objective account, without losing the essential Mapham that makes his prose so very engaging.

Finally, with the kind permission of Neville Mapham's family, I have also made use of most of his original maps, which have been modified by a cartographer to improve legibility.

Once more, I am also indebted to the curators and staff of various museums and libraries who have been so helpful with my enquiries. I must specifically mention the staff of The National Archives, Kew, the National Army Museum, Chelsea and the Campbell Collections in Durban; Jeff Peires and his staff in the Cory Library at Rhodes University, Grahamstown; and 'Moose' van Rensburg at the Fort Beaufort Museum. The curator at the Museum of the 'Royal Green Jackets' was kind enough to supply me with an extract from 'The Records of the 2nd Battalion, King's Royal Rifle Corps'.

Peter Ewart once more bravely accepted the burden of editing the work. His very careful exertions again allowed me to escape many grammatical pitfalls, for which I am most appreciative. As usual, I have tinkered after his labours, so that any errors which may be found must be laid at my door, and not at Peter's.

Ken Thompson, a fine cartographer living in Adelaide, South Australia, prepared, or modified, a number of maps for this work.

Finally, my appreciation is again due to my good friends Julie and John Parker of Durban, who have once more endured my visits, always with a smile.

If I have omitted thanks due to any other helpful person or institution I trust they will excuse me.

Keith Smith
Northern NSW, Australia

Meet Lieutenant-Colonel Henry George Wakelyn Smith, later to be better and more famously known as Lieutenant-General Sir Harry Smith, Baronet of Aliwal. Within this account he becomes henceforth one of the most extraordinary personalities of all, dashing, vain, self-glorifying, reckless, somewhat mad, and often ludicrous, as well as silly.

Noel Mostert, Frontiers, p. 658

Introduction

Just as there was a Hundred Years' War in Europe, so there was something similar at the Cape of Good Hope in South Africa. However, this extended period of warfare was between the indigenous peoples of the Cape and the Caucasian colonists. Like its European counterpart, the war was not continuous but consisted of a number of discrete periods of conflict. Between 1781 and 1878, no less than nine such wars occurred. The first two involved the Dutch settlers, while the remainder were against British colonists.

The greatest of these frontier wars, the eighth, was fought between December 1850 and March 1853 and it is remarkable for both the duration of the war, and the dedication of the Xhosa to defending their land and heritage. It is the story of this war that I propose to tell.

The so-called War of Mlanjeni was the longest conflict in South African history until the second Anglo-Boer War at the beginning of the twentieth century. The loss of life of the indigenous combatants was substantially heavier than that of the Zulu War of 1879 and the political after-effects of it 'were immeasurably greater than those that followed the Zulu War'.[1] It is a sobering thought that while the Zulu War has, through the many accounts written of it, glorified the courage of both sides, the silence surrounding the Eighth Frontier War is deafening.

The war sits squarely at the centre of a decade of conflict at the Cape. The Seventh Frontier War, known as the War of the Axe, was fought in 1846–7.[2] The later event was a period of great internal turmoil among the Xhosa, but which also had a flow-on effect for the colonists. This was the great Cattle Killing of 1856–7.[3]

In telling the story of this Eighth War, the voices of the Xhosa themselves will be almost mute; they were, for the most part, illiterate people and their only recourse to recalling their history was an oral tradition. Nor was there, unlike the huge work of James Stuart, which recorded the oral tradition of the Zulu people far to the north, any substantial record of this oral tradition. We therefore have little to tell us of their opinions on matters concerning the war, nor can we read their words spoken in the many councils which must have taken place. Their voices, therefore, may be heard only through their actions.

In 1850, the administration of the colony was the responsibility of the governor, Lieutenant-General Sir Harry Smith, who was a serving senior military officer, as all of his predecessors had been. The governor was assisted in his work by a Legislative Council consisting of five government officials and five to seven colonial residents chosen by the governor. This government structure was a relatively recent innovation, having been introduced by Sir Benjamin D'Urban in April 1834.[4]

One cannot compare the simple nature of the government of that day with that of the modern era. The number of government departments was few: the governor's office, treasury, customs, judiciary, etc. Department heads had very small staffs, most of whom were clerks, and there would be numbers of people writing letters by dictation, and then writing the final copies 'fair'. They would also have to re-write a number of copies of correspondence for other recipients or for filing.

Military affairs were usually controlled by the governor, who also acted as the commander-in-chief of the colony's troops.[5] The military forces at the Cape consisted of line regiments from Britain supported by artillery and engineer units, and a local mounted force called the Cape Mounted Rifles (CMR). This force was made up of white officers and some white troopers, the remainder being of mixed race. These forces were supplemented by occasional volunteers consisting of mounted units of white settlers, or burghers, and African infantry levies, often drawn from a people loyal to the Crown known as the Mfengu.

The population of the Cape Colony in 1852 was just a little less than 300,000.[6] This was made up as follows:

	Coloured	White	Total
Western Cape	49,109	65,777	114,886
Eastern Cape	135,857	34,536	170,393
Total	184,966	100,313	285,279

It will be noted that the non-white population of the Western Cape represented only 42 per cent, while in the Eastern Cape indigenous people represented 79 per cent of the inhabitants.

The Xhosa Warrior

The Xhosa of the 1850s, like all other Africans in the Eastern Cape, were reared to a rugged life, in many ways reminiscent of that of Sparta: manliness and athletic prowess were revered.

From childhood a boy would herd cattle, first following older boys and then, at a surprisingly young age, being given responsibility for a herd of his own. To pass the time as the cattle grazed, the boys would play games, all with the aim of making them more proficient as fighters. Thus, any object or animal that moved or could be pushed downhill or which floated downriver would be pelted with sticks or stones and any hits acclaimed. Then there was the duel: the boys would fight each other holding the middle of one stick in the left hand as a shield and the end of another in the right hand as a club. This game was played, and still is, from the age of five through to manhood and they became proficient in those intuitive skills known to boxers and fencers.

They were naked till adulthood and learned to ignore pain: a boy leading a team of oxen would run unflinchingly through a thorn bush if it were in his way. In his late teens, he would be initiated into manhood if he were fit, and in the ceremony he would be publicly circumcised, each cruel cut being accompanied by the question 'Are you a man?'; a clear and firm affirmative response had to be given.

For weapons the Xhosa used the throwing spear, with which he could hit a man 70 per cent of the time at thirty paces. For close-quarter work he used the shorter stabbing spear, sometimes breaking the shaft of a throwing spear to create one in a mêlée; then he had that versatile 'mace', the knobkerrie, which could be used either as a club or as a missile, bringing his quarry down when flung spinning at its legs. An ox-hide shield was used when fighting in the open but it was not used in the bush-fighting of the 1850 war. A small percentage of the Ngqika had outdated muskets but they were poor shots and only occasionally hit their targets; they were also very short of ammunition. It was for their musketry skills that the great Ngqika military leader Maqoma wisely courted the people of mixed race, the Khoikhoi.

The Xhosa leadership was wielded through its chiefs. There was no king, instead there were two principal chiefs. These were the paramount chief of all the Xhosa people, who was also head of the Gcaleka Xhosa. The other was the sovereign chief of the Rharhabe Xhosa, who was also chief of the Ngqika clan. No chief, however, had exclusive power. Instead, his power was shared with his council, which might even dictate its own terms to the chief. Similarly, if clan members did not favour their own chief, they were free to leave and seek the shelter of another.

The Xhosa did not, unlike the Zulu far to the north, gather their young boys into age groups; nor did they subsequently form those age groups into the lethal regiments so ably used by the Zulu kings. Instead, their fighting groups were their immediate family members, followed by their clan members, led by their elders and the chiefs. It was all very informal, and quite unlike the efficiently organised regiments.

Xhosa warfare was originally somewhat stereotyped, whereby warring parties ranged opposite each other and hurled insults and spears; the weapons used were largely the long throwing spear and the knobkerrie, with a light shield made from cow-hide for protection. Under conditions of close-quarter fighting, the shaft of the long spear might be broken so that the now-short weapon could be better used in close proximity to the enemy. A chivalrous feature of their warfare was the exclusion of women and children, who, unlike those of the Zulu, were never attacked.

This method of warfare had to be changed as a result of the use of firearms by the white man, so guerrilla, or hit-and-run, tactics were used. As the Xhosa acquired their own firearms, old though they were, they developed the ambush, to seize convoys of wagons, a stratagem at which Maqoma excelled.

The British Government

The government in London at the time of the Eighth War was led by the First Lord of the Treasury, Lord John Russell,[7] whose Whig party had been in power since June 1846. In February 1852, the Whigs were defeated by the Conservative, or Tory, party at an election, following which the Earl of Derby became the leader of the government.

The minister responsible for colonial matters was the Secretary of State for War and the Colonies and the incumbent from July 1846 was Henry, the third Earl Grey. Sir John Pakington took office as Secretary of State in February 1852 after the electoral defeat of Lord Russell's government.

A constant subject for often heated debate between governors of the Cape and the various colonial ministers during this period, and later, was the very high cost of keeping imperial troops at the Cape. The expectations in London were that, first, the Cape government should provide for its own defence, and second, that the number of imperial troops at the Cape should be reduced significantly, while the cost of those remaining should be borne by the Cape government.

The British Army of 1850

From a wider perspective, the decade of the 1850s was greatly overshadowed in European military history by the war in the Crimea, fought between the French and British on one side and the Russians on the other. The Russians chose to ignore an Anglo-French ultimatum on behalf of Turkey and war was declared between them in March 1854.

For Britain, the Crimean War was both a disaster and an embarrassment. It lost many thousands of its redcoated soldiers, most of them to hunger and disease. They were poorly led, badly supplied and were compelled to bear the most severe privations, especially during the Russian winters. The army administration, or, more correctly, maladministration, was principally responsible for these problems. It is also true, however, that for decades the army had been dominated by the Duke of Wellington, who obstinately refused to countenance any of the many army reforms that were advanced in the later years of his life.

The army was nominally under the care of the sovereign, Queen Victoria, a duty which she took very seriously. In practice:

> . . . five agencies dealt continuously with matters of major administrative importance connected with the regular army: two government ministers (Secretary of State for War and the Colonies and Secretary at War), two military officers (C-in-C and Master-General of the Ordnance) and one civilian department (the Commissariat, under the Treasury), although another civilian department (the Ordnance) was responsible through the Board of Ordnance to the Master-General.[8]

This complex structure was further surrounded by other peripheral departments, such as the Army Medical Department, which had varying degrees of influence, so that the whole administration was a vast, unwieldy machine.

It was this organisation which controlled the army in the Crimean War of 1854, and it was this same administration, and the same army, which was called upon to fight the Eighth Frontier War in South Africa four years earlier in 1850.

The British Soldier

During the 1850s a newly appointed infantry subaltern received no training, serving an 'apprenticeship' under his captain and at the hands of his sergeants instead. If he was lucky, these 'masters' would have seen active service, could teach well and the regiment could easily cover their mistakes. If, however, several levels of officer ranks were unblooded, then the inexperience of the regiment would show up in its performance, as was to happen to the 2nd (The Queen's Royal) Regiment.

Officers' commissions were usually purchased, making promotion on merit very infrequent – Harry Smith being a rare example. With ability not a consideration, training suffered; gentlemen did not need to be trained, their 'breeding' gave them all the knowledge that was required. Inevitably, when it came to fighting, initial reverses often occurred as the unfit officers were eliminated, taking their men with them. Promotion of officers was strictly by seniority, rarely on merit. This was the reason for the publication of army lists, both by the War Office and also by such entrepreneurs as H.G. Hart, because they allowed officers to see where they ranked in seniority in their own regiment. Furthermore, because promotion was purchased, the more affluent an officer, the more likely he was to achieve promotion to the higher ranks.

Promotion, even by purchase, however, was a slow process, depending on the retirement or death of more senior officers before those below could achieve their 'step' to a higher rank. Thus, when a major was killed in combat, or a lieutenant-colonel retired through ill-health, all those who were next in seniority were able to move up one rank, while the lower ranks moved up in seniority.

Private soldiers were treated very impersonally by their officers, who regarded them as having no feelings, since they had been reared in an environment where any sensitivity they might have possessed would have been eliminated by its brutality. They believed that soldiers were there to do as they were told, they were lazy and stupid and, unless you were careful, they would get the better of you; your only hope was to rule by fear. Their habits were coarse and dirty – even unspeakably disgusting. Camp followers, although they made a filthy mess of the place, were a necessary evil as they helped to dissipate the men's tensions and calmed them down in camp. For the same reason, sodomy was unofficially condoned.

The private soldier joined the army for a number of reasons: he was out of work, he was starving, he wanted to escape hanging for stealing a sheep, or most probably, he was in search of excitement and adventure. He accepted the Queen's shilling and bounty money – which was immediately lost to the recruiting sergeant and collaborating inn-keeper – and he was well clothed, usually well fed, the work was easy, if sometimes dangerous, the company good and the responsibility nil. The fact that the officers rode while he walked, slept in tents while he slept in the open and kept him awake at night with their drunken songs – well, it was no worse than the treatment they received from the squire or mill owner.

The men served for twenty years and were trained to be automatons, machines that obeyed the orders of their officers implicitly, enforced by their sergeants. Initiative was effectively eliminated by punishment, most usually flogging. They were trained to fire percussion muskets, which had now replaced the unreliable flintlocks; they were also rigorously and effectively trained in the use of the bayonet. The average private was short, muscular, tough, unflinching in the face of death and superbly suited to set-piece battles after the style of Waterloo. But this was not the sort of fight to which he had been invited at the Cape.

Chapter 1

Setting the Scene

The Indigenous People

It would be a grave error to imagine that the land at the southern tip of the African continent was empty of people when the Dutch arrived in 1652 to establish a settlement there. There were, in fact, two numerous peoples already in occupation, as they had been for thousands of years.

The nomadic San, or Bushmen, were perhaps the oldest inhabitants of South Africa and were widely distributed. They were a small race physically and depended upon hunting and gathering for subsistence. The men hunted game using spears and poisoned arrows while the women foraged through the bush searching for wild fruits, berries, tubers and other edible plants.[1]

The Khoikhoi, known to the new settlers as 'Hottentots', were very distant descendants of the San and their language included the same 'clicks' found in their ancestors' tongue. They were, however, a little more sophisticated, being herdsmen of cattle and goats, which they considered represented their individual wealth. The men hunted and the women engaged in agriculture but the people remained quite primitive. While not a nomadic people, they did move with the seasons to take their cattle to better grazing, a process known as transhumance.[2]

A third people, who lived far to the east of the Cape, were the amaXhosa,[3] a part of the numerous Nguni, a Bantu sub-group which had gradually moved south from the sub-Sahara.[4] The central part of the country was high plateau, arid and sparsely grassed, thus requiring the Nguni to follow a broad coastal path.

The Nguni shared a common language, including the clicks of the San and Khoikhoi, but as separate clans were established, so the language of each took on variants. Even so, the many different Nguni people such as Zulu, Mbo, Mpondo, Thembu and Xhosa, could still understand each other's speech without much difficulty.

The Xhosa were the most numerous people to be found on the periphery of the nascent Cape colony. Like many other Nguni, the constituent clans were often named after a male ancestor in the remote past, a name known as a patronymic.

They were culturally little different from the Khoikhoi, their lives also being dominated by cattle, their external form of wealth, and the land on which the cattle grazed. Ownership of the land did not rest with individuals but was controlled by the chiefs, who made it available to their people. In short, it was a feudal society. The men did little work, the tending of the herds being the responsibility of youths and boys, while the women cared for their families and tended the gardens in which they grew Indian corn (maize or mealies) and other vegetables. Their diet also included honey, wild figs and berries. Compared with the Khoikhoi, however, their skills in animal husbandry and simple agriculture were more highly developed, and they were also able to fashion iron tools and weapons.

There were two essential features which governed relationships in Nguni, and therefore Xhosa, society. The most important was that of exogamy: marriage was not permitted between members of the same extended family, thus ensuring that the blood line remained open. Xhosa chiefs, for example, frequently took Thembu wives. (The Thembu were also a Nguni people who lived on the northern periphery of the Xhosa, especially the Gcaleka. Their life-style and weapons were much the same as the Xhosa.)

The second significant feature was that inheritance of the chieftainship was not based upon simple primogeniture, that is, inheritance by the first-born male, but by a more complicated method through the 'chief son'.

According to Xhosa custom, the chief's first wife was known as the founder of the 'Right Hand House' because of the position of her hut in the *umuzi* (homestead) relative to that of the chief. However, the chief was succeeded, not by the first wife's son but by the oldest son of the 'Great Wife' whom he often married later in life, thus creating the 'Left Hand' or 'Great House'.[5] This son was normally named as the chief's successor before his father's death. This means of succession was perhaps the single most frequent cause of disharmony in families and clans, frequently leading to conflict.[6] It is a discord that we shall see often as our story unfolds.

The Cape Settlement

On 7 April 1652 the Dutch East India Company (Vereenigde Oostindische Compagnie, or VOC) founded a settlement at the Cape of Good Hope, under the leadership of Jan van Riebeeck, on the small plain on the shore of

Table Bay, in the shadow of the rugged mountains almost encircling it. Its purpose was to enable ships en route to or from the Company's colonies in what is now Indonesia, to re-provision with fresh water, meat and vegetables. Repairs could also be made to vessels if required. The men who served under van Riebeeck were employees of the Company and were not therefore free to do as they chose.[7]

The Khoikhoi were obstructive to the settlers and initially refused to trade with them. In time, however, they were seduced by the trade goods that the white newcomers had to offer and, over the first century of white occupation, lost touch with their heritage, being reduced to the status of workers for the colonists.

Unlike the San, the Khoikhoi were eventually prepared to intermix with other races, including white men, and between these two and the (often Asiatic) slaves who escaped from the colony, founded what can only be called a coloured mixed race. Some of these people drifted off to the north, where they established themselves as a people known as Bastaards, or Griqua.

The early settlement at the Cape consisted of two simple elements: a mud-brick fortress near the shore of Table Bay and a large rectangular garden nearby for the growing of food. (Remarkably, much of this garden remains: it is at the centre of Cape Town, and is still known as the Company Garden.) Grazing land was also appropriated for the few cattle which were brought in, and the inhabitants lived in hovels that were quickly thrown up. The old fort was eventually replaced by a larger one, built of stone, in 1679.

The early years of the settlement were miserable indeed and the inhabitants were frequently close to starvation. They were timid and suspicious, making them slow to establish trade relations with the indigenous population; those San remaining in the area were quick to move away from the white men.

In 1656 van Riebeeck decided that instead of binding the settlers to the Company, some should be allowed to take up their own land to develop private farms. The spirit of free enterprise quickly took root. The Khoikhoi were subsequently even more severely affected by this extension of European grazing land – land which they themselves had used since time immemorial.[8]

During the following ninety years, the settlement expanded to become a substantial colony, expanding progressively as far as the high plateau to the north and taking over a considerable amount of land to the east, though never seeming to have enough of that precious commodity. This was not as surprising as might be thought: each 'Boer', or farmer, demanded one or more farms of at least six thousand acres, plus farms of the same size for each of their sons, in order to compensate for the frequently poor quality grazing. This occupation of land was always, of course, at the expense of the aboriginal owners. Over time the troublesome San had been hunted down or driven to the mountainous or arid fringes of the expanding colony and the Khoikhoi had become totally subservient to their new masters.

The administration of the Cape had, during this period of rapid expansion, recognised that it must exercise some control over the burgeoning colony and in 1743 had set the eastern boundary at the Brak River. The Boers, however, anxious both to escape the control of the Company and to appropriate new lands, had progressed still further east. In 1770 the border was moved to the Gamtoos River and only five years later it was placed on a line from the Upper Great Fish River through the Bushmans River to the sea – but still the Boer farmers outran it.

Between 1775 and the end of the century, the Dutch fought two wars in defence of their new frontier: the first was in 1781 and the second was in the years 1789–93. Both of them were against the new obstacle to their expansion – the Xhosa. Both wars had their origins in the scarcity of two resources: land and cattle. The Xhosa had always enjoyed a tradition of cattle theft among themselves and, in meeting with white settler-farmers who also raised cattle, their theft extended to the animals of the Boers. It was also very unsettling for a Boer farmer to awake one morning and find his farm overrun by Xhosa, busily building their *imizi*, or homesteads, on what they had thought to be their land.

By the eighteenth century the Xhosa had roughly divided into four great families, all descended from a remote common ancestor, Tshawe. These families were the Tshawe themselves, the Ntinde, Mdange and Gwali. Much of Xhosa history prior to the incumbency of chief Tshiwo, a great-great-great-grandson of Tshawe, is shrouded in myth and the early genealogies remain uncertain.

When Tshiwo died in the early eighteenth century, he was survived by his brother Mdange and a son of the right hand house, Gwali. Tshiwo had taken a great wife but she had not yet borne him a son, so Gwali became the new paramount chief. But at the time of Tshiwo's death, his great wife was carrying his child and Mdange hid her, and subsequently her newborn son Phalo as well. Years later, Mdange revealed the existence of the boy and claimed the paramountcy for him. Gwali refused to accept him and in the battle which followed Gwali was defeated and fled south-west across the Kei River, accompanied by Ntinde and his people.

Meanwhile, Phalo took up his role as the new paramount chief of the Tshawe. Mdange eventually followed Gwali across the Kei, leaving Phalo to his own devices. In coming years Phalo had a number of sons, the two most significant of whom were Rharhabe, son of the right hand house, and Gcaleka, of the left hand house and thus the heir to the paramountcy, each of whom were to found their own chiefdoms.

Tensions between Rharhabe and Gcaleka developed because the latter was declared to be a diviner. Rharhabe claimed that this would bring dissension to the clan because diviners were usually common people who dared not 'smell out' a chief. Gcaleka, on the other hand, being a chief himself, might have no such qualms. The situation eventually moved to war and in the subsequent battle Rharhabe was defeated and made a prisoner. On his release he too moved into a region that was later called the Ciskei.[9] Here, Rharhabe tried to gather together those people who had previously crossed the Kei River. Only the Dange and Gqunukhwebe resisted him. (The Gqunukhwebe was a clan that was originally Khoikhoi but which had, through the services their chief had rendered to Tshiwo, been admitted to the Xhosa.)

In 1775 Phalo, a weak ruler anyway, died and Gcaleka became the paramount chief. He did not survive long either, dying in 1778. Rharhabe chose this moment to attempt to seize the paramountcy for himself, but Gcaleka's heir Khawuta drove Rharhabe away. In his frustration, Rharhabe hurled himself on the Dange and drove them west across the Great Fish River.

In 1782, Rharhabe was involved in a dispute with the Thembu and died during an invasion of their territory, together with his heir Mlawu. He was survived by his eleven-year-old son Ngqika, whose uncle, Ndlambe, took on the role of regent. Thus we find the paramount chief of the Xhosa, Gcaleka, on the east bank of the Kei River while the Rharhabe, under Ngqika, with the lesser clans, were in the Ciskei to the west.

Ndlambe was the second son of the house of Rharhabe. He was a clever and ambitious man who immediately took up his father's mantle and challenged the remaining people who had obstructed Rharhabe in his quest to bring all the Ciskei Xhosa under his influence. Ndlambe first brought Langa of the Mbalu under his power, then both of them attacked the Gqunukhwebe, who also then moved still further west across the Fish River in June 1779.

The Xhosa continued their migration west across the Fish River and Boer complaints of theft and conflict continued to assail the administration at the Cape. Finally, in December 1780, instructions were issued to the field cornet at the frontier, now designated 'Commandant of the Eastern Country', to negotiate with the Xhosa, setting the Fish River as the boundary between the two races. However, these negotiations were often with minor chiefs and any agreement thus reached would not bind any other chief, nor eliminate further conflict.

* * *

The next major event was the decision by the British to take over the Cape. This step was taken to forestall, they thought, a French bid for the colony. On 11 June 1795, a British fleet sailed into False Bay and landed troops. The small Dutch garrison capitulated only after three months of negotiations and threats and, assuming the title 'Commandant of the Town and Settlement of the Cape of Good Hope', Major-General James Henry Craig took command of the administration.[10]

In 1799, the British fought the brief Third Frontier War (and their first) against the Xhosa, although, not knowing how to contain the enemy, the acting governor, Major-General Francis Dundas, used one of the remaining Dutch administrators to negotiate a peace.[11]

Far away in Europe, events were taking place that would have a dramatic effect in South Africa. A peace was declared between the French and British, together with their allies, and on 25 March 1802 the Treaty of Amiens was signed. One of its provisions was that the Cape Colony should be returned to its original founders, and the new Dutch administration arrived at the Cape on 23 December 1802.[12]

A British Colony

This situation did not prevail for long. In July 1805, intelligence reached London that the French again planned to seize the Cape. The Admiralty was also greatly concerned that the Americans too were casting covetous eyes in that direction. In response to these stimuli, a fleet of no fewer than sixty-one ships was prepared in secret and on 31 August it departed with an army of seven thousand troops under the command of General Sir David Baird. By 3 January 1806 it was standing off the South African coast. By the end of February Britain was again master of the Cape, this time permanently.

Between 1806 and 1847 Britain fought three more frontier wars against the Xhosa and, as each was won, so more Xhosa land to the north and east was swallowed up. The Fourth War was fought in 1811–12, the Fifth in 1818–19 and the Sixth in 1834–6.[13]

During those wars the Xhosa quickly learned that their spears would not win them any battles against firearms, and they abandoned their traditional fighting methods in favour of hit-and-run, or guerrilla, tactics. Their ability to remain almost invisible in heavy bush was soon found to give them a considerable advantage, since the more heavily burdened white soldiers found it difficult to move and fight in such an environment and the invisibility of their foes generated considerable fear.

*   *   *

Around the same time as the second British seizure of the colony, a major change was also taking place in the fortunes of the Xhosa. Ndlambe had been under severe threat from Ngqika. The change in the Cape administration, therefore, was of concern to Ndlambe, who was now potentially exposed to attack by a combination of Ngqika and the British.

Ndlambe had taken a new wife, Thuthula, reputed to be a great beauty, and now Ngqika had her abducted and brought to his homestead or 'Great Place' where he succeeded in seducing her. Two reasons have been offered for his action: either he might have hoped that Ndlambe would pursue her across the Fish River and thus fall into Ngqika's power, or Ngqika was simply gratifying his appetite for beautiful women. Whatever motive impelled him, it was too much for his people, who saw the union as incestuous. His people left him in droves. Mdushane, one of Ndlambe's estranged sons who had been very close to Ngqika, also left him and became reconciled with his father. Ngqika's chiefs rose in revolt against him and Ndlambe, together with Hintsa, the new paramount chief of the Xhosa, seized the opportunity to send a Gcaleka army to assist them. Ngqika was defeated and fled into the Amathola Mountains in fear of his life, while his people defected to Ndlambe. The confident young man of earlier days was now reduced to a state of fear and indecision, desperately trying to maintain the protection of the British – something he had hitherto secured merely through the power of his personality.

Over the ensuing months, the pendulum of popularity gradually moved away from the elderly Ndlambe and back towards Ngqika. Discussions between the two chiefs resulted in Ndlambe finally acknowledging Ngqika's leadership of the Rharhabe.

Thus the two principal chiefs then were: Hintsa of the Transkei Gcaleka, who was also paramount chief of all the Xhosa, and Ngqika, chief of the clan of the same name and sovereign chief of the Rharhabe.

Lord Charles Somerset arrived at the Cape in early 1814 to take up his appointment as the new governor. He had subsequently decided not to pursue the Xhosa further and, aware that Ngqika had lost favour with his people, arranged to meet him to bring his popularity more into balance with that of Ndlambe. It was a policy that seemed bound to re-kindle old rivalries.

In April 1817, a magnificent panoply of British power was displayed on the banks of the Kat River. When the formalities were completed and discussion began, Lord Charles Somerset proposed that if stolen cattle were traced to a particular Xhosa homestead, that homestead should be held responsible for the theft, even though the cattle might not still be found there. This was later to be known as the 'spoor law', a bad pun even then. Ngqika readily assented to this proposal. However, he refused the governor's demand that he accept personal responsibility for returning all stock and slaves that were found in his country. His argument was that although he was the sovereign chief of the Rharhabe, all the lesser chiefs should accept their own responsibilities. Lord Charles was adamant, claiming that he would not recognise any chief other than Ngqika. It is said that Ndlambe, standing close by, urged Ngqika to acquiesce, lest the white man become angry. Having received his agreement, Somerset brought the meeting to a close by giving the chief presents, upon receiving which Ngqika departed the scene without thanks or further ado.[14]

One of the oddities of Xhosa history is the occasional emergence of a sage who was able to influence the people, including their chiefs, sometimes to dramatic and tragic effect. One such mystic now made an appearance in 1818. His name was Makanna but he was nicknamed Nxele, meaning left-handed. The Boers translated this into the Dutch 'Links', which the British anglicised as Lynx. Nxele, coincidentally bearing some Gonaqua blood, had been exposed to missionary sermons and was drawn to Christianity, although it was very much his own brand of it.[15] His charisma among his people made him widely known and he was eventually accorded the rank of a chief. His message was that the white people were the original sinners and the Xhosa, under his leadership, would drive them into the sea.

In the months following the meeting with the governor, Ngqika began to feel the effects of his agreement when increasing numbers of claimants descended upon him demanding that he make good their losses. A commando arrived in early 1818 demanding his assistance in recovering some stolen cattle. When Ngqika vacillated they went off and raided Ndlambe's homesteads instead. Ndlambe, encouraged by Nxele, plotted the destruction of his nephew. Men were sent to raid Ngqika's chiefs for cattle as a reprisal and the chiefs demanded that Ngqika take his army and destroy Ndlambe permanently. Ngqika's own seer, a man name Ntsikanna, warned against this course of action but Ngqika found himself with little choice. He sent a message to the British and received a supportive response, then sent his army down the Tyumie River to meet his arch-enemy in battle.

In November 1818 the two armies met on a plain in the Debe Valley, some fifteen kilometres west of modern Dimbaza. From the heights, Ngqika watched with satisfaction as his warriors drove back the enemy, spaced across the plain in small groups. But these were inexperienced decoys, set out as a lure to ensnare the Ngqika warriors in a trap. As they advanced, veteran warriors from the Ndlambe, Gcaleka, Gqunukhwebe, Dange, Mbalu and

Ntinde, led by Ndlambe's son Mdushane, rose up from the tall grass and attacked the Ngqika from all sides.

The battle of Amalinde raged from noon until nightfall and the shattered remnants of Ngqika's force were pursued from the field by the victorious Ndlambe in darkness. Fires were lit on the battlefield to enable the victors to find the wounded and kill them. This action, named after the many shallow depressions (*amalinde*, caused by giant earthworms) found on the battlefield, was the greatest set-piece battle ever fought between factions of the Xhosa people.[16] The battle was also the trigger that would bring upon the Xhosa the Fifth Frontier War with Britain.

One of the leaders of the Ngqika at Amalinde was a young man named Maqoma.[17] He was born in 1798 and was thus about nineteen years old when Lord Charles Somerset's boundary treaty was imposed on his father. Maqoma could claim to be of royal blood as he was the great-grandson of Phalo, the first paramount chief of the Xhosa known to Europeans. Maqoma is described as being well built, of average height and having a fine, friendly, open face. He had a great following among his own people, being the archetypal hero whom the Xhosa worshipped.

He was a born fighter and his courage at the battle of Amalinde was well remembered: he was acclaimed for the viciousness of his attack and his persistence even after receiving many wounds. For the next nine years Maqoma lived in the Kat River Valley with his own followers, the Jingqi, close to his brother Tyhali in the nearby Tyumie Valley, and while there he made himself a continual nuisance to his white neighbours by his frequent raids on their stock.

Both brothers lost their homes and land through this boundary treaty and both were to turn against Ngqika's former ally the British and become the vanguard of the struggle of the next generation of Xhosa. Three years after their eviction, Maqoma and Tyhali quietly slipped back to occupy their mountain valleys, where they remained, noticed but unmolested by the administration.

This internal Ngqika war was a conflict in which Nxele played a considerable part, and he was also responsible for the most astonishing effrontery yet witnessed. With Nxele's encouragement, the Fifth Frontier War began with a massive irruption of Xhosa into the colony; they began seizing cattle and destroying farms. The situation was very difficult to control and lasted for several months.

On 23 April 1819, Lieutenant-Colonel Thomas Willshire, commanding in Grahamstown, received a perplexing message from Nxele that the mystic would take breakfast with him on the following day.[18] After the dramatic defeat of Ngqika at Amalinde, Nxele had been transformed into the commander of the Xhosa army and his confidence now brought him to confront the British on their own ground – he would attack Grahamstown itself.[19] Thus was fought the battle of Grahamstown, a battle in which the Xhosa were heavily defeated. By the middle of the year, Willshire had led three columns across the Fish River and harried the Ngqika in their own land. Willshire even went so far as to cross the Kei and deliver a stern warning to Hintsa for supporting the Ngqika people. The war was quickly over and it only remained to deal with the seer.

Nxele was sentenced to life imprisonment on Robben Island but on the night of 9 August 1820 he and some fellow prisoners were able to escape by stealing a boat. Approaching the mainland shore, the boat tipped its occupants into the surf and Nxele was swept to his death.[20]

As a result of this war, the frontier boundary of the colony was moved from the indefensible Great Fish River to the Keiskamma River. The country now appropriated by the British between the two rivers was to be known somewhat ironically as the 'Ceded Territory', since the Xhosa had 'ceded' it to the British.[21]

Lord Charles Somerset recognised that the eastern frontier lacked sufficient settlers for its adequate defence. At his suggestion, the British government embarked on a great migration programme of British settlers to the colony. The British economy was in a parlous state, with serious inflationary pressures leading to high unemployment. To this was added the great number of soldiers returning from the war against Napoleon, further adding to the number of unemployed. In July 1819 Parliament appropriated funds for the emigration of five thousand Britons to the Cape.

By April 1820, the first of some four thousand British settlers had begun to arrive at the Cape. The new immigrants, however, were poorly served, both by the colony's administration and by their political masters in London. They were landed on the beach at Algoa Bay, carried by wagon to their assigned property many miles away and abandoned to begin farming. Henry Dugmore described his own experience:

> It was a forlorn-looking plight in which we found ourselves, when the Dutch waggoners had emptied us and our luggage on top the greensward, and left us sitting on our boxes and bundles . . . There we were in the wilderness; and when they were gone we had no means of following, had we wished to do so . . . This thought roused action – the tents were pitched – the night-fires kindled around them to scare away the wild beasts, and the life of a settler was begun.[22]

Lacking the knowledge or wherewithal to farm, many were soon forced from their land to nearby Grahamstown to seek what employment opportunities they could. Mostert himself described the operations as 'probably the most callous act of mass settlement in the entire history of empire'.[23]

Changes also occurred among the Xhosa. Ndlambe passed away in February 1828 and was succeeded by his son Mdushane, the hero of Amalinde, who survived him by only a year when he, too, died. The Ndlambe were then ruled by another son, Mhala, and went into decline thereafter. In the following year Ngqika himself died, on 14 November 1829. It was said that liquor had caused his death. He was succeeded by his son by his Great Wife, Sandile but, because he was then only nine years old, Sandile's much older brother Maqoma was appointed regent until he came of age.

Sir Galbraith Lowry Cole, who served as governor from 1828 to 1833, again expelled Maqoma from the Kat River Valley in 1829, the force used for the task being under the command of Colonel Henry Somerset.

Henry Somerset was born on 30 December 1794, the eldest son of Lord Charles Somerset. He was commissioned a cornet on 5 December 1811 and lieutenant on 30 December 1812. He fought in the Peninsular War and with the 18th Hussars at Waterloo, serving as aide-de-camp to his uncle Lord Edward Somerset. He purchased the rank of captain on 6 October 1815. In 1817 Somerset proceeded to the Cape Colony, where his father was governor, and took service with the Cape Mounted Rifles. After his father's resignation of his position as governor, Somerset stayed on at the Cape. He was promoted major on 25 March 1823, and on 17 July 1824 purchased the rank of lieutenant-colonel.

The second eviction from his home added fuel to Maqoma's burning hatred, especially when his beloved valley was later given to the Khoikhoi on the establishment of the Kat River Settlement.

Enter Harry Smith

Henry (Harry) George Wakelyn Smith was born in Whittlesey, Cambridge-shire, on 28 June 1787. His father was John Smith, a local surgeon of very modest means. It was, therefore, rather unusual that the relatively poor Harry Smith should have chosen the army as his career, in which the first com-mission and subsequent promotions to the rank of colonel were normally obtained by purchase. (Having once gained a colonelcy, promotion beyond that rank was based firmly on seniority.)

On the whole, then, birth was likely to be a help and wealth was of great importance. Smith had nothing of the first and little of the second, but there remained ability and patronage, both likely to be more effective if supplemented by self-confidence and luck. As will be shown he had all four of these, though he was inclined to ascribe his success entirely to his own exertions.[24]

In 1804, in a military climate influenced by the Napoleonic War, and under the threat of a French invasion, the seventeen-year-old Harry Smith accepted a commission as ensign in the Whittlesey Yeomanry Cavalry. In the spring of 1805, his unit was inspected by Brigadier-General the Hon. William Stewart, a co-founder of the Corps of Riflemen,[25] who was obviously impressed with Smith. Stewart was forming a second battalion and was looking for likely officers. He offered Smith a commission as second-lieutenant, an offer which was immediately accepted. Only three months later, in August 1805, a lieutenancy became available and Smith was required to purchase this 'step' for £100, a sum gathered together by his father.

Smith served in a number of campaigns, including the attack on Monte Video and Buenos Aires; Sir Thomas Moore's brief invasion of Portugal and Spain, leading to the evacuation of the force from Corunna; and the Peninsular War under Sir Arthur Wellesley, later Duke of Wellington. It was during the latter campaign that Smith rescued, and shortly thereafter married, fifteen-year-old Juana Maria de los Dolores de Leon.

Smith also served in the American War of 1812 and returned to Europe following Napoleon's escape from Elba, being present at Napoleon's final defeat at Waterloo on 18 June 1815. Smith remained in France as town major of Cambrai, Wellington's headquarters, until his return home in October 1818, having cemented as much of a friendship with Wellington as rank permitted – a relationship for which some of the credit belongs to Juana, as she charmed everyone she met.

Smith's meteoric rise was sponsored by several senior officers, including Colonel (later Lieutenant-General) Thomas Sydney Beckwith, Colonel John Colbourne and Lord Fitzroy Somerset. Evidence of the speed of his rise is supported by his record of promotion:

Captain	February 1812
Major	September 1814
Brevet Lieutenant-Colonel	June 1815

During much of his service, while often serving 'in the line' with great distinction, Smith had also acquired considerable staff experience, and was regarded as a very talented staff officer.

Following his return from Cambrai, Smith served in several posts before being sent to the Cape of Good Hope at the request of the governor, Sir

Lowry Cole, with whom he had served in the Peninsular War. Colonel Harry Smith arrived in Cape Town with his wife Juana in March 1829 as the new deputy quartermaster-general. There followed the happiest years of his life, and perhaps the quietest.

At the expiry of Sir Lowry Cole's term as governor he was succeeded by Sir Benjamin D'Urban, who was sworn in on 16 January 1834, and with whom Smith built a close relationship.

Smith's peaceful life evaporated in 1835 when, having chafed at the bit for so long, an opportunity arose for him to show his fighting mettle once more. Although D'Urban was aware that there was some unrest on the eastern frontier of the Cape, where Colonel Henry Somerset was in command, it was not until the arrival of a despatch from Somerset on 28 December 1834 that he finally became aware that another Xhosa invasion of the colony was actually in progress. It was the commencement of the Sixth Frontier War.

Harry Smith was the second most senior officer at the Cape and was at once ordered by D'Urban to take ship with reinforcements to assume command on the frontier. Smith eschewed the ship and made his celebrated thousand-kilometre ride from Cape Town to Grahamstown in six days, arriving on 6 January. (Smith was inordinately proud of his achievement and would have been profoundly disappointed to learn that Henry Somerset had made the same journey, in about the same time, in 1828.[26])

There he found the town in the grip of panic, with rickety barricades thrown up in the main street, the town full of refugees from the countryside and many of the outlying military posts abandoned by Somerset.

On the day following his arrival, Smith, with plenipotentiary civil and military power on the frontier, exploded into action. Martial law was declared and all males between sixteen and sixty years of age were required to register for military service. At the same time he ordered the dismantling of the town barricades, which Smith regarded as ridiculous. Next, he dealt with the messages from the Xhosa leaders: after learning that they offered no hope of peace, he sent a message to them ordering them back behind their boundaries after surrendering all their plunder and stolen cattle. Smith's credo was that attack was the best form of defence and he applied his doctrine immediately.

The regular troops were ordered out of their barracks to retake the abandoned border forts and Major William Cox, whom Smith discovered to be a fellow officer of the Rifle Brigade, was given command of a force with the object of taking back Fort Willshire.

Smith next took decisive steps to secure the border area. Patrols were sent out to re-occupy the abandoned forts and to set up new ones. Somerset was sent to secure the road to Port Elizabeth, whence Smith expected his supplies and reinforcements to arrive. By 20 January, when Governor D'Urban arrived at Grahamstown, the first phase of the fight-back was concluded and the Xhosa had, for the most part, returned across the Great Fish River boundary.

D'Urban now determined that the fight must be carried across the Fish River into the Xhosa heartland and prepared four columns of troops to undertake the reprisal invasion. Smith had suggested that the Fish River was not a satisfactory boundary for the colony because of its vast mantle of bush. Instead, he proposed the Buffalo River as being more suitable since it was more open.

Throughout the remainder of January, and the whole of February, Smith, now Chief of Staff to D'Urban, laboured to prepare the invasion force. On 29 March, a general order was issued identifying the troops assigned to each of the four columns, numbering some two thousand men in total, of whom eight hundred were mounted. The thrust was directed towards the Amathola Mountains, where the chiefs were said to have concentrated.

The governor quickly tired of directing the clearance of the mountain fastness and decided to press on with two of his divisions, leaving the remainder to continue the difficult task of clearing the mountains. D'Urban led his troops through Ngqika country to the banks of the Kei River in order to invade Hintsa's country, in what was later to become known as the Transkei.

On 15 April, D'Urban reached the Kei. He then crossed and proceeded some thirty kilometres to the area now occupied by the town of Butterworth, near the site of an abandoned Wesleyan mission station, where he set up his camp. Here they found a swelling mass of refugees who were finally identified as Mfengu.

The origins of the Mfengu are still in dispute, but I shall here advance the view which has, until recently, long been held. They were refugees from Natal, mostly Mbo, who had been dispossessed during the *mfecane* in the late 1820s.[27] The name was given to them by the Gcaleka Xhosa who had received them in their country but, instead of taking an equal place in Xhosa society, they were treated almost as slaves, being called by the Gcaleka their 'dogs'.

Their weapons were much the same as the rest of the Nguni people, including the Xhosa, although under British tutelage they became familiar with firearms, especially when they later served as auxiliary troops.

They had rebelled against their erstwhile masters, the Gcaleka, and now wished to attach themselves to the British force, together with many thousands of Gcaleka cattle, to go with them to the Cape Colony. Both D'Urban and Smith recognised their utility as a buffer against the Xhosa and welcomed them into the British fold.

Meanwhile the Gcaleka chief Hintsa, who was very suspicious of the white men, had finally agreed to meet the governor. In the discussions which followed, D'Urban demanded that Hintsa cease giving aid to the Ciskei Xhosa and surrender fifty thousand cattle and one thousand horses as a fine. He demanded hostages against the speedy delivery of the animals.

Harry Smith was eventually able to convince Hintsa that he must accept what the chief saw as very severe terms. He also agreed to accompany Hintsa on an expedition to collect the cattle for the fine and return with them to D'Urban's camp.

On 10 May the governor ordered his troops into a large square facing inwards. Hintsa, his brother Bhurhu and son Sarhili were brought into the centre of the square and there listened to D'Urban proclaim the new border of the colony, naming the country between the Keiskamma River and the Kei as the province of Queen Adelaide. All the rebellious Xhosa were to be transported across the Kei to the Gcaleka country, leaving behind only the Gqunukhwebe[28] and the newly transplanted Mfengu. A new military headquarters town was to be established on the upper Buffalo River and given the name King William's Town.

That same day, Harry Smith left with a large force for a destination known only to Hintsa, who accompanied him, where the promised cattle were to be delivered. Hintsa twice asked Smith to clarify the chief's position, to be told that should he attempt to escape he would be shot. Otherwise, peace would be established when the requisite number of cattle had been delivered.

After two or three days of frustrating travel, Smith became suspicious of Hintsa's intention. Suddenly the chief bolted and Smith quickly pursued him. The colonel was able to catch the chief and tip him from his horse, after which Hintsa ran off into the bush pursued by the force of guides which were supposed to be watching him. Hintsa was eventually cornered in a creek under some rocks and there he was killed by a shot to the head.

Callously disregarding Hintsa's murder, and leaving his body lying in the bush, Smith continued to gather up Gcaleka cattle and had taken more than three thousand before he at last turned back to the Kei River and the governor's camp. D'Urban was greatly shocked by the news of Hintsa's death and anxiously considered the reaction that might be received from the Colonial Secretary in London.

Following his father's tragic death, Sarhili (known to the British as 'Kreli') became the new chief of the Gcaleka people, who lived on the eastern bank of the Kei River, seemingly quite remote from the centre of violence around King William's Town. He was, however, more than just a chief – he was the paramount chief of all the Xhosa, including Sandile and his Ngqika.

As a result of the manner of his father's death, Sarhili remained suspicious of white men for the rest of his life and could never trust their word. He was described by John Milton thus:

> In the years since his father's slaying the son of Hintsa had grown into a tall, handsome, dignified man, much loved by his people, and admired and respected by the few Europeans who had actually met him. Unfortunately to most colonial folk he was a spectre, distant and dangerous, the dreaded Paramount Chief of the Xhosa. Suspicious and hostile, they created a myth about him: he was wily, crafty, devious, dangerous, a savage warrior endlessly plotting and scheming to invade their country and sow ruin and destruction throughout the land.[29]

D'Urban's proclamation of the Province of Queen Adelaide was vetoed by Earl Grey and the governor had to abandon his work, to his great embarrassment. Smith was hurt in a rather different way – he had to give up his hopes of being master of the new province and return to Cape Town to prepare for his defence of his actions in the death of Hintsa. In the whitewash enquiry into Hintsa's death which followed, Smith was cleared of any wrongdoing.

Sir Benjamin D'Urban was replaced in January 1838 by Sir George Napier but the former would remain at the Cape in a private capacity until 1846, the city of Durban being named after him. Harry Smith, meanwhile, who had thought that his military career was finished, received news in 1840 that he had been appointed adjutant-general of the British forces in India and left the Cape immediately.

Also in 1840, a senior British officer was visited by a number of chiefs, who introduced him to a twenty-year-old youth with a withered leg. This was the new chief of the Ngqika and sovereign chief of the Rharhabe Xhosa, Sandile (known to the British as Sandilli), who had only recently undergone his coming of age ceremony. He had done so with some bitterness on the part of his older brother Maqoma, who had served his people as regent since the death of Ngqika in 1829. Maqoma's dependence on alcohol had increased in recent years – especially after Sandile assumed his leadership of the Ngqika – and it was not unusual for him to be found in the canteens of Fort Beaufort. He and Tyhali had gone their separate ways, Tyhali being disgusted with his brother's alcohol dependence.

Mostert describes Sandile, who by now had begun emulating his older brother's intemperance, as having 'a more difficult personality to penetrate than most'.[30] Other historians were less generous, Meintjes recounting:

Character assessments of Sandile are not flattering. Cory described him as weak-minded. Theal says that he was 'a wretched stupid sot'. Brownlee also calls him weak, as well as irresolute and foolish. Soga says he was a weakling, pliable, 'and without a settled or reliable mind'.[31]

Brownlee's assessment must have been quite accurate, as the two men had grown up together. While these descriptions may be correct, they may also reflect the conditions under which he lived during his minority, being in the shadow of his more dynamic and influential brother Maqoma. Certainly the events that follow indicate that he was making an effort to cast off Maqoma's dominance and assert his own personality. One might also suggest that his withered leg, the result of infantile paralysis (poliomyelitis) might have induced a reserve in him as a youth which bred a lack of confidence as he grew older.

The Kat River Settlement

The mixed-race Khoikhoi people were employed in domestic service and on white farms throughout the colony, many of them in the Western Province. Another name for these people was Gonaqua Khoikhoi, with the sobriquets 'Totties' and 'Gonas' being frequently applied to them in contemporary accounts.

The Khoikhoi people, as I shall call them, had also long fought with the British against the Xhosa and had proved loyal and courageous fighters. By the middle of 1829, legislation was passed to allow 'Hottentots and free persons of colour' to own land and, when the Kat River Valley was settled by these loyal people, it was at the expense of the original Xhosa inhabitants once again. The population of the Kat River Settlement quickly swelled to more than four thousand people and became a thriving farming community, regarded enviously by white and Xhosa alike. Inevitably, however, coloured squatters were also attracted to the settlement and they formed a substantial proportion by 1850.

Many of the Kat River settlers were men who had retired from, or were still serving with, the Cape Mounted Rifles (CMR) or other ad hoc units called upon in times of need. The dependants of those still serving were given 'rations' by the government because their men were away from home and could not provide for them.

Among these was a man who will feature later in our story. He was Hermanus Matroos, whose name would be most strongly attached to the alienation of the settlers of the Kat River Settlement.

At one point he had been under death threat from Maqoma, whose plans for a campaign of resistance against the British he betrayed. He had served as an interpreter to the British since 1819, notably in the wars of 1835 and 1846. It was he who warned the British that Hintsa was plotting to escape from Harry Smith's custody. He was rewarded with a fine double-barrelled gun at the end of the war, as well as one of the best farms in the Kat river valley. The son of a runaway slave and a Xhosa mother, he was . . . one of the great outsiders of the South African frontier, those who belonged neither truly with their own kind nor with those alternative societies through which they also freely moved.[32]

The arrangement for supporting the dependants of the coloured men who served with the British and were away from their homes, without pay, was that they too were given rations. In January 1847, when the then governor, Sir Peregrine Maitland, had declared the end of the War of the Axe, he had ordered all rations to the Kat River Settlement to be stopped, effective from 1 February.[33] It is clear that Maitland's order was not carried out, apparently on the 'verbal orders' of Henry Somerset.[34]

On his arrival at the frontier in February 1847, the new governor, Sir Henry Pottinger, found that his predecessor's peace announcement had been premature and that the war was not, in fact, finished. Mostert described Pottinger as 'a violent-tempered martinet, greedy and ambitious'. This seems to be demonstrated by the fact that he agreed to take the governorship of the Cape 'on the "express understanding" that the post was seen as temporary and did not interfere with his "prospects" for India'. Mostert goes on to note:

Pottinger's physical discomfiture [caused by a kidney ailment] obviously added many degrees to his permanent condition of hot displeasure with the world about him. The shoddy disorder and makeshift way things were managed on the Cape Colony's frontier, the venality, crookedness and subterfuge that lurked behind the shabby facade, permanently inflamed his mood. His rage was cumulative, overheated by impatience, by contempt for the way things had been left and by the shortcomings of those with whom he had to deal.[35]

As part of his plan to bring an end to the conflict, Pottinger ordered four hundred men to be called up from the Kat River Settlement. The response was poor, with Major Sutton of the Cape Mounted Rifles reporting 'the spirit of insubordination which has been evinced by the men of the Kat River Settlement . . .'[36]

Pottinger's expectation was, in fact, unrealistic, as the following report from his military commander-in-chief, Sir George Berkeley,[37] shows:

The population [of the Settlement] consists of 3700 women and children, and 1000 adults, 900 of whom are effective and doing duty, 400 at present in the field, and 500 garrisoning the important posts in that district; under the general rule, the wives and families of the 400 men in the field only would receive rations; but, from the nature of the duties of the remaining 500, although not actually with me in the field, they are wholly prevented from attending to their agricultural pursuits, or in any other way providing for their families, as I conceive the posts they hold too important to be abandoned at the present crisis, I beg to submit to the favourable consideration of your Excellency the recommendation of Colonel Somerset, that for the present the wives and families of these men also should be allowed rations, furnished through the Commissariat at the expense of the Colonial Government.[38]

From this assessment it is plain that the men of the Settlement were already fully stretched and could not send more. But they were also suffering severe privation, as Cory was to record:

In consequence of the war, all had left their allotments and for nearly a year had crowded round such places as Fort Armstrong and Elands Post fort – now the town of Seymour. The men had been [away] from their homes and thus had been prevented from working for the support of their families. Further, having served *without* pay,[39] but merely for a ration of bread and meat, all were in semi-nakedness in consequence of the want of the wherewithal to purchase clothes.[40]

The result of these reports was that that settlers' dependants were granted rations, whether their men were on active service or not, but an issue of clothing was refused. Nevertheless, the refusal to provide adequately, either for the men or their families, left a sour taste in their mouths and their privations were to make them reconsider the value of their loyalty.

True to his word, Pottinger left the Cape after less than twelve months, to take up an appointment in India. It now became necessary for the incumbent Secretary of State for War and the Colonies, Earl Grey, to find a replacement.

Time had obviously healed the suspicion attached to a soldier newly returned from India, Major-General Sir Harry Smith, a baronet, the victor of the battle of Aliwal and a national hero. Seeking someone to replace Pottinger, Grey approached Smith about the matter, having previously sought his advice on instructions to be sent to Sir Henry before his departure. Here, then, was a man whose military prowess was firmly established and who had enjoyed a considerable period of service at the Cape. Furthermore, it was plain that the frontier was now less stable than it had been when D'Urban and Smith had been there ten years earlier.[41] In typical style, he was already making known to those in power just what he would do if he were there. It was all very impressive and Grey was convinced he had found his man. What he did not consider was Harry Smith's worst fault, and one which he had so far been able to keep under control: hubris. In the rarefied environment at the Cape, where he would be the most senior officer of government and the military, the genie would soon slip out of the bottle.

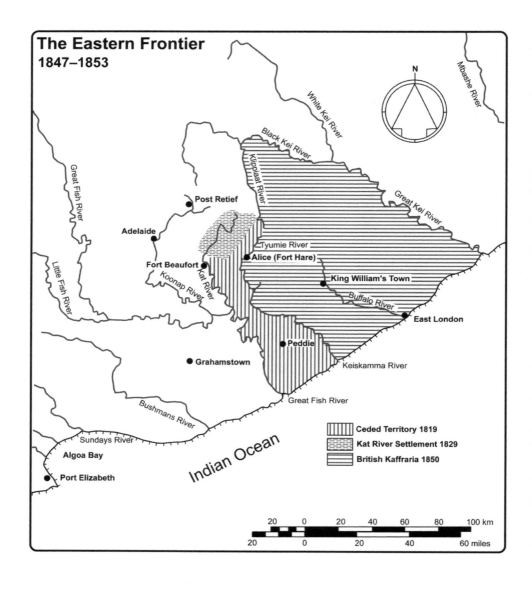

The Eastern Frontier
1847–1853

N

Mbashe River

White Kei River

Black Kei River

Klipplaat River

Great Kei River

Great Fish River

● Post Retief

● Adelaide

Tyumie River

Fort Beaufort ●

● Alice (Fort Hare)

Koonap River

Kat River

● King William's Town

Buffalo River

● East London

Little Fish River

● Peddie

● Grahamstown

Keiskamma River

Great Fish River

Bushmans River

Indian Ocean

Sundays River

Algoa Bay

● Port Elizabeth

	Ceded Territory 1819
	Kat River Settlement 1829
	British Kaffraria 1850

| 20 | 0 | 20 | 40 | 60 | 80 | 100 km |
| 20 | 0 | | 20 | | 40 | 60 miles |

In spite of some initial objections to Smith's appointment by the Duke of Wellington, the governorship was finally offered by Grey in the following terms:

> Your experience in the former Kafir War & the distinguished success with wh. you then (& since) conducted the military operations entrusted to you, together with your knowledge of the general affairs of the colony point you out as far the fittest person that would in my judgement be selected for this important Govt. which I trust you will not refuse.[42]

There were a couple of hitches regarding Smith's appointment. The first was that, as usual, Smith was short of funds and to remedy this lack he was given both the salary of governor and that of a lieutenant-general. This was still not enough to cover his needs, however, and his problem was relieved through the generosity of Miss A.G. Burdett-Coutts.[43]

Rather more serious was the haste with which Smith was hustled off to the Cape, which caused him to outrun the bureaucracy: the Letters Patent for his appointment had not been signed by the Queen.[44]

At noon on 23 September 1847, Sir Harry Smith went aboard HMS *Myrtle* with Juana for their second voyage to Cape Town.[45]

Chapter 2

I Will Be Governor

Aucto Splendore Resurgo[1]

On 1 December 1847, there was a formal reception for the new governor of the Cape of Good Hope. Now elevated to lieutenant-general (local rank), Sir Harry Smith had returned to the seat of his discredit in triumph, having won a name for himself in India, earning a baronetcy and the epithet 'Hero of Aliwal'.[2] Furthermore, he returned as the most senior officer at the Cape, governor and high commissioner. This latter title, first bestowed on his predecessor Sir Henry Pottinger,[3] gave Smith the same additional power, authorising him to deal with 'the settling and adjustment of the territories adjacent or contiguous to the eastern or north-eastern district of Our said settlement and its dependencies'.[4] No doubt the extra pay also helped to ease Smith's money problems.

Smith was of small stature and by nature he was somewhat unconventional. He had already demonstrated that he was a fine, dynamic soldier with great personal courage. He was, however, no longer a young man, having been born in June 1787. He was thus sixty years of age in 1847 and his eccentricities had come to dominate his personality: 'Within this account [Smith] becomes henceforth one of the most extraordinary personalities of all, dashing, vain, self-glorifying, reckless, somewhat mad, and often ludicrous, as well as silly.'[5] Thus did Noël Mostert introduce this remarkable character, who was to bring down on himself, the colony and his country yet another war during his second sojourn in South Africa.

Sir Henry Pottinger had failed to bring the War of the Axe to a final conclusion. Thus his replacement was first required to put an end to this latest (seventh) war. In fact, the war was all but over anyway: Ngqika's older son Maqoma was in virtual exile in Port Elizabeth and his much younger brother Sandile, sovereign chief of the Rharhabe people, was already a prisoner of the British. He had attended what he thought were to be peace talks on the Keiskamma River but was instead seized and brought to Grahams-town under heavy guard by Captain John Jervis Bisset.[6] Sandile regarded this seizure as a great betrayal on the part of the British and never forgave them. Nor did he forgive Bisset, it seems: 'Sandile never ceased to speak of this case as one of gross treachery, and in order to commemorate it gave to a son born during his captivity the name of Bisset.'[7] Smith and his wife Juana arrived at Cape Town on the morning of 1 December 1847, where he received an ecstatic welcome from both citizens and local dignitaries. Smith quickly displayed his idiosyncratic nature:

> Menzies, J., and Mr. Montagu almost ran a boat race, through the South Easter of the day, to board the 'Vernon'; when before Sir H. Smith, he soon found out they were not Friends and would say, and do, nothing till he had made them shake hands, a form, I fear, between them – like the Prize-fighters – who no less heartily, immediately afterwards, try to knock each other's head off. Some such feeling has continued, I believe, to prevail between them, and equally perhaps on either side.[8]

After being sworn in as 'Administrator of the colonial government' (since he lacked the Letters Patent)[9] almost the first action he took was to permit the departure for home of the two companies of the 62nd Regiment, detained en route from India.[10] This was almost certainly a sop to Earl Grey, who had impressed upon him the need for economy in the matter of the expense of British troops at the Cape.

At the time that Sir Harry became governor, Colonel Henry Somerset was in command of the Cape Mounted Rifles and also the other frontier forces. Captain Thomas Lucas described him at this time:

> He was a fine specimen of an old soldier, frank and loyal in his bearing, and the beau ideal of a cavalry officer of the 'old regime.' He had served at Waterloo as a subaltern in the 11th Hussars, and had made himself conspicuous in the different Kaffir campaigns by his bravery and intimate knowledge of the country, and of the bush tactics so necessary in that exceptional warfare. He was a fine looking old man, a regular *vieux d'Afrique*, his bronzed complexion and fine features well contrasted with his large moustache which, with his hair, was snowy white.[11]

Somerset was not, however, altogether a moral man. Captain William King-Hall, RN, of HMS *Styx*, noted in his diary entry of February 3rd 1851:

> The Cape Corps is a species of family monopoly to him, having his relatives in it as Officers, and they also say as men, bastard children, in his ranks . . .

They also publicly report that he has three or four prostitutes – Hottentots – with him, and from the care he takes of himself, travelling with every luxury and convenience, these patrols are a species of pleasure picnic to him with the knowledge of his getting out of debt by the prolongation of the war. It is an undisputable fact that during the previous war (1846–47) many wagons hired by him were his own, under the names of others.[12]

As well as being a venal individual, Somerset was also indolent and frequently dilatory and, by being so, sometimes put his troops in harm's way. He did, however, possess great personal courage.

In addition to these traits, Somerset inherited still another from his family – nepotism. His son, Charles Henry Somerset, was a brevet major in the CMR and his daughter Fannie was married to William Sutton, also a senior officer of the CMR.

On the Frontier

Ten days after his arrival at Cape Town, Sir Harry left by ship for Port Elizabeth, where he was again greeted by jubilant crowds. Among the throng outside his hotel was a mounted Maqoma, his old adversary. Smith glared at the chief and drew his sword halfway out of its scabbard. Then with a flourish, 'he drove it back again with an expressive gesture of anger and scorn'.[13] Maqoma started back in alarm and the crowd laughed at his discomfiture. However, worse was to come for Maqoma:

> His Excellency afterwards saw Macomo, whom he bitterly upbraided for his treachery, and derided for his folly. As he uttered his reproaches, he ordered him to kneel prostrate before him, which he did, unwillingly enough. 'This,' said Sir Harry Smith, placing his foot on the neck of the conquered savage, 'this is to teach you that I have come hither to teach Kaffirland that I am chief and master here, and this is the way I shall treat the enemies of the Queen of England.'[14]

An interesting Xhosa variation of this account shows Maqoma resisting Smith's action, saying, 'You insist on behaving like a dog because you are a dog; Queen Victoria did not send you to do this.'[15] Whichever version resembles the truth, Smith's hubris was to the fore.

Mostert described Smith's humiliation of Maqoma as 'an act of unfathomable coarseness and stupidity',[16] while Rev. George Brown said that it was 'one of his unaccountable freaks.'[17] This single demonstration was to sound the death knell of Smith's governorship almost as soon as it began, because Maqoma never forgave, nor forgot, this public degradation and would eventually take his revenge. For Maqoma, however, vengeance was a meal best taken cold and in order to wreak it fully he gave up his dependence on alcohol.

The governor continued his triumphal progress to Grahamstown, arriving there on 17 December. After acknowledging the cheering crowds from the steps of St George's church, he went to his official residence, where he sent for the imprisoned Sandile.

> On his Excellency's arrival at Government house, he sent for Sandilla, whom he addressed in severe terms. Sandilla, of course, admitted, in the old style, that he had been in error. On Sir Harry asking him who was now the 'Inkosi Enkulu', (Great Chief) of Kaffirland, he, after a pause, in true Kaffir style, and closely observed by his councillors, replied 'Kreli.' [Sarhili, son of Hintsa.] At this Sir Harry broke forth, in terms of great anger. 'No!' said the governor, 'I am your paramount chief – I am come to punish you for your misdoings – your treachery – and your obstinate folly. You may approach my foot and kiss it, in token of submission, but not until I see a sincere repentance for the past, will I permit you to touch my hand.'[18]

In spite of his outburst, the governor allowed Sandile to go free – and gave him a baton confirming his effective reduction from sovereign chief to quasi-magisterial status.

While the rest of the town was celebrating his appointment, and presence, Harry Smith himself was working feverishly to complete his early plans for the colony: 'Three o'clock on the morning of the 18th found him at his desk, which he scarcely left till five in the evening.'[19]

In two despatches to the Secretary of State, Earl Grey, he set out these plans in detail, while at the same time preparing a series of proclamations to announce them to the public. They were remarkable proposals for a governor who had been in office for less than two weeks. The first was announced immediately: the eastern boundary of the colony was formally extended from the Great Fish River to the Keiskamma and Tyumie rivers and all treaties with the Xhosa chiefs were declared null and void.[20] The annexed land formed what was hitherto known as the 'Ceded Territory', to be occupied only by the military, under a determination by Lord Charles Somerset in 1819. The only concession made to the Xhosa chief at that time, Ngqika, was that he could continue to live in the Tyumie Valley in the north. Maqoma too had fared quite well: he had been removed from his homeland in the nearby Kat River area several times but each time he had been permitted to return by Lord Charles's son, Colonel Henry Somerset. Later, after the departure of Lord Charles Somerset, the Xhosa were allowed to remain on the land by Lieutenant-Governor Andries Stockenström, under 'a loan in perpetuity'.

The newly annexed area was to be known as the Division of Victoria and a chief commissioner was appointed 'to reside at Alice Town, a rising town on the Chumie [Tyumie], near Fort Hare'.[21] The post was originally given to Rev. Henry Calderwood, who had previously served as assistant commissioner to the Ngqika people.[22] He was, however, replaced in that position by twenty-six-year-old Charles Pacalt Brownlee.

Brownlee was born in March 1821, was close in age to the Ngqika chief Sandile and they had known each other for most of their lives. His father, Rev. John Brownlee, had founded a mission station for the London Missionary Society in the Tyumie Valley in 1820, and his son inherited his father's talent for languages, quickly becoming fluent in Xhosa, and later in what became Africaans. Physically, Charles was very tall, again like his father; he was a burly man who sported a luxuriant beard. He had considerable sympathy for the Xhosa people and this showed in his kindly treatment of them. His choice, therefore, as commissioner to the Ngqika was a particularly happy one.[23]

In his new position, Charles Brownlee took up residence at Fort Cox, with his brother James as his clerk: both men had small cottages there. His choice of Fort Cox was understandable too, because the fort was close to Burnshill, where Sandile and his mother Suthu lived (and where Ngqika's grave still lies).

It should also be noted that Captain John Maclean was serving as commissioner to the Ndlambe people and Mr W.M. Fynn was at this time appointed as assistant commissioner under Maclean.

In that first despatch of 18 December, the governor had casually mentioned a further change in the boundaries of the colony. 'The eastern frontier as designated is indispensable; and I trust your Lordship will not regard the northern limits as extensive.'[24] The proclamation announcing this change, supported by a report from the surveyor-general, was equally enigmatic:

> . . . and whereas the northern limits of the colony, as the same purport to be settled by the proclamation of the Government, bearing date the 21st of February, 1805, are ill defined and uncertain, and it is expedient to adopt in that direction a clearer and better boundary; Now, therefore, I do hereby, in the name of Her Majesty, and subject to her Royal confirmation, under and by virtue of the several powers and authorities in me vested, proclaim, declare, and make known, that the boundary landwards of the colony of the Cape of Good Hope shall, from and after this date, be as follows – that is to say, from the mouth of the Keiskamma river, ascending along the western bank of the same, up to its confluence with the Chumie river; thence up the western bank of the last mentioned river to its northernmost source, thence along the summit of the

Katberg Range to the centre of the Luheri Mount or Gaika's Kop; thence to the nearest source of the Plaats river, and down the left bank of the same to its junction with the Zwart Kei river . . .[25]

What was not said, anywhere, was that the land to be annexed was that of the Thembu chief Maphasa, who had struggled long and hard against British incursions during the previous war. As a result of white settlement of the area, and in particular the establishment of the village of Whittlesea,[26] Maphasa began a series of raids against the settlers.

On 19 December 1847, Phato, chief of the Gqunukhwebe, finally surrendered – the last to do so. The War of the Axe, it seemed, was finally over. Smith left for King William's Town on the same day, arriving there on the 23rd. In his second despatch to Earl Grey, he described his action towards the Xhosa chiefs and notables assembled there to meet him:

> A custom of great antiquity prevails among them, the obeying all mandates by messengers bearing a long stick of the Chiefs; and to disobey a mandate thus conveyed, entails outlawry. This custom I maintained when formerly in command in this province – a species of magic wand they well understood; and I rode into the circle formed by their followers, the Chiefs having all assembled in the centre, bearing in the right hand a serjeant's halberd, well sharpened, the emblem of war; in my left, my baton of peace and authority, surmounted by a brass knob. I directed each Chief to come forward and touch whichever he pleased – it was immaterial to me – they all most cheerfully touched the symbol of peace. I then in a very impressive manner read and explained the proclamations, with various comments, threats, and promises, as the tenor of the documents turned; which being concluded, each Chief came forward and kissed my [stirruped] foot; a custom of their own in doing homage; exclaiming, 'Inkosi Inkulu!' (great chief).[27]

Mostert summarised the characteristics Smith had exhibited since his arrival at the frontier as: '. . . the dangerously impulsive immaturity, the foolish posturing ego, the unsure and distinctly ungrand little man who was for the moment concealed under the cocked hat and behind the glittering medals and sash of office'.[28]

The Xhosa chiefs were not, of course, impressed with Smith's theatricalities; on the contrary, they were at pains to suppress their contempt for both him and his performance, while maintaining the external appearance of servility simply to stroke the great man's ego. They were biding their time.

So was Maqoma. Once again, he had sharp words with the governor at this meeting. A newspaper report alleged that Smith had said to the chief, 'in four days I can have my ships at the Buffalo with thousands of soldiers to punish all bad men who stir up the country to strife and war'. Maqoma had quietly asked the governor if he had any ships 'that can sail into the Amatholas'.[29]

Having, as he thought, sufficiently impressed and cowed the chiefs, the governor made the remaining announcements of his plans. The second proclamation was to cause great consternation among the Ngqika: the country between the new eastern border on the Keiskamma River and the Great Kei River was declared to be 'vested in Her Majesty the Queen', while not formally becoming a part of the colony. The area was to be 'held by the Kaffir Chiefs and people from, and under, Her said Majesty . . . under such rules and regulations as Her Majesty's High Commissioner . . . shall deem best . . .'[30]

In creating this new zone, to be called 'British Kaffraria', Smith was making two statements. First, he was correcting what he had always thought to have been a great wrong when, in 1835, Lord Glenelg had vetoed Sir Benjamin D'Urban's establishment of Queen Adelaide Province in the same area, while Smith was the administrator of the new province. It was at that time that Smith established his headquarters in the newly founded King William's Town. Second, he was demonstrating his new authority, that of high commissioner, and asserting his power over 'adjacent territories'.

Sound the Tocsin

Next, Smith announced the establishment of 'military villages' in the newly annexed land between the Fish and Keiskamma, which were thrown open to occupation by retired soldiers.[31] Four of these villages were eventually established in early 1848, in the area of the upper Tyumie and Kat rivers, and were named Woburn, Auckland, Ely and Juanasburg, the latter named after the governor's wife. These villages were to occupy land resumed from the Xhosa without recompense. Each village was to be administered by a superintendent and the process by which the village of Woburn came into existence was described to historian George Cory by Captain Godfrey Armytage.[32]

On 1 January 1848 twenty-two-year-old Lieutenant Armytage, of the 6th Regiment, applied for the position of superintendent of Woburn military village and accordingly underwent an interview with Sir Harry Smith. Having then been appointed, Armytage went out to find a site for the village, accompanied by Rev. Henry Calderwood and a land surveyor, Captain Robert Bates of the 45th Regiment. Armytage, with the agreement of his colleagues, decided on the site of the future village at a spot in the Tyumie Valley about thirteen kilometres from Lovedale.

Discharged soldiers who wished to find a place at the village had been ordered to march to Fort Hare. On 12 January, Armytage went to the fort and found seventy-nine men ready to go with him. Accordingly, with 'a wagon and a very inadequate supply of spades and carpenter's tools and also a small supply of seeds and potatoes for sowing', they went off to their new home.

After homes and gardens had been started, a series of setbacks reduced their enthusiasm: promised implements and seed did not arrive; poor surveying caused men to make their gardens in the wrong place; single men decided that they were unsuited to such a settled life of labour. Finally, a three-day rainstorm flooded gardens and home foundations, bringing everything to a halt. Armytage relates that, after payment of a first £5 instalment on their properties, thirty men left the settlement. By March 1849, after their free rations had stopped, the number of men at the vllage dwindled to twenty-four. The situation in the other villages must have been very similar. After six months, even Armytage had had enough and rejoined his regiment, his place being taken by a Captain Stacey. (Armytage subsequently married Charlotte Emily Blackburn of Wynburg, on 6 February 1849[33] and purchased his captaincy effective 26 December 1851.[34])

A series of further announcements followed, appearing in General Order No. 124:[35]

1. Lieutenant-Colonel George Henry Mackinnon, CB, was appointed colonel on the staff and commandant and chief commissioner of British Kaffraria.
2. Captain John Jervis Bisset, Cape Mounted Rifles, whom we shall meet later in these pages, was appointed brigade-major in British Kaffraria, through whom all correspondence for Mackinnon was to pass.
3. The 7th Dragoon Guards, and the 27th, 90th and 1/91st regiments were told off for home service. This was clearly a response to pressure from Earl Grey to further reduce the expense of maintaining British troops at the Cape. It was a decision which was also to come back to haunt the governor.
4. Announcements were made concerning existing forts within the colony, and new ones to be erected in British Kaffraria, among them Fort White and Fort Cox.

Colonel Mackinnon was an unattached officer at the Cape serving, like Harry Smith before him, as assistant quartermaster-general. He had been commissioned as cornet on 22 March 1810 and had then been promoted to lieutenant on 4 November 1824, and captain in February 1828. Mackinnon had never held the rank of major but was promoted directly to the rank of lieutenant-colonel on 24 April 1840. He had seen little or no active service in his forty years of military service, and this was to become quite evident.

Within a month of taking office, Smith had already alienated the Xhosa people in a number of ways. First, he had publicly humiliated the two great chiefs, Maqoma and Sandile. Then, he had confiscated a huge parcel of land – the Ceded Territory – which they, being in possession once again, had retained great hopes of retaining permanently. He had established military villages, to be settled by ex-soldiers, on land appropriated from Chief Tyali's sons, Feni and Oba. (Tyali was a half-brother to both Sandile and Maqoma.) Finally, he had continued to reduce the status of the chiefs by removing many of their powers and handing them over to white commissioners. Xhosa morale fell to its lowest ebb.

The Kaffir Police had first been formed by Sir Peregrine Maitland as long ago as late 1846, when Lieutenant David Davies of the 90th Regiment had been appointed superintendent of police and given orders to train fifty Ngqika for the purpose.[36] This establishment was increased by Sir Henry Pottinger to two hundred men and subsequently, as a result of the success of the unit, he authorised an increase of a further two hundred men, in a second division under the command of Captain C. Mostyn Owen.[37] On 1 January 1848, Sir Harry Smith confirmed these arrangements, under the same superintendents, together with the stations of the two divisions.[38]

Each division was to consist of four African sergeants, eight corporals and four hundred privates. Provision was also made for fifty-four horses, so that a quarter of the force should be mounted. (Quite how one hundred men would be mounted on half that number of horses remains a mystery.) The first division was to be placed at Fort Cox, with detachments at Forts Hare and White, the second at Wesleyville, with detachments at King William's Town, Fort Waterloo and Fort Murray. In a report to Earl Grey, Smith noted that the Kaffir Police 'is most obnoxious to the Kaffirs; hence its loyalty and attachment are perpetuated'.[39]

On the same date, a general order was promulgated which gave the conditions under which British ex-servicemen could qualify to take up residence in one of the military villages announced earlier.

On 7 January 1837, Smith had called a great meeting of the Xhosa chiefs, in the newly established King William's Town, to describe to them how they were to be governed. Eleven years later, on that same date in 1848, he called them together once again. Among those present were Sandile and his brothers Anta and Xhoxho, Feni and Oba, sons of Tyhali, all Ngqika chiefs; Mhala of the Ndlambe, Stokwe and Sotho, sons of Nqeno; the brothers Thola and Bhotomane of the Dange; Phato of the Gqunukhwebe and Tshatshu of the Ntinde. All were there, except one man: Maqoma, who was represented by his son Kona.

Once again, the governor described the assembly, and his words to the Xhosa chiefs, to the Secretary of State in London. Among his declarations were two which stand out:

> The day I arrived at King William's Town, the 23rd December, I read to you the Proclamation in the name of Her Majesty the Queen of England, which described your true position, the consequence of the wicked and unprovoked war which you had made upon the colony, viz., that conquest has deprived you of all right to the country upon which you are now permitted to build; that between the Keiskamma and the Kei is 'British Kaffraria;' . . . and that in future you hold these territories of and from Her Majesty; that all your political independence as a people is at an end; that no treaties will ever again be entered into with you; that you shall acknowledge no paramount chief but the (Jukosi Jukulu [Nkhosi Nkhulu]) Great Chief, whom Her Majesty of England places over you, from whom you hold your lands, and not in any right of your own; for you well know that war, the war you made, has deprived you of them for ever.
>
> . . . Hear! I am your 'Jukosi Jukulu [Nkosi Nkhulu],' and no chief of your own; no 'Kreili!' no 'Sandilli!' no Macomo no Seirani! [Siwani] no Umhala! but I shall keep each chief at the head of his own tribe, and I will make English and good men of you. Now you great chiefs come forward, and touch my Stick of Office. The Stick of War I have thrown away.[40]

The climax came when, as he drew to the end of his harangue, he made a great demonstration of British power:

> He then worked himself up into a storm of wrath – or pretended to do so – and shouted: 'And you even dared to make war, you DARE TO MAKE WAR, you dare to attack our waggons! See what I will do if you ever dare to touch a waggon or the oxen belonging to it. Do you see that waggon, I say? Now hear my word, FIRE!'
>
> Before the meeting, preparations had been made for a thrilling theatrical effect which was to be introduced at this part of the proceedings. At some little distance from the assembly, stood an empty ox-waggon, which, though in the sight of all, had most probably been unnoticed. Under it was a considerable heap of gunpowder and a train was laid to a convenient spot. When the word, 'fire,' was given a spark was put to the train, and in a moment, there was a

deafening report. When the volume of smoke had cleared and the shower of waggon fragments had ceased to fall – it was seen that the waggon had disappeared.[41]

One is left to wonder what Earl Grey might have thought of such an inane pantomime but his replies remained mute on the subject.

On 14 January 1848, Smith announced the resumption of the mouth of the Buffalo River as a port, with a radius of two miles from that point, to be named East London.[42] This was an important military step because it greatly reduced the time required to move troops up to the frontier from Cape Town or Port Elizabeth, although the Ngqika would have regarded the annexation as yet another theft of their land.

In a despatch to Grey on 15 February, Smith announced the foundation of the four planned military villages, only three of which were for white settlers, the other being for 'Hottentots', presumably on lines similar to the Kat River Settlement.[43] They had a planned total of three hundred residents, a target which was never to be reached.

The Grand Tour

In his role as high commissioner, Smith embarked on a great tour of the territories adjoining the Cape Colony, beginning on 10 January 1848. He was accompanied only by his private secretary John Garvock, High Commission Secretary Richard Southey and his aide-de-camp Edward Holdich. He travelled with such a small retinue because he wanted to demonstrate his trust in the Boers across the Orange River, who were to be his most important hosts. His unstated purpose was to bring the recalcitrant Boers back into the British fold.

Between that date and 13 February he visited Adam Kok in Griqualand West, Mshweshwe of the BaSotho and Bloemfontein in Trans-Orangia. He also held a conference with the Boer leader Andries Pretorius at the foot of the pass from the Drakensburg plateau into Natal, and then proceeded to visit Pietermaritzburg and Durban.

The most significant occurrence during this tour was his proclamation of 3 February 1848:

> Now, therefore, by virtue of the several powers and authorities in me vested, and subject to Her royal confirmation – I do hereby proclaim, declare, and make known, the sovereignty of Her Majesty the Queen of England over the territories north of the Great Orange river, including the countries of Moshesh, Moroko, Molitsani, Sinkonyala, Adam Kok, Gert Taaybosch, and other

minor chiefs, so far north as to the Vaal river, and east to the Drakensberg, or Quathlamba mountains.[44]

The proclamation is breathtaking because it demonstrates the confidence which Smith had in his own abilities and the considerable forethought which had clearly gone into such an action, even to the extent of carrying with him the text of the annexation which was handed to Pretorius before his departure.

The newly proclaimed Orange River Sovereignty remained quiescent for the first few months but on 22 July the governor received a message from Major H.D. Warden, the new British Resident of the Sovereignty, to the effect that Pretorius had entered Winburg with five hundred men and was fomenting rebellion. On 29 July, Smith left Cape Town to take a small force into the sovereignty,[45] arriving there only on 22 August after being delayed by floods.

On 29 August 1848, Smith and his column caught up with the Boer rebels near the farm 'Boom Plaats'. The battle began soon afterwards and ended with a victory for the governor, the Boers fleeing from the field 'in twos and threes'. The governor finally arrived back in King William's Town on 6 October 1848. But this was only the beginning of Smith's troubles with the Orange River Sovereignty – things were going to get worse.

Another crisis inflicted on Smith was brought about by the actions of the home government. It has little bearing on military matters but concerned Earl Grey's attempt to settle Ticket of Leave convicts at the Cape in 1849.[46] Once again, Smith managed to anger Grey by supporting the colonists in their opposition to the proposal, even including his criticism in an official despatch. Grey's response was very cold:

> I do not think that an officer of your high position in Her Majesty's service ought in a public Despatch to have condemned the existing system of military punishment if you had no better suggestions for its improvement to offer than those which I have mentioned. I must add, that this indiscretion has been aggravated by your having thought fit to publish that Despatch, as in your subsequent one of the 31st of July you informed me that you had done. I feel it to be my duty to express my strong disapprobation of the step you have thus taken, and which the reasons you have assigned for it do not seem to me to justify.[47]

Despite this, and his previous threats to persevere, Grey finally dropped the matter and freed the colony from the shadow of the convict.

Reduction of Troops

There were repeated reminders to earlier governors of the Cape regarding the expense involved in maintaining imperial troops there. It was a well-worn argument that either the Cape purse should pay for their upkeep or they should be returned and the Cape authorities recruit, and pay for, their own forces from local resources. Sir Harry Smith was no exception to these entreaties and his instructions on his appointment reminded him of this expectation.

Smith, unlike most of his predecessors, took notice of the injunctions and did, indeed, send back many troops to England in the period between his appointment and 1848. His early despatches are replete with his determination to act as Grey demanded.[48]

On 18 March 1848, the governor sent a despatch which included complete details of his efforts in this regard, showing the following troops to have been sent home to the end of March:[49]

27th Regiment	287
62nd Regiment	146
90th Regiment	398
91st Regiment	264
Medical, RA, RE	11[50]
Total	1104[51]

In addition, a further 313 were to be sent home on 1 April, consisting of elements of the 7th Dragoon Guards, RE, 1/91st Regiment and the Rifle Brigade, totalling nearly 1,500 men. The 7th (The Princess Royal's) Regiment was sent back in late April 1848.

All this, of course, was welcomed by Earl Grey but the reduced garrison must also have been noted by the Xhosa. The major forces remaining in April 1848, omitting artillery and engineers, were:[52]

Cape Town	6th Regiment	505
Frontier posts	91st Regiment	531
British Kaffraria	45th Regiment	522
	73rd Regiment	514
	Rifle Brigade	510
Total		2582

The other battalion of the 45th was in Natal, while the Cape Mounted Rifles amounted to a further 680 men.

Rise of Mlanjeni

We have already noted that at times of great stress among the Xhosa, mystics emerged who were able to assume considerable power, Makanna/Nxele among them.

Now another such individual appeared whose name was Mlanjeni of the Ndlambe. The first official notice of him appeared in a letter from John Maclean, commissioner to the Ndlambe, from Fort Murray:[53]

> I have the honour to report that Umlanjeni, a Kafir of Umkye's [Mqhayi's] tribe and location, has lately revived the witch-doctoring craft, and great numbers have attended his meetings from all parts of Kafirland; in consequence of which I ordered him to appear before me, also his father Kala (at whose kraal Umlanjeni had erected several witchcraft poles). Both parties failed to appear; I therefore ordered the second division Kafir police to apprehend them, and to seize two head of cattle for their disobedience.
>
> The police apprehended Kala and seized one head of cattle, but they found Umlanjeni so weak and emaciated that he could not leave his kraal without assistance; they, however, pulled down all his witchcraft poles; and I have had him removed to the immediate vicinity of Umkye's kraal, near Mount Coke, in order that I may keep him under observation.[54]

The next report came from the chief commissioner, Colonel Mackinnon to Sir Harry Smith:

> A very considerable degree of excitement has been occasioned in Kafirland by the proceedings of a prophet named 'Umlanjeni' in Umkye's [Mqhayi] location; and the colonists on the immediate border have been much alarmed by all sorts of warlike rumours which have been spread abroad. I have directed that he shall be seized and placed in confinement, but I delay any official Report until I can report the result of the attempt to catch him. He is aware that it will be made, and therefore he has no fixed place of residence. We have spies out to try and get sufficient information as to where he passes the night. I am unwilling to risk a failure, as it would only increase his influence, and therefore if we find that the attempt is not likely to succeed at present, I shall defer it for some time. . . . Great numbers from all parts of Kaffirland are constantly visiting him, but it is very difficult to obtain any direct evidence of what has taken place at the meetings. He directs that all bewitching substances at present in possession of the Kafirs be destroyed, and points to some great event impending. The only way to check the evil, as remonstrance with this credulous people is vain, is to send him out of the country, and this I will do the moment I catch him.
>
> We are terribly ill off for want of rain. The country is as dry as a bone, and the cattle like skeletons.[55]

It is perhaps no accident that Mlanjeni's appearance coincided with still another of the many droughts with which the country was bedevilled.

'Mlanjeni, the Riverman, was about 18-years old in 1850, and so weak and emaciated from fasting that he could not walk about unaided.'[56] The new seer was reported to have spent a long period of time immersed up to his neck in an enchanted pool, and to have emerged speaking the words of spirits.

This, and other, reports eventually found their way to Sir Harry Smith's attention and his response was to instruct Mackinnon to arrest Mlanjeni as soon as practicable. It did not happen and rumours of war compelled Smith to go to the frontier himself in October 1850.

A letter from an 'Inhabitant of the Frontier' to the Cape Legislative Council, dated 8 October 1850:

> Last year Sandile made a tour through the country and laid before the Chiefs the position they were in: not only faced with the prospect of losing their country to European aggression but also their power as chiefs, especially their right of 'smelling out' enemies amongst their own people which enables them to confiscate cattle and supplement their revenues.
>
> Sandile's half-brother Maqoma, as a result of being driven from his home in the Blinkwater, bears a lifelong grudge against the White man. Recently Maqoma made a personal visit to many Ngqika chiefs, showing each of them the necessity of a combined attack on the Englishmen. He prevailed on them to assemble and consult the Prophet Mlangeni and accept his decisions.
>
> The question the Chiefs asked Mlangeni was, what were they to do? The English had taken their land and were treating them like dogs, even drying up the country with the sun, and if left alone would starve the Ngqika to death. Mlangeni replied that he had talked about this matter to the Spirit, Mthlogu, before they came and would tell them in the morning what the Spirit had said.
>
> Next morning he reported that war was in the land. He then made the Chiefs assemble in two groups, those with muskets on one side and those with assegais (spears) on the other. The musket party represented the English and those with assegais the Ngqika. Mlangeni then placed the two groups opposite each other and told the assegai group to lie flat on their faces. Turning to the others he told them to fire their muskets, then he immediately ordered those with assegais to run and seize the muskets with their hands before they could be reloaded. This was the way he told them to fight the English.
>
> Mlangeni next invested Maqoma and Mhala as the two Great Commanders; no other was to give orders but these two. The signal for the outbreak of war was to be an attempt by the English to seize him, and they were then to make a rush for the Colony.
>
> After the meeting messengers were sent to all Ngqika, including those in the Colony, recalling them and their wives and children. All were told not to steal, as this would break the spell, and also to preserve the utmost secrecy.

What Smith failed to understand was that the Xhosa reaction to Mlanjeni was caused by the policies of the governor himself. He had seized the Ceded Territory and handed it over to the Mfengu and new settlers; he had forced the Xhosa across the Keiskamma River into the new British Kaffraria; he had usurped the power of the chiefs and given that power to Mackinnon and his commissioners; finally he had tried to force the Xhosa to adopt European ways at the expense of their own culture. Little wonder, then, that they should pay attention to a new seer who recognised the troubles they were enduring, and offered a solution.

On 26 October, Smith convened another conference of the Xhosa chiefs but Sandile failed to appear. Brownlee was instructed to compel Sandile's presence but again the chief declined to attend, claiming that he had received a similar summons once before, as a result of which he had been arrested and locked up in Grahamstown. He said that he feared that the same thing would be attempted again. Sandile's refusal, and his reason for doing so, at once ignited Smith's anger and on 30 October he issued a proclamation announcing that Sandile was deposed as chief of the Rharhabe and appointing Charles Brownlee to act in his place.[57] Finding nothing more to detain him at the frontier, he returned to Cape Town on 24 November.

In a report of 2 December 1850, Mackinnon told Smith that Maqoma had left his homestead near Fort Hare to join Sandile in the bush.[58] With considerable foresight, he went on to say, 'I am still not apprehensive that the Kafirs will make an attack on the colony, but that they will endeavour to drive us to some act which shall give them a pretext for rising.' He did not have long to wait for such an event to occur.

Smith soon found that his presence was again necessary on the frontier and on 5 December he took ship to the new port of East London, taking with him reinforcements from the 73rd Regiment. On the same day, Mackinnon reported a state of tranquillity on the frontier: 'I have the satisfaction of informing you that matters look more peaceable in Kaffirland and that I have no apprehension that any attack will be made in the Colony . . . I have not given the ill-disposed the pretext which they desire for openly resisting us and thereby raising a war cry.'[59]

In contrast to Mackinnon's soothing opinion, when the governor arrived at King William's Town, he found the farmers in a state of panic, many of them having already abandoned their farms for safety in laagers. To stabilise the frontier and reassure the colonists, on 14 December he issued orders for the formation of three large military columns. The left, under the command of Lieutenant-Colonel Eyre, 73rd Regiment, was to move to the Kabousie Nek; the centre, under Colonel Mackinnon, was to be based, with headquarters, at

Fort Cox 'for the purpose of penetrating the Amathola Mountains'; the right, under Colonel Henry Somerset, was to concentrate at Fort Hare.

On 14 December a meeting of Boer farmers was held, at which it was agreed that they should abandon their farms and trek. The reasons given in their subsequent resolution sent to the governor were:

1. Rumour of war emanating from Kafirland.
2. The absconding of nearly all Kafir servants . . . without warning, and in many instances leaving their wages behind . . .
3. The knowledge that the British had been opposed, defied and trampled upon in Kafirland . . .
   Accompanied by the recollection that they had twice suffered ruin before . . . as well as all hopes of assistance from Government being denied.[60]

Smith issued a proclamation on 16 December under which he offered a reward of £500, or two hundred head of cattle, for the capture of Sandile and £200, or one hundred head of cattle, for the capture of his brother Anta.[61] During a speech the following day, addressed to the people of King William's Town, he made it clear who was now in command:

But gentlemen, though assailed, I ultimately triumphed and again appear on the scene to resume and carry out the very measures which were rendered abortive . . . The Kaffirs shall be prostrated under our feet and the occurrence of war shall be prevented. Let it be understood, I WILL BE GOVERNOR.[62]

On 19 December, Smith called a conference of Rharhabe chiefs at Fort Cox, Sandile and Anta not attending, which he opened by dramatically brandishing his Staff of Peace, complete with bedpost knob, after which the chiefs pledged their loyalty to the Crown. At this meeting the chiefs pressed Smith to accept Sandile's mother Suthu to rule the Ngqika rather than Mackinnon, a view which Smith shared, and he acceded to their request.[63] The governor also assured the chiefs that he would not hunt down Sandile. He then launched into one of his long harangues, as a result of which he sowed doubt in the minds of the chiefs with regard to his undertakings. He also verbally attacked Maqoma:

. . . he spoke of Macomo, who was present, in terms of a very irritating nature, stating that he did not care whether he touched the stick of peace today or not; that he might have been a great man, but he was now a drunken beast and had to be turned out of the colony, and a number of things, which I lamented as they seemed to be uncalled for.[64]

By then almost everyone in the Eastern Cape knew that war with the Ngqika was imminent. The only exceptions were Sir Harry Smith and

Colonel Mackinnon. But it was these two men who were to precipitate the colony into conflict.

On 23 December 1850, Sir Harry Smith, also at Fort Cox, having heard that Sandile was at his homestead, ordered Colonel Mackinnon to take his column the short distance north to Burnshill, and there to arrest the recalcitrant chief – so breaking the undertaking that he had given to the Rharhabe chiefs only four days earlier.

Chapter 3

War's Grim Visage

Ambush at Boma Pass

Lieutenant-General Sir Harry Smith's blood was up. Strutting up and down his room at Fort Cox like a white-headed cock-sparrow, he cursed Sandile, chief of the Rharhabe branch of the Xhosa, in language honed to perfection in Buenos Aires, Corunna, Salamanca, Toulouse, Washington, New Orleans, Waterloo and Aliwal:

> Who the *** did Sandile think he *** was to defy the commands of Her Majesty's representative at the Cape, with dominion over the whole *** sub-continent of Africa if he wanted it; and here was that shrivel-legged *** chief of a petty tribe *** of thieves and cutthroats DEFYING him! Treating him with CONTEMPT![1]

Turning to Colonel George Mackinnon, chief commissioner of British Kaffraria, Smith peremptorily ordered him to take all the men he could find and arrest the scoundrel; let him have a taste of what it meant to defy the power and wrath of the British Empire.

Mackinnon quietly demurred, pointing out that a show of force might provoke Sandile to war: they should proceed cautiously. But this was the wrong thing to say, the wrong time to say it and the wrong man to whom to say it.

At 2 a.m. on 24 December 1850, Colonel Mackinnon and a force of nearly six hundred men,[2] with rations for three days, left Fort Cox and marched up the Keiskamma River Valley. After covering four kilometres they came to Burnshill, where Sandile and his older half-brother Maqoma had been born, and where 150 army supply-wagons had been lost to the Ngqika only four years before. Burnshill was also the burial place of Ngqika and the Great Place of Sandile, and Mackinnon expected to find him here. He was not but was reported to be in Keiskamma Hoek, so the column pressed on. Their route lay through thin bush; there was no road, only tracks made by cattle driven to and from their grazing ground by naked herd-boys of Sandile's Ngqika. The order of march was: the Kaffir Police leading, then the predominantly Khoikhoi Cape Mounted Rifles (CMR). They were followed by the pack horses carrying spare ammunition, medical supplies and officers' comforts, together with their attendants and guard. Finally came the infantry: the 6th Regiment (known as the 'Doylers' as a large percentage of them were Irish lads, refugees from the potato famine) led by Captain J. Elphinston Robertson, and lastly a company of the 73rd Regiment, the 'Cape Greyhounds', which, under the diligent command of Lieutenant-Colonel William Eyre, was rightfully regarded as the finest regiment in South Africa.[3] Strict orders had been given that muskets were not to be loaded and no one was to fire a shot.[4]

Twenty-nine-year-old Brigade-Major John Jervis Bisset was riding with Colonel Mackinnon at the head of the CMR. As they walked their horses, Bisset remarked on the large number of Ngqika gathering on the surrounding hills. He also commented on the absence of the usual crowd of men, women and children who habitually gathered along the roadside during patrols, peddling their wares or asking for *basela* or alms. In fact, only one man came, offering a basket of curdled milk, and he, Bisset thought, had probably been sent to spy out the land. Bisset, who had served in the two previous frontier wars, concluded that these were hostile signs, but Mackinnon had made up his mind: the Ngqika were not going to attack.[5]

After marching twelve kilometres the column halted for breakfast on the open ground just south of the Wolf River. Following a two-hour rest, which gave ample time for the men to bathe, the column fell in and proceeded to cross the river. The stones of the drift were slippery and the infantrymen were considerably delayed thereby, causing breaks in the column. Quite a few men were thoroughly soaked by 'accidental' falls.

The Boma Pass lies one kilometre north of Wolf River, and, before reaching the pass, Bisset told Mackinnon that it would be a formidable position if occupied by an enemy. The men would have to march in single file, the path being narrow and intersected by huge boulders that had fallen from the krantzes (cliffs) above the pass to the left, and there was excellent cover behind the large trees and dense undergrowth. Mackinnon, however, was so serenely confident that there would be no ambush that the men entered the pass with their muskets still unloaded and their bayonets unfixed.

Bisset described the pass as follows:

A little on the left was a high precipice, something in the shape of a crescent, its two horns falling away to a ledge. The far end one abutted on the Keiskamma

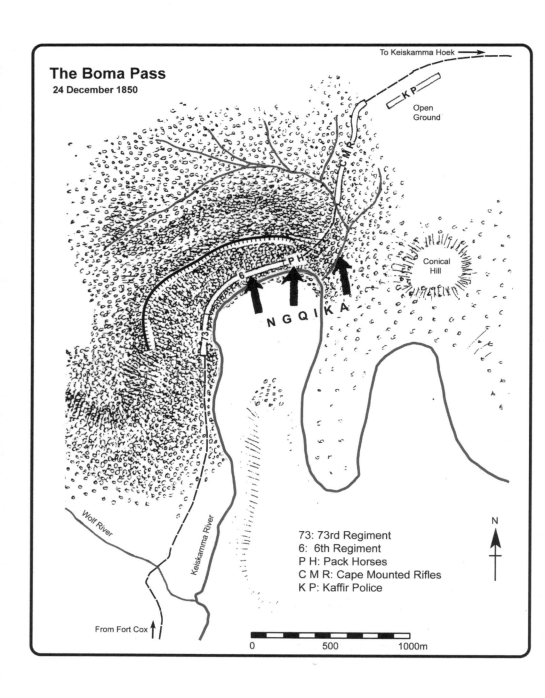

The Boma Pass
24 December 1850

To Keiskamma Hoek →

K P

Open
Ground

C M R

Conical
Hill

6

P H

N G Q I K A

73

Wolf River

Keiskamma River

N

73: 73rd Regiment
6: 6th Regiment
P H: Pack Horses
C M R: Cape Mounted Rifles
K P: Kaffir Police

From Fort Cox

0   500   1000m

River, which ran on the right hand side of the track and conformed to the shape of the precipice, leaving a narrow belt of forest-wood between the rocky mountain and the river. The road or track wound through this forest of large trees, rocks fallen from the perpendicular cliffs, and tangled underwood. There were boulders as big as castles, and you had to serpentine and make your way through these as best you could. On the opposite side of the river there was a peninsula-shaped spit or tongue of land sloping down to its banks, with conical-shaped hills at the far end of the tongue; this slope was covered with bush and large olive-trees, as was also the rocky mountain on the left, and in fact the whole of the country around the pass itself.[6]

Ensign Thomas J. Lucas was laughing and chatting with Assistant-Surgeon William Stuart,[7] both of them in the CMR, as they approached the pass. They agreed that the grass under the shady trees on the banks of the mountain stream, gurgling as it rushed over its rocky bed, would make a jolly place for a picnic. Their reverie was interrupted by an excited CMR trooper who drew Lucas's attention to piles of stones at intervals along the roadside, each pile made up of successively smaller stones placed on top of each other. The man told him that this was the work of Mlanjeni,[8] the Xhosa prophet, for the purpose of casting an evil spell over the patrol. He then pointed out an Ngqika scout standing on top of a krantz on the north side of the pass, who withdrew as soon as Lucas looked up at him – proof positive, the CMR man said, that mischief was at hand. Lucas was beginning to feel anxious when Dr Stuart's servant rode up and told him that his medical supplies had slipped off his pack horse. Stuart rode back immediately, and that was the last time Lucas saw him alive.[9]

Lieutenant Godfrey Armytage was riding near the centre of his regiment, the 6th.[10] He too had noticed the absence of spectators and he was also puzzled by the piles of stones. Lucky stones? He queried his fellow officers, but no one could offer an explanation. Before entering the pass, Armytage saw a group of Ngqika on a krantz, halfway up a conical hill to his right front, who were alternately standing up and hiding again.

Through his telescope he thought he recognised Sandile and pointed him out to Lieutenant Robert Provo Norris, also of the 6th. They both thought the sighting should be reported to Colonel Mackinnon, but how could they? He and his staff were far ahead at the front of the column.

Colour Sergeant Thomas Golding, CMR, formerly of the 6th Regiment, had an old friend in that regiment, Private John Payne. Both were from Coventry. Four days previously he had written home: 'My old Regiment and John Payne are here with me at Fort Cox. Please tell his mother he is quite well.'[11] Now they were together on this patrol, and it seems that Payne was walking with Golding in the ranks of the CMR.

About an hour after its vanguard had entered the pass, the column was spread out to its maximum extent. The Kaffir Police had emerged from the bush onto open ground, about one kilometre beyond the pass, and Mackinnon and Bisset were just riding out at the head of the CMR, which extended back to the bottom of the ravine. Then came a 500-metre gap to the pack horses, which were slowly struggling through the narrow spaces between the boulders and trees in the pass. Behind them came the infantry, spread out over perhaps a kilometre, many of the men sitting and talking while waiting, including Lieutenant Armytage, who was holding the reins of his horse and chatting with a group of fellow officers some distance from his own company.

It was while the column was in this – its most vulnerable – position that a single loud musket shot was heard, its echoes rolling along the whole length of the pass. Lieutenant Armytage was immediately on the alert, thinking it was a signal, but someone muttered that it was probably the CMR shooting game. Ten seconds later a musket ball whizzed past his head, and then the shooting became general. Taking his horse firmly by the bridle, Armytage ran back to his company and ordered his men to take cover behind trees and boulders. Finding that his commanding officer, Captain Robertson, was in the rear, Armytage took charge of his own men and ordered them to load their weapons and make their way forward as fast as possible. A heavy volley was heard in front and before long they came to the remains of the ammunition guard: all except one man had been either killed or wounded and the pack horses had vanished. Advancing further, they were attacked at close quarters by the enemy, who discharged muskets and threw assegais at the troops, their fire coming only from the British right – the river side. The men could not see the enemy as they were hidden, not only by the undergrowth, but by the acrid, blinding smoke from the muskets, which, in the still air, filled the enclosed spaces beneath the trees.

Major Bisset heard the single shot, followed shortly afterwards by a continuous discharge of musketry, coming from the pass behind him. He immediately asked Colonel Mackinnon's permission to return and take charge of the infantry, but Mackinnon would not at first believe that the Ngqika were attacking. Eventually, Bisset managed to convince him and, calling his mounted orderly to follow, he rode back, passing the mounted men with difficulty. At the bottom of the ravine he pushed clear of the CMR and soon reached the ridge at the head of the pass. As he prepared to go down the side of the ridge his orderly shouted '*My Got! Meneer, moet nie ingaan nie!*' (My God! Sir, do not go in!) and, looking up, Bisset saw, on the tongue of land in the fold of the Keiskamma, 'thousands' of Ngqika running in his direction with the obvious intention of heading off the infantry. As he admitted afterwards, it was only the thought that his honour was at stake that made him go on, and it says much for the discipline of his Khoikhoi orderly that he in turn followed. Bisset pressed his forage cap down on his head, set his teeth, brought his double-barrelled carbine to the 'advance' and forced his horse down the slope. Almost immediately they were both nearly knocked down by three pack horses which rushed past at full gallop, bleeding from wounds and with their packs hanging under their bellies. The two men then had to run the gauntlet of shots from Ngqika lying in ambush behind rocks waiting for the *Rooi-Baadjies* (Red-Jackets) to come. Further on Bisset saw the heads and shoulders of five Ngqika behind a boulder with their muskets pointing at him. He spurred his horse but at that moment he was hit by a musket ball which entered low down on the outside of his left thigh, the ball passing upwards and, narrowly missing vital parts, coming out just below his right hip. The shock was like a blow from a sledgehammer and even his horse staggered. Bisset fired one barrel at the Ngqika but the ball struck the top of the rock, scattering splinters in all directions without any apparent effect. One of the Ngqika, a plumed warrior, stood up and shouted in Xhosa, 'I have hit him.' Bisset then fired his second barrel and the ball hit the warrior in the chest; Bisset heard himself replying, illogically and also in Xhosa, 'I have got it.'[12]

They now met the first of the infantrymen who were working their way forward, in spite of continuous fire from the Ngqika – which they were stoically returning, although not one of the enemy could be seen. Bisset halted for the first time when he saw his friend Dr Stuart leaning against a boulder, blood pouring from a wound in his chest. As he rode up to him a second ball struck Stuart in the head, his brains spattering over Bisset's face and jacket.[13]

It seemed to Bisset that a standing fight where they were was impossible, as the path wound round the boulders so that the men could not tell whether they were facing friend or foe. There was no alternative but to press on and get the men out of the pass as quickly as possible. Turning round, he led perhaps half the infantrymen as they fought their way out. It was a long drawn-out struggle, and even on the ridge they had to drive back a large number of Ngqika who had come at them from the base of a conical hill.

Ensign Lucas was completely surprised on hearing the outburst of firing in the pass, followed after an interval by what he surmised was a volley of musketry from the infantry. While he and the other CMR officers waited for orders, Major Bisset galloped by on his way to the rear and ordered the CMR to dismount and scatter into the bush. After waiting impatiently, Lucas and a

brother officer, Ensign James C. Grant Kingsley, both of them bursting with
excitement, rode back to the pass. They tried to catch a wounded ammunition
pack horse that was galloping wildly about, without success. Then they met
Colour Sergeant Golding, who called out that Dr Stuart had been shot and
that they must not attempt to go any further as the pass was full of Ngqika.
He had hardly finished speaking when Major Bisset was seen coming back
towards them, struggling to sit upright, blood dripping from his wound down
his horse's flank onto the path, and his face ashen. He called out to Lucas and
Kingsley to follow and support him and this they did, although disappointed
at missing the action. The major managed to get as far as the open ground,
where he fell from his horse, exhausted. He would have bled to death – a ball
having pierced the femoral artery – had not Captain George Jackson Carey,
CMR, happened to have two little web tourniquets in his pouch. These were
immediately applied to Bisset's thigh and the bleeding partially stopped.[14]
Golding wrote two days later:

> Poor John Payne and Doctor Stuart were the first shot. Poor John was not
> dead when the troops left; he said, 'for God sake comrades don't leave me here',
> but alas we had no alternative. I had to assist Major Bisset out of the Kloof
> wounded in two places and when I again returned, the troops had retreated, and
> that poor boy's fate must have been awful.

Lieutenant Armytage, still in the midst of the fighting, saw one of the
6th Regiment's Grenadier Company men shot and killed. He lifted the
man on to his horse to carry him out but he fell off on the other side. As
it was imperative that Armytage should lead the men about him out of the
bush, he had to leave the dead man and his horse behind. Further on their
progress was delayed by a group of Ngqika behind a large boulder but these
they overwhelmed, Armytage shooting two of them himself. Eventually they
managed to get clear of the pass, mainly by keeping up a steady fire to their
right whenever there was the slightest sign of their opponents.

At the ridge Armytage saw that the path down to the ravine and up the
other side was thick with Ngqika. After some discussion with his brother
officers, his view that they should not go down prevailed so they cut through
the bush to their left and, in a surprisingly short time, came out onto the open
ground, somewhat to the left of the CMR.

Soon after Bisset had been made as comfortable as possible Dr Fraser, the
second medical officer, arrived but he was in such a state of shock that, on
kneeling down to dress Bisset's wounds, he fainted.[15] It was not from the sight
of the wounds, he explained later, but from the mental stress and anguish
of having to leave the wounded and dying in the pass to be tortured and

mutilated by the Ngqika. Bisset, who always carried a flask of cold tea with him on the march, managed to take it off and force some of the contents past Fraser's lips. The tea soon revived him and his first words were: 'Oh, my God! I had to leave Stuart!' He then explained that he had kept hold of his horse with the medical supplies until it had been killed by a bullet. He had then hurried on to catch up with the rest of the men and it was while passing the dying that he heard a voice cry out, 'For God's sake, Fraser, don't leave me'. Fraser knew that if he had hesitated for a moment his throat would have been cut, or worse, so he was forced to ignore the cries for help.

Somehow Fraser thought that it was his colleague Dr Stuart who had called out and this made the agony of his perceived desertion more acute. It was of little comfort to have Bisset point to his own jacket and ask what the spots were. On Fraser seeing that they were human brains, Bisset told him they came from Stuart's head.

Meanwhile, Fraser had been dressing Bisset's wounds, plugging up the holes and adjusting the tourniquets. Before he had finished, a man ran up to say that Captain Charles Parker Catty of the 6th Regiment was badly wounded and dying. Bisset insisted that Fraser go, but he soon came back; he could be of no help to Catty, he said, three musket balls had entered his right side and had passed into his intestines.[16]

While the troops were gathering on the open ground, a large number of Ngqika were seen assembling on the conical hill to the east. Mackinnon extended the Kaffir Police on his right, or eastern flank, but the Ngqika fortunately did not attack.

The column eventually continued its march for the remaining four kilometres through comparatively open country until they reached the Rev. Mr Niven's mission station, Uniondale, near the present town of Keiskamma Hoek. No stretchers were available as these had been lost with the medical supplies so the wounded suffered badly. Major Bisset had to be carried by three men; two took hold of his arms with their elbows in his armpits while the third man walked between Bisset's legs, well up into the crotch, with a thigh under each arm. Bisset's face was towards the ground and he was carried the whole four kilometres in this fashion, suffering agonies from his painful wounds, and indignities from mimosa bushes and brambles scratching his face.

A camp was formed at Niven's – if lines of soldiers lying down in a square with their muskets facing outwards can be called a camp. Here Fraser again attended the wounded. Captain Catty did not die: none of the musket balls had entered his intestines after all. One had struck a small rib and had immediately come out again, while another, also striking a rib, had run up

under the skin and had lodged high up his chest where Fraser cut it out.
Catty was well within two weeks while Bisset was on crutches for two years.[17]

At 5 a.m. the following morning, Christmas Day, the column made its way
slowly and painfully towards Fort White via Baillie's Grave, thirty kilometres
to the south. Golding was in charge of the rear guard: '. . . consequently we
had the worst of it, the Kaffirs attacking our rear at 10 past 5 and fought us
for 9 hours, never permitting us to obtain even a drink of water and the sun
actually skinning our hands and face. Such an awful day I never saw . . .'

Armytage was particularly chagrined to see Sandile mounted on his own
(Armytage's) charger and wearing his military coat with red lining. Lucas was
incredulous when they were again ordered to unload their muskets and to
refrain from firing in case they provoked a war; the Boma Pass affair, it was
said, was just the disaffection of a particular tribe. Lucas continued:

> The column moved on as sorrowfully as might be. No Kaffirs made their
> appearance until we halted for breakfast on the top of a high hill [Red Hill
> Pass], lined on either side with impenetrable bush, when we observed them
> in great numbers creeping along the jungle on our flank, with the evident
> intention of lining the road by which we were to pass. How we came to halt
> in such an exposed spot I cannot understand, especially as it gave the enemy
> plenty of time to make their arrangements to circumvent us. No sooner,
> however, did the column fall in and commence the descent on the other side,
> than we were once more trapped, and shot after shot came pouring in. Unable
> to see our enemy, and finding it impossible to make our way through the
> dense thorns, we were literally obliged to run the gauntlet and get out of it as
> best we could.[18]

The column finally managed to make its way down past Baillie's Grave
to the open ground below.[19] But the Ngqika had one more surprise for
Mackinnon's column. In Lucas's words:

> As we passed through a mimosa-covered flat, which traversed the main road, I
> was riding in front with the advanced guard, when I encountered a horrible sight.
> Stretched out in fantastic positions across the path, lay the bodies of thirteen
> infantry soldiers in hideous array, horribly mutilated, the agony expressed in
> their glassy, upturned eyes showing that they had met with a lingering death by
> the sharp assegais of the Kaffirs.[20]

These men, Lucas later found, had formed the guard of a convoy on their way
to Fort Cox. The careless escort allowed an attack to penetrate too closely and
thus capture the wagons. The casualties for the two-day operation, apart from
those men found on the Debe Flat, were:

Killed   Assistant-Surgeon Stuart and eleven other ranks.
Wounded   Major Bisset, Lieutenant Catty and seven other ranks.

On arriving at Fort White,[21] not far distant from their tragic find, the column halted while Colonel Mackinnon rode to Fort Cox with the CMR to see Sir Harry Smith. The governor had been incredulous that the attack on Mackinnon could even have taken place,[22] so he was dumbfounded when he learned the truth.

The colony was too stunned by the events on the outbreak of the war to comment on the handling of the Boma Pass affair. A few days later the Kaffir Police and some of the Khoikhoi men in the CMR deserted, and this prompted reports that placed the blame for the fiasco on the 'treachery' of the Kaffir Police. It will not have escaped the reader's notice that the Kaffir Police and the CMR had both emerged from the pass before the attack began and thus escaped any injury.

> Reflecting on what had happened during the day, the behaviour of the Cape Corps and Kaffir police struck me as somewhat peculiar and suspicious. It was afterwards discovered that there had been some consultation between the hostile Kaffirs and our Kaffir police as to whether the latter should not join in the attack of the enemy upon us. They decided not to do so, as their wives and families were at Fort Cox. The time for desertion was not yet, though it was not far off.[23]

The *Grahamstown Journal* spoke of the patrol being 'inveigled into a narrow and difficult pass by the native Police . . .' This, of course, was nonsense. Colour Sergeant Golding was nearer the mark: 'My old Regiment behaved very bad [sic].'

The disaster was, however, clearly due to the incompetence of Colonel Mackinnon, who was entirely convinced that the Ngqika would not attack, in spite of repeated warnings to the contrary. Having told the world that there would be no war – and he was the Ngqika commissioner – his pride would not allow him to admit that he was wrong and so men died. However, there also seems to have been an element of fear in Mackinnon: the fear of provoking the enemy to attack. Later, in September 1851, Mackinnon refused to allow the bugle to be used to recall a scattered patrol in the Fish River bush, 'In case the enemy might hear it and attack' – the result was that eight men of the Queen's Regiment went missing and were never found.

Captain William King-Hall, RN, after recording the successes of Lieutenant-Colonel Eyre and General Somerset in his diary of 9 January 1852, noted:

Not a word was said about Mackinnon's patrol who, it is generally supposed, will do nothing to speak of. I have never heard anyone mention him except to accuse him of great incompetency and only fit for an office.

Ensign Hugh Robinson of the 43rd, serving under Colonel Eyre, wrote on 16 March 1852:

We went through the terrible Boome [sic] Pass, of unfortunate memory, and being the first troops there since the passage at the beginning of the war, we found skeletons with morsels of red cloth which the jackals could not digest. So admirable were our chief's [Eyre's] dispositions that not a shot was fired at us that day.[24]

About twenty-five years later Colonel Gawler of the 73rd Regiment lectured on the subject of fighting Africans. He had not been at the Boma Pass, but he was with Colonel Eyre throughout the war; he made these comments:

Some months after the Boomah [sic] Pass affair the 73rd marched through the Pass and my company moved without any difficulty from one end to the other in skirmishing order through the bush with one flank in the river and the other under the precipice.
    Should an officer by accident or neglect ever find himself ambushed, the only safe plan is to dash straight at the enemy. This not only scares him at the moment but gives him a lasting respect for you.
    I will lay down as a rule that a British force should never be surprised either in camp or on the march. I always reconnoitered in small parties in all directions to long distances, and frequently by night.
    On the march by footpath through a bush so dense that flanking skirmishers cannot be used, the leading file must turn to the right, get as far as he can into the bush, kneel and look well under the bushes; the next file in about five paces turn to the left, the next to his right, etc. Thus the whole force is inverted and extended on both flanks at ten paces. As the rear-guard approaches the files rise in succession and close by sections, moving along between halfed [sic] sentries. I first saw this done in 1851 by Col. Eyre of the 73rd in going through a ravine in the Fish River where a large number of another regiment [the 6th] had been killed two days before.[25]

The one remarkable fact is the low number of casualties suffered by the infantry; only one man of the seventy-five in the detachment of the 73rd Regiment was killed, yet they were in the rear and were exposed longest to attack. The most probable explanation for the low casualty figure is that the number of Ngqika was quite small. It is just not possible for the men of the 73rd to have traversed one kilometre of bush virtually unscathed if they had been attacked by 'thousands' of enemy warriors, as Major Bisset had it: common sense would dictate that their number was only a few hundred. The troops' musketry also produced a magnificent smokescreen which helped them make their escape. Finally, the Ngqika rarely came to close quarters, and their poor performance with the old muskets with which they were armed left much to be desired. This left them with only their throwing spears, which had a very limited range and poor accuracy.

Massacre in the Military Villages

On that same Christmas Day, the three white-occupied military villages of Auckland, Woburn and Juanasburg, which had been deliberately located inside Ngqika territory, were attacked without warning while the families were preparing their Christmas celebrations.

> Woburn was situated on the present main road from Alice to Seymour, then called Eland's Post, and about eight miles from Lovedale. Auckland was about twelve miles further on in the beautiful valley on the right and near the foot of the luxuriantly-wooded Hogg's Back [sic] mountain. Juanasberg (so named after Lady Juana Smith) was situated more towards Eland's Post and near the Lushington mountain . . .[26]

The fourth village, Ely, was occupied by coloured settlers and was located halfway between Alice and Fort Beaufort. This village was not attacked.

Three men of the CMR arrived at the village of Juanasburg about an hour after sunrise on Christmas Day 1850.[27] It was the smallest of the villages and had only eight men living there. The visitors brought a circular letter from Colonel Henry Somerset addressed to the superintendents of the military villages in the Tyumie Valley. The letter stated that war had broken out, and that the men of the military villages were to concentrate and, if they could not hold their position, they were to fall back upon Fort Hare. Captain J.M. Stevenson, the superintendent at Juanasburg, was absent on that day, having gone over to Woburn to spend Christmas with his friend, Lieutenant Stacey.

The three CMR men then moved on to Auckland, where they delivered the same letter. The people in the village gave the message little attention – it was, after all, Christmas. The messengers then proceeded to Woburn, where they were attacked by a party of Ngqika. Two of them were captured and deprived of their horses and arms, stripped naked, and then allowed to escape to the Gwali mission station. The third man escaped with his horse and arms.

In Juanasburg, meanwhile, Henry McCabe had immediately saddled up a horse and started for Woburn to acquaint Captain Stevenson with the contents of the letter. A further three men left either shortly after the message was received, or when they saw the neighbouring village of Woburn on fire. On his way, McCabe came across a large body of Ngqika assembled on the Gwali mission station land.

When he saw them, McCabe turned back but saw a number of the Ngqika were following him. He found his horse was unable to manage the heavy bush that he needed to enter to shake off his pursuers, so he abandoned the beast and continued on foot. He eventually threw himself into the Juanasburg stream, where he waited for two hours, up to his shoulders in water, during which time he heard gunshots. He eventually left the stream and made his way safely to Alice. About eight o'clock in the morning the firing ceased, and then the houses were sacked and burnt. Three men were killed in the village and a further four, including McCabe, escaped.[28] They were from a variety of regiments, including the 7th Dragoon Guards, which had left the Cape in April 1848. The eighth man in the village was Captain Stevenson who, as we have seen, was visiting Woburn at the time of the attack.

The next village to be attacked on that Christmas Day was Woburn, which contained sixteen men but no women. About 9 a.m. the village was surrounded by Ngqika, and the first alarm was sounded by the shooting of a Mr Thomas Shaw while seated in his garden smoking his pipe.[29]

Some days previously, at a spot on the main road leading from the village to Auckland, where two abandoned houses stood, one on each side of the road, the village superintendent, Lieutenant Stacey, had erected bars across the road, which, with the two houses, formed a rectangle. Lieutenant Stacey, Mr Philips (the superintendent of Ely), Captain Stevenson (the superintendent of Juanasburg) and sixteen other men now entered the house on the eastern side of the road in order to defend themselves.

After the first man was shot in his garden, the Ngqika did not bother those barricaded in the houses at first but chose instead to pillage other empty houses. Only after completing that work did they turn their attention to the men of the village, and attacked the barricaded houses, throwing stones into the unroofed buildings at first, the inhabitants firing their muskets in return.

Stevenson saw at once that when their ammunition was exhausted the rebels would be able to enter the houses at will. He therefore suggested to Stacey that they leave the barricade and make for Alice, 'by which movement he might at least have saved half of his men'. The superintendent refused, saying: 'The Government placed me here to defend Woburn, and I will do so to the last.'

Stevenson made up his mind to leave alone for Juanasburg, having thoughtfully saddled his horse earlier. He shook hands with the others, saying, 'You will all be dead by midday', and rode off to the accompaniment of catcalls, shots and assegais from the rebels down the Auckland road, before shortly afterwards turning in the direction of Alice. He eventually arrived at the Gwali mission station, where he remained until the emergency was over.[30]

The Rev. George Brown happened to witness his arrival there and his comments were hardly positive:

> I had scarcely [unsaddled my horse], when a man was observed coming at the full speed of his horse, from the direction of Woburn. We went down to know who it was, and what tidings he had brought. It was Stephenson, superintendent of one of the military villages, and field cornet – that is the most petty office in the Colony. He was a very overbearing man, not at all of a disposition to undervalue his commission, and far enough from being a favourite with the natives. He told us that he had gone over to enjoy Christmas eve with the superintendent at Woburn, and had stopt [sic] all night; that in the morning the men were just going out to have a Christmas game at cricket when the cry, 'the Caffres' was given. They had no time to run for their firearms, or to in any way organise themselves, and it was his conviction that ere now there was not a living man in the village . . .[31]

When the fighting was finished in Woburn, all sixteen men lay dead, including Stacey and Philips. Every man was from the 90th Regiment. Stevenson was never forgiven for his cowardice in deserting the men of the village.

The rebels' principal target was Auckland, the largest of the three villages, containing twenty-two men and thirty women and children. It was a death trap, with little avenue of escape once the village was occupied. Worse still, it had no view of either Juanasburg or Woburn, so that no warning smoke from the attacks on those places could be seen.

About two o'clock in the afternoon of 25 December, a large group of Ngqika rode into Auckland under the leadership of a man named Xaimpi, a grandson of Tyali. The latter's people had been displaced by the villages, and Tyali's Great Place was at no great distance from them.

Xaimpi and some of his men tried to reassure the villagers, particularly the women. One of these, Sarah Bailey, described their arrival:

> About 2 o'clock, I observed a considerable number of Kaffirs enter the village; they were headed by Xaimpi, who said they were his friends, and that they had all come on a friendly visit. We thought nothing of this number of Kaffirs coming into our village, as it was a common occurrence. As there was a report of the probability of war Mr. Farquhar Munro, the acting Superintendent, called a meeting of the military settlers, but requested them not to bring their arms,

as it might irritate the Kaffirs, and lead to them to suppose they intended to fight. While Mr Munro was engaged in reading a letter from Mr. Calderwood, brought by two Cape Corps men, to the military settlers, who were at the time mixed up with the Kaffirs, seven or eight strange Kaffirs came up from the direction of the Drift. When Mr Munro asked David Gibson, the interpreter, to inquire from her who those strange men were, Xaimpi replied that they were like themselves, yes, friends. The front one was his brother . . .[32]

Whilst the women became somewhat lulled, the men were still suspicious and rightly so. At that very moment, Xaimpi threw aside his blanket and gave a piercing whistle. Sarah Webster takes up the story:

> The Kaffirs then rushed upon the settlers, and stabbed and shot them down in every direction. I saw my father shot, but cannot say what Kaffir shot him. At this time also, my brother, David Gibson, was pulled down by the Kaffirs and ripped open. The Kaffirs then told us (the women and children) to go on, and they would follow us. We then retreated into an old ruin, where a few of the survivors were still alive, and firing on the Kaffirs.

Johanna Auld gave her version of what took place:

> Xaimpi, Tshatsu and all the Kaffirs had short assegais, and some guns concealed under their blankets. I saw Xaimpi and Tshatsu stab my husband, Alexander Thompson, who immediately fell. I then retreated to my house, to look for my child, and afterwards went for protection to some old walls where a number of women were assembled. At this time, ten men of the settlers were assembled under cover of the walls, attempting to defend themselves against the Kaffirs, who kept up a heavy fire. We remained there during the night. Next morning, at the dawn of day, a very great number of Kaffirs were assembled, and renewed the attack with greater fury, when three of the men were shot dead, and some of them wounded. About 3 o'clock on the afternoon of the 26th December, the women called out to the Kaffirs to cease firing, in order that they might come out with their children.

In most cases, the rebels stripped the women and stole their clothes, barely allowing them sufficient to retain their modesty. After the surrender at the ruined building, Sarah Bailey recorded:

> The next day, about 3 o'clock in the afternoon, the Kaffirs permitted us to come out, and when they had stripped us nearly naked, allowed us to proceed with our children to the Gwali mission station, which place we reached about sunset. The Kaffirs plundered us of all our property. Before I left the walls, I saw Donelly, Spiron and MacRobert fall, and several others were wounded.

Mary Ann McCarthy gave her version of events:

The Kaffirs kept up a fire on the position [inside the walls] during the whole night; and, by the break of day the next morning, their numbers were greatly increased. About 8 o'clock in the morning they made a furious attack. Three of our men were killed, viz., Donelly, Spiron and MacRobert. About 3 o'clock of the afternoon of the 26th of December, the Kaffirs called to the women and children to come out. They then rushed upon the walls, and I came out by climbing over the walls. They then commenced stripping me, when a Kaffir came up and told them not to strip me until such time as Xaimpi gave the order. They desisted for a moment, but recommenced stripping me. They took nearly everything off me. One of the Kaffirs then led me by the hand in front of one of the burnt houses, and told me to remain there, until the other women and children should come. Mrs. Drennan and Mrs. Donnelly came up shortly after. They then wanted to drag me up to the Bush, and told us that Mrs. Clarke and Mrs. McGeary were there, waiting for us. We did not go to the bush but asked the Kaffirs to allow us to go to Fort Hare. We had not gone more than a mile (by this time all the women and children except Mrs. Clarke and Mrs. McGeary were with us) when two young Kaffirs came up, and made us halt. One of them insisted upon my taking off the few articles of clothing which still remained upon my person. I hesitated in taking off my petticoats, when he struck me with a knobkerrie a violent blow on my left arm. I then took all my clothes off with the exception of my shift, which they allowed me to retain. They partially stripped two other women, viz., Mrs. Donnelly and Sarah Gibson. After this they let us go, and we reached the Gwali [mission station] that night, and Fort Hare on the morning of the 27th December, 1850.

Twenty-eight men were killed at Auckland, of whom eleven were married; the women and small children survived.

Also on 25 December, someone noticed a curious individual in Fort Beaufort:

He was about 50 years old, well built and with a dark, wrinkled skin and kinky hair. It was Christmas morning in Fort Beaufort and he was going from store to store, knocking at doors trying to buy ammunition. At R's he stopped to chat. He offered Mrs R. two goats, saying she could keep them in her stable. When R. asked him where he stood in the event of war he replied that he had long been a friend of the English and that he would fight for them again. Then pointing his finger to the sky he said ambiguously, 'God above will tell me what I should do.' On leaving he shook hands with R. in a most friendly manner.

He called himself Hermanus Matroos when dealing with Europeans but to the Xhosa he was Xoggomesh; he was of mixed Hottentot–Xhosa ancestry. He had been of good service to the Government on several occasions and had been rewarded with a farm about twenty kilometres north of Fort Beaufort in the Blinkwater Valley. He had, however, abused this privilege by allowing a lot of Gonas (Khoikhoi who had adopted Xhosa manners and customs) to collect around him and these had repeatedly raided the neighbouring settlers, running off with their stock.[33]

It was thus with some alarm that the Rev. John Ayliff heard that Hermanus was persuading Lieutenant-Colonel William Sutton, the ranking military authority in the town, to let him have arms and ammunition. Sutton pointed out that they had recently supplied the people of the Kat River Settlement with five thousand rounds, to which Hermanus responded: why not then the Gonaqua who would add to the defences against their common enemy the Ngqika? Ayliff publically denounced Hermanus as a traitor and managed to persuade Sutton to reduce his contribution to a token ten muskets and hundred rounds. Only a short time after Hermanus had left, an express message arrived with the news of the massacre of the military villages. By then Hermanus and his arms could not be found.

The Governor Besieged

Sir Harry Smith, rather than being the aggressor, now found himself besieged in Fort Cox.

> This fort was situated on an eminence which was encircled on three sides by a horse-shoe bend of the Keiskamma river. Around it there towered very high and steep hills, which perhaps might be called mountains. These were covered with a dense bush which gave cover, at this time, to the thousands of natives who infested it and invested the fort. The greatest danger was incurred in venturing outside the gates.[34]

Smith only had a modest force in the fort with him but he was constrained by limited food supplies. Other than that, there remained only the exhausted and dispirited column at Fort White which had so recently escaped the trap in the Boma Pass.

The governor managed to send a message to Colonel Somerset at Fort Hare with orders to undertake a series of activities designed to continue the war:

> These consisted in the declaration of martial law in the districts of Albany, Uitenhage, Somerset, Fort Beaufort, Cradock, Graaff-Reinet, Victoria and Albert and the calling upon all the male inhabitants between the ages of 18 and 50, in those districts, to enrol themselves for the defence of the country; in ordering up from Cape Town all the available regular troops, amounting only to about three or four hundred; in authorising the organisation of levies who

were to take service for six months, to receive a bounty of £2, to be clothed, and accoutred, to receive sixpence per day and the usual rations, to receive a liberal share of the cattle captured and their families to be rationed in their absence; and finally, in sending a message to the Lieut.-Governor of Natal asking him to send forward three or four thousand Zulus to attack the Gaikas in the rear.[35]

During his enforced confinement, Sir Harry delegated to Colonel Somerset the authority to act in all these matters as commander-in-chief. But Somerset, as he himself soon discovered, was scarcely in a better situation than the governor:

On the night of the 28th [Somerset] endeavoured to get some despatches through to Fort Cox by means of a small party of the C.M.R. At a distance of a few miles from Fort Hare, the messengers became aware of a great number of the enemy ahead of them. They therefore hastily returned to the fort. The next day, 150 of the 91st regiment and 70 of the C.M.R., with a three-pounder gun – a force which Col. Somerset, in his ignorance of the true state of affairs, considered more than sufficient to overawe any opposition – went forth with the despatches. Their route lay round the base of Sandilli's Kop in the direction of Middle Drift. When they had marched about six miles, they beheld vast numbers of Kaffirs assembled on the ridges in the vicinity of the Yellow Woods river. The military party came to a halt and opened the guns upon them. But though it did good execution, the enemy was in such overwhelming numbers that the troops found it expedient to commence a retreat.[36]

Heeding a message sent to him by Somerset, Smith finally escaped from Fort Cox on 31 December: dressed as a trooper of the Cape Mounted Rifles, he led his cavalry in an attempt to reach Fort Hare. He was intercepted by a large Ngqika force and, instead, was compelled to change direction, arriving at King William's Town just after noon.

It was the end of a difficult year, and the defection of the Kaffir Police and many members of the CMR to the rebel Ngqika made the prospects for 1851 most discouraging.

Battle for Fort White

It was not only the governor who was besieged. Fort White was also isolated, containing only the small garrison and the wounded men brought back from the Boma Pass affair, with Dr Fraser to care for them.[37] The fort was commanded by Captain John Craven Mansergh and 120 men of the 12th Regiment; Ensign Francis Smyth had with him a detachment of his CMR. Captain Henry Thomas Vialls and a detachment of his 45th Regiment, who had previously manned the fort, had proceeded to Fort Cox with Mackinnon's column.

On the day of their arrival, Christmas Day, the fort had been attacked and all the slaughter cattle driven off, leaving few provisions to sustain the people there.

> The wounded were accommodated in wattle-and-daub huts, but every available man was set to work to build or erect an earthen parapet, breast-high, between each hut, and to construct a couple of flanking bastions at corresponding angles of the square. This precaution was not taken too soon. On the second day [27 December] the post was attacked by an innumerable horde of savages, led forward in three great columns, Sandilli and his chief councillors directing the whole movement, but themselves remaining out of gunshot. He was riding Colonel Mackinnon's cream-coloured charger, captured a few days before.[38]

Mansergh organised a magnificent defence of the fort with what limited resources he had available, the volley fire of the infantry stopping the Ngqika rebels in their tracks. At a vital moment in the defence, while the CMR was drawn up to defend 'the lower intermediate angle of the post', the sergeant and two troopers ran forward holding their weapons aloft, and joined the enemy. The wounded Bisset wrote that Ensign Francis Smyth, leading a CMR detachment, missed an opportunity in not shooting the three men down. It immediately became imperative to disarm the remainder of the CMR until Bisset could identify those that were most reliable. The weapons of these few were then restored and they joined the firing line, while the remaining 'cowardly rascals fell to praying aloud'.[39]

Mansergh, with his disciplined volleys, was eventually able to see the attackers off, though they remained in nearby gullies and crannies for another three hours before all gunfire ceased. They were constantly under threat, and were attacked most of the following days, but managed to stem the tide each time.

Bisset became seriously ill during this time, having suffered a massive haemorrhage from the ruptured artery in his thigh. He was sustained, it seems, by a daily egg from a turkey brought into the fort by a Mrs James. The remainder of the post were first reduced to half-rations, and then to quarter-rations as the siege drew on.

The siege of Fort White lasted for some six weeks, when it was finally lifted by the arrival of a column of troops escorting a convoy of supply wagons from King William's Town.[40]

Chapter 4

Desertions and Incursions

Harry Smith was reeling. Not only had the Ngqika under Sandile gone to war with the colony, after all he had done for them, but the hitherto-loyal Khoikhoi men of the Kat River Settlement had joined him. It came as a still greater surprise when the Kaffir Police deserted their posts on 27 December, pausing only long enough to gather up their families and possessions, including arms, before joining Sandile.

> The progress made within the last three years induced every one to hope that the wildest barbarians are capable of appreciating kindness, and that just and liberal treatment will develope [sic] the nature of man, and prove that he is created for civilized, not savage life. But no people can evince more determined, reckless, and savage hostility, than do the Kafirs at this moment.[1]

Despite these serious threats to the well-being of the colony, however, the governor could do little more than declare martial law on the eastern frontier.

The Waterkloof Triangle

All the action to be next described took place in a triangular piece of country which has Post Retief at its apex, Adelaide on the left and Fort Beaufort on the right; the sides of the triangle each being about thirty kilometres long.

Post Retief lies in a valley between two mountains: sensuously shaped Little Winterberg to the west, which looks like a leopard couchant, and to the east knobbly Didima, which soldiers claimed had a profile resembling that of Queen Victoria. The post was built in 1836 to protect the Winterberg farmers against marauding Xhosa. Authorisation to build it came as a result of agitation led by Piet Retief, of Voortrekker fame, who then sold the land to the government, was awarded the contract to build the post and had it named after himself. The post had been abandoned after the Seventh Frontier War of 1846–7 and by 1850 only the old officers' quarters were still in use.

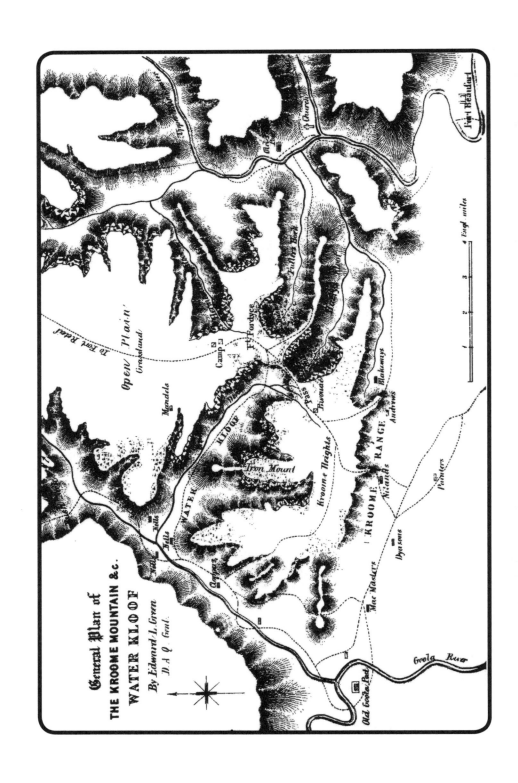

General Plan of
THE KROOME MOUNTAIN &c.
WATER KLOOF

By Edward L. Green
D. A. Q. Genl.

The incumbent was the Rev. Joseph Willson of the Anglican Church, who married, baptised, buried and gave spiritual comfort to a small and widespread flock of the '1820 Settlers' and their descendants.

A rolling, grass-covered plain spreads out to the south of Post Retief. Its eastern side is marked by an escarpment which drops steeply down to the Blinkwater Valley, part of a beautiful and fertile group of wide kloofs and valleys from which the Ngqika sub-chief Maqoma had been expelled in 1829. This made room for an ambitious scheme to prove to the world that the mixed-race people descended from the Khoikhoi were equal to white men in industry and religious devotion – the Kat River Settlement.

Further south, at one of the hairpin bends of the Kat River, the defensive works of Fort Beaufort had been laid out in 1822, and by 1850 a prosperous little town had developed, occupied by about sixty soldiers, five hundred white civilians and several thousand Mfengu, a people physically and ethnologically indistinguishable from the Xhosa.

On the southern side of the triangle there is also an escarpment, known as the Kroome Heights, running towards the west from Fort Beaufort. Near the base of this range lay the prosperous settler farms of Blakeway's, the two Gilbert farms and Niland's farm. Then came the rudimentary village of Adelaide at the junction of the Koonap River and its tributary the Gqwala. Adelaide consisted of a Dutch Reformed Church, a store and two houses serving the farmers in the Koonap, Mankazana and Cowie River valleys.

The Gqwala forms the western side of the triangle. Its source lies at the foot of the Little Winterburg and from there it flows through Kaal Hoek (Bare Corner) past the farms of Eli Wiggill, Isaiah Staples and John Austin, over the falls at William Bear's, down the rapids at Bush Nek and then ambles slowly past Nel's farm at the entrance to the Waterkloof to join the Koonap River at Adelaide.

The Waterkloof itself is a deep valley which runs eastwards from Nel's farm for about ten kilometres, making a gash in the triangular plain as if aeons ago a great gully had been cut by some gargantuan flood. A climb up the bushy sides of the Waterkloof does not lead to the usual ridge between valleys but, unexpectedly, to a grassy plain. Many references to the Water-kloof in our sources do not refer to the valley itself, but to the more extended area within this triangle, particularly the plateau to the north of the Kroome escarpment.

It was within this triangle, and especially in and about the Waterkloof, that the severest and most exasperating fighting of the war was to take place. The severity, in terms of the number of men killed, was puny compared with what Europe could do, but in exasperation it brought famous regiments to near mutiny, shattered the reputation of 'England's finest general' and materially contributed to the fall of a British government.

A correspondent of the *Grahamstown Journal* in Fort Beaufort wrote:

> The Authorities treat the reports going about very lightly . . . but they ought not to be treated so. Nearly all the Xhosa in the service of the farmers about here and the Koonap River have left and gone to Kaffirland – many of them having left nearly a year's wages behind. Some told their masters to trek as the Ngqika intend to make war.
>
> I hear strange reports about this Prophet Mlangeni. One is that some Kaffir Police were sent to take him and when they arrived at his place they all fell dead. A Chief said: 'You are too soon, my son, we are not yet ready for war', whereupon Mlangeni went through some antics and the dead men came to life again. Now as this is believed throughout Kaffirland, he will have great influence in the minds of these superstitious people and they will do anything at his bidding.
>
> I was at Roux's today – he has one wagon in front of his house with furniture [this was probably G. Roux of the neighbouring farm 'Brakfontein']. I went in and the room was nearly bare except for one table and a couple of camp stools. Roux looked miserable and the children huddled up in one corner of the room – it was a distressing sight to see.

On 28 December, Siyolo attacked the Line Drift Post on the Keiskamma River with five hundred men.[2] The Khoikhoi men of the CMR holding the post deserted to the Xhosa and the only two white men there, Sergeant Matthew Kelly and a storeman, fled for their lives to Fort Peddie.[3] 'From what I could see, the whole of the Cape Corps [CMR] were in league with the Kafirs, with the exception of the sergeant and the corporal.'[4]

On 1 January 1851, Colonel Somerset reported that the whole of the Kaffir Police had deserted and joined the enemy, taking with them all their arms, ammunition and equipment.[5]

The governor also had cause to mention the activities of Hermanus Matroos:

> 4. The Kafir 'Hermanus,' who had for years been tolerated within the colony, a large tract of country upon the Blinkwater having been granted to him by Sir Benjamin D'Urban, has turned rebel and traitor, and has committed serious devastations and murders in the district of Fort Beaufort. Major-General Somerset, when I last heard from him, for our communication is very interrupted, was endeavouring to collect a burgher force in order at once to crush the rebel.[6]

1. Sarhili, paramount chief of the senior eastern Gcaleka branch of the Xhosa nation, as he was in the 1850s.

2. Sandile, sovereign chief of the amaNgqika branch of the Xhosa, upon whose people much of the brunt of European expansion on the eastern Cape frontier fell.

3. Sandile's elder brother – who acted as regent during his minority – Maqoma. A brooding portrait of a man most white observers found to be unprepossessing – but whose military flair was to prove Harry Smith's undoing.

4. A British column on the march. The Xhosa were adept at exploiting the terrain to good effect to disadvantage the cumbersome British columns.

5. In this representation of the ambush at Boma Pass British troops are lost in a confusion of smoke and bush and at the mercy of well-placed Xhosa.

6. A disguised Sir Harry Smith and a small escort of Cape Mounted Riflemen make their escape from Fort Cox.

7. A Xhosa warrior in classic fighting pose, blanket wrapped round his left arm for protection, right arm drawn back to throw his spear.

8. The sudden outbreak of war left many settlers on exposed farms vulnerable to attack; here a family is over-run as they try to trek to the safety of the nearest fortified village.

9. British troops carrying their wounded on improvised stretchers through the wooded depths of the Waterkloof.

10. During earlier clashes on the Cape frontier the British press found nobility in the images of Xhosa chiefs.

11. Early romanticism withered under the grim reality of warfare in the bush.

12. The descent of Niland's Pass. (*Africana Museum, Johannesburg*)

13. Men of the 74th Highlanders - in their distinctive field uniform of locally made hunting smocks, forage caps and trews - skirmish with Maqoma's warriors on the high ridges above the Waterkloof.

14. The death of Colonel Fordyce.

15. The dynamic, ruthless and vengeful Colonel Eyre and his men in the field.

16. A skirmish between settler volunteers and the Xhosa in deep bush - a scene typical of the sweeps through the Waterkloof.

In fact, after the date of the despatch, 7 January, Hermanus would no longer be a problem to him.

In Kaal Hoek, a farmer who had been in Fort Beaufort on Christmas Day returned home bearing the news of war. Five men later volunteered to go to Fort Beaufort with a wagon to replenish their stock of ammunition; the five were Thomas Eastland, John Austin Jr, George Gibbons, James Holt and John Edwards. They arrived on 27 December and must have become livid with rage at government stupidity on finding that the civil commissioner, Thomas Stringfellow, refused to allow the ammunition to leave the town in case it fell into enemy hands.

Four of the men left for home while Thomas Eastland stayed behind; we do not know the reason for this but he thereby twice saved his own life. The road to Kaal Hoek goes up the Blinkwater Valley and there, some twenty kilometres from Fort Beaufort, a group of Hermanus's men waylaid the four men. While some cut the oxen loose, others attacked the men riding on the wagon. James Holt, a young man recently from England, was on the driver's seat when they came at him with assegais from both sides of the wagon. He was stabbed four times before he could dive under the canvas cover, jump out of the back of the wagon, plunge into the nearby Blinkwater River and elude his assailants. After dark he made his way on foot back to Fort Beaufort to raise the alarm. Two of the other men, George Gibbons and John Austin, were killed, the latter leaving a wife and three children. Somehow John Edwards managed to escape and carry the news of their first fatalities of the war to the Kaal Hoek farmers.[7]

Kaal Hoek, 28 December

Isaiah Staples, wagon maker and farmer, was hurriedly trying to convert his farm 'Cold Valley' into a defensible camp with the help of his family and servants. They were so intent on their work that they were completely unprepared when at about midday someone shouted: 'The Kaffirs are taking our stock!' A great deal of confusion followed as men rushed to fetch their muskets and tried to find their mounts. Unfortunately, the enemy had taken most of the horses, but eventually some were found and five men started off in pursuit. But, as Staples said afterwards, what could five men do against hundreds? One flock of sheep, the rearmost, seemed to offer the only chance of recovery and even they were being driven away by about fifty of the enemy. The five men charged and the enemy scattered, allowing the sheep to be recaptured and Staples had to be satisfied with these. Fortunately, some oxen that had been kept near the house were also saved.

Later in the day, while Staples was searching for stray cattle that might have escaped capture, he came to the ridge overlooking the Eastland brothers' homestead on their farm 'Kaal Plaats'. To his surprise he saw a man running towards him from an intervening strip of bush; Staples urged his horse on. 'It's all up with poor Eastland,' the man said, 'look at the smoke,' and Staples saw the house on fire with hundreds of red-painted Ngqika around it.

The man, whose name was Leary, told Staples that the brothers Thomas and James Eastland had allowed the Ngqika to camp on their farm because they claimed they wanted to remain loyal and were afraid to stay in Blinkwater. On the morning of that day Leary had noticed that the Ngqika seemed excited about something but he went about his work as usual, as did James Eastland; Thomas was away in Fort Beaufort.

Suddenly Leary heard a shout and, looking up, saw the Ngqika stab James to death. Leary ran for the house and got his musket out in time to kill two of the Ngqika as they came towards him. The rest took shelter behind the house and then set fire to it. After reloading his double-barrelled musket Leary waited until the smoke in front of the house formed a big enough screen, then he ran for the bush. The bush was two hundred metres away and he had covered only half the distance when he heard his pursuers closing in on him. He turned and shot the first man dead then ran on again. As he reached the bush he turned and shot another, then plunged in with nothing but an empty musket. Fortunately, the Ngqika gave up the chase and Leary was just emerging from the opposite side of the bush when he saw Staples.

Leary had left his wife and six-year-old stepson, James Murphy, in the house, but the Ngqika allowed her to go unharmed, though the poor woman had to beg hard to keep them from killing her son.[8]

On arriving back at his farm, Staples found that all except two of his Khoikhoi servants had deserted. They had marched off in a body, taking with them the muskets he had supplied for the defence of his camp. Their reason for deserting, he learned, was that the defences of Cold Valley were too weak. Staples was very depressed as the realisation came to him that they now had to fight 'the whole kaboodle, Kaffirs and Hottentots'.[9] Reluctantly, he and his men decided to join William Bear's camp at 'Ellington', five kilometres to the south-west.

Bear was a fine old settler who was much respected by Staples. As a fighter he was memorable for the way he would charge the enemy, with his long grey locks flying like regimental colours.[10]

Bear's Farm, 29 December
The combined force at Ellington consisted of fifteen white men, ten Mfengu and two loyal Khoikhoi; too few, Staples thought, to make a stand against thousands of Ngqika and Khoikhoi rebels living only ten kilometres away.

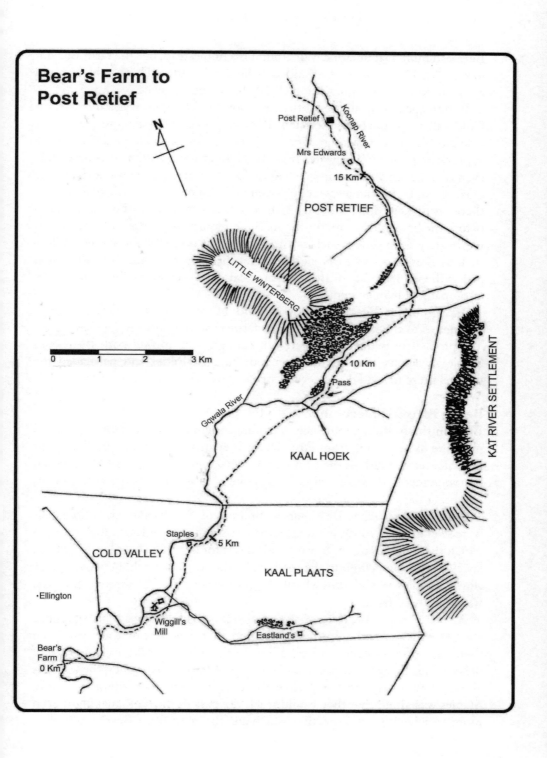

Bear's Farm to Post Retief

N

Post Retief

Koonap River

Mrs Edwards

15 Km

POST RETIEF

LITTLE WINTERBERG

0   1   2   3 Km

10 Km

Pass

Gqwala River

KAT RIVER SETTLEMENT

KAAL HOEK

COLD VALLEY

Staples

5 Km

KAAL PLAATS

·Ellington

Wiggill's
Mill

Eastland's

Bear's
Farm

0 Km

Bear had built a stout stone wall around his homestead, but the farm was not in a good position, being surrounded by hills and scattered bush, which would allow the enemy to approach too closely before being seen.

In retrospect, it would seem that the move to Ellington was a mistake, for Cold Valley was the better position. There are three essential requirements for a defensible camp: nearby grazing, water for the stock and a good view of the approaching enemy. The water must be close at hand so that it is accessible even if the enemy surrounds the camp, for stock must have water daily. The grazing can be further away, yet close enough to defensible cattle pens so that there is sufficient time, after seeing the enemy, to drive the cattle into the pens before the enemy can capture them. These requirements preclude the use of moderately deep valleys such as Bear's farm but favour shallow, open valleys such as Kaal Hoek. Nearly eighteen months later, the Rifle Brigade would realise the vulnerability of Bear's farm to cattle thieves, even when guarded by a company of regular soldiers.

The group at Bear's farm decided to move to Post Retief, seventeen kilometres to the north, where fifteen farmers were known to have gathered. The problem was that there were not enough oxen to pull both Bear's and Staples's wagons. One of the men rode to Post Retief and persuaded the farmers there to send down several spans of oxen and an escort of ten men.[11]

Bear's Farm, 31 December
Early in the morning, four men, including Isaiah Staples, left Bear's farm to meet the oxen coming from Post Retief. They met at 11 a.m. on a ridge about five kilometres south of the post – and so began a day that was to be hard on everyone involved. Staples afterward spoke of it as 'a day that was as long as two other days'.

On their way back to Bear's farm, hundreds of Ngqika and Khoikhoi rebels were seen heading towards a treacherous pass on the farm Kaal Hoek through which the road then ran. It was an ideal site for an ambush as a strip of bush lay close to a long climb in the road where the wagons would be moving very slowly. Staples was gloomy about the prospect of getting through the pass without a hard fight.

Arriving back at Bear's farm, the usual delays in preparing a train of wagons were experienced and it was not until 2 p.m. that they were on their way. Even then, soon after starting, a wheel of one of the wagons broke, causing further delays. Thus by the time they reached Staples' farm, Cold Valley, the sun was already low on the horizon, while the pass was still four kilometres away. Staples was afraid that they would reach the pass in the dark, making it even more treacherous, so a meeting was held. The men from Bear's wanted to outspan for the night where they were and continue in the morning but those from the post objected strongly; they refused to leave the post's defences in its weakened state overnight and threatened to return there on their own if the wagons did not continue. So they all had little option but to push on and this they did as fast as possible, arriving at the ridge overlooking the pass just as the sun was setting.

All the men, ranging in age from William Bear at sixty-seven down to John Wiggill at sixteen, made preparations for the fight. They checked their muskets, mostly flintlocks, which were older and less reliable than the percussion-capped weapons that the enemy was known to have – muskets either purchased by the rebels from unscrupulous traders or weapons actually issued to them by the authorities. Then the stirrups and girths had to be checked for the charge, for the men were determined to take possession of the bush or die in the attempt, as this was their only chance of getting control of the cover and so enable the wagons to pass through. The farmers, by clearing the way before sending in vulnerable ox-wagons, showed an intuitive grasp of military tactics that is refreshing.

They made a detour to the left of the road and then, while on the blind side of the enemy, they began their famous charge. To Staples that gallop was the most thrilling experience of his life: he knew he was doing his utmost to get to grips with a hated opponent, taking inordinate risks in running his horse at full speed over rough ground and he experienced that tingling sensation known only to those who have lived through the expectation of receiving at any moment a volley of musket fire. The thrill was keenest when they were almost onto the bush, all of them knowing that many of the coloured rebels were old soldiers who had been trained to hold their fire until the foe was within close range – but not a single shot came from the bush and, to Staples's utter amazement, not a single Khoikhoi or Ngqika was to be found. Still disbelieving their luck, they drove the oxen hard until the wagons reached the ridge at the head of the valley leading down to Post Retief. There they rested the oxen until hundreds of the enemy were seen pouring over the escarpment from Blinkwater. However, perhaps daunted by the absence of cover, for the valley was clear of bush, the enemy did not attack and the wagons reached Post Retief safely. Staples learned much later from a rebel that they had waited at the pass until late in the afternoon and then, thinking that the wagons would not attempt the pass till the morning, they had returned to their settlement to feast and carouse in anticipation of the morrow's haul of booty. As the gates of Post Retief closed after the last wagon, Staples found himself staggering with exhaustion. He had a meal and turned in for a well-earned rest.

But a rest he did not have, for the enemy, chagrined at their failure at the pass, had followed the wagons at a distance and had quietly surrounded the post; as the New Year came in, the sleepers were awakened by the sound of heavy firing from all four quarters of the compass. The attackers could not be seen in the dark so the only recourse the defenders had was to fire at the flashes of their muskets. The attack continued for about an hour, whereupon the enemy's fire ceased and all was quiet for the rest of the night.

In the morning a rebel was found dead and there were traces of blood where others must have been wounded. On the defenders' side, one Mfengu had been killed and a farmer slightly wounded. Not expecting an attack so soon, the men from Bear's had left their sheep outside the post and the morning brought the painful news that all had been stolen, including the small flock that Staples had saved from the raid on his farm.[12]

After the loss of their sheep, the defenders at the post still had about two hundred head of cattle remaining to supply their needs for milk and beef, and much thought went into ways of guarding them. The enemy made several attempts to drive the cattle off but each time the men rode out and thwarted the attempt. Then the wily rebels lit upon a stratagem which succeeded only too well. One night they hid in an orchard about a kilometre from the post, near where the cattle were known to graze. The next morning, as soon as the cattle approached the orchard, they rushed out and drove them off before anyone at the post realised what had happened. Some fifteen men saddled up and went off in pursuit but they met a large body of the enemy and were forced to return empty-handed for fear of having their retreat cut off.[13]

The defenders' circumstances were now grim. The only stock left was one span of oxen that had fortuitously been kept at the post to draw wood for fuel, and a few sheep: not much to feed seventy mouths for an indeterminate time. The rations were reduced to dry bread and coffee made from roasted wheat without milk or sugar. Worse still, the supply of ammunition was dangerously low, yet it could not be conserved as they had to defend themselves daily against attacks.

There had been no news from Fort Beaufort since John Edwards had escaped from Hermanus's gang, but all knew of the massacre of the men and boys of the military villages and it looked as though those at Post Retief would share the same fate. Fortunately for their morale, the Rev. Mr Willson seems to have been a man of strength; Staples appreciated his spiritual ministrations, which ensured their continued deliverance from many perils, but he did think him rather 'High'.[14]

Fort Beaufort

Sarah Ralph, the twenty-three-year-old daughter of a town councillor, rose early on Christmas morning to ride towards Alice. At a point ten kilometres out of town she halted to wait for relatives who were coming to celebrate the day with her family. She waited for a long time until, worried and disappointed, she returned home feeling that something dreadful must have happened. At 9 p.m. the news of the massacres in the military villages was heard.[15]

Benjamin Booth was a wealthy farmer living with his wife Matilda, the daughter of the editor of the *Grahamstown Journal*, on their beautiful farm 'Hammonds', thirteen kilometres west of Fort Beaufort. After some indecision Ben had sent most of his sheep to Somerset East and had reluctantly made preparations for the war that everyone, except those in authority, knew was coming. He and his wife had stored all their furniture and possessions in the main rooms of the house and had the doorways bricked up. They had then moved to Fort Beaufort, leaving the house and remaining stock in the care of their faithful Khoikhoi servants, who assured the Booths that they could defend the loopholed, fortress-like building against any Ngqika attacks.

William Gilbert's farm, 'Sipton Manor', was well known for the excellence of its defences – its original plans had in fact been published by the authorities as a model of what a fortified farm should be like. The house and a hectare of ground were enclosed by a high rectangular wall with a tower in one side on which was mounted a swivelled, two-pound cannon.[16] Inside the wall there was a spring of good water for the house and stock, and a fruit and vegetable garden. There was also a stone house filled with a year's provisions, including forty sacks of potatoes and ten sacks of onions. The enclosed area provided enough space for the Gilberts' remaining span of oxen and five hundred sheep, the rest of their stock having been sent to Port Elizabeth for safety. Gilbert was obviously a man of foresight and he had made Sipton Manor virtually unassailable against Xhosa attack by training a staff of faithful Khoikhoi to man the defences; he and his wife were determined to stay.

The village of Fort Beaufort had no defences other than a Martello tower, on which was mounted a small cannon, and a strongly built military barracks. The tower, with its beautifully cut and fitted masonry, still stands in almost perfect condition. The barracks, although now incorporated into a psychiatric hospital, remain identifiable; the first floor had six rooms in a row, each eighteen metres long, while the second had three large and twelve small rooms. A defensible guard house had been built at one of the barracks and there was a blockhouse in front. The officers' mess has been preserved intact and is now the home of Fort Beaufort's excellent military museum.

The defences were manned by a small detachment of the 91st Regiment under Captain James M. Pennington, a few Sappers and Miners, and a detachment of the CMR. The whole force, numbering fifty or sixty men, was under the command of Lieutenant-Colonel William Sutton, of the CMR. Sutton was a veteran of twenty-four years' service at the Cape and, since martial law had been declared, was the senior authority in the town and district. He and his wife Fannie, second daughter of General Henry Somerset, lived in the officers' quarters. Ensign Lucas, whom we last met in the Boma Pass affair, knew Colonel Sutton well, having served under him in the CMR:

> About this time Colonel Somerset was made a Major-General and K.C.B.[17] The consequence was that we lost him. The command of the regiment now devolved on Colonel S[utton], who was away on leave at the time far in the interior on a sporting tour. Reports had come down of the number of large game he had demolished, and hippopotami were, we were told, becoming scarce on this account. I was quite prepared, therefore, to see a mighty hunter . . . 'full of strange oaths and bearded like the pard.' Full of strange oaths I must confess he was, but there the resemblance ended. He was a very little man, about five feet four, with a sharp-featured bronzed face, and a high-dried look about him, and had not an ounce of superfluous fat on his frame. Though small in person, he was large in gesture, walked like a heavy dragoon, as if his limbs were inconveniently large for him, and seldom opened his mouth without an expletive. One peculiarity of his was that, without intending to be witty, he made use of such odd phrases and incongruous metaphors . . . that even in his vituperative moments, which were numerous, he was irresistibly ludicrous, and sent us off into convulsions of suppressed laughter.[18]

> There was a tradition in the regiment that he once sentenced a private, who would not get his hair cut short enough to please him (this was always a serious cause of offence) to be confined to barracks for the remainder of his natural life and to have his hair cut every two hours!
> . . . But, with all these eccentricities, he was a highly educated, agreeable man in society, and was a thorough sportsman. His foibles were the result of old associations, and the fashions of an obsolete regime.[19]

Fort Beaufort, along with all Cape districts, was required by a (not very strictly enforced) law to provide a burgher force when called upon to do so by the governor. The white citizens of Fort Beaufort had formed two corps, the Mounted Volunteers, a group of young men who rode and shot well, and another corps of volunteers, unmounted. Both groups performed regular guard duty, having their headquarters at St John's Anglican Church on Campbell Street.

The Mfengu who lived north of the village formed by far the largest force at the disposal of Colonel Sutton. Six hundred had been formed into a levy corps under Commandant James Verity, superintendent of the Mfengu Sunday School, assisted by his two lieutenants, Mr Gee and Mr Clarke. The Mfengu were not armed with muskets on orders from Sutton but retained their traditional weapons, assegais and knobkerries. Many of their womenfolk were similarly armed and could be quite violent when provoked. The task assigned to the Mfengu was to guard the three drifts across the Kat River: Johnson's, the one below the hospital, and Stanton's, as well as a magnificent stone structure built by the Royal Engineers in the early 1840s, the Victoria Bridge.

28 December

It seemed to William Gilbert that his Khoikhoi servants, who were always prone to inebriation on a Saturday, were more than usually difficult on this particular day; it was almost as if there was a spirit of rebelliousness amongst them. He sent a letter to Colonel Sutton appealing for eight or ten white men to come to his assistance, but his request was refused. Gilbert then set about rearranging his defences so that they could be handled by six of his most reliable Khoikhoi as well as himself and an elderly relative, a Mr Hogben – in all there were eight firearms.

At 2.30 p.m. on that Saturday the inhabitants of Fort Beaufort were startled to hear the cry, 'The Kaffirs are coming.' The volunteers hurried to arm themselves and run to their posts; Colonel Sutton ordered arms and ammunition to be issued to the Mfengu from the tower, and the women and children hurried to their assigned place of safety, the barracks. The attack on the town itself never came, for the enemy, Hermanus's rebels, were after cattle. They captured all of Commandant Bovey's and five groups belonging to the Mfengu, in all about 350 head. By 5 p.m. the excitement had died down and Sarah Ralph, for one, was quite thankful to be able 'to sit down and have a comfortable cup of tea'.[20]

29 December

The Mfengu were forcibly and loudly expressing their dissatisfaction with Colonel Sutton's order that the arms issued the day before had to be returned. As they piled the muskets they let it be known that they would in future stay with the cattle and fight off attackers with assegais, knobkerries and even stones – white Fort Beaufort could look after itself. Some of the civilians remonstrated with Sutton and he then allowed those who had been issued with arms to keep them, but he would issue no more. Later in the day, an express message arrived from Colonel Somerset ordering all the Mfengu in the levy to be armed – an order which, Sarah wrote in her diary, 'gave general satisfaction as most of his orders does [sic]'.[21]

Fort Beaufort had three places of worship: St John's Anglican, with the Rev. Mr Wiltshire; the Independent Chapel, with the Rev. Mr Gill; and the Wesleyan Chapel, with the Rev. John Ayliff. On this Sunday night all three reverend gentlemen noted with satisfaction a marked improvement in attendance.

30 December

It was only 8 a.m. and the cattle had been out grazing for only half an hour when the herdsmen were seen driving them back as fast as they could run. Sarah heard the Mfengu women shouting that the enemy were coming, so she ran up to the second floor of the barracks where she had an unobstructed view for about five kilometres in the direction of Blinkwater. She was surprised to see so many of the enemy on horseback.

The Mfengu women had by this time armed themselves and were helping to drive the cattle in. Sarah thought they looked quite formidable as they ran up the street brandishing their knobkerries and assegais.[22]

William Wynne, a mounted volunteer, had just finished eating breakfast when he too heard the cries. He rushed out, saddled up his horse, rode down D'Urban Street and crossed over Stanton's Drift. There he found himself alone with only a few Mfengu men, but proceeded to look around to see how he could cut off the attackers. He was about to join a group of men about a hundred metres away when a Mfengu rode up to ask for a charge of gunpowder and told him that the men were Gonaqua. The powder was no sooner handed over than two balls, uncomfortably close, whistled by his head. Wynne fired a shot at the group, but could not see the result as his horse had become restive, this being the first shot of the day. He tried to reload but failed, so he rode back to join three white men who had just ridden out of town. After Wynne had dismounted to reload, all four, along with a group of Mfengu, chased after the enemy who were driving the cattle away. The mounted volunteers chased the raiders for about four kilometres, every now and then dismounting and firing, but without success.

At one point Wynne found himself separated from the other horsemen, having gone a little too far ahead with some of the Mfengu, when suddenly a group of rebels came down a small kloof and started firing at them. All the Mfengu jumped up and ran off, at the same time frightening Wynne's horse so that he could neither remount nor reload his musket. The rebels were only fifty metres away by the time a thoroughly scared young man was up and galloping to join his comrades.[23]

It had been a spirited affair: the enemy had daringly ridden down almost to Victoria Bridge and the defenders had fired until a shortage of ammunition had forced most of them to retire. Hermanus Matroos had his horse shot dead under him and, in his hurry to get away, had left his tobacco pouch and his saddle and bridle behind, which the Mfengu brought in. Three of the enemy were found dead – one was a Khoikhoi, not a Gonaqua, and for the first time the inhabitants realised that the Kat River Khoikhoi people, whom Sutton had so recently armed, were in league with Hermanus. Eighteen places were found where marks on the ground showed that bodies had been dragged away.[24]

On the side of the defenders, one Mfengu had been killed and two wounded, one of them mortally. Several hundred cattle had been taken. Captain Wynne criticised the poor organisation of the counter-attack: the Mfengu had been without leaders and Sutton had delayed sending any of the CMR until near the end of the attack – and even then only ten of them, half of whom hadn't fired a shot. The four mounted volunteers did, however, receive a vote of thanks from the colonel.

For the next two days Fort Beaufort was left in peace. It seemed as if the enemy were replenishing their courage by attacking lesser game – the outlying farmers.

Sipton Manor

1 January 1851

Early in the morning, William Gilbert sent his herdsman out as usual with the stock but told him specifically not to go too far and not to go in the direction of Blinkwater. Later, to his intense frustration, Gilbert saw that the herdsman, a Khoikhoi, had gone towards Blinkwater after all and he was there now with twenty-two other men, some on horseback, driving his stock away: all the goats, eleven oxen and five horses. There were too few of his own men at the house at this time so Gilbert was only able to recover two flocks of sheep that were within range of the cover provided by his two-pounder.

For the rest of the day Gilbert's remaining Khoikhoi seemed uneasy, and repeatedly asked him to give them ammunition. This he refused to do, telling them that he had it on hand in case of an attack. Privately, he felt that if he had given the ammunition out they would have deserted him. When night came, he made all preparations to repel an attack, placing the Khoikhoi in positions where his few more-trusted men could watch them. One of the latter, a man named Andreas, had been asking all day for permission to go and fetch his mother who lived in the Waterkloof, where, he said, she was in great danger. Gilbert eventually allowed him to go, thinking that to keep him against his will would make him of little use in an attack.[25] He was expecting an attack, for Khoikhoi and Gonaqua were all around, and he had not been able to cut forage for his remaining horses even from the field in front of his house. The first half of the night passed quietly.

2 January

At 3 a.m. the Gilberts were woken up by the barking of their dogs and someone knocking at a side gate close to the house. Looking through a loophole Mrs Gilbert recognised Andreas and saw behind him many men, poised as if ready to rush in when the gate was opened.[26] William Gilbert promptly told Andreas where he could go, whereupon the men opened fire on the house from three directions, at the same time calling on his Khoikhoi hands to come out and join them – and to Gilbert's distress he saw that only two of his men were returning fire. The attack continued until daylight when the enemy, having broken open a gate, went off with nine hundred fat wethers. Gilbert was left with only four horses which had been tied to a wagon near the tower.[27]

At 9 a.m. they saw Booth's wagon passing over the hill on the way to Fort Beaufort, so Gilbert took the opportunity to write a note to the civil commissioner reporting the mutiny of his Khoikhoi and his parlous state. He sent a Khoikhoi on horseback with the letter, but as soon as the man reached the wagon Gilbert realised his mistake. The wagon was in the possession of the enemy and it was loaded with the Booth's possessions, and they also had his cattle, sheep and goats; they were on their way to Blinkwater. The man delivered the note to the rebels, who promptly tore it up and seized him and the horse. After some discussion, they allowed him to return on condition that he and all Gilbert's Khoikhoi join them on the hill. The man was crying when he came back; he had to leave in an hour, he said, otherwise the rebels would cut him up. He confirmed that Andreas had led the attack and that there were a great many Khoikhoi with the Gonaqua.

All of Gilbert's men had by now packed their belongings and, although he begged them to stay just long enough to get a message to Fort Beaufort, they refused. He tried using a gold sovereign to persuade one of the Khoikhoi women to go; Mrs Gilbert even offered to walk to the town herself if some of the women would accompany her, but none would do so. Finally, all the Khoikhoi laid down their arms and walked off towards the rebels. William Gilbert, his wife and old Mr Hogben were alone.

They had no other choice but to leave their proud home and, as the rebels came to meet his once-faithful servants, William Gilbert began to destroy his ammunition. Just then Mrs Gilbert saw a man on horseback coming towards them with two other men on foot. Hurriedly looking through his telescope, her husband saw that the horseman had a white face while the other two were Khoikhoi. The Gilberts' hopes surged – help was at hand! He turned out to be an Englishman by the name of Jones who worked for Booth and was with a group of volunteers sent out from Fort Beaufort with an escort of fifty Mfengu. Their purpose was to bring the Gilberts in and at the same time take three Englishmen to the Aytons who had hired them to help defend their farm 'Rietfontein'. At William Gilbert's insistence, Jones went back to the escort to persuade it to return and pick up a box of clothes for Mrs Gilbert. At the same time, Gilbert sent the two Khoikhoi running after his own people, one of whom had his wife amongst them, to tell them to return as help was at hand. Jones came back with the message that the escort could not be deflected from their orders. In desperation, Gilbert sent him back to the wagon again and even fired the two-pounder to attract their attention to his plight but they would not come. Nor would his Khoikhoi return.

Sadly, Gilbert buried the ammunition in the empty sheep-pen, took the locks off the spare gun and then the three of them mounted the three remaining horses and followed the wagon to Ayton's, who was Gilbert's brother-in-law. The Khoikhoi whose wife had been with Gilbert's people followed with his family. The night was spent at Ayton's.[28]

Fort Beaufort

3 January
All who saw the two wagons come in agreed that it was one of the saddest sights they had ever seen, many of the women among the spectators weeping.[29] The Aytons had changed their minds about defending their home and had loaded their stone-wagon with bedding and some of it was trailing on the ground as it came up the street. The other wagon was full of children, while the women rode on horseback. It was one of the hottest days anyone could remember and the men driving Ayton's and George Gilbert's sheep reported that many had dropped dead on the way: Ayton had started with two hundred kid goats but only twenty arrived at Fort Beaufort.

4 January
At daybreak the mounted volunteers went out with William Gilbert to Sipton Manor to bring in some of his more valuable possessions. Colonel Sutton had offered to send fifty Mfengu and a wagon but, as they didn't arrive, a small cart was loaded with clothing and the arms and ammunition Gilbert had

buried. The two top floors of the tower were filled with Gilbert's valuables and the doors were then battened down, leaving the ground floor empty.[30] They returned to town at 1 p.m. and a strange sight they were, each man loaded with as many of Gilbert's possessions as they could carry. Jones had persuaded five men to go with him to Hammonds and brought sad news for Mrs Booth. Afterwards, she wrote to a sister in Grahamstown:

> In Pa's room they had broken down the brick work, forced open the door and turned everything upside down.[31] They have taken out of that part of the house two mattresses, one feather bed, bed clothes, all his clothes and his telescope.
>
> In my own wing of the house there is nothing left save the chairs and bedstead. I left everything behind, except my clothes, thinking them perfectly safe under the protection of our own people. My work box, desk, and all my other little things I valued, are all gone. My saddle is also taken and the horse-hair mattress of the little sofa is gone and all the chintz torn off.
>
> Mr Bell brought me in those verses our dear mother wrote and also my scrap book. Who would have thought of our own people deserting us, old Jan the wagon driver whom we had known for so many years and Piet whom we had brought up from a child?
>
> All the people here feel very much for us; Savory's, our big store, say that so long as they have anything themselves we shall share it with them, no matter whether they are ever paid.[32]

After dark, two large fires could be seen in the exact direction of Booth's and William Gilbert's homes.[33] Both Gilbert and Booth had been party to a government commission that had investigated Hermanus's iniquities so the worst was feared.

5 January
It was quiet all day. Church services were held, but everyone in Fort Beaufort was on the alert in case of an attack. Three hundred Mfengu, incensed at Hermanus Matroos, wanted to go out and attack him at night but Colonel Sutton would not hear of it.

That night fires were again seen burning in the direction of Booth's and Gilbert's.

6 January
Twenty-five mounted volunteers left early for Ayton's with a wagon and a second span of oxen to draw a new wagon hoped to be still at Sipton Manor, which they could then load with some of Gilbert's possessions. This time Sutton promised faithfully to send an escort of Mfengu to meet them at Sipton Manor.

The enemy had not been to Ayton's so they were able to load up the wagon with bedding, provisions and a piano. One of the mounted volunteers was Peter Campbell, a thirty-eight-year-old farmer and a friend of the Aytons. He had served in the two previous frontier wars and was to captain an Mfengu levy in this one. In his view, Ayton made the great mistake of serving liquor while the wagon was being loaded. The liquor began to affect some of the men, especially his own servants. Campbell cautioned several who were helping themselves rather too freely but their reply was that there were no rebels around and that even if there were they were quite game to take them on. The result was that by the time they left Rietfontein most of the fellows were intoxicated. Before leaving, Ayton told everyone to help themselves to the poultry and soon many had dead ducks or geese stowed about their persons.[34]

From Ayton's they went to Booth's and found that the place had not been burnt down, after all. The bedsteads were still there as well as the tables and chairs, but Mrs Booth's easy chair had been taken outside and broken to pieces. Ben Booth loaded a carpet, a rug, a small Pembroke table and a box of books onto the wagon.

At Gilbert's they found that the place had been burnt down and that the enemy was in the vicinity in great force. The rebels had also loaded Gilbert's wagon with furniture and were in the process of inspanning the oxen when the volunteers arrived. As there was no sign of the promised Mfengu help, all the volunteers could do was to fire at the rebels as they left in triumph, their infantry escorting the wagon in military order while their cavalry attacked the volunteers.

Now the trouble began. One poor volunteer begged and prayed to be lifted into the wagon or he would die, while another got off his horse and asked where the rebels were as he wanted to have a shot at them; Campbell's two Khoikhoi servants, Smidt and Arnolus, managed to get the volunteer on his horse and pointed in the right direction. Another fellow jumped off his horse and ran for it, leaving his steed standing in the middle of the wagon road. As he ran he emptied his pockets of the ducks and geese which were impeding his struggle through the bush; Smidt and Arnolus had them for supper that night. The majority of the escort made for a place of safety and it was left to a few to maintain an almost hand-to-hand fight with the rebels; at one time they were firing at each other across the wagon road. Campbell shot one rebel at ten paces as he was aiming at one of his servants. Then one of the rear oxen got out of its yoke and this held them up considerably, for there was no chance of getting it in again and they had to drive on regardless or lose their wagon. In the skirmish Campbell fired fourteen rounds – as he was a fair shot some of them must have met their mark. For about an hour the volunteers retreated steadily towards town without anyone receiving a scratch. The nearest the enemy came to doing any bodily harm was to put a ball through the crown of Mr Ayton's hat.[35]

At about 3 p.m. Matilda Booth noticed a good deal of activity about town and learned that shots had been heard coming from Gilbert's farm. Fearing an attack on the wagon, a group of horsemen started off immediately, followed shortly afterwards by an unofficial body of Mfengu, cheered on by their womenfolk. They were too late, however, to inflict any damage on the enemy, who were seen taking a route that kept them well clear of Fort Beaufort. Mrs Booth, Sarah Ralph and everyone in town were delighted to see the volunteers and their wagon winding their way towards Victoria Bridge. As they came up the street they were followed by a hundred Mfengu women dancing to their victory song and brandishing their arms at an imaginary enemy. That night Campbell was publicly thanked at Berry's hotel by the captain-in-charge for his part in the affair.

The Booths were just settling down in the room at Savory's when Colonel Sutton came in and told Savory that an express message had arrived from General Somerset, written in French and hidden in a Dutch tinder box. All men were to be under arms immediately as the general had positive information that Hermanus would attack either that night or early the following morning.[36]

William Wynne went to bed that night having made his own personal plan of action: if the enemy came during the night he would not go outside, as there were too many men in town who would fire at the first object they saw. If, however, the attackers came by daylight, it would not be long before he was amongst them.

Chapter 5

The Colony Fights Back

The Battle of Fort Beaufort

7 January

In the early morning, Hermanus Matroos halted his force of five hundred Khoikhoi rebels on the flat about two or three kilometres north of Stanton's Drift. Gathering his men around him, he repeated his instructions: the first division was to attack at Stanton's Drift, the second at the drift below the hospital and the third over the Brak River at Johnson's Drift. The last two divisions were to go to their positions and wait for the signal, which would be the sound of musket fire from Stanton's Drift. As soon as they entered the town they were to kill all the Englishmen; he himself had a knife in his hand which he was going to use to cut English throats. Those without muskets were to drive all the cattle back to this place, where they would be divided – those who fought hardest would get a larger share. Afterwards they could do what they liked, kill Mfengu men, take their women; he himself was going to have the white women serve him tea on Mr Holliday's stoep,[1] where he would sit with the young ladies and then afterwards . . . He had great power in Kaffirland and if anyone failed to fight to the utmost, Mlanjeni, who was his friend, would know about it and great would be that man's punishment. Remember, he told them, approach with the utmost silence and wait for the signal.

Mr Mewett was looking forward to being released from guard duty at 4.30 a.m. It had been a boring night in spite of the warning that Hermanus would attack. All was quiet, the women and children were asleep in the barracks, twenty Regulars were on duty in the guard houses and the Martello tower, and the Mfengu were on the river banks, supposedly alert. Mewett's guard duty was just about over and he was ready for a good sound sleep when he heard musket fire coming from Stanton's Drift.[2]

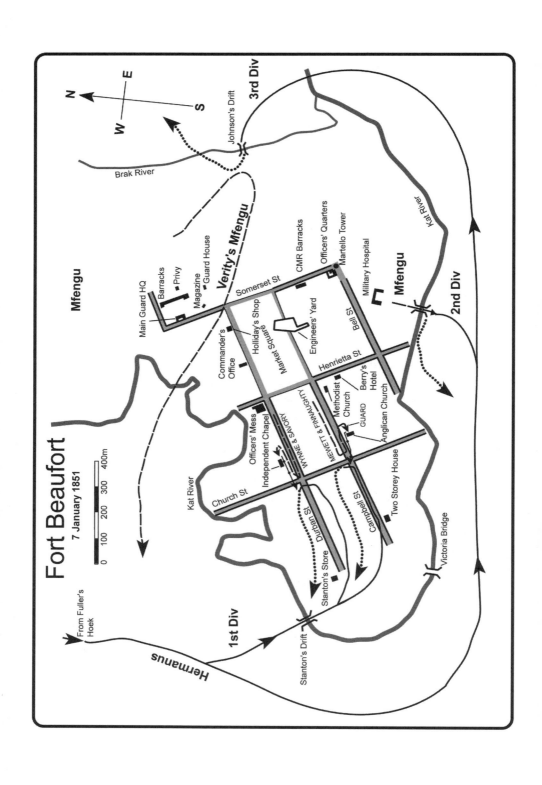

Fort Beaufort
7 January 1851

0 100 200 300 400m

Mfengu

3rd Div

Brak River

Johnson's Drift

Kat River

Verity's Mfengu

Main Guard HQ
Barracks
Privy
Magazine
Guard House

Somerset St

CMR Barracks
Officers' Quarters
Martello Tower

Mfengu

2nd Div

Military Hospital

Commander's Office
Holliday's Shop
Market Square
Engineers' Yard

Bell St

Henrietta St

Officers' Mess
Independent Chapel

WYNNE & SAVORY

MEWETT & FINNAUGHTY

Methodist Church
Berry's Hotel

GUARD
Anglican Church

Kat River

Church St

Durban St

Campbell St

Two Storey House

Stanton's Store

Stanton's Drift

Victoria Bridge

1st Div

From Fuller's Hoek

Hermanus

N
E
S
W

William Wynne was awakened by the sounds of three shots. He sat up, but as there were no more he lay down again, cursing the guard for celebrating their last turn of duty for five nights. He was just dozing off again when he heard four more shots so he jumped out of bed, dressed, collected his arms and was out on the street within two minutes.[3]

Sarah Ralph woke up just before daylight and realised with a warm feeling of relief that there had been no attack after all. Turning over, she was falling asleep again when she was startled to hear the report of a musket and then four more shots in quick succession. She woke the women around her and they dressed to the sound of continued firing. They then climbed on the beds close to the wall and peered through the high windows of the barracks from which they had an excellent view of the town – although at that moment it was still dark and all they could see were the flashes of muskets towards Stanton's Drift and below the hospital.[4]

Hermanus's first division had by now taken several houses in the lower end of the town without opposition. At Stanton's house near the drift the rebels had called out to his Mfengu maids, ordering them to hurry up and make plenty of coffee.

Out on the street Wynne met Captain Savory and, as there was no time to saddle horses, they both ran down D'Urban Street towards the scene of the firing; they were joined on the way by four volunteers. At about the same time Mewett and fourteen more volunteers also ran down and so did Mr Finnaughty and twenty others. Before any of them got very far they met a herd of cattle being driven by their Mfengu owners towards the centre of town. Wynne and Mewett both shouted to the Mfengu to leave the cattle and join in the fighting, and most of them did.

As the volunteers and Mfengu approached the houses occupied by the enemy, Wynne found the firing so heavy that he and his men had to take shelter behind a house near the Independent Chapel and wait there for opportunities to take pot shots at the 'rascals'. It was still scarcely light and Wynne could see nothing clearly except the flash of the enemy's muskets. They waited until Hermanus's men began to show themselves and then they fired. Wynne himself knocked one fellow over, and Savory another, as the enemy moved to take up better positions.[5]

Savory and Wynne were able to hold their ground but Mewett, also behind a house, found the balls, which were flying around like hailstones, too much for him so he and his men had to retreat to St John's Church, where they found themselves reinforced by thirty-seven other volunteers. This augmented force of Mfengu and volunteers took up positions along Church Street and Campbell

Street and poured volley after volley into the approaching enemy, who had made a sudden dash for the Rev. John Ayliff's house. Their fire not only halted the enemy's approach, but turned the tide and forced them to retreat.[6]

Five minutes after the firing began, it became light enough for Sarah Ralph to see everything that was going on, apart from in the lower part of the town, which was partially obscured by the smoke from musket fire. She had a good view of the attack below the hospital: the Mfengu stationed there attacked Hermanus's second division so ferociously that they had to retreat before they even entered the town and she last saw them running in all directions with the Mfengu chasing after them.[7]

The enemy's third division at Johnson's Drift had the honour of being led by Hermanus himself. The Brak River, although impassable to anyone on foot after storms, is hardly more than a dry watercourse in the summer. Hermanus's men were crossing it when the Mfengu and several volunteers under Captain Verity rushed down from the upper part of town and drove them back. This division now found itself in the worst possible situation: to its front Verity's men were pressing vigorously, on its left flank refugees of the second division were arriving, crying out that the Mfengu were coming. Worst of all, though unknown to Verity, Hermanus himself had been killed. The men of the third division gave up all thought of attack and scattered as fast as their legs could carry them.

It was at this time that an inspired tactical move took place. Captain Verity did not follow the fleeing third division – instead he took his men back through the upper part of town, crossed over the Kat River behind Mr Holliday's shop and ran onto the flat ground to the west of town to attack the left flank of the rebels' first division.

Meanwhile, the Mfengu and volunteer attack on the first division in the lower part of town had forced them to retreat across Stanton's Drift where about a dozen were killed, half of them being Khoikhoi, while the rest went streaking back towards Blinkwater.

By 5 a.m., half an hour after the battle had begun, the enemy were in full retreat on all three fronts. Sarah Ralph went home to prepare coffee for the menfolk's return and the Rev. John Ayliff went out with a canteen of wine and water to succour the wounded. Wynne and ten mounted volunteers returned to saddle their horses and then went off in hot pursuit, taking Captain Savory's horse with them, he having gone ahead on foot. Colonel Sutton ventured out of the barracks, gave orders that prisoners were to be secured and then went back into the barracks again.[8]

The rebel first division was in trouble: Verity was racing to cut off their retreat, and more Mfengu and volunteers were coming at them from Stanton's

Drift and from the south. Meanwhile, remnants of the second division were fleeing north with the Mfengu behind them. The enemy's reaction was to get away as quickly as possible. So rapidly did they run that neither the Mfengu nor the mounted volunteers at full gallop succeeded in catching up with them. The main body of the rebels took the route over the hill on Major Blakeway's farm 'Olive Cliffs' and here they made a stand, pouring several volleys into the pursuing Mfengu. But the latter, excited to the utmost, raced up the hill and dropped several of the enemy without losing a single man. The volunteers on foot could no longer keep up with the pace set by the Mfengu and returned to town, some perhaps to enjoy Sarah Ralph's coffee though most went to the canteens. A message from the mounted volunteers asking for more ammunition was handed to Colonel Sutton and he sent out six of his CMR with two thousand rounds in their haversacks, although they were given strict orders to return immediately to the barracks after the ammunition had been delivered – this was the regulars' sole contribution to the battle.[9]

On reaching the Blinkwater River, the fleeing Gonaqua and Khoikhoi turned left towards Hermanus's camp at Fuller's Hoek. There the pursuers divided, the Mfengu following them up Fuller's Hoek while the mounted volunteers went on to attack a group of enemy cavalry at the derelict Blinkwater Post. The enemy horsemen taunted the volunteers to come on, which they did, and as soon as the rebels saw them coming they turned and fled into the mountains. The volunteers stayed at the post, where they could protect the Mfengu against any possible counter-attack from the north.

Meanwhile the Mfengu were having the time of their lives. Gonaqua and Khoikhoi were everywhere and many were killed, one even in Matroos's own hut. They found eight wagons still loaded with household goods from Booth's, Ayton's, Gilbert's and other looted farms. The Mfengu ransacked everything and brought away all they could carry, then set fire to the rest. On their return they had with them twelve hundred head of cattle, several hundred sheep and goats, six horses, including Matroos's favourite piebald, five muskets and a carpet from Matilda Booth's house. The victorious return was covered by the mounted volunteers.

About five kilometres from Fort Beaufort, the victors met Colonel Sutton and the CMR. Then at 10 a.m., two kilometres out of town, just as the first lot of cattle were being driven over the hill from Major Blakeway's, Captain Carey with his CMR arrived from Fort Hare – all the men that General Somerset could spare. Sarah Ralph thought highly of Captain Carey: 'Good and attractive, the right sort of man for Kaffir warfare was he not so bound by military orders, which must be obeyed.'[10] There was, however, no romance: she married a parson, but her assessment was correct for, as the story of the war progresses, it will be seen that Carey was an officer of considerable quality.

The dead at Johnson's Drift were being identified when, about two hundred metres east of the drift, someone turned over a big fellow and found him to be Matroos; it was the first any of the defenders knew of his death. He was thrown over one of Booth's horses, 'Browny white', and brought to the market square in, Sarah declared, 'a state of nudity', wearing only a woman's black crepe bonnet. He was placed under the market bell, on which a Union Jack had been raised, for all (except, we hope, the ladies) to see that it really was Hermanus Matroos.[11]

They remembered the thrill, the emotion, and the tears of joy and relief at the sight of the returning victors that noon for the rest of their lives: the mounted volunteers, the cattle, the Mfengu and then the exalted Mfengu women, dancing and clapping their hands to a deafening chant, '*Mlangeni gedaan* (Mlanjeni finished), *Mlangeni gedaan, Mlangeni gedaan, Mlangeni gedaan* . . .' It was hypnotic.

About eighty Gonaqua and Khoikhoi rebels had been killed. Of these, thirty were lying in the open while the rest had crept away to hide and had died of their wounds. Many of the rebels were well known and Ayton and William Gilbert recognised several who had worked for them. Another, a Gonaqua, was a deacon in the Rev. Arie van Rooyen's church, a man formerly employed by Sarah Ralph's father and 'one of the last anyone would have thought would have become a rebel'.[12] The Rev. John Ayliff was able to assist one wounded man, not with wine and water but by his presence.[13] He was an old Khoikhoi, Figland Fransman, who was being beaten to death by Mfengu women and boys.

The biggest catch was Klaas Botha, who had the best singing voice in the Kat River Settlement, and was the son of Andries Botha, the field cornet and rebel leader. During the chase, Thomas Berry had been aiming his musket at a group of the enemy when a ball struck an intervening branch; the ball was deflected but the branch struck Berry in the eye. This caused him to fire at random and, on opening his eyes, he was surprised to find that he had struck Klaas Botha in three places with buck-shot. Mr A. Ferguson, a 'son of the sod', showed his humanity by bringing in a broken-legged Gonaqua across the pommel of his saddle and taking him to the hospital. Two young Ngqika had also been taken prisoner.

On the side of the defenders, two Mfengu had been killed, one by the treachery of a Khoikhoi and the other by his own haste for plunder. Three Mfengu were slightly wounded but not one of the hundred volunteers involved was even scratched. It had been a great victory, boosting the morale and confidence of both black and white inhabitants enormously.

One of the Ngqika prisoners reported that Sandile was in the neighbourhood and it had been his intention to join in the attack but Matroos had begun too soon. It was Wynne's opinion that 'If he had come we should perhaps have had him too!'[14]

8 January

Colonel Sutton suggested to the Rev. Mr Ayliff that a united thanksgiving service be held that evening by the three ministers and their congregations. The obvious place was St John's Anglican, the largest of the three churches, so the Rev. Messrs Ayliff and Gill waited on the Rev. Mr Wiltshire. He, however, was quite shocked at the idea, he set his face against it altogether, 'It was quite against the rubric.' Sarah Ralph also heard that many of Wiltshire's congregation were very much displeased with his attitude, while the dissenters were sorry that he should have raised objections. The service was held at 5.30 p.m. in the Wesleyan Chapel and the congregation was a large one which included many Anglicans.[15]

The news of Sandile's presence sent the men to their posts and the women and children to the barracks again that night, but no attack came, nor did any come on subsequent days; it had been Fort Beaufort's last battle.

Inevitably there were recriminations. Sutton allowed the Mfengu to keep all the booty, following a sensible precedent set by the authorities. It paid in the long run, for it ensured their loyalty and dedicated service in much the same way as prize money did in the Royal Navy during the Napoleonic wars. Nevertheless, it was not easy for the Booths and the Gilberts to see Mfengu dressed in their fine clothes, hawking their belongings about the street, and harder still to see their stolen cattle given away. Some questioned the legality of Sutton's action – did not the regulations apply only to cattle captured outside the colony?

But the matter which rankled long afterwards was the inactivity of the military – particularly Colonel Sutton. Mewett, in a letter to the *Grahamstown Journal* reporting the battle, stated:

> We had no assistance from the military who were ordered to remain in the barracks and protect our wives and children. We were well supported by our officers, Savory, Sands, Higgs and Finnaughty, but we cannot say so much in favour of our Commandant (Bovey), he not having joined until some time after the fighting commenced.[16]

Mewett later found he had a libel suit on his hands.

Nor was the anger of the inhabitants in any way dissipated when they read the general order reporting the battle:

> Major-General Somerset had obtained information of [Hermanus's] intention, and having communicated it to Lieut.-Colonel Sutton, *that officer was prepared, and his posts of defence occupied accordingly* by the gallant men of Fort Beaufort, the Christian Kafirs, Fingoes, and others, with a detachment of the 91st regiment, which was, however, *very judiciously held in reserve*. A detachment of the Cape Mounted Rifles *was brought into action and behaved nobly*. Hermanus led the attack in person, and was killed in the square of Fort Beaufort. The attack was repulsed on all points.[17]

Sir Harry Smith also used the occasion to refute the power of Mlanjeni:

> This signal success, at a moment when certain of the coloured classes were combining to annihilate the white man, is everywhere, of the greatest importance, as it destroys the charm of protection to the black given out by the prophet Umlanjeni.[18]

Loss of Fort Armstrong

On 22 January, Hermanus Matroos's successor, Willem Uithaalder, led his Kat River rebels in an assault on Fort Armstrong. The fort was built on a peninsula of land some thirty kilometres north of Fort Beaufort, almost entirely surrounded by the Kat River except for a narrow access to the north-west only three hundred metres wide.

Strategically well-placed, it was 'a square enclosure of stone walls [and] had a large, square, loopholed tower astride one of its corners'.[19] There were no troops there, the fort having been abandoned in 1847, but it was occupied by loyal Khoikhoi, missionaries and British settlers who had taken shelter there. Mostert continued:

> This racially mixed defensive post pressed into double duty as refuge became, during the first three weeks of January 1851, an uncomfortable, fearful place of mistrust and suspicion, the focal point of all the tragic divisions and differences within the Kat river district and community. The whites in the fort were frightened of the Khoikhoi and 'coloureds', and uncertain of the commanders of the fort, [Andries] Botha and [Christian] Groepe. The 'coloureds' were mistrustful of one another and apprehensive of both Xhosa and settlers.[20]

A letter signed by J.H. Wienand, magistrate of the Fort Armstrong area, began:

On Wednesday, the 22nd instant, the rebel Hottentots and Kafirs appeared with hostile intentions before Fort Armstrong in considerable force, both mounted and foot, armed with guns and assegais surrounding in every direction the fort. A large body commanded by Willem Uithaalder, appeared on the heights; and in consequence of a message sent in by the insurgents a parley took place between the rebel chiefs and the Rev. Mr. Thomson, Field-Commandant Groepe, Field-Cornets Gobus Fourie and Andries Botha, the purport of which is contained in the document signed by the parties, and which I had the honour of presenting to you yesterday.[21]

Following these discussions, the rebels withdrew 'without firing a shot', although Wienand notes that had the settlers fired on the rebels, many of the coloured people would have turned their arms against them.

The next morning, the British settlers held a meeting at which they decided that, should no aid arrive before sunset, they would leave for Whittlesea, leaving their families behind. This they did, with an escort of burghers from Philipton, as Groepe refused to provide one.

The majority of the coloured people now defected to the side of the rebels and in view of the general air of unease at the fort, Wienand also sent the British families off to Philipton, leaving with them himself. The camp then descended into anarchy, with Commandant Groepe turning a blind eye to everything that occurred – Fort Armstrong was lost.

The Thembu Rebellion

The governor being under siege in Fort Cox, Mr John Montagu, Colonial Secretary in Cape Town, maintained communication with Earl Grey in London on his behalf. On 11 January, Montagu wrote that 'Madassa [Maphasa], the chief of the Tambookies [Thembu], whose tribes occupy the country adjoining our extensive colonial boundary . . . has revolted.'[22] Thus did Maphasa reinforce his displeasure with Smith's casual annexation of a part of Thembu land within days of his arrival at the Cape.

It was fortunate for the British that Second Captain Richard Tylden, Royal Engineers, who was undertaking a survey in the area, assumed command at Whittlesea. He gathered around him men of the loyal Gqunukhwebe under Phato's Christian brother Kama, who had also been attacked by Maphasa, a body of three hundred Mfengu and seventy mounted burghers under Thomas Bowker. Between them, they were able to drive off an attack by the marauding Thembu on 26 January. The attackers regrouped, to be joined by a party of Kat River men from the mission station at Shiloh, three kilometres to the south. The new alliance of Khoikhoi and Thembu engaged Tylden and his men on 31 January, when they were again driven off.[23]

Tylden made a sortie to Shiloh but found it heavily occupied by Khoikhoi rebels and retired. Nevertheless he persisted and again approached the village at dawn on 1 February, before it could be reinforced. The attack was only partially successful, burning down the missionaries' house. The rebels and Thembu, including perhaps Maphasa himself, were driven into the church but this could not be put to the torch due to the wet clay which lined the roof. Tylden's losses, after more than six hours' fighting, were eight Mfengu and one burgher killed, with seventeen wounded. He thought that the enemy had suffered some forty killed and wounded, and he drove off six hundred cattle.

On 3 February, the Thembu and rebels made an attempt to recover some of the lost cattle when they made an attack on the Mfengu. They failed completely, losing three dead, while the Mfengu lost two.

A shortage of ammunition now caused Tylden to send an urgent message to Cradock some two hundred kilometres away. Luckily, the rebels did not attack the next day, nor the day after that. On the morning of 6 February, however, Tylden was puzzled to see a great herd of cattle approaching the village. He quickly understood, however, when he saw many rebels and Thembu following behind, screened in part by the dust. The attack began and Tylden was compelled to hold his fire due to the shortage of ammunition. Finally, he could wait no longer and gave the order to fire, and the cacophony deafened him. The attack did not waver and Tylden must have thought that the village would fall.

> Then suddenly – in the proverbial nick of time – horsemen were seen careering down a distant hillside. Running the gauntlet of a storm of gunfire they came galloping into Whittlesea leading pack-horses loaded with powder and shot. They were the men of the Cradock Mounted Volunteers, hereafter to be known as the Cradock 'Bricks'.[24]

The next day, the wagon-train entered the village, escorted by 180 burghers.

The daily skirmishes stopped quite suddenly as the result of an unexpected armistice. It seems that several of the Khoikhoi went down to the Kat River Settlement, where they were interviewed by the Kat River Loyal Burgher Association, after which the two missionaries, W.R. Thompson and J. Read, sent a letter, dated 4 February, to General Somerset, deploring the destruction of life and property at the mission station of Shiloh. On 7 February, Somerset responded by giving an order that attacks on the Shiloh Khoikhoi must cease, and they did, although skirmishes with the Thembu were unremitting.[25]

This armistice caused such an uproar outside the settlement that the matter was finally taken for adjudication to Sir Harry Smith. This resulted in his decision by proclamation:

> I hereby proclaim, declare, and make known that the Shiloh Hottentots are thus proved to have been guilty of rebellion, and the punishment inflicted upon them has been of their own seeking, and the evils and horrors of war been brought on by themselves. And whereas my Proclamation of the 10th January last, as also the Notice of Major-General Somerset, of the 3rd January, and the various friendly communications made by that able officer, are proofs of my desire to receive those who submit, I hereby proclaim, declare, and make known, that unless the misguided men of the Shiloh institution proceed to Whittlesea, individually or in small parties, lay down their arms, and take the oaths of allegiance, they must still be regarded as enemies. And whereas this line of obedience and submission is open to them, Captain Tylden, commanding the Cradock and Victoria districts, is hereby authorised to restore to any men their arms in whose future loyalty he may consider he can confide.[26]

The brief period of the armistice, which ended with Smith's finding, allowed sufficient time for the Shiloh Khoikhoi to pack up and move. Cory records that a patrol which visited the mission on 26 February found it 'quite deserted'.

Although Captain Tylden was not aware, the Boers in the Orange River Sovereignty had begun their own attacks on the Thembu in January, thus drawing off many of the attackers on Whittlesea. On 2 February, there was a large engagement between the two when a great number of Thembu were killed, with no loss to the Boers. The Boer pursuit continued until 11 February, when another engagement took place, where the Thembu again lost heavily, both in lives and cattle.[27]

With the Shiloh emergency over, on 3 March Captain Tylden assembled, on his own initiative, a small force in the square at Whittlesea to take the fight to the Thembu. He had 176 of Kama's Gqunukhwebe, two hundred Mfengu and twenty-three European volunteers. All the Africans had white bands tied round their heads to distinguish them from the enemy. The force set out before dawn the next day and, after a long march, found the enemy in a strong position on a nearby mountain. This was joined soon after by another group coming up from their base. In the engagement which followed, the Thembu were driven over the nearby Klaas Smits River, although when Tylden tried to follow the fugitives, he found himself outnumbered by new Thembu reinforcements. There was a running fight all the way back to Whittlesea, which was reached after at least twenty-three hours of marching and fighting.

Tylden's force suffered five killed and six wounded while the Thembu loss was counted at forty-three, although the total dead was not known.[28]

Subsequently, the Thembu rebellion petered out, and Maphasa was killed shortly afterwards during fighting with the Boers.

Post Retief

On 17 January Sarah Ralph heard that two Mfengu had brought news from Post Retief of a very gloomy nature – the post had been attacked twice and unless supplies and reinforcement were received they would soon be forced to surrender. However, relief was not sent, the excuse being that there would then be too few men in Fort Beaufort to repel another combined enemy attack.[29]

The news that the Mfengu brought back was a severe disappointment to those at the post. Another message was sent to Fort Beaufort but it never arrived and Staples concluded that these Mfengu had been captured and killed. In desperation, three men were sent up-country to try and get help and supplies, especially ammunition. The men were John Edwards, William Armstrong and Peter Marshall.[30] At McKay's farm in the Mankazana, Peter Marshall was wounded by a sniper and thereafter progress became difficult as one of the other two men had to support him continually on his horse. Fortunately they met a patrol from a nearby camp who took them to a farm, 'Nettle Grove', where the ball was extracted by Dr Armstrong of Cradock. The three men eventually struggled back to Post Retief bearing welcome assurances of relief.

Subsequently forty mounted men arrived at the post and forthwith decided to teach the enemy a sharp lesson by riding off to Blinkwater to recapture some cattle.[31] Staples thought they had inflated views of their powers; while complimenting them on their bravery, he was smug about their precipitous withdrawal when the rebels came at them like an angry swarm of bees. Staples, however, made a valid point: there is no shame in running away when the enemy is overwhelmingly stronger. The forty, their ardour dampened, left the post to return home but held out the hope that they would return with a stronger force. It must be assumed that they had supplemented the defenders' supply of ammunition.

6 February

The severest test of the war for the post came on 6 February 1851. The day began with fifteen men, including Staples, riding out to shoot buck for meat. When they had travelled some distance, they saw a group of about fifty men going towards the post and, afraid of being cut off, the hunters galloped back, reaching safety just in time. After caring for their horses and having a meal, the men noticed that the rebels had not retired as usual but were assembling in increasing numbers with the evident intention of making an attack. The hunters took up their muskets again and went out on foot to meet the enemy, taking up a position about two hundred metres from the post where they could find some cover. Both sides began popping away at each other but it soon became apparent to the hunters that the rebels were sending back three bullets to every one of theirs and that they were gradually closing in. There was only one way out and that was to make a bolt for the post gate as fast as possible; in spite of a fusillade, all arrived safely.[32]

They now invested the post, taking up positions all round it and firing continuously. The defenders could only reply occasionally as they still had to be careful with their ammunition, taking only 'sure' shots. The firing continued all afternoon and, as night approached, the more fearful thought that the rebels would climb the walls in the darkness and overwhelm them. Staples, however, had his own views of their pluck and he was right: apart for an occasional shot, the night passed uneventfully.

7 February
Next morning, however, the bullets came whistling as thickly as before and, because the post was built on a hillside, the enemy was able to fire from above into the enclosure. Rather than resulting in consternation, however, this fire seems to have caused some amusement – such as the sight of a man dodging about to avoid low-velocity bullets as he went from one place to another on essential personal business.

The next trick of the rebels, though, did cause consternation, for they diverted the water in the artificial channel flowing just below the post by opening a sluice gate, and thus draining it. As the river was two hundred metres away and very much exposed, it seemed that disaster would ensue. Fortunately, the day before, prudent housewives had filled all available utensils with water so that, with care, they had enough for three or four days, although there was none for the poor animals.[33]

No one could tell how long the siege would last but the indications were that the rebels were in earnest. Wagons now began to arrive bringing the besiegers' womenfolk, and the defenders were entertained to a dance outside the post, the performers dressed in looted finery. After this overture, the women set to work on three large sacks of wheat belonging to Mrs Edwards; the sheafs were carried to hard ground where they were threshed and the grain loaded onto the wagons. Those at the post could only watch, frustrated, because the distance was too great for their muskets. Nor could they take any offensive action as the enemy still surrounded them.

Some time later, a mysterious object was dragged up to the high ground overlooking the post. While everyone was guessing what it might be, it suddenly belched out smoke, gave a loud boom and a shot bounced onto a zinc roof in the post and then bounded away: it was William Gilbert's two-pound gun from Sipton Manor. Fortunately the Khoikhoi were no artillerymen and the only damage the shot did was to dent the roof.

That afternoon the clouds gathered and a splendid downpour fell, enabling the defenders to replenish their water supply. Even better news was that, as soon as the rain was over, the attackers began to move off, laden with produce from the surrounding farms. The men at the post, in their haste for revenge, went after them on foot. They were unable to inflict any casualties but were able to harass them sufficiently to gather a welcome supply of hastily abandoned fruit.[34]

'Hartebeestfontein'

8 February

It is greatly to the credit of those marooned at the post that they should have cared enough for their fellow men to do more than just wonder what had happened at Smith's camp.[35] On 8 February, the day after the relief of Post Retief, seven men volunteered to ride out to see how the Smiths were faring. The only names of the seven that are known are young John Wiggill[36] and his uncle, Francis Bently; one of the seven was an Mfengu. On reaching 'Hartebeestfontein', they found all to be well and so, after the usual pleasantries, they left to return to the post.[37]

On the way back, a Khoikhoi was seen standing in a hollow and, as they approached, he called to the horsemen, saying that he wanted to talk to them. There was some discussion amongst the seven but eventually four of the youngest, including John Wiggill, rode down to hear what he had to say. While they talked he appeared friendly enough, but suddenly a band of Khoikhoi and Ngqika ran out from behind cover and surrounded the four men. They were disarmed and led away with riems around their necks.[38]

The three wiser Post Retief men somehow overheard that the band was on its way to join in an attack on Smith's camp so they rode back towards it. They were too late, however, for the camp had already been surrounded by Khoikhoi and Ngqika under their captain, Andries Botha, another son of the Kat River leader. On his arrival, Botha had called to all the Khoikhoi on the farm to leave immediately and told Smith that he had until midnight to lay down his arms and surrender or the camp would be sacked. All seventeen of Smith's Khoikhoi went over to the enemy and he was left with only ten white men and three Mfengu and their wives and families. To their surprise and joy, that night they were reinforced by the three horsemen from Post Retief.

9 February

The next morning, at break of day, the attack by about three hundred Khoikhoi and 150 Ngqika began. Most of the firing took place between the mill occupied by the rebels and the house occupied by Smith's men. Smith, in his report of the attack, says that the back of the mill was only a few yards from the front of the house. This odd statement cannot, unfortunately, be checked for nothing now remains of these two buildings.

The enemy's musket balls riddled the house. They came through the doors and windows, struck the roof beams and knocked the plaster off the walls in all directions; many spent balls fell on the beds occupied by the women and children. No one was hurt until 1 p.m., when George Wilkinson was killed by a ball through the head; he was buried under the floor. The rebels made two attempts to fire the house but on both occasions their men were wounded while advancing with fire brands. The burnt stumps were later found lying on the ground with trails of blood leading away.

10 February

The attack continued into the night and only ceased the following morning, the 10th, when the rebels, evidently finding they could make no impression on the house, turned their attention to plunder. The rebels broke in at the back of the mill and, having brought a wagon with them, loaded it with twenty-six bags of wheat as well as meal and other items. Wool had been stored in the mill and this was scattered all over the place to free more bags for carrying the booty. They also took the stock – 985 sheep, thirty-two oxen, eight cows, five calves and six horses. Three other horses were shot, one of which was a valuable animal belonging to Smith's son-in-law.

During the twenty-eight hours of the attack, none of the men left his station, being served breakfast, dinner and supper by old Mr Smith himself and the women and children.

Meanwhile, when the seven men failed to return on the evening of the 8th, those at Post Retief became worried, for all were experienced enough to know that some disaster must have occurred. Staples found the terror amongst the men's relations pitiful, for they were convinced that their menfolk were either dead or in enemy hands.

There was still no news the next day, the 9th, but the sound of firing from the direction of Smith's camp gave hope that the men had somehow found it impossible to return and were taking part in the fight. There was still much anxiety, however, for it was well known that Smith's camp was not secure. Their ultimate fear was that, should his camp fall, the enemy would then attack the post, where, with seven men short, their chances of survival were slight.

Just after noon on the 10th, anxious eyes at the post saw about thirty or forty rebels approaching over the mountains from the direction of Smith's camp. Their conclusion was that Smith's had been taken and that these were the vanguard of rebels coming to finish them off. Preparations were made to give them as good a reception as possible, although Staples for one was inwardly beginning to lose heart; they were so terribly alone and without any hope of relief.

Then, to everyone's astonishment, the rebels produced a white flag. Its meaning baffled the defenders; certainly the rebels, who had so far had it all their own way, were not going to ask for a truce, so the only conclusion was that they were going to offer terms of surrender. But everyone agreed they would not surrender and all said they would rather die. As the rebel body came nearer, it was seen that they had a few prisoners with them; about four hundred metres away, on the other side of the stream, they halted and called for a parley. John Sweetnam, the field cornet, also carrying a white flag, went out to meet their representatives, Spielman Kieviet and van Beulen. He found they had three prisoners, two white lads, one of them being John Wiggill, and an Mfengu; the rebels wanted to exchange them for all the Khoikhoi at the post – three or four men and their families. Sweetnam's reply was to agree to the terms but he would not force his Khoikhoi to go; they had been faithful and were fighting well. The Khoikhoi at the post, with one exception, flatly refused to go and told Sweetnam they would rather have him shoot them instead. One said that he would go for the sake of the 'children', as he called the prisoners.

Whether this was from self-sacrifice or a desire to join the rebels, Staples didn't know. He had all along had some doubt about the man's loyalty, but perhaps wrongfully. The parley was now at a stalemate, the rebel Khoikhoi insisting on the exchange, the loyal ones refusing to go.

So anxious was Mrs Susannah Wiggill[39] to hear news of her son John that she, with a sister, Elizabeth, and a servant, went out to where the men were talking. When the Khoikhoi saw Mrs Wiggill, some who knew her called out to her to come over, and she would not be harmed. She insisted on seeing the prisoners and found her son, stripped of nearly all his clothes. The rebels told her that he was not being held prisoner, he had been given his liberty on condition that he promised not to take up arms against them but he had refused to do so.

John told his mother how he and the three others had been captured and how the Ngqika had insisted that they be killed. However, the Khoikhoi had recognised him and had surrounded the prisoners so closely that the Ngqika could not get at them. They then threatened to tell Sandile but the Khoikhoi replied, 'We don't care, he's not our chief.' John's feelings during this tussle for his life are not described; his only comment was that the Ngqika stared at them over the shoulders of their protectors and called them 'Satans'. The prisoners' champion was a Khoikhoi named Diedrich, who had at one time been employed by Mrs Wiggill's parents. Diedrich had managed to prevail over the other Khoikhoi with the persuasive argument that John's father was well known to them all, that he was a good man who had never done them any harm and that as a wagon builder he would be indispensable in their future Khoikhoi kingdom.

The rebels took the prisoners with them to Smith's and thereafter to an empty Boer house where Diedrich and others could more easily protect them from the Ngqika. The rebels had also brought sheep into the house and John was appalled at the cruel way the sheep were slaughtered – the Khoikhoi either falling on them like a pack of wolves or throwing assegais into their bodies and then letting the sheep run around painfully wounded. It was the time of year when the grapes in the vineyards were ripe, so John and his fellow prisoners lived on a diet of grapes and mutton, a lot better fare than they were used to at the post. Later, when John was released, Diedrich gave him a leg of mutton to take to his grandmother.

When the negotiations were on the point of collapse, the men at the post made up their minds that they would not allow the prisoners to be retained in captivity. Although realising the risk they were taking, fifteen men saddled their horses and loaded their muskets, ready for a rescue attempt should peaceful means fail. It was at this critical moment that yet another last-minute rescue occurred, which convinced the more religious-minded that a spiritual providence was controlling their affairs.

A large body of mounted men was seen approaching from the south. At first those at the post thought it was more of the rebels and that now all chance of rescuing the prisoners was gone. Their despair did not last long, however, for the rebels at the parley started showing signs of restlessness, and suddenly the approaching men were recognised as burghers. There were about eighty of them under Commandant William Monkhouse Bowker from Somerset East and Captain William W.D. (Dods) Pringle from the

Mankazana. Bowker and Pringle immediately went down to where the negotiations were taking place. Sweetnam, according to Bowker, asked him whether he should deliver up the Khoikhoi at the post. Bowker told him to let the rebels keep the prisoners and do with them what they liked, and shortly afterwards the prisoners were released unconditionally. The rebels stated that they had long fought on the side of the English government and did not kill prisoners because they knew the law. Bowker asked van Beulen and Kieviet whom they were fighting under and they replied that they fought under their own commandant and that Sandile was their chief.[40]

Mrs Wiggill was still with her son when Bowker arrived and, when the rebels decided to release him, she promptly also asked for her riding horse, a fine mare that John had ridden. According to John's father, Eli Wiggill, one of the Khoikhoi replied, 'No, no, Missis, you have got your boy, be satisfied.' She begged them to be kind to her horse and caressed it affectionately as she said goodbye.[41]

It was learned from the rebels that Smith's camp was still holding out, so those at the post were eager to go to their aid but Bowker refused as both his men and his horses needed rest, so it was decided to camp for the night and start early in the morning. There was some grumbling at this decision as some felt that the rebels would break off the attack and escape but, in a matter such as this, Bowker's decision had to be respected; his record as a commander was excellent.

Sure enough the rebels had left, which was just as well, for the camp was in a pitiful condition. Someone estimated that four hundred bullets had hit the house and all thought it was a miracle that only one man had been killed and none wounded. With all the stock gone, there was not much point in maintaining the camp, so arrangements were made to move to the post. Smith had seven wagons and they were all drawn in, two at a time, by the eight oxen remaining at the post. The first wagons carried the women and children; it took two days for the poor oxen to complete the move.

John Joseph Smith was proud of his victory. Seventeen men had successfully withstood an attack by 450 well-armed, well-trained and determined men which lasted for twenty-eight hours, with only one casualty. It was an epic defence which ranks with the Alamo and Rorke's Drift and deserves, like them, to be immortalised.

Chapter 6

The End of the Beginning

Balfour and Fort Armstrong

Before going to Post Retief, Commandant Bowker went to see General Somerset at Fort Hare.[1] There he received orders to assemble as many burghers as possible for a punitive action against the rebels in the Kat River Settlement. Everyone, including the authorities, was now convinced that the settlement lay at the heart of the revolt and was the source of most of the raids on farmers over a wide area, as far afield as Cradock. Many also thought that, without the support they had been promised, the Ngqika would never have started the war. The objectives of the campaign were now, therefore, directed towards the destruction of the rebel camp at Balfour and the recapture of Fort Armstrong, taken without opposition by Willem Uithaalder on 22 January 1851.[2]

The plan was as follows: Commandant William Monkhouse Bowker, with seven hundred burghers and Mfengu, would overcome Balfour, and then move some four kilometres south-east to Fort Armstrong. Meanwhile, General Somerset, with two howitzers, two squadrons of CMR and twelve hundred levies would approach Fort Armstrong from Fort Hare via the Lushington Valley.[3] A two-pronged attack would then be launched on Fort Armstrong, Bowker from the north-west and Somerset from the east. After taking the fort the combined force would proceed to Philipton, the focus of the revolt, and evacuate and destroy that village.[4]

Post Retief, 21 February

About three hundred mounted burghers and four hundred Mfengu were gathered together at Post Retief: many must have slept outside the post on that night of 21 February 1851, relying on pickets to keep foraging Khoikhoi away. It was a convivial gathering; a Grahamstown volunteer wrote of the high spirits and the expectation of 'active work' on the morrow;[5] while another young burgher, a Graaff-Reinet Englishman, expressed his gratitude for much kindness from the Rev. Mr Willson and especially from Mrs Edwards, who baked bread for him and his comrades and offered to look after their kit while they were on patrol.[6] Isaiah Staples recalled that, in spite of the order to start at midnight, with the preparations and excitement few of them slept.[7] Commandant Walter Currie was more sombre. He had attended divine service held by the Rev. Mr Willson in the morning and then a meeting of the Commandants in the afternoon to decide on the method of attacking Balfour. 'For a wonder', Currie wrote, 'all were unanimous.'[8] The burghers' spirits were high; whereas up to the present the rebels had been living off the fat of their labours, the burghers now had the opportunity of taking their revenge and the urge was great. While everyone was eager for the fight, they also knew it was not going to be easy and some of them would not return. The rebels had a four-to-one advantage in numbers; they were also mostly Khoikhoi and Gonaqua, who could use a musket, as many of them had been in the CMR. They were well supplied with ammunition and had muskets superior to those of the burghers. Also, Balfour had many strong points, with its bushy ravines and dongas, from which it would be difficult to dislodge the rebels. Finally, Fort Armstrong itself, although abandoned by the military in 1847, was still in good condition with its loopholed walls and a virtually impregnable tower.

Bowker's force left Post Retief about midnight just as the new moon was rising. They moved up the valley to the ridge overlooking the upper Blinkwater and then turned east and rode along the ridge extending to Balfour. After covering twelve kilometres of reasonably open and level country the going became rougher. There was no road, and in the pale moonlight the difficulty of descending the steep, rocky, bushy hillside was so fraught with danger that Staples thought it was a miracle that they all got down safely.

During the descent the enemy's camp at Balfour was clearly visible, lit by numerous camp fires over a wide area. This camp consisted mainly of Gonaqua and Ngqika under their leader Jan Hermanus, son of the Hermanus Matroos killed at Fort Beaufort. There was much singing, dancing, clapping and beating of hides, the sounds of revelry disturbing the cattle in nearby kraals who bellowed in sympathy, reminding many of the burghers of their once-prosperous farms.[9]

Balfour, 22 February

Bowker's force arrived at the base of the ridge just as day was breaking, the inhabitants of Balfour still completely unaware of their approach. He had split his men into two groups for the attack: Dods Pringle, Walter Currie and the Mfengu took the left or northern flank, while Bowker and the rest of the burghers approached from the right, the enemy being caught in-between.

Balfour and Fort Armstrong

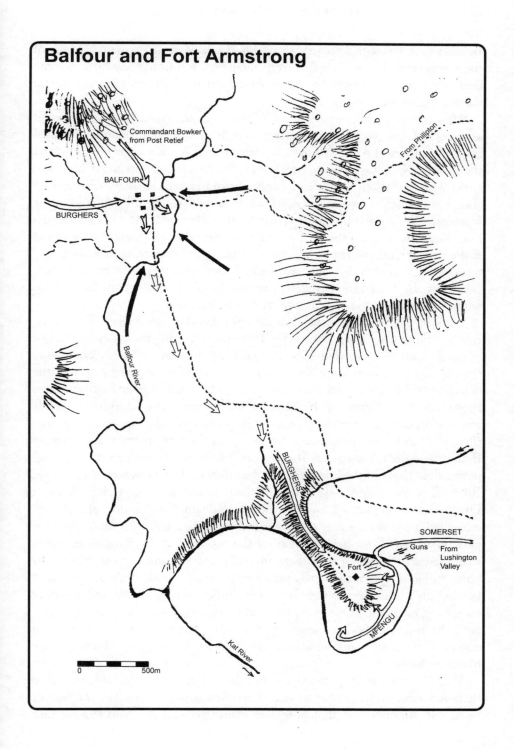

Commandant Bowker
from Post Retief

From Philipton

BALFOUR

BURGHERS

Balfour River

BURGHERS

SOMERSET

Guns

From
Lushington
Valley

Fort

MFENGU

Kat River

0   500m

Bowker gave the signal to attack and hundreds of muskets roared. Many of the rebels were shot as they fled from their fires and from their huts into the bush – many more would have been killed but the half-light made accurate shooting difficult.

After the attack commenced a few of the rebels managed to arm themselves and opened fire, but with little effect, and the attack soon became scattered as the burghers and the Mfengu separated into small groups chasing after the fleeing rebels. One group, which included Staples, cut off about fifteen of them who had taken refuge in a bush-covered ravine. There all fifteen were shot, but not before one of the rebel bullets caught young John Niland in the forehead, killing him outright.[10] Other rebels had taken shelter in cattle kraals built along the edge of the bushy ravine and the Mfengu thought they would make a great haul, but the Ngqika, as befitted a cattle-revering race, fought so tenaciously that they not only succeeded in getting away with most of their cattle but also forced the Mfengu to retreat. In all, about thirty or forty of the enemy were killed, the rest disappearing into the bush.

Looking round in the now-clear daylight, Bowker saw a large body of the rebels coming from Fort Armstrong. These men, making their way up the bed of the Balfour River, started firing from behind the cover of its banks. Bowker then observed another large body, mounted and on foot, come down from the direction of Philipton and take possession of the buildings at Balfour, where they made life difficult for the Mfengu and Graaff-Reinet burghers. Shortly afterwards, Bowker saw still more, the majority mounted, approaching from the east – and they commenced firing on his force from the ridge between Balfour and Fort Armstrong. The muskets of the rebels had greater carrying-power than those of the burghers and the effect on Bowker's men was serious. Riley, Thompson and Baker from Graaff-Reinet were wounded. A stout Dutchman sitting on an anthill next to William Ainslie, one of Pringle's men, had a narrow escape, a musket ball making a mark on his scalp. One participant could not help comparing the coolness of the English burghers with the excited state of the others around them: the one party lighting their pipes and joking about the 'pale pills' being administered, while involuntarily bowing their heads very respectfully to the bullets as they passed, and the other entreating everyone to avoid exposure as much as possible. 'Our engagement with these several bodies continued from daylight until about 10 a.m., not one loyalist out of many hundreds said to be in the Kat River having come to our assistance.'[11]

Thus hemmed in by perhaps five hundred of the enemy, unable to return their fire effectively, unable to take Fort Armstrong unassisted for fear of being cut off, uncertain that Somerset would ever come – and cursing him for being already two hours overdue – the morale and discipline of Bowker's force broke.

A large body of men, chiefly Dutchmen, began a disorderly retreat up the ridge back towards Post Retief. Commandant Currie was thoroughly disgusted with the five deserters from his group. '[They] fled', he wrote to the *Grahamstown Journal*, 'with a number of Dutch and have not been seen since. I only hope they will be cut off to a man . . . You may publish the names of the deserters of mine: Manuel Thorp, Wm Edwards, Wm Noble, Fred Noah and Kirkman; they should be brought to justice by the public.'[12] Yet there were also acts of courage. Riley, although desperately wounded, sat on his horse and would not allow the doctor to come near him until another wounded man had been attended. Although nearly fainting from pain and loss of blood, Riley cheered and exhorted the men around him to stand fast to the last gasp 'for the honour of their name as Britons'.

The worst fire was now coming from the river and Bowker and the other commandants seemed at a loss to know what to do, when suddenly a young Dutchman, Hermanus Bertram, shouted 'Let's charge them!' Bowker and Currie immediately got their men together: the Graaff-Reinet Englishman heard the call 'Bowker's men, turn out, turn out!' Only thirty responded but they, with a loud 'Hurrah', charged the rebels behind the river bank and speedily dislodged them. While following the fleeing Khoikhoi, four of the men, including Bertram and Staples's brother Sam, found themselves face to face with thirty rebels whom they had mistaken for burghers. At forty paces they saw their mistake too late and the Khoikhoi rebels poured a volley into them, killing or wounding their horses and wounding Sam Staples. A deep donga ran nearby so the four men jumped into it and managed to keep the rebels at bay with their muskets. The Khoikhoi did not like exposing themselves in order to take shots at the four men but taunted them instead, telling them to look at the sun for this would be the last time they would see it. The four men, however, by skilfully creeping back up the donga, eventually got within the shelter of the muskets of the main group of burghers and so prevented the Khoikhoi from following. All four escaped but lost their horses and kit, for which, by the rules of their service, they received no compensation.[13]

The effect of the charge was surprising, for the enemy was seen to be giving way in all directions, many of them running towards Fort Armstrong, and in a matter of minutes the field was clear. It was then realised that the enemy had seen the dust of Somerset's force coming down the Lushington Valley. Some of the burghers thought the dust was Sandile coming with reinforcements and this threw them into an even greater state of panic and led to renewed desertions. However, the dust was eventually recognised as that of Somerset's column, whereupon Bowker gathered his men together and galloped towards Fort Armstrong, followed by the waverers and, in the rear, by some of the deserters who had changed their minds.

General Somerset and his column of artillery, CMR and irregulars, had left Fort Hare between 2 a.m. and 3 a.m. the previous day.[14] On reaching the Tyumie River they had off-saddled while the artillerymen repaired the drift so that the two howitzers could be taken across. The column had then marched to Tyumie Hoek where Somerset had made an early halt for the night. No enemy had been seen except for a few Ngqika on Peffer's Kop and the Amathola Mountains.

The column was on the move again at 3 a.m. following the road which rose steeply as it crossed over the mountain range separating the Tyumie from the Kat River Valley. Near the crest of Peffer's Kop, Ngqika poured a heavy fire on the head of the column. This was promptly returned and they were forced to leave their position. The Ngqika then ran down the mountainside and attacked the centre and rear of the column and here the levies opened up a heavy running fire and the enemy was routed. The column's losses were one horse killed, one wounded and two men wounded. According to Somerset, the attack delayed the march 'some short time'.[15]

The column, after crossing the ridge along a very rugged road, eventually reached the Lushington Valley, which they descended unmolested. On the way down, the sound of heavy musketry was heard from the direction of Balfour so the general, seeing a few Ngqika on a nearby hill, ordered one of the howitzers to be fired at them with the added purpose of signalling to Bowker's force that they were at hand. There is no record that anyone in Bowker's force heard the shot. Somerset left his infantry at Hertzog, some four kilometres from Fort Armstrong, to recover from their exertions and continued with the two howitzers and the CMR to the ridge to the north-east of Fort Armstrong. Here they had a good view of the fort; it had been built on a loop of the Kat River and could be approached either from the open end along a narrow ridge from the north-west, or over a drift from the north-east. The fort itself was surrounded by mud-walled, thatched-roofed structures used as homes and trading stores. Rebels were seen running to the fort from the direction of Balfour and there was considerable activity within the fort itself.

Fort Armstrong, 22 February

Commandant Bowker had ridden over to the general for orders and was told to form his men up on the narrow ridge about three hundred metres away from the fort, out of musket range. Somerset then sent his Mfengu levy over the drift with orders to take up positions in the bush on the banks of the river; as they went they shouted their war-cry in anticipation of the coming slaughter.

At this moment a man came out of the fort bearing a white flag. He was a Khoikhoi by the name of Christian Groepe and it reflected the confused state of Khoikhoi loyalties in this rebellion that he was the commandant of the Kat River burgher force which, under his command, had done effective work during the 1835 and 1847 wars against the Xhosa. Groepe was apparently still loyal, for his purpose in coming out was to negotiate a safe passage for the women and children in the fort.[16] He was met by Major Charles Somerset[17] who, after communicating with the general, gave him permission to proceed with his rescue operation.[18]

As soon as the women and children were clear the general ordered Lieutenant Field, RA, to start shelling the fort. This was not at all to the liking of the Khoikhoi and many saddled up and made for the bush, followed by others on foot. However, if they thought they were going to escape they were deceived, for some of the burghers had taken up positions that covered the southern slopes and the CMR had crossed over the river and were lining up to attack from the north-east; even if the rebels did escape the burghers' bullets, they had then to face the menace of the Mfengu in the bush. The bombardment of the fort and the surrounding buildings continued and the latter were soon demolished, while many shells were lobbed into the fort itself. Somerset now decided that the fort could be taken directly, so he ordered the CMR and the burghers to attack.

A squadron of CMR led by Lieutenant Joseph Salis galloped up the hill under continual and harassing fire from perhaps a score of Khoikhoi in the fort and tower. On reaching the fort, the CMR and burghers entered by the gate and by climbing over the walls, killed all in the fort itself.

Isaiah Staples was with the mounted burghers who attacked from the west. They were in a dense body as they rode along the narrow ridge and then galloped straight for the loopholed walls of the fort from which the rebels were firing continuously. Yet, in spite of being easy targets, 'not a single burgher was hit.' Staples attributed this incredible result to the rebels' inability to keep cool under pressure and he offered as evidence the fact that they sometimes forgot to load their muskets with ball before firing.[19] On reaching the fort, the burghers dismounted and sprang up on the walls where, together with Salis's men, they killed fourteen Khoikhoi. Staples was disappointed in the small numbers in the fort for his 'blood was up', but most of them had fled to the bush.

The tower, still in the possession of the enemy, presented a problem. It is an immensely strong stone structure with walls nearly a metre thick. It has two floors, the vaulted ceiling of the top floor supporting a roof on which a cannon had originally been mounted. The roof has a parapet and the second floor is loopholed with alternately three and four loopholes on the four sides. Strangely, it is not possible to fire from the loopholes on anyone approaching directly on the corners. The stoutness of the tower is confirmed by the fact that today, nearly 150 years after being built, not a stone is damaged or out of place. Like the Martello tower in Fort Beaufort, the masonry is superb. There are two small doorways, 0.5 m by 1.5 m, into the tower, one facing east and the other south. In 1851 the doors must have been made of thick, solid wood.

The attackers were even more determined to take the tower after the rebels were so foolish as to wave a white flag out of one side while still firing from the other; the flag was speedily shot down by infuriated burghers.

The only way that the tower could be taken was to blow one of the doors open with cannon fire, so Major Charles Somerset obtained permission to take one of the howitzers across the drift and place it just out of range of the rebel muskets opposite the eastern face of the tower. It took only two or three shells aimed by the skilled hands of Lieutenant Field to burst the door open.

The first to enter was Hermanus Bertram followed by Brown, Rabedge, Commandant Currie and Lieutenant Jesse, RE. These men, especially Bertram, exhibited considerable courage in going through a small door into a dark, cavernous room known to contain armed, desperate, and cornered men. Soon after their entry, those outside were astounded to see about twenty women come out as well as one man dressed in woman's clothes who, as soon as his sex was recognised, was immediately shot down.

There were twelve men in the tower, including three Englishmen. Five of the occupants were killed and one of the Englishmen committed suicide on top of the tower as soon as he saw that the day was lost; only the day before Sandile had appointed him one of his captains. After removing the prisoners, combustible material was thrown into the tower and all the woodwork burnt.[20]

The casualties for both sides were:

Attackers	
Men killed	4 (2 Mfengu and 2 burghers)
Men wounded	21 (5 Mfengu; 14 burghers, 2 CMR)
Horses	14 killed and wounded
Defenders	
Men killed	120 (counted)
Prisoners	150 men

The following day Somerset's force, augmented by burghers, proceeded to demilitarise the Kat River Settlement. The village of Philipton, six kilometres to the north, was cleared of all inhabitants, loyal, rebel and missionary. A great deal of loot was recovered, including John Edwards's new wagon, which had been captured by Hermanus's men at Blinkwater. John Wiggill found his Uncle George's telescope, as well as his mother's mare in poor condition.[21]

The next day, the whole Kat River Settlement was cleared and it remained cleared of the enemy for the rest of the war. Many of the rebels, however, escaped to take refuge in the Waterkloof fastness while others returned to the fold, signing up in Her Majesty's newly created Kat River Levy. The remainder formed small bands of brigands, which were quickly hunted down.

State of the Colony

At the end of February 1851, Sir Harry Smith, governor and high commissioner of the Cape of Good Hope, could look around him with more satisfaction, and much less trepidation, than he had felt just two months before. It was not the end, as Winston Churchill would one day famously say: 'It is not even the beginning of the end. But it is, perhaps, the end of the beginning.'[22]

The news was mixed, but the good news outweighed the bad and there was nothing that was desperately bad. For example, Phato of the Gqunukhwebe had declared himself loyal to the Crown and undertook to keep open communications between King William's Town and East London. It was a promise that Phato would honour to the end of the war.

In his despatch to Earl Grey dated 27 January 1851,[23] Harry Smith was also pleased to announce that he would receive 'Hottentot levies from the Western Districts, amounting to 1600 men', thanks to the exertions of the Colonial Secretary John Montagu. He also expected another body of similar strength shortly thereafter. He was able to tell Grey that he had managed to raise a small 'Hottentot corps' of 348 men locally, although their loyalty must have been considered, at best, suspect.[24]

Other good news was that an attack on Fort Hare on 21 January by two to three thousand Ngqika had been foiled by Henry Somerset. The attack was made to screen an attempt to steal a substantial number of Mfengu cattle in the area. The Mfengu, aided by the CMR, managed to fight off the attack, supported by artillery. After two and a half hours, the Ngqika withdrew, lucky to have managed to capture about two hundred of the five thousand cattle then grazing.[25]

On 30 January, Colonel Mackinnon took out a large force, numbering some 2,200 men, in an attempt to convey supplies to Forts White and Cox.

Some eight miles from Fort White, his column was attacked by a considerable number of Ngqika, but the attack was repulsed. A second attack was made as the column crossed the Debe Nek, but was again deterred by the accurate firing of the artillery. Mackinnon entered Fort White without further hindrance and was able to re-provision the fort with supplies for six weeks. Mackinnon's column continued to Fort Cox with the same intention, reaching the fort without interference. He was then able to return to King William's Town, via Fort White, without further molestation.[26] On 3 February, Mackinnon again marched out, this time to punish Siyolo for his destruction of the Line Drift Post.

In a despatch of 18 February, the governor was able to provide Earl Grey with a complete analysis of the status of his forces at the Cape. This reveals that at that time, Sir Harry Smith had command of the following imperial troops:

6th Regiment	560
45th Regiment	403
73rd Regiment	472
91st Regiment	479

This strength may appear to be substantial but their effectiveness was reduced by their distribution in small groups throughout the frontier, the only solution to a war fought over a very wide area. Thus, the 6th Regiment was based principally at King William's Town, but there were also detachments at Forts Murray (near King William's Town), Grey (near East London) and White. Similarly, the 45th was based at Fort Hare but had detachments at Forts Cox and White. The 73rd was the only exception, being wholly based at King William's Town. The 91st was split between Fort Hare and Fort Beaufort, with further detachments at Forts Cox, Brown, Peddie and at Grahamstown. However, the governor could not complain of a shortage of imperial troops because it was he who had only recently sent about half of them home.

The strength of the Cape Mounted Rifles was more than eight hundred men, but it too was spread across the country at virtually every fort that was manned.[27] There was, of course, little alternative to this strategy so it is not surprising that the governor found it difficult to place a large force in the field without the support of levies, especially those of the Mfengu.

One serious problem that remained was the shortage of mounted volunteers, though the lack of burgher forces, in any numbers, was not so surprising. Smith had made a number of appeals for volunteers but farmers were especially reluctant to take part in the war, simply because their Khoikhoi workers had left them to join the rebels, or were suspected of wishing to do so.[28] They therefore either trekked or stayed at home to defend their farms from the depredations that were occurring daily. This is not to suggest that there were no volunteers: there were some, but entirely insufficient to fill the need. Once again, Harry Smith had shot himself in the foot.

Losses and Gains

The CMR Deserts
In mid-March, Harry Smith received some news which again shook his confidence. Things had been going well until he received a report concerning the CMR:

> About half-past twelve o'clock on the night of the 13th instant, Colonel Mackinnon and Lieut.-Colonel Napier came to me to report that 3 non-commissioned officers and 45 men, including many of the oldest and best soldiers of the regiment, had deserted in the most clandestine manner; and that others had been preparing to follow, but a discovery having taken place they were prevented from doing so. The deserters were accompanied by their wives, and they took with them their double-barrelled carbines, their field equipments, and whatever they could carry; but not their horses.[29]

The court of enquiry which followed this desertion found that there was evidence of previous disaffection in the CMR and that 'the causes that have led to this desertion are not of recent origin, and are connected with the spirit of disaffection that has shown itself among the rebellious Hottentots on the Kat River'.[30] As a result of the court of enquiry, Smith ordered a general parade of the unit and disarmed a further 161 men, 'being nearly the whole levy', and another company of the Albany Levy. Such was the reduction of his mounted force that he transferred a hundred horses, double-barrelled carbines and horse equipment to a hundred men of the levies to make them up. He hoped that Earl Grey might be able to send out four hundred young Englishmen, similarly armed, who could boost his mounted force still further.[31]

Reinforcements
In March 1851, Earl Grey received Smith's December and January despatches, with their news of the rebellions then in train. As a result, he told Smith:

> I am commanded by Her Majesty to express the very great concern with which she has received this intelligence; the Queen deeply laments the loss sustained by her troops (of whose conduct, it is however satisfactory to find, that so

favourable a report can be made both by yourself and by Colonel Somerset), and
also that many of her faithful and peaceable subjects have been murdered, and
much valuable property destroyed by the Kafirs, in a rebellion as unprovoked as
it was treacherous.[32]

Grey continued that it was thought their duty 'not to defer for a single day
making arrangements for sending out a powerful regiment'. Accordingly, the
74th (Highland) Regiment would immediately embark for the Cape.

The month of May saw further mention of additional imperial troops being
sent out to the Cape.[33] In his despatch, Earl Grey noted that he had 'entered
into communication with the Commander-in-Chief and with the Lords
Commissioners of the Admiralty, with the view of being able . . . promptly to
forward further reinforcements to the colony'.

In fact, there is considerable evidence to suggest that much of the drive
to send more troops back to the Cape was on the initiative of the Queen
herself, and there was considerable correspondence between Her Majesty and
the Duke of Wellington on this subject. Two requests from Victoria for troops,
which were acted upon very quickly, were for the 2nd (The Queen's Royal)
Regiment, together with replacement drafts for the other regiments, to be sent
out,[34] as well as the 12th (The Prince of Wales's) Royal Regiment of Lancers,[35]
better known then as the 12th Light Dragoons. These conversations between
the Queen and Wellington continued throughout 1851, with predictable results.

The first unit to arrive at the Cape was the 74th (Highland) Regiment
under the command of Lieutenant-Colonel John Fordyce, accompanied by
the promised drafts to complete the other regiments.[36]

Fordyce, a very wealthy man, had purchased every step in his military career,
beginning with his first commission as ensign in December 1828, through to
his lieutenant-colonelcy of the 74th in July 1846. He was a disciplinarian but
not a martinet and the fact that he was not married allowed him to devote his
life to his regiment.

> I well remember a young soldier who had been sentenced to be flogged; his
> court-martial was read out, he stripped, and the drummers fastened his legs and
> arms to the triangle; the drum-major stood ready to count the lashes, and the
> sergt.-major stood nigh, with memorandum book in hand, to note each ten that
> the erring soldier was about to receive. Fordyce stepped forward: 'Young man,'
> said he, 'I think it a pity to disgrace such a fine back as that of yours; let this be
> a warning to you. Drummers, take him down.' The order was obeyed, and I do
> not remember this act of leniency ever being abused.[37]

> Our colonel was an officer whom I never saw on horse-back during his short
> but eventful career in the colony, though he was an excellent horseman. His

hobby was, at all times and in all places, at home or abroad, when with his own regiment and in command, to take a strong walking-stick in his hand; having given the word of command to his regiment to march, he placed himself at their head, and led them on by giving them the proper time to march.[38]

It was incidents like these that drew his men to him.

Fordyce also knew how to enjoy himself when not on duty, as the following anecdote attests. Prince George, Duke of Cambridge and cousin to Queen Victoria,[39] was a guest in the mess of the 74th when he invited Fordyce to demonstrate the sword-dance on the mess table. He did so to the skirl of the pipes, his pace accelerating as the audience, and the Duke, urged him on. 'The crystal began to keep as good time as the music', and decanters and glasses began to leap off the table.[40]

Apart from three skirmishes between forces commanded by Colonel Mackinnon and General Somerset, with rebels under Siyolo and Stokwe of the Mbalu, no major engagements were reported in March or April.

Operations in May involved patrols in the Amathola Mountains and around Eland's Post with the aim of suppressing the continuing raids and threats to communications. These patrols were undertaken by a Captain Fisher at Eland's and Major H.E. Wilmot, RA. A larger force under Colonel Mackinnon, involving elements of the 6th and 73rd regiments, CMR and mounted and foot levies, scoured the Kabousie area as far as the Kei River, the domain of Toyise, a grandson of Ndlambe. Only minor skirmishes were reported, without serious casualties on either side.[41]

On 24 May, three columns left to harass the Ngqika further in the Amatholas, under Colonels Mackinnon and Eyre, and Major Wilmot. Mackinnon first took supplies into Forts White and Cox, then moved his column to the north of the latter. He had a brief engagement on the 26th, suffering three casualties, then moved on towards the Hog's Back. There, a rebel camp was destroyed and a reconnaissance of the area was made from the Hog's Back ridge. Mackinnon next moved into the Tyumie Valley, then on to the area between Forts White and Hare, finally moving on to Forts White and Cox. He ended his foray in King William's Town, arriving there on 30 May.

Lieutenant-Colonel William Eyre had accompanied Mackinnon as far as the area north of Fort Cox and, on the 26th, he parted company and moved into the Amathola Valley. Eyre had purchased his first commission as ensign in April 1823, and bought his lieutenant-colonelcy in September 1845. He now commanded the 73rd Regiment, known in South Africa as the 'Cape

Greyhounds'. Stephen Lakeman admired the 73rd and Eyre greatly, stating: 'By their training they had become the most effective fighting regiment at the Cape, and had never left a wounded or dead man behind in the hands of the foe. As might be expected, Colonel Eyre himself was a most daring, energetic officer.'[42]

William Ross King was intrigued by the relationship between Colonel Eyre and the Mfengu. The latter skirmished with unusual activity because of their awe for *'inkhosi ameshlomani'* (Chief Four-Eyes), for Eyre wore spectacles, to which they attributed his vigilance and sharpness. Whenever the Mfengu showed the slightest hesitation in obeying, the colonel rode at them laying his sjambok about their shoulders and driving them before him.[43] They did not, however, have that same awe for every officer: on another occasion, when a young levy officer tried to do the same, he was unceremoniously tumbled off his horse into a thorn bush.[44]

Eyre gradually became more ruthless in his approach to the war, unlike his early view:

> One day I remarked to him that about three miles from his camp was one of the best places of the whole line to waylay [ambush]. He said it was both unsoldierlike and un-Englishmanlike to waylay. I said, 'Well, Sir, my idea is to destroy all the enemy without being killed myself or losing my men and shall continue that plan as long as I have anything to do with the war.'[45]

Noel Mostert observed:

> In spite of his stiff, predictable initial response to Stubbs's way-laying proposals, Lieutenant-Colonel Eyre was to prove an apt pupil, one of the first regular British commanders to discover a military school for himself in the South African bush. He was to become, if anything, a more ruthless exponent of waylaying than Stubbs himself, with no scruples at all about shooting black men, in dark or in daylight. What he absorbed from Stubbs and then proceeded to expand upon himself was to make a significant difference to the conduct of this war on the British side. He was everything that the twentieth century was to consider a guerrilla or special forces commander should be: tough, violent, merciless with foe and his own men alike. He was to be the most interesting, resourceful and ruthlessly successful of the British commanders, the only original tactician of the war; the best soldier, and a fierce hater of black men.[46]

In time, Eyre became the terror of Khoikhoi and Xhosa rebels alike, hanging them from trees as an example of the rebels' fate if they fell into his hands.[47]

*   *   *

On this patrol Eyre was fired upon by the concealed enemy, as witnessed from the hills above by Mackinnon. This caused some disorder among the levies and Eyre ordered the men of the 73rd 'to lie down, pending this confusion, and until I could reconnoitre a little the position of our invisible foe'. After identifying the location of the Ngqika, Eyre advanced against them until, reaching more open ground, he was able to extend the infantry into skirmishing order. The Ngqika broke off the engagement with loss, Eyre suffering few casualties.

He then moved to the Tyumie Nek below the Hog's Back, fighting off attacks on the rear of his column by reforming his skirmishing line. He finally linked up with Mackinnon's column again at the foot of the Hog's Back Mountain.

From here he was ordered to retrace his steps through the Tyumie Valley to the Amathola Valley. There was another engagement on this march in which he was quickly able to defeat the enemy. He finally returned to King William's Town with Mackinnon's column, having suffered one man killed and seventeen wounded.

Major Wilmot marched towards Keiskamma Hoek via Baillie's Grave and the Red Hill Pass, where he arrived without incident at 1 a.m. on 26 May. After a three-hour rest, he marched again, this time to the ridges 'dividing Keiskamma Hoek from the Amatola Basin' where he spent the night. On the 27th, he returned towards the Red Hill Pass but was intercepted by a large Ngqika force before he reached the summit. The force engaged the enemy, who were eventually sent scuttling towards the Boma Pass. Having received a message from Mackinnon that 'he had no further occasion for my co-operation', Wilmot left the Keiskamma River and, on 28 May, moved off towards the Kabousie Nek, thence on to King William's Town via the Yellowwoods River. He arrived back from his patrol on 30 May.[48]

On 29 May, General Somerset had also attacked Khoikhoi and Ngqika rebels in the area of Philipton, where he had successfully engaged them, driving them off and destroying their camp.[49]

Rebellion at Theopolis

Sir Harry Smith might have been forgiven for thinking that the defection of Khoikhoi troops was at an end but he was sorely disappointed when he learned that the CMR at the mission station at Theopolis, some forty kilometres from Grahamstown, had also revolted on 31 May. Quite by chance, however, General Somerset had gone to Grahamstown to guide the newly arrived 74th Regiment from there to Fort Hare. He was thus able to send men to the scene of the revolt immediately.

A mounted levy under Captain Thomas Stubbs was sent in advance to give assistance and came up against the deserters driving eleven wagons. The mounted men attacked the rebel position near Bushmans River where they recaptured seven of the wagons. They were not able to follow up their success, however, due to the death of Field Cornet William Grey and the wounding of Stubbs's brother, William, whose arm had to be amputated, Commandant Johann Pieter Woest, shot through the thigh, and four others. They therefore returned to their camp.[50]

Meanwhile, Somerset had sent two companies of the 74th with a similar objective and, on hearing the bad news from Stubbs, sent off two more companies to assist the first two.[51] Smith was incensed when he heard that Somerset had sent the two companies of the 74th on this mission, and was furious when Somerset's second report told him that a further two companies had also been sent off, telling Somerset that he was 'greatly opposed to any serious diminution of [his] force at Fort Hare'. He finished Somerset's admonition thus: 'I must again impress upon you the necessity there positively is that the burghers of Albany take the field, and that every soldier of the 74th Regiment marches to Fort Hare.'

Despite this injunction – which, in fairness, Somerset may not have received in time – he attacked the rebel camp with three hundred men of the 74th, fifty CMR and one hundred Mfengu. The camp was taken without difficulty and the rebels ran off into the surrounding forest. Considerable quantities of grain and cattle were recovered. Somerset reported that the men of the 74th had returned to Grahamstown to continue their march to Fort Hare,[52] but not before one company had become lost in the attack on the rebels.[53]

Later reports by Somerset were not encouraging, advising that the rebels had returned to Theopolis and burnt every building, including the chapel, to the ground. He also noted reports of numbers of Xhosa taking refuge in the Kroome Mountains between Adelaide and Fort Beaufort.

The Amatholas

Since Somerset was to return to Fort Hare with the 74th, the governor ordered Colonel Mackinnon to form two columns, under himself and Major Wilmot, to prevent the Theopolis rebels from joining up with their fellows around Fort Beaufort. Mackinnon was to march towards Fort Willshire on 6 June while Wilmot would go to Breakfast Vlei via the Tamacha Post, leaving on the 5th. There he would be joined by a force from Fort Peddie. The two columns would then work their way up the Keiskamma River, also devoting some attention to Stokwe in the process.[54] The patrol met with only light resistance and saw nothing of the Theopolis rebels.

Harry Smith next planned a major offensive against the Ngqika lodged in the fastnesses of the Amathola Mountains. It was to consist of no fewer than four divisions 'converging to a centre'. The divisions were to be led by Somerset, Mackinnon (who became sick and delegated his command to Lieutenant-Colonel Michel of the 6th Regiment), Lieutenant-Colonel Henry Cooper, 45th Regiment, and Captain Tylden from Whittlesea.

The plan was for Somerset and Mackinnon to drive from the south and north respectively while Cooper would advance from Fort Cox and Tylden would take a position at the Windvogelberg to intercept any rebels who slipped through the net.

First Division

Somerset moved out of Fort Hare on 24 June with a force comprising two guns (a twelve-pound howitzer and a six-pounder) the 74th Regiment and two companies of the 91st under Lieutenant-Colonel Fordyce, together with 230 CMR and other European mounted and foot levies, and nearly six hundred Mfengu. The column marched north through the Tyumie Basin, and, having rested during the day of the 25th, moved off again on the 26th for the 'Amatola Hoek'.[55]

In the days that followed, Somerset patrolled over a wide area of the western Amatholas bounded by the Isinuka [Zingcuka] River in the west, the Hog's Back range in the north, the Keiskamma River in the east and Mount MacDonald to the south, engaging the enemy in several severe clashes. This is extremely difficult country for such fighting and the rebels had a considerable advantage. Nevertheless, Somerset received offers of surrender if time was given, but he allowed only thirty minutes, after which he resumed his operations. He was unable to give the number of enemy killed but he suffered the quite heavy loss of six men killed (three of the 74th) and fifteen wounded, including Lieutenant W.W.J. Bruce, 74th, and Captain Melville of the George Levy. Two of the rank-and-file died of their wounds later.

Somerset returned to Fort Hare on 29 June, sending in wagons loaded with the wounded men. Colonel Fordyce took his 74th, and a detachment of the 45th, into Fort Cox on 4 July, where he left the men of the 45th, bringing away the detachment of the 91st. The main body of Somerset's division returned to Fort Hare on 5 July. Throughout this patrol, Somerset observed that he had seen nothing of the column from Fort Cox.[56]

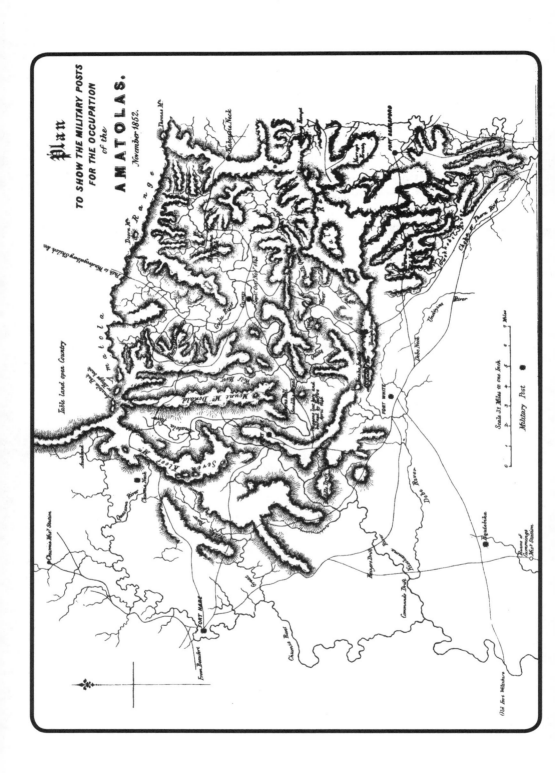

Plan
TO SHOW THE MILITARY POSTS
FOR THE OCCUPATION
of the
AMATOLAS.
November 1852.

Scale 3½ Miles to one Inch

■ Military Post

Second Division

Colonel Mackinnon's division left King William's Town on 24 June and marched via Baillie's Grave (and presumably the Red Hill Pass) to the Gwili Gwili River. He had with him four companies of the 6th Regiment under Colonel Michel, five of the 73rd under Colonel Eyre, forty-seven marines, 170 CMR and an assortment of other mounted and foot levies, including 170 Mfengu. His force totalled more than two thousand men.

After bivouacking overnight, he moved further up the Gwili Gwili, where he left three hundred men to guard his camp and divided the remainder into two equal brigades. He took one of these along the left bank of the Keiskamma to its confluence with the Wolf River not far from the Boma Pass. He too had expected to find Colonel Cooper from Fort Cox but Cooper was not there. He subsequently returned to his camp on the Gwili Gwili, encountering a small party of Ngqika on the way who were quickly brushed off.

The second brigade, under Colonel Michel, moved down to Keiskamma Hoek along the Gulu [Gxulu] River. Michel returned to the camp the same evening without incident, other than spotting some cattle.

The division rested on the 27th; on the following day, as Mackinnon was ill, he ordered Michel to make a night march to swoop on the cattle seen earlier. Michel penetrated deep into the maze of kloofs around the upper Gxulu, taking the Ngqika entirely by surprise, and returned to Mackinnon's camp on 29 June, having captured some fifteen hundred cattle, five hundred goats and twenty-two horses.[57]

We have twice mentioned the fact that Colonel Cooper of the 45th, whose column should have left Fort Cox to support the other two divisions, was not seen by either of them. Cooper's report lacks detail, merely stating that a diary of his activities between 20 and 30 June was attached but this document has been omitted from the official record.[58] From this omission, it might be considered that Cooper's contribution was less than expected. Intriguingly, the regimental history is also silent on the subject, merely observing: 'Again, between 20th and 30th of June, [Cooper] was out patrolling, but nothing notable occurred.'[59]

Captain Tylden was unable to complete his patrol as ordered, as he was 'obliged to return abruptly to Whittlesea, having received a report that it was threatened by a large force of Tambookies [Thembu]'.[60] Nevertheless, Tylden was still able to capture three hundred head of cattle.

A Loss of Confidence

The reader will recall that, during his enforced isolation in Fort Cox during late December 1850, Sir Harry Smith had sent a message to the then Colonel Somerset requiring him to forward a request to the lieutenant-governor of Natal for him to send forward 'one, two or three thousand Zulus' to attack the Ngqika in the rear.[61] On 17 January, Lieutenant-Governor Pine had responded to Smith's appeal, giving an undertaking to send not three thousand, but five thousand – Theophilus Shepstone considering that the lower number would be 'too small to be marched with safety'.[62] Pine stated that some recent disaffection would cause their departure to be delayed, and cautioned that the Zulu might pursue the Xhosa and their cattle into adjoining territories 'and thus be the means of exciting such tribes to take part in the rebellion'.[63]

Earl Grey had fully approved of this step but Smith was eventually compelled to admit defeat when he reported to the Secretary of State that the enterprise had failed, and had asked Shepstone to disband any Zulu he had already gathered together. There was to be a cost to the imperial chest of £2,000, which had been paid to the government of Natal.[64]

A more serious blow to Smith's self-esteem was the news delivered to him by a despatch from Earl Grey advising the appointment of two special assistant commissioners who were to help Smith in his role as high commissioner.[65] Grey's stated reasons for these appointments were that he was convinced that the rebellion of, first, the men of the Kat River Settlement, and then large elements of the CMR, evinced 'symptoms of some deeply seated evils in the existing state of society'. He went on:

> I am led to infer that one of the principal causes of the difficulty which has been experienced in maintaining peace and order on the colonial frontier has been the prevalence of disputes as to the occupation of land. Such disputes naturally arise among people of pastoral habits, and seem to have been aggravated at the Cape by the want of any effective and satisfactory arrangements for their decision when they occur, and of any sufficiently clear definition of the respective rights to land, either of individuals or of the different small communities into which the population is divided. It is obvious, from your Despatches, that there are many difficult and complicated questions as to these rights, which require to be carefully investigated and determined; and I believe that, if this could be done in a manner which should be felt to be just by the different parties concerned, and if at the same time arrangements could be made for enforcing the decisions which had been pronounced, and for giving for the future prompt redress to those whose rights may be infringed, the main cause for discontent and for the disturbances which too often occur would be removed.

Smith would have been quite shocked by such words, bearing in mind the difficulties now being borne by the colony in containing, and trying to end, the current state of war. But Grey had the answer to that too:

It is impossible that, with the laborious duties imposed upon you by the civil Government of the colony, and the military command of the large force under your orders, you should yourself attend to all the details of these arrangements; further assistance will obviously be required by you in doing so, and I have judged that the best mode of affording it will be to join with you in the commission which you already hold as Her Majesty's High Commissioner for settling the relations of the colony with the frontier tribes, two gentlemen who will be appointed either Assistant-Commissioners or Second and Third Commissioners under you, for the above purposes. The precise form of the appointment will require some further consideration, and will be made known to you in a future Despatch.

Reading between the lines, however, one is compelled to agree with Harington that Grey's action 'was an indication of dwindling confidence and what he had said to the contrary was not absolutely true'.[66]

The Secretary then went on to name the two commissioners as Major William S. Hogge and Mr Charles Mostyn Owen, both of whom were already known to the governor. Oliver Ransford calls them 'two mysterious bureaucrats', and continues: 'Reading the history books of the period, we find their names appearing constantly in the text; but we never discover very much about Hogge and Owen, and they leave us with an impression of faceless men fumbling about with a problem which is much too big for them.'[67]

In fact, had Ransford searched a little more diligently he may have discovered more about them. Hogge, for example, had served in the War of the Axe, 1846–7, as commanding officer of a Khoikhoi levy.[68] During that time, he met Sir Henry Pottinger, who 'found him by far the most intelligent, practical man with whom I have conversed since I landed'.[69]

Owen had also served at the Cape, but as the commanding officer of the second of two divisions of Kaffir Police formed by Sir Henry Pottinger in 1847.[70] It is likely that both men were serving officers of regiments then at the Cape, and returned to England about the same time as Pottinger or shortly thereafter.

They both had, therefore, seen military service in the Cape Colony, and were thus familiar with its problems, 'without being among its permanent inhabitants'. Owen particularly commended himself to Grey because he had 'the advantage of an acquaintance with the Kaffir language', a deficiency for which Grey had been critical of Colonel Mackinnon in his position as commissioner of British Kaffraria.

Still another, perhaps more serious, problem for Grey was the Orange River Sovereignty. He had objected to its annexation after the event but was bound by Smith's fait accompli. It was becoming increasingly clear to him, however, that the sovereignty would have to be abandoned, a proposal which mortified Smith. A more immediate issue was the poor performance of Major H.D. Warden as Resident of the Sovereignty, based at Bloemfontein. In March 1851, for example, he had responded to a request for assistance from the commissioner of Albert, south of the sovereignty, by sending a force of 150 men and two six-pounder guns – as a result of which a mixed Basotho–Thembu force had suffered a severe defeat,[71] thus potentially harming relations with Mshweshwe of the Basotho. Warden was also thought 'a weak character and rather easily offended'.[72] These matters, together with one or two others – not least of which was the governor's constant praise for Somerset and Mackinnon, concerning whom Grey was receiving other, less flattering, advice – were beginning to sap Grey's confidence in his governor, and things were only going to deteriorate further.[73]

Chapter 7

The New Battleground

The Ngqika, with their Khoikhoi partners, having effectively been driven from the Kat River area and the Amathola Mountains, had repaired to the fastness of the Kroome escarpment. This feature runs parallel with the Fort Beaufort–Adelaide road for a considerable distance and is accessible from the south via only two passes: Niland's Pass and the Tenth Pass, both of which are still difficult to negotiate. The extensive tableland which forms the top of the escarpment is scarred by four heavily wooded valleys with steep sides. On the western side lies the Waterkloof, while to the east there are three more, these being Arie's Hoek, Fuller's Hoek and Schelm (or Hermanus's) Kloof. The north-pointing Blinkwater Valley lies further to the east. Maqoma had his homestead in Fuller's Hoek and his people gathered round him there. To a large extent, they were masters of the plateau and thus dominated the Blinkwater, from which the Khoikhoi rebels had also been driven by the British. The farms at the southern foot of the escarpment, and the properties to the west and north running from Adelaide to Post Retief had already been attacked and, in many cases, destroyed. Sir Harry Smith now recognised that the Ngqika and their Khoikhoi allies must be driven from their heavily wooded valleys.

The Fox's Lair, July 1851

14 July
The force for this attack consisted of two columns. The main column, under Henry Somerset, consisted of the 74th (Highland) Regiment of some four hundred men (Lieutenant-Colonel John Fordyce), one six-pounder gun (Lieutenant Field, RA), about one hundred CMR and several levies, both mounted and on foot, totalling about 560 men.

The flanking column, commanded by Major Charles Somerset, Henry's son, contained another hundred CMR and an Mfengu levy of some 250 men. Another 250 to 300 men, including two companies of the 74th Highlanders,

The Waterkloof

14 July 1851

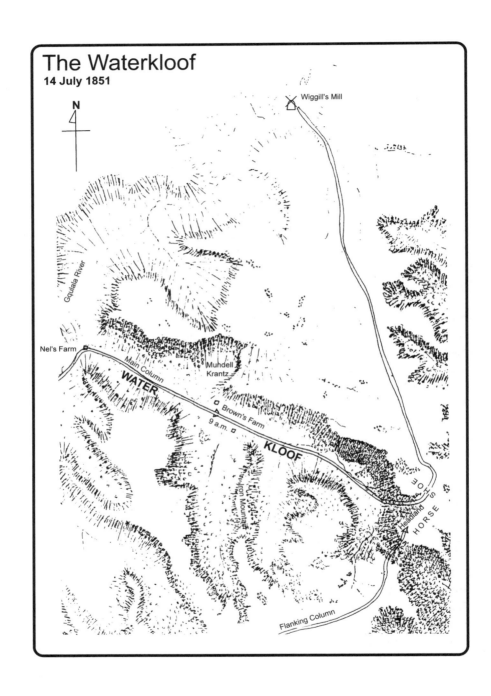

stayed behind to guard the camp at Adelaide. Lieutenant King was among them.[1]

The plan was that the flanking column of CMR and Mfengu would leave Adelaide at dusk on Sunday 13 July and camp for the night at Painter's farm, 'Yellowwood Trees'. Early in the morning of 14 July, this column was to climb the Kroome Heights via Tenth Pass, march across the plateau to the heights overlooking the Waterkloof and then hold the position, pending the arrival of General Somerset's column.

The main column was to leave at 3 a.m. on the 14th and march up the Gqwala Valley to the entrance to the Waterkloof.[2] It would then proceed up the Waterkloof to the head of the valley, then scale the heights to the plateau above under cover of the flanking column. The enemy was to be attacked wherever they showed themselves. After uniting, both columns would proceed to the farm 'Thorn Hill', to bivouac there for the night, returning to Adelaide on the following morning.

The troops crossed the Gqwala River soon after leaving Adelaide and then settled down to a steady march, the horses keeping pace with the Highland infantrymen.

This was the life that artist Thomas Baines relished: a good horse, a rifled musket, his sketch book and journal, the companionship of men and the exciting anticipation of the hunt made more exhilarating by the sure knowledge that the hunted would fire back. He had been under fire before – in fact quite recently, in the Amathola Mountains – but only at the extreme musket range of several hundred metres; now it would be different for, of his own free will, he was going into a known enemy stronghold where he would meet wrought-up Ngqika warriors at close range in the bush.

Baines's main concern was to look good in the eyes of the men, to make them look up to him with respect and to avoid being accused, at whatever cost, of showing fear. For respect was what Baines badly needed. He was now thirty-one years old and nearly penniless; he had only just been saved from an ignominious retreat back to England by officers of the newly arrived 74th who, on seeing his unsold paintings in Grahamstown, had persuaded him to apply to General Somerset for the post of war artist. Somerset, to our everlasting gratitude, had approved, provided it didn't cost him any money. Baines was to serve without pay but he could draw ammunition and rations for himself and his horse. To Baines's chagrin, however, his secret hope of being invited to the officers' mess was denied him; instead he messed with Abel Hoole, interpreter and guide to Somerset.[3]

The smell of burning manure diminished as they left behind them the cattle pen from which it emanated and, shortly afterwards, as day was breaking, the column arrived at the junction of the Waterkloof and the Gqwala rivers, thirteen kilometres north of Adelaide. Here lay the ruins of Adriaan Nel's homestead, the stone walls of the house still standing, though the weeds were growing over the door sills and the roof was gone. The outhouses were also in ruins and the orchard that ran down to the river was rank with tall weeds, which almost hid the fruit trees in their winter bareness. The sight of the house was peculiarly unpleasant to Sergeant James McKay of the 74th's Light Company and he was glad when the order came to continue the march up the Waterkloof. McKay thought it a dank and gloomy valley; its northern slope, in shadow, was covered with dense bush for the whole ten kilometres of its length, the only notable feature being a high krantz named after Mundell, the owner of the farm on the plateau above. The southern slope was quite different: being exposed to the sun, it was semi-arid and covered with mimosa and scrub.

As the column marched along the wagon track on the southern side of the little river a light blue mist lay in the valley, leading the soldiers to think that it was smoke from Maqoma's hearth-fires; further excitement was generated when the fresh dung of horses and cattle was seen on the wagon track. At 9 a.m. the column halted for breakfast at another burnt-out farmhouse and derelict orchard. This was Brown's farm, which McKay described as being opposite the entrance to a large, south-going kloof.[4] There are actually two kloofs leading southwards here and along the ridge between them are two conspicuous features: a conical hill jutting into the Waterkloof and south of it a hill crowned with a red krantz, attached to the Kroome Range by a peninsular ridge. The Dutch guides called the mountain 'Ysterberg' and the name was immediately anglicised to 'Iron Mountain'.

After a two-hour rest, during which a mess tent was erected for the general's comfort, the march was resumed. Half an hour later Baines found himself riding under an avenue of trees whose branches met overhead and here he was amused to hear Somerset, whose reputation as a philanderer was well known, say that it was the sort of place where lovers might breathe their vows.[5] As they came out of the avenue, about fifty of the enemy were seen on the headland directly in front of them and moments later shots rang out from the bushy slopes to the right. The general promptly ordered some of the 74th and the Mfengu into the bush and soon afterwards Ngqika were seen running up the side of the mountain. The general also ordered the CMR to cover the valley on the left flank, while the reserve were told to shelter until further orders. The six-pounder had been ordered up and a round shot was fired at the group on the headland; it had been well aimed and made the enemy scurry for shelter. Next followed two explosive shells which sent up small clouds of white smoke as they burst a hundred metres short of the target, each liberating about seventy high-velocity musket balls, though by this time the enemy had disappeared.

During the shelling, three or four musket shots had been fired into the headquarters party by a rebel perched on a krantz about two hundred metres to the right. Colonel Fordyce and others of the staff tried to shoot the sniper with their rifles but could not dislodge him and he maintained the annoying fire until the column was out of range. Strangely enough no one was hurt.

On reaching the head of the Waterkloof, the column saw before it the steep termination of the valley rising to the headland on which the enemy force of fifty had been shelled. A narrow slip-path used by timber workers to transport logs on sleds ran up the slope through dense bush. Baines saw yellowwood trees with their bare, straight stems and scanty foliage towering above other species: iron-wood, white and red pear, assegai wood and sneeze-wood. In between, there was a jungle of branches, bushes and entwined vines that made progress, other than by the path, difficult. The slip-path itself was in a bad state, being strewn with boulders, stumps and other debris from bush working. Baines found the prospect of climbing the path daunting: the Ngqika on the headland had not been killed and were still about, probably waiting for him in ambush, but up he had to go. The way was so steep and difficult that those who were riding horses had to lead them, slowly following the gun.

As the artillery horses struggled up the slope, it soon become evident that the load was too great for them; the general was about to send the gun back to Adelaide with an escort when Fordyce volunteered the services of his regiment. The gun was unlimbered and the horses sent up with the limber only, while the gun was man-handled. It was hard work, for the 'light' six-pounder still weighed half a tonne, but drag it up they did. Ropes and riems were tied to the gun and then, with some men pulling and others turning the 1.5-metre-diameter wheels, with much hauling, shoving, grunting, heaving and sometimes lifting over obstacles, the gun was slowly moved up the slope. None of the men could maintain the pace for long, especially when laden with thirty kilograms of kit, so they worked in relays and it took nearly two hours of effort. All this time, perhaps aware of their vulnerability, General Somerset stayed near the gun, revealing his concern by calling out occasionally, 'Now, my men, pull away', and all the while the skirmishers on either side of the path fired steadily into the bush; they nearly succeeded in killing one Mfengu who had, it seemed, lost his way. Still the enemy did not appear.

Baines was mystified on seeing a horse, recently dead, alongside the path; no one could explain its presence there. Just before reaching the top they passed beneath the krantz forming the headland. This was where everyone expected to be heavily attacked and the skirmishers redoubled their firing, but they only succeeded in stirring up a flight of lowries, splendidly plumed in green and crimson, much to the delight of an ornithologist in the headquarters party. As the main column emerged from the bush, they passed through the dense smoke of huts which had been set alight by the men of the flanking column. On getting clear of the smoke the 74th sank down thankfully onto the grass, eager to hear the news.

Major Somerset's flanking column had been sharply engaged by the enemy but had managed to beat them off. They had lost one CMR trooper wounded, Surgeon Hassard, CMR, had had his horse shot under him, one of the sergeants' horses had been killed and another troop-horse had been wounded. Captain Thomas Hare had been hit in the leg by a spent bullet but was not in the least hurt by it. Major Somerset himself had been temporarily blinded by ground coffee which had been knocked out of a sack carried by a man riding in front of him.

While the Highlanders rested, a few Ngqika were seen a long way off and the Mfengu amused themselves by shooting at them – quite ineffectively, however. The men now formed up again in columns and marched northwards through a narrow belt of bush that stretched across their path. As soon as the last man had passed through this belt, though, shots were fired from it, one coming close to Baines's head. It had a peculiar sound, something like a sharp body cutting through water rather than the shrill whistle of a musket ball: it had presumably been fired from a rifle.

A little further on Baines saw a fine-looking Ngqika standing boldly on a ridge about five hundred metres to the east, shouting in derision at the Mfengu efforts at musketry and thinking himself perfectly safe. The soldiers challenged Baines to show what his rifle and fancy conical bullet could do,[6] so, dismounting and giving the bridle to one of them to hold, he advanced a little and tried a shot. The line was good but it fell short. Elevating the sight a little he tried another, whereupon the Ngqika dived like a bushbuck behind the ridge. He showed himself again for a moment and then vanished. Satisfied, Baines returned to the headquarters party just as they reached the high ground of the plateau. Here was a spectacular view: to the south-east lay the white-painted houses of Fort Beaufort glistening in the sun, just north of east the flat top of Ngqika's Kop, to the north-east the untidy crest of Didima and just west of north the great Winterberg, perhaps brooding over man's insatiable lust for violence towards his fellow men.

A group of Ngqika had in the meantime been quietly gathering on a nearby ridge. The six-pounder was quickly brought to bear and a round shot thrown well amongst them. A shell followed, not quite so accurately directed, but before another could be prepared the Ngqika took cover behind the ridge.

From the high ground above, the plain resembled a horseshoe due to a tongue of bush jutting into its otherwise semi-circular shape and this name was immediately given to it. The surrounding area was named Mount Pleasant, after that of a nearby farm, and this was subsequently used in official despatches; later the soldiers named the area Mount Misery instead, because of the killing and maiming that occurred there, and the dreadful weather. The whole area also took on the name Waterkloof, a misnomer which was later to result in political acrimony due to the ambiguity of the statement 'The Waterkloof has been cleared of the enemy.' Today the names Horseshoe and Mount Misery are, along with those who used them, forgotten – the Horseshoe is now covered in pines and is known as the Fort Fordyce Forest Reserve.

As the column marched northwards along the bush-workers' road, many of the men thought the patrol had been a wild goose chase, so light had been the enemy activity. Was this all that the great Maqoma could do?

At sunset they arrived at the ruins of Wiggill's mill and the Austin's homestead, on the farm 'Thorn Hill', and here they bivouacked for the night. Some of the captured cattle were slaughtered for the evening meal, which the men must surely have relished – after a gruelling day, there being few pleasures greater than a camp fire with meal cakes and grilled beef to fill the aching void, followed by coffee and a pipe in a cold, clear, moonlit night.

After caring for his horse, Baines crawled contentedly between his blankets; he had carried himself well, he had shown no fear under fire and he had displayed some skill with his rifle in front of the men. The last entry for this day in his journal reads: 'I was shewn the second volume of a large edition of the Bible and another illustrated work which had been found in one of the Hottentot laagers during the day.'

15 July
It was clear and frosty as Baines broke the ice for his morning wash in the frigid water of the Gqwala stream. While there, an Englishman in the CMR came up and congratulated him on his shot on the previous day. 'I think I frightened him,' Baines replied modestly, at which the man laughed. The Ngqika, he said, had not risen after falling the second time and, much to Baines's satisfaction, this statement was corroborated by several other men around.

They left Wiggill's mill at 11 a.m. after a leisurely breakfast. Turning south they descended the pass at Bush Nek, marched past Nel's farm at the entrance to the Waterkloof and then, following the course of the Gqwala River, reached their camp at Adelaide without further adventure.

Further Arrivals

Another despatch from Earl Grey further enlightened Sir Harry Smith as to the expected duties of his two new assistant commissioners. The despatch ended with platitudes:

> I have only to add, that I rely with the utmost confidence upon your disposition to avail yourself of the services of the gentlemen who are now proceeding to join you as Assistant Commissioners in the manner intended by Her Majesty's Government, and on their receiving at your hands all the consideration which is their due. I have not failed to impress upon them the duty on their side of acting towards you with that deference, and in that spirit of subordination, which is prescribed by the positions you respectively hold as servants of the Crown.[7]

Major Hogge and Mr Owen arrived in the Eastern Cape in early August 1851, where they immediately set to work. In mid-August, Owen sent Smith a satisfactory report of the state of the Khoikhoi in the area of Swellendam and Caledon.[8] Much less satisfactory to Smith, and an indication of what would follow, was a brief report on the nature of communications between the chiefs and the executive. Hogge noted that, for the second time, he had expressed the view that such communications should be 'through the Commissioners of the respective tribes, the Chief Commissioner of Kaffirland [British Kaffraria] and by no other channel'. He complained that, instead, Sir Harry 'adheres to the expediency of private and personal communication through the natives'. Hogge continued that he desired that a copy of his memorandum be forwarded to the Secretary of State,

> for though the Assistant Commissioner is bound to aid his Excellency the High Commissioner in the carrying out of his decisions, even should the opinions upon which those decisions are founded unfortunately differ from his own, he cannot but deem it essential that his dissent on all subjects of paramount importance should be systematically recorded.[9]

When one reads the governor's curt reply to this memorandum, one can readily imagine that it was written with firmly pursed lips – Smith was not amused:

> The High Commissioner is very much obliged to Major Hogge for the record of his opinion, a mode he desires to court upon all occasions. The practice

pursued is one dictated by long experience with the Kafir character, as well as the mode for authority to obtain information by every practicable and honourable means, in all situations.[10]

He also acknowledged that a copy would be sent to Grey.

It was plainly time to get these trouble-makers out of his way. The concomitant deterioration of the situation in the Orange River Sovereignty resulted in Smith's decision to send his assistant commissioners to that place, in company with the troops he also proposed to send.[11]

In July, the service period of the Khoikhoi levies from the Western Cape expired and Smith was compelled to allow them to go home, though not without urgent requests that more be sent to replace them.

More welcome to Smith than Hogge and Owen were the troops that continued to arrive at the Cape. In June, Grey had given Smith permission to call upon the services of the reserve battalion of the 12th (East Suffolk) Regiment, then in Mauritius. In acknowledgement of that authority, Smith advised the Secretary of State that he had sent a steamer for the battalion immediately.[12]

The arrival of the 2nd (The Queen's Royal) Regiment was fraught with difficulty, even before it had entered the fighting zone. The transport vessel arrived at East London in mid-July 1851 but only a part of the regiment had managed to disembark before a sudden storm caused the master of the ship to seek shelter at sea. It was a further two weeks before the remaining men were able to go ashore. The headquarters division of the regiment marched into King William's Town on 20 August.[13]

Baptism of Fire

The deployment of the 2nd Queen's to the frontier was to prove a severe trial for the regiment's officers and men. On 30 August, Major John Burns, 2nd Queen's, marched out of King William's Town in command of a column to deal with rebels in the Fish River bush. His force included 180 officers and men of his own regiment, together with elements of the 6th Regiment, CMR and auxiliary troops, in all totalling eighteen officers and more than four hundred other ranks.[14]

He arrived at Breakfast Vlei, via Fort Willshire, on 1 September, where he left his cattle and pack horses, then moved on to the heights overlooking Kommitjie Drift. During the ascent he was involved in a heavy engagement with Ngqika which lasted three hours. He fought his way out and returned that night to Breakfast Vlei where he calculated the 'butcher's bill'. He thought that he had killed at least twenty-three Ngqika but had paid a heavy price for so doing: he had suffered fifteen men wounded, two of them mortally.

On 3 September he sent his mounted men out again well before dawn. Their instructions were to scour Chief Thola's country as far as the Tyumie junction but nothing was found.[15] He took the remainder of the column back to Fort Willshire and joined up with his cavalry at their bivouac in the late afternoon. Burns's column returned to King William's Town on 4 September, having received a bloody nose at the hands of the Ngqika rebels. In a separate report, Major Burns gave his casualties as follows:

Engineers	four wounded, one of whom died later.
2nd Queen's	eight wounded, one of whom died later.
6th Regiment	one man wounded.
CMR	one man wounded.
Armstrong's Horse	one man wounded.[16]

Sergeant McKay, of the 74th, later offered an explanation for the heavy casualties in the 2nd Queen's:

Five of the 2nd's bandsmen were killed or wounded. These men all wore their white regimental jackets, with brass epaulettes. Previous to setting forth on the patrol, they had been furnished with arms and distributed among the different companies; and, no doubt, the Kafirs imagined them to be men of a superior grade, as they picked them out from the men of the ranks.[17]

The rough handling of Burns's force must have rankled with the commander-in-chief because, on 5 September, Sir Harry Smith sent instructions to Colonel Mackinnon and Colonel Eyre which expressed his dissatisfaction with the number of rebels who had 'collected in the fastnesses of the Fish River Bush, especially about Kommitjie's Heights'.[18]

When the remainder of the 2nd Queen's Regiment finally arrived at King William's Town, Colonel Mackinnon was ordered to take another patrol to the Fish River bush. His force was much stronger than Burns's, consisting of the following in two divisions:

2nd Queen's	398
6th Regiment	419
73rd Regiment	152
Royal Marines	52
CMR	33
Armstrong's Horse	29
Catty's Rifles	64
Levies and Guides	105

Mackinnon's force therefore numbered some 1,250 men.[19]

On 6 September, Mackinnon marched out of King William's Town, with Kommitjie Drift on the Fish River as his destination. His instructions were to clear the area of rebel Ngqika gathered there. During the day, he detached Colonel Michel's division near Fort Willshire, which included his own 6th Regiment. Mackinnon then continued with the other division and the supply wagons by Line Drift.

On 7 September, 'the whole force met at Fort Williams'. The next day, Mackinnon moved to 'Foonah's Kloof', during which march he spotted a number of Ngqika driving some cattle into a deep valley which led down to the Fish River.

Early on the morning of 9 September, Mackinnon set out to capture the cattle he had seen the previous day. Leaving a sufficient force to defend his supply wagons at the overnight bivouac, he marched out at 3.30 a.m. He sent Michel, with his 6th Regiment, Catty's Rifles, Armstrong's Horse and fifty of the levy, to the right side of the valley. Mackinnon himself took two companies of the 2nd Queen's, a detachment of the 73rd and the CMR to the left side of the valley, attempting a form of pincer movement. He directed Commandant Davies to take the remaining fifty men of his levy, supported by the other two companies of the 2nd Queen's under Captain William Joseph Oldham, down the centre of the valley, to follow the spoor of the cattle.

Mackinnon bent his steps towards some high ground on the left side of the valley, about three kilometres away, from where he could observe the movements of Davies's detachment. Before he reached that point, however, he saw a large number of Ngqika and Khoikhoi rebels to his left, and moved to engage them. He extended the two companies of the 2nd Queen's in skirmishing order, keeping the 73rd in reserve. The 2nd drove hard into the enemy, forcing them back towards the Fish River. Here the imperial infantry found themselves at a disadvantage, as the enemy were able to fire up at them. Mackinnon then extended the 73rd into skirmishing lines, withdrawing the 2nd Queen's through them. As a result of this manoeuvre, the Ngqika thought that the British troops were retreating and came into the open to follow them up, instead falling victim to the waiting 73rd. Mackinnon then continued towards the high ground he had been moving towards before the engagement.

Mackinnon reached the high ground about 10 a.m. but was too late to see what had become of his centre detachment: he heard no firing and saw no one in the valley. 'I concluded that Commandant Davies and Captain Oldham had scoured the valley, and had effected their junction with Lieut.-Colonel Michel.'[20] Mackinnon then found that the rebels had stolen round his flanks with the intention of preventing his movement back towards the mouth of the valley and his camp. He drove them off, the enemy fighting with less spirit than in the earlier engagement. When he arrived at the road between Fort Peddie and his camp, he found Captain Tainton waiting for him with about 180 Mfengu, having been detained at Fort Peddie and thus arriving late.

It was about 11 a.m., Mackinnon had suffered a number of wounded, and he now received a report that eight privates of the 2nd Queen's were missing. His infantry were too exhausted to retrace their steps, so he sent Tainton's Mfengu and the CMR to search for the missing men. The men were not found, nor were they ever seen again. Mackinnon returned to his bivouac, arriving there by 12.45 p.m.

Colonel Michel returned to the bivouac about four hours later. He had worked his way along the heights of the valley and, after twice crossing the Fish River at its end, returned through the valley, where, about 9 a.m., he came across the detachment under Davies and Oldham at a most critical moment:

> It appears that the enemy attacked the rear of this detachment soon after they entered the valley, and that they met another body of them in their front. The Levies and guides outmarched the Queen's, and the latter got separated, Captain Oldham with one company leaving the path down the valley and losing his road. He was surrounded by Kaffirs, was killed himself, and his men suffered severely. The loss of this detachment was, one Captain and 19 rank and file of the Queen's, and Quartermaster Ebden and two rank and file of the Levy, killed. Twenty rank and file of the Queen's and Commandant Davies, one serjeant and one private of the Levy, and two Kafir guides wounded. The opportune junction of Lieut.-Colonel Michel's column enabled the detachment to bring away their wounded in safety.[21]

On 10 September, Mackinnon took his battered force back to Breakfast Vlei, expecting to rendezvous with Colonel Eyre. Eyre, however, had fought an engagement of his own that morning and was only able to reach the bivouac later in the day. From there, he moved on to Fort Williams, from where he sent off his wounded to Fort Peddie.

Mackinnon allowed his men to recover on the following day, moving off on the 12th back to Foonah's Kloof. Here he made arrangements to scour once again the valley where his column had been so badly mauled only three days earlier.

On 13 September, he again detached Colonel Michel to repeat his traverse of the right side of the valley, while he ordered Major Armstrong and his mounted men, one hundred of the 2nd Queen's and Tainton's Mfengu levy to the heights on the left. Mackinnon himself took a hundred of the Queen's, the 73rd and the remaining Mfengu down the centre of the kloof.

It rained hard all day and as a result few of the enemy were to be seen. The whole valley was searched as far as the Fish River with little result, and Mackinnon linked up again with Michel near the river.

The next day, the 14th, Mackinnon led his column back to Breakfast Vlei and on 15 September he moved on to Kommitjie Drift, near where Colonel Eyre had fought his engagement on the 10th. A strong group of the enemy drew up to oppose him but 'were quickly routed by the 6th and 73rd regiments'.

On 16 September, he sent the wagons under Colonel Michel, with the 6th, two companies of the 2nd Queen's and Armstrong's Horse to King William's Town via Line Drift. Mackinnon took the remainder of his force via Tamacha Post and arrived in King William's Town on the 17th.

Mackinnon's casualties for the expedition were very heavy:[22]

	Killed	Wounded	Missing
2nd Queen's Regiment	24	23	8
6th Regiment	1	1	
73rd Regiment		6	
Royal Marines		2	
CMR	1	1	
Armstrong's Horse		2	
Levies and Guides	3	4	

Once again, the combat inexperience of the officers of the 2nd Queen's is revealed in their casualties.

Terror at Niland's Pass

General Somerset had taken most of his division, which was stationed at the farm 'Rietfontein' ten kilometres south of Fort Beaufort, to the Fish River bush to help suppress the troublesome raids from that enemy fastness. Lieutenant-Colonel John Fordyce was left in charge of the camp with about six hundred men and, as McKay put it, 'With Fordyce in command, something must be done.'[23] He therefore ordered that all the available men in camp be prepared for an unauthorised patrol to the Kroome Heights.

Fordyce's force comprised: four companies 74th Highland Regiment; thirty-eight CMR under Lieutenant-Colonel Sutton; a small European levy of fourteen men attached to the grenadier company of the 74th; fifty-eight mounted levies; eighty-one foot levies; and 216 Mfengu levies. Totalling only some 560 men, it was quite inadequate for the task it was about to undertake, and Fordyce had no real plan for the assault. It also left the Rietfontein camp exposed, with few remaining to guard it.

7 September

Fordyce's column left Rietfontein a little before sunset, with each infantryman carrying sixty rounds of ammunition and three days' rations. The immediate objective was to cross over the top of the ridge to the north in the dark and thereby prevent their movements being seen by the enemy. After marching in the dark for ten kilometres across a rolling plain, accompanied by myriads of fireflies, they reached William Gilbert's farm, Sipton Manor, which lay on the 'Clu Clu' [Xuxuwa] River. Here the men were allowed to rest but were ordered to be ready to turn out at a moment's notice. The horses were tied to a broken fence around the derelict flower garden and the men lay down in companies with their arms piled in front of each rank. Even though it was cold, fires were forbidden so as not to alert the enemy.[24]

Sergeant McKay slept restlessly, waking up at the slightest noise; shortly after midnight he heard the sound of horsemen arriving and wondered who they were.

8 September

It was bitterly cold as they fell in at 2 a.m. in quarter-distance column, at the east gate of Sipton Manor near the tower. McKay was astonished to see the 74th's much esteemed bandmaster Hans Hartung, a native of Germany, on a borrowed horse. The noise he had heard during the night was the arrival from Fort Beaufort of Colonel Sutton with the eight men of the CMR and Captain Wynne with men of the Fort Beaufort Mounted Volunteers. Hartung had mistakenly thought Sutton was on his way to Rietfontein, which he wanted to visit, and he was now very much vexed at having to join the column instead. It would have been dangerous for him to have ridden back to Fort Beaufort alone but, as things turned out, it might have been better for him had he undertaken it.[25]

Fordyce led the column westwards along the foot of the Kroome Range towards Thomas Niland's farm, Mount Pleasant, where the enemy had reportedly established a camp. There, however, they found that they had departed with all his cattle, leaving only a large grass fire behind. A halt was called while the surroundings were reconnoitred, the men meanwhile feeling the cold intensely. Fordyce then ordered the column to about-turn and return along the foot of the Kroome Range to Blakeway's farm, Longnor Park, which

Upper Waterkloof
7 September 1851

N

Eastland's Farm

Mundell's Farm

MUNDELL'S KRANZ

WATERKLOOF

SCHELM KLOOF

WOLF BACK RIDGE

HORSE SHOE

TENTH PASS

FULLER'S HOEK

ARIE'S HOEK

ARGYLE PASS

KROOME HEIGHTS

Andrew's Farm

Niland's Farm

Blakeway's Farm

they subsequently reached at 8 a.m. and had breakfast there. Lieutenant King found the farm beautifully situated in a warm, sheltered kloof through which a small stream wound its way. He was delighted to see numerous bushbuck, which had been disturbed by their arrival, scudding across the open flat below. While at breakfast some excitement was generated by the report 'The Kaffirs are coming', but it turned out to be a group of Fort Beaufort Mfengu taking a short cut.[26]

Fordyce and Sutton had a long discussion about their next course of action. Fordyce was in favour of getting at the enemy in the Waterkloof by the easiest and quickest route, but Sutton thought the force had insufficient men. He also pointed out that they had no artillery and only two thousand rounds of extra ammunition – about three rounds per man. The two colonels compromised and agreed to climb to the top of the Kroome Heights where there was open and safe ground for a camp. From there they could descend at night into either Arie's Hoek or Fuller's Hoek where the enemy was reported to be concentrated. While at breakfast, one of the 74th's fires got out of hand. It was midwinter and the grass was long and dry, so within seconds the flames were as high as a roof, threatening to engulf men, muskets and ammunition. Never did a column start more promptly.[27]

The ascent of the Kroome Range was by a bush-workers' slip-path running along the top of a ridge, known from its profile as Wolwekop or 'Wolf's Head', with wooded precipices on either side dropping with frightening steepness down to deep ravines below. The lower half of the climb was through shadeless brushwood and mimosa and the troops, in contrast to the cold of a few hours before, perspired profusely in the heat of the sun. The upper half of the climb was steeper but shaded by the tall trees which supplanted the scrub and made a refreshing change for the men. At the summit, the tall trees give way to an open, undulating, grass-covered plain about two kilometres wide, crossed by several gentle ridges and shallow valleys, the whole being surrounded by bush. The Kroome Heights are separated from the area called the Horseshoe by a nek through which runs a narrow, rocky road known as Tenth Pass.

A large number of the enemy were seen collecting around the edge of the nek, apparently with the intention of blocking any attempt to use Tenth Pass. Fordyce's opinion was that, while the nek could be forced during daylight, the advantage to be gained was doubtful, especially as neither the Waterkloof nor Fuller's Hoek could be examined closely until they had crossed over, and any attempt to cross over at night was unwarrantable. He therefore decided not to attempt the crossing but to descend the Kroome Range after dark by another pass to the west of Wolf's Head which led down to Niland's farm.

The column marched over the plateau and halted in a shallow valley through which ran a small stream of good water. Pickets were mounted on two adjoining ridges, sentries were posted, the horses were knee-haltered and turned out to graze nearby and the men were free to do as they pleased; some lay down under blankets thrown over piled arms while others lit fires to cook their rations. The Fort Beaufort Mounted Volunteers captured two oxen grazing nearby, which were immediately slaughtered – McKay was given one of the kidneys as a present. It was now midday and the men who had been hard at work since dawn were at last able to relax in anticipation of a meal of stewed beef and biscuit.[28]

Several officers had gone to the top of a ridge in the direction of Tenth Pass with their telescopes. Suddenly at 3 p.m., they came back shouting, 'To arms', and reported breathlessly that hundreds of Ngqika were running at full speed towards the camp from the pass. The men immediately rolled up their blankets, collected their arms, caught and saddled their horses and emptied the untasted contents of the soup kettles onto the grass. Lieutenant King, as duty officer, doubled out with the advance guard and extended in skirmishing order along the ridge facing the pass. Soon shots were being exchanged at very short range, the crouching enemy almost hidden in the long grass as they fired. The numbers were overwhelming and King's advance guard was gradually forced back until Captain James Duff reinforced them with his Grenadier Company. Bayonets were fixed and with a wild Highland shout they charged the dense black horde, which promptly retreated into the bush.[29]

The grenadiers and the advance guard rejoined the rest of the column, where Fordyce had formed the infantry in extended order behind a ridge. Three companies of the 74th were placed on the right with the right flank near Wolf's Head Pass. Next came the dismounted Kat River Levy, then the Mfengu and finally Captain John Henry Borton's No. 7 Company on the left flank, thrown back to face the north. The infantry thus formed a semicircle with the mounted men under Colonel Sutton remaining in the shallow valley in the rear, ready to support or attack.

The enemy, who had advanced out into the open again during this movement, once more came running and yelling their chilling war-cries. Fordyce found it difficult to estimate the number of the scattered, irregular groups of the enemy but guessed that there were nearly two thousand on the open ground. They came on with the speed of greyhounds and, as soon as they were within extreme musket range, dropped to the ground and started firing. They kept up a continuous fire but it was more noisy than dangerous and it was vigorously returned by the infantry who, being well covered by the ground, could fire deliberately without exposing themselves.

One huge Xhosa ran at top speed towards the right along the ridge behind which the enemy lay. Ignoring the bullets which flew past him he kept straight on towards Wolf's Head Ridge, shouting and encouraging the others to follow him. Fordyce saw this as an attempt to cut off his retreat so he ordered his bugler to sound 'Take ground to the right', and also had Sutton's cavalry gallop to the front where a volley from their carbines effectively checked this movement. This skirmish lasted about half an hour, by which time the enemy appeared to have had enough, as they withdrew back into the bush. Their attack had been repulsed with no loss to the 74th, except Fordyce's horse which had been shot under him; three Mfengu were killed and three wounded.[30]

Fordyce now had to decide whether to remain on the heights until nightfall or retire immediately down Niland's Pass. He had to take into consideration that half their ammunition had been used, that no more fresh meat could be obtained as there was no chance of capturing any more cattle, and that the Ngqika were almost certainly still in the bush, running to cut off the passes by which he could descend. If he did not act quickly, Sutton said, they would be finished. Reluctantly, Fordyce gave the order to retire and sent Sutton to secure the head of Niland's Pass. At almost the same time a mounted chief, thought to be Maqoma, with three hundred mounted warriors, came out of the bush to the north and also raced towards Niland's Pass. Sutton, however, gained the head of the pass first without opposition and so Maqoma re-entered the bush further to the west.[31]

The enemy emerged from the bush again as soon as the retreat began and firing commenced on both sides as they came closer. The retreat must have been at a fast pace for McKay tells of seeing a seventy-year-old man of the European levy lagging behind. The men of the Grenadier Company did all they could to bring him on but he continued to fall behind until he was surrounded by a black mass of 'merciless savages'. McKay and those around him fired in desperation into the black mass, but the European was seen no more.[32]

Niland's Pass, like Wolf's Head, runs along the top of a ridge descending to the plain below. The passes are similar: a narrow track, steep hillsides, tall trees above and scrub below. The mounted men and the baggage horses descended first. Their pace was that of a slow walk as they were hampered by piles of lumber, some nearly two metres high, which lay strewn across the slip-path. No. 5 Company entered next, followed by No. 3 and the grenadiers. The enemy, as expected, were in possession of the bush and kept up a steady fire on the retreating Highlanders, though as yet with little effect, with only one man being wounded at the top of the pass.

The men in the rear, however, were feeling the pressure. The enemy were closing in behind while the companies in front seemed to be in no hurry to move. Captain Borton's No. 7 Company could wait no longer and entered the bush to the west of the path, leaving the Kat River Levy and the Mfengu behind. While among the tall trees, Borton was able to travel faster than the grenadiers, but further down, when he encountered the scrub, he was forced back to the slip-path where his presence further hampered progress.[33]

In these circumstances it is not surprising that, in spite of their officers' efforts, the discipline of the Kat River Levy and the Mfengu in the rear broke down. Shrieking and firing their muskets in all directions, they ran headlong down the narrow path, knocking down and trampling the Highlanders. The enemy, ever ready to take advantage of any weakness, fell on the confused Highlanders, first hurling their light spears and then closing in and stabbing with their short heavy ones, the famed *untsuntsu*.[34] It seemed to Lieutenant King that the bush swarmed with Ngqika. Some were perched in trees firing from above, others rushed up in hundreds from the bush below, yelling in a most ferocious manner, hissing through their teeth, their blood-red faces, brawny limbs and enormous size terrifying the Highlanders, each of whom had nothing but his bayonet and the butt-end of his musket to use as a club.[35] The pungent smoke from musket fire on both sides hung in the still and sultry air, making it difficult to tell friend from foe. There was confusion everywhere; some called out to pass the word to the head of the column to come in support, others roared out the order to march on.

Yet the Highlanders' response was magnificent: Private Karrigan ran one Ngqika through with his bayonet, shot another and killed a third with the butt-end of his musket. Private Hall was caught by the straps of his blanket and thrown down the steep side of the ravine.[36] When his senses returned, Hall found himself caught in a bush on the steep slope down which he had been hurled. Crawling out of the bush he picked up his musket, which was lying nearby, and carefully climbed up the slope, keeping still whenever he heard the sound of bare feet on the path above. When all was quiet he stepped out onto the path and, looking about, was distressed to see no sign of his comrades. Hall ran downhill as fast as he could until some men of the 74th saw him when, predictably, they fired at him. He fired into the air then raised his musket and waved it. Fortunately he was recognised and was able to rejoin his comrades, where he was revived with a shot of brandy by Doctor Fraser. Ever afterwards Hall suffered from nightmares, frequently shouting 'There they are, murder! murder!' – much to the consternation of his tent mates.[37]

Corporal Everleigh was struck in the back with a spear and did not have it drawn out until he reached the bottom of the pass. McKay heard Fordyce call out an order to his bugler. The boy raised the bugle to his lips and sounded the 'advance', the last notes being blown straight into the face of a Ngqika who was grasping for the boy. The boy dodged away and the African stumbled and fell; as he rose McKay shot him.[38] Three Ngqika caught one Highlander by his blanket and were dragging him into the bush when the straps slipped over his shoulder and released him. Unarmed, he threw himself on to the nearest man and wrestled with him for his spear. Over and over they rolled, struggling on the ground, but the well-greased, naked body had the advantage over the clothed and belted soldier and he was stabbed to death.[39]

Slowly the descent continued, the grenadiers in the rear meeting attack after attack from an enemy that was fighting with ferocious madness. After each attack, the path was left strewn with black corpses with, here and there, the still form of a dead or dying Highlander, eight of whom fell in all.

About three-quarters of the way down, the grenadiers overtook bandmaster Hartung, struggling to lead his obstinate mount. The men begged him to let his horse go, for they had seen the enemy and he had not. He, however, stubbornly insisted that, as it was a borrowed horse he must return it. Not long afterwards, as he lagged further and further behind, Hartung was seen surrounded by Ngqika, who took his horse and then seized him by his arms and legs and carried him bodily away. The grenadiers were helpless and could only fire shots at his captors until the thick smoke hid him from view.[40]

When the grenadiers at last reached the bottom of the pass they could see mounted men and levies stretching far into the distance towards Niland's farm, while the 74th collected together in a confused mass until their officers and NCOs set about forming a rear guard. The pitiful two thousand rounds of reserve ammunition were distributed, but the pressure of the enemy was such that, by the time the 74th reached Niland's, even these rounds had been used up. Fortunately, at this point the Ngqika decided to break off their attack and return to the bush, having inflicted upon them what McKay could only describe as a 'disgraceful affair'.[41]

Now that the excitement was over, Lieutenant King suddenly felt desperately tired and he had to force his legs to carry him along after seventeen hours of almost uninterrupted exertion. He was extremely depressed; the day had not been a success and his depression was increased by the groans of the wounded men near him as they were borne along on stretchers. The evening's long shadows increased the gloom of the dreary scene and it was quite dark by the time he reached Sipton Manor.

A mounted express was despatched to Rietfontein for more ammunition and a wagon to carry the wounded, who in the meantime had been made as comfortable as possible in an old shed. Fires were lit and King lay down once again amongst the bricks, utterly exhausted.[42]

The casualties of the day were fourteen dead and fourteen wounded.[43] The dead had all been left behind.

For many months the 74th was ignorant of the fate of their bandmaster, then one day a Xhosa woman named Numkani was captured by Lieutenant-Colonel Eyre's brigade. She gave a sworn account of what became of Hartung to the Fort Beaufort magistrate. Later still, another eyewitness, a handsome maid named Nomini, the friend of Sergeant-Major James Cooper of the 74th, corroborated her story.

On the day following his capture, Hartung was paraded in front of a gathering of Ngqika and Khoikhoi on the Kroome Heights. Maqoma presided, attended by his son Kona and a head-man named Queque. Maqoma, not wishing to become involved, declared that those who had lost relatives could take Hartung and do with him as they wished and he was led away to a nearby homestead. There he was stripped, Queque taking his clothes, and the men then formed a ring around him and danced and sang and brandished their spears and mocked him. Tiring of this sport, they took Hartung to a grassy spot and stretched him out on his back. Two stakes were driven through his wrists into the ground and his ankles were fastened to a third stake at his feet. His cries were terrible and this angered the spectators who threatened to kill him if he didn't stop screaming. The women now took up the dancing, but eventually they retired to their huts leaving Hartung in the hot sun, his snow-white skin blistering and his wounds oozing blood.

Towards evening the women came back and began dancing again. One of them understood Hartung when she heard him say 'water' and went to fetch some, but was prevented from giving it to him by the arrival of the men. One man took a knife and cut a vein in Hartung's arm but little blood flowed. He next cut a vein in his thigh and filled a calabash bowl with blood but by this time Hartung had fainted. On recovering, Hartung again called for water whereupon the bowl was held to his lips, but as he raised his head to drink, the whole coagulating mass flopped over on to his face. That night he was carried into a hut for protection from hyenas.

The next day his captors amused themselves by cutting Hartung's arms and legs and taking off the joints of his fingers. He screamed fearfully when cut. To everyone's amazement he was still alive the following morning. One man asked if he would like something to drink and, receiving what he thought was an affirmative answer, cut off Hartung's penis and stuck it in his mouth. The spectators found the sight of a man apparently drinking from his own dismembered penis so incredibly funny that they rolled on the ground convulsed with laughter.

At some time during the third day of his capture, peace came to Hartung, late bandmaster of the 74th Regiment and a fine musician.[44]

With regard to the Kroome operation, Major-General Somerset later noted that:

> The very judicious and able disposition of the forces made by Lieut.-Col. Fordyce, when engaged with so superior a force of the enemy, who had every advantage the local circumstances of so strong a position would give them, will no doubt meet with the Commander-in-Chief's high approbation.[45]

Perhaps the most remarkable fact of this engagement is the very low casualties suffered by Fordyce's men, considering the ordeal they had undergone in their retreat down Niland's Pass. The casualties published named eight men of the 74th killed, to which should be added Bandmaster Hartung, missing, believed killed. The regiment also suffered ten men wounded, including Lieutenant John Joseph Corrigan.

Chapter 8

October on the Kroome Heights

First October Campaign

Three brigades were to take part in this attack. The first was led by Major-General Somerset, who also had overall command. He had with him five six-pounder guns under Lieutenants Campbell and Field of the Royal Artillery, and about three hundred men of the CMR under Major Charles Somerset.

The second brigade was led by Lieutenant-Colonel John Fordyce, whose 74th Regiment of Highlanders was included in his column. He also had with him two companies of the 12th Regiment. His mounted units included over seventy men of the Graaff-Reinet Mounted Levy and twenty-nine men of the Fort Beaufort Mounted Volunteers. He also had the Fort Beaufort Mfengu Levy of some 260 men.[1]

Lieutenant-Colonel John Michel, commanding his own 6th Regiment, led the third brigade. Michel had purchased every step in his military career, from ensign in April 1823 to lieutenant-colonel in April 1842. The 6th, and its commanding officer, were described by Sergeant McKay thus:

> A rag-a-muffin, devil-may-care lot of Irish boys formed the 6th Foot . . . They were commanded by an experienced, able officer, one who was a father and friend to them – Colonel Mitchell [sic]. This day was the first time I had ever seen him, and he was busily engaged pointing a gun which was loaded with shell at a group of Kafirs in a valley. His shirt sleeves were turned up to his elbows, his wide-awake [hat] cocked on one side, strong Blucher boots on his feet, and a pair of corduroy trowsers on his legs. He appeared to me the beau-ideal of an able campaigning commander, willing to brave the difficulties and dangers of the campaign with his men, upon the same fare and clothing.[2]

As well as his own men, Michel also had some companies of the 2nd and the 91st regiments. The latter contribution was three companies, commanded

by Lieutenant-Colonel Charles Cooke Yarborough, six years junior to
Michel. The brigade's auxiliary troops included about a hundred mounted
men of Armstrong's Irregular Horse and a hundred of Catty's Rifles. There
was also a number of Mfengu from Peddie and Port Elizabeth.

The plan of attack was elegantly simple: Fordyce would traverse the Kroome
Heights from its western end to the Tenth Pass, where he was to await the
arrival of the other columns. The other two brigades would move together
down to the area of the Horseshoe from the north, following a circular march
from the Blinkwater. On General Somerset's arrival, Fordyce was to cross
over Tenth Pass to the Horseshoe and join the general attack on the enemy
in the surrounding bush.

13 October

Fordyce's brigade left its camp near Fort Beaufort at 1 a.m. and, after a march
of twenty-four kilometres via the Xuxuwa River, arrived at the Yellowwoods
River at 6.30 a.m., where they rested for three hours. Fordyce then continued
the march, rather than make camp, as he was not sure whether there would
be a sufficient supply of water before reaching the Koonap River.[3] He also
felt that the nearer they came to their destination the better, as the following
day's work could be long and arduous. As they tramped along the dusty road
running parallel to the Kroome Range towards Adelaide, the heat from the
sun became intense. Lieutenant King found that any metalwork, such as the
barrel of a musket, was too hot to touch. After eight kilometres they reached
McMaster's farm, 'Mimosa Park', just short of Adelaide, at 11.30 a.m., where
the men were told to rest until midnight. Everyone lay down gratefully in
whatever shade they could find.

Captain Cowie of the Fort Beaufort Mfengu Levy went up to Colonel
Fordyce and told him that their guide had never been up the proposed route
to the top of the Kroome Range. Cowie himself knew this route and judged it
impassable for pack horses. As usually happens to those who volunteer advice,
Cowie was promptly made the new guide.[4]

October in the Eastern Cape is a month of extremes of heat and cold, as if
summer and winter are vying with each other for mastery over spring. Thus,
as evening came, the heat of the day was replaced by a cold rain and the men
lay wet and shivering on the muddy ground, 'a confused mass of steaming
blankets'.[5]

General Somerset, with the 1st Brigade and part of the 3rd, had left Fort
Beaufort the day before, with the 91st Regiment making up the bulk of his
infantry. On reaching the junction of the Kat River and the Mankazana (not
to be confused with another Mankazana River thirty kilometres to the west)

Somerset was joined by Lieutenant-Colonel Michel and the rest of the 3rd Brigade consisting of the 2nd Queen's and the 6th regiments.

The first to appear were the 2nd Queen's in their red jackets and light blue trousers. Baines, who was with the general, was surprised to notice that they carried their blankets in the form of a long roll thrown scarf-wise round their necks and strapped to their waists. 'How', he mused, 'can they fire their muskets with a blanket roll in front of their shoulders?' Many of the Queen's had lost their regulation caps in the recent, unfortunate patrol in the Fish River bush and they now appeared in a variety of headgear such as Jim Crows (forage caps with leather peaks), red night-caps and large handkerchiefs.[6]

The 6th, the Royal Warwickshires, had also been heavily involved in a number of skirmishes and reminded Baines of Falstaff's regiment: he had never seen a more ragged lot of men. Their uniforms were stained and tattered, their red coats and filthy white trousers were patched with leather, canvas and cloth of many colours.

The combined force under Somerset marched through the Kat River Settlement and Baines thought the rebel Khoikhoi had been very foolish to abandon such a paradise, where everything that man could plant seemed to thrive, in order to live like bandits in the bush. After climbing Blinkwater Hill the force halted for the night on a grassy slope near the little Gqwala River, the Mfengu taking up separate quarters on the opposite side. As soon as the soldiers had piled their arms there was a general rush for two small patches of bush and within a few minutes they were stripped of everything that could be used for firewood.[7]

Lieutenant B., an officer of the Queen's, described their camp:

> As we lighted fires, a heavy drizzle of rain came on, and continued throughout the night . . . An hour sufficed to kill, distribute, cook, and eat the tough rations of beef doled out with the illiberal hand by the contractor's agent; and after that time, cold, wet and miserable as we were, thankful indeed we were to rest awhile before a renewal of our labours.[8]

14 October

It was a little before midnight when Lieutenant King was woken up to continue the march. Although he had spent a very uncomfortable night, it was with the greatest reluctance that he crept out of his plaid to face the drizzling, bitterly cold, foggy night.[9] The route chosen by Captain Cowie was over an outlying spur of the Kroome Range, but even this ascent was so steep that the mounted men had to walk their horses.[10] King watched his pack horse anxiously, for his sustenance and comfort for many days depended on preventing that animal from falling or losing his pack. He was more than half asleep as he stumbled along. Every now and then an unevenness in the ground would unbalance him and he would wake up momentarily, only to lapse again, struggling against the temptation to let go and sleep. Bearing the load of leadership, he forced himself to keep awake by pinching his arms 'black and blue'.[11]

They reached the summit as day dawned and a halt was called for breakfast but all the men had to eat was dry, black biscuit. The horses fared as badly, for all the grass had been burnt by a recent fire. The mist still hung around, making it impossible to see anything of the general's forces. It also saturated the men's canvas blouses and made everyone so cold that they were glad to move off. The march towards the east along the top of the Kroome Range started at 7.30 a.m. and shortly afterwards the boom of a gun was heard. In a gap in the mist, red coats and gleaming arms could be seen on the Horseshoe, howitzers belched out their smoke and moments later the bursting of shells over a group of huts was clearly visible. Cavalry moved forward followed by a battalion of infantry – and then the mist closed in again. The sound of firing continued to be heard, generating a great deal of excitement among Fordyce's men.[12]

At 10.30 a.m. the brigade reached its destination, a spot about a kilometre from Tenth Pass and here they halted. Lookouts were stationed along the edges of the bush to watch for any of the enemy who might attempt to escape. Mfengu were sent into the surrounding bush where they burnt some huts and did a lot of firing but, according to Fordyce, without object or effect.[13]

The men retained their arms in case of sudden attack and, besides cooking and resting their tired limbs, they talked. The main topic was the affair of 8 September, for they had halted on the same ground from which that less-than-glorious retreat had begun.

The brigade waited for an hour and a half, then Captain Carey with his troop of CMR and some of the 91st came through Tenth Pass with orders for Fordyce. Everyone crowded eagerly around them to hear the news.[14]

Somerset's force at Kaal Hoek was awakened at midnight and each man was issued with three days' rations, except for beef, which would be supplied on the hoof.

A thick mist covered the ground and the artist in Baines was fascinated by the play of lights and shadows from across the stream. As the Mfengu passed in front of their fires, gigantic shadows of the upper half of their bodies would be projected on the intervening clouds of mist. Below these images sparks flickered from flint and steel as the ranks of soldiers, invisible in the dark, lit their pipes.

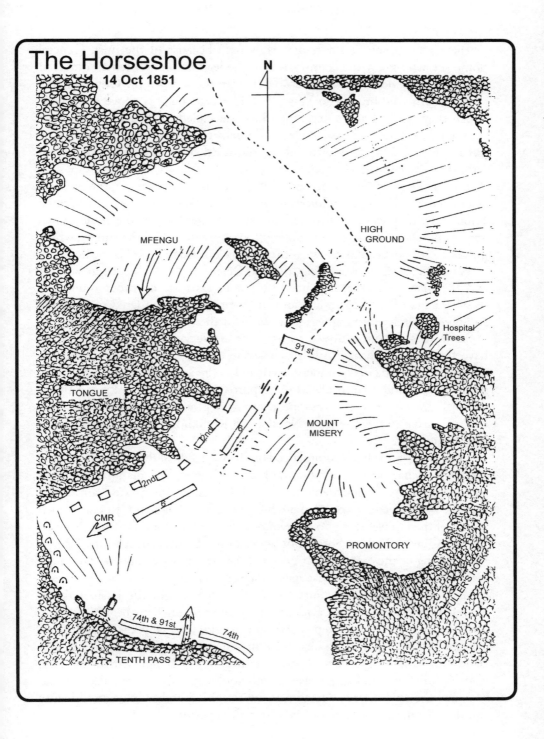

The march began at 1 a.m. at a slow pace because of the mist. General
Somerset, who knew the country, was in the lead and he posted an officer at
each turn to guide those who followed. He led them down the Gqwala River,
past the 74th's old bivouac at Wiggill's mill, to the heights above Bush Nek,
which they reached at 5 a.m. Here a halt was called for half an hour in the
vain hope that the mist would clear.[15] Somerset then led them in an easterly
direction, past Mundell's farm, along the northern rim of the Waterkloof
until they reached the Horseshoe at 7.30 a.m.

The artillery under Lieutenant Field was now turned on the Ngqika
assembled on the eastern promontory and, as soon as the mist cleared
sufficiently, they were shelled and driven into the bush.[16] The mule-drawn
guns of Michel's division came up and took over from Field's artillery, which
moved to support the infantry on the Waterkloof side of the Horseshoe.

While the artillery was firing, the 2nd Regiment, with the 6th in support
and the 91st in reserve, had been posted in skirmishing order round the
western edge of the Horseshoe and the men had been ordered to lie down
and take cover. Everything was now ready for the work of killing to begin.

Somerset's tactical plan was to have the artillery shell the bush and then
have the infantry charge in to disperse the enemy. The enemy's method of
defence was to hide in the undergrowth and to fire at the soldiers from behind
boulders and large tree trunks as they approached. Once the soldiers entered
the bush, the enemy would disappear into its depths. Later, when the soldiers
had to retire into the open, the Ngqika and Khoikhoi rebels would return to
attack their rear.

The attack on the bush commenced on the west side of the Horseshoe. Men
everywhere charged the surrounding bush with wild 'hurrahs' and Highland
shouts and soon the inevitable happened: Captain Thomas Addison of the
Queen's was severely wounded in his left arm, Lieutenant Robert Provo
Norris of the 6th was dangerously wounded in the chest and Colonel Burns of
the 2nd Queen's had his horse shot under him.[17] Lieutenant Edward George
Mainwaring of the 91st, at great personal risk, rescued a wounded man of his
regiment who would otherwise have fallen into enemy hands.

Captain Ayliff took his Port Elizabeth Mfengu into the bush high up
on the Waterkloof side, at a point where there seemed to be little enemy
concentration. He then swept down and round, attacking the enemy from
behind. Two half-naked Ngqika were driven out into the open and at first
Baines and those around him thought they were Mfengu with a message
from Ayliff. The Ngqika, however, calmly took a circular route back into the
bush and the onlookers had to admire their coolness and courage on suddenly
coming face to face with an overwhelmingly superior foe.[18]

Captain Carey and his squadron of CMR had been sent by the general to the edge of Tenth Pass to summon Fordyce's brigade. Unfortunately, the bugler did not know the 74th's 'advance' call, so he tried that of his own regiment, and as many of the other regiments' as he could remember. He made the kloofs echo with the 'assembly', the 'ration' and the 'dinner' calls, all without response. At last the general, annoyed at the delay, ordered Carey and some of the 91st to cross over and deliver the message to Fordyce in person.[19]

Lieutenant King was not impressed by the road through Tenth Pass, which he found strewn with rocks and so narrow that the men had to march in single file. The forest on either side, however, was dense with tall, straight trees, luxuriant undergrowth and immense creepers with 'monkey ropes' hanging from branches twenty metres overhead, right down to the ground. Because of the path's narrowness the head of Fordyce's brigade had already emerged from the bush and was out on the Horseshoe before its tail had entered the pass. In this vulnerable state, so reminiscent of the Boma Pass, those in the middle received a volley of musket fire from a dense clump of bush ahead and above them. The shots caused the forest to ring as the balls whistled by, striking the trees and sending splinters flying. The column, however, continued to advance, with the men firing at every puff of smoke that came from the bush – their only indication of the whereabouts of the enemy. On coming out into the open the men in the middle of the column again came under fire, now from the bush to their left. King thought the fire seemed to be concentrated on each officer as he emerged but fortunately no one was injured, though some suffered damage to their equipment.[20]

As the head of the brigade moved across the Horseshoe to join the general, the alarm was given that the men of the 12th Regiment and the pack horses still in the pass were cut off. The 74th, who were in open column, doubled back and extended along the edge of the bush on either side of the pass and here a brisk skirmish took place. The ground in the vicinity was strewn with rocks and the 74th and 91st were able to fire from behind cover. The enemy, who had erected breastworks on the edge of the bush in front of their huts, replied strongly.

In the midst of this intense fire, Ensign Frederick Walter Ricketts of the 91st was carried off, dangerously wounded in the chest, while the 12th cleared the pass. Half a dozen mounted men were also wounded and several riderless horses galloped wildly by.[21]

The artillery now opened fire, hurling round shot and shell over the heads of the men into the bush around Tenth Pass. To King, the shells made a disconcerting whirring noise as they passed overhead and then splintered trees as they exploded with deadly effect. The skirmish lasted for a quarter of an hour, after which the enemy's fire ceased and the bush suddenly seemed deserted. The 'recall' was heard and the skirmishers slowly reformed into columns and regiments; the heavy masses of infantry then moved in from all sides of the Horseshoe towards the general's position on the high ground. Soon after the recall, the enemy magically reappeared and, seemingly from behind bush and rocks in every direction, kept up an incessant fire which was returned with doubtful effect by the infantry and artillery. Each position, as it was abandoned, was re-occupied by the enemy with such rapidity and boldness that it drew murmurs of approval from the general and his staff. The Graaff-Reinet Mounted Levy in the rear came under heavy fire as they retired, five of their horses being killed. Some of the pack horses, also in the rear, broke away from the hands of the men and the enemy gained a lot of precious ammunition.[22]

As the columns withdrew, the Ngqika became bolder until Captain Carey judged that they had come far enough from the safety of the bush – then he charged. The Ngqika ran, followed by the galloping CMR, who discharged their carbines and trampled many bodies underfoot. This charge, the only bright spot in a tiring day, thrilled all who witnessed it. It was fortunate for the Ngqika that the CMR did not have their sabres – they had been left behind, being regarded as useless in the bush – otherwise the slaughter might have rivalled that of the great charge at the Gwangqa River in 1847. Carey was later honourably mentioned in a despatch from General Somerset to the governor.[23]

After this charge the enemy ceased attacking and the long column moved northwards at 3 p.m. over the rolling plains towards their bivouac at Mundell's farm, 'St Lawrence'.

Lieutenant B. of the 2nd Queen's noted the utter exhaustion of his men:

On reaching [Mundell's farm] the troops were in a state of utter exhaustion, having been under arms, in patrol order, since midnight without food, and, with little intermission, warmly engaged with the enemy from daylight. This, too, after a day's march of eighteen hours over a mountainous and harassing country, under a burning sun.

Such indeed was the state of fatigue in which the men were, that, in more than one instance, the skirmishers, when ordered to halt for a moment whilst under fire, dropped asleep, through sheer inability to keep themselves awake, and were supposed by their officers to have been killed. Notwithstanding these hardships, the men, one and all, bore them admirably, and not a single murmur was ever heard.[24]

The wounded men were placed on wagons to be sent to Post Retief but, by the time they were ready to leave, it was getting too late so it was decided to postpone the journey until the morrow.[25]

15 October

Fortunately for the men, the brigades stayed at the ruined Mundell's farm all day, giving them a much-needed rest, for it took that long to fetch a fresh supply of ammunition from Post Retief. The Khoikhoi rebels again carried out cavalry movements well outside gun-shot range.[26]

In the afternoon Lieutenant Norris was buried in the north-east corner of a small patch of bush near the skeleton of a long-dead elephant.[27] Lieutenant King attended:

> The corpse lay by the side of the open grave, sewn up in a blanket through which oozed the blood from his death wound; around stood uncovered a reverend crowd of officers and men: grey-headed colonels, a host of younger, bronzed and weather-beaten faces . . . the soldier-like old General, with his snow-white hair and drooping, grey moustache. The 'funeral party' of the 6th, their red coats patched with leather, canvas and cloth of all colours, with straw hats and wideawakes, long beards, tattered trowsers and broken boots revealing stockingless feet, leaning their sun-burnt cheeks on the butts of their 'arms reversed' . . . Scarcity of ammunition prevented the volley being fired over the grave, and we turned away and dispersed in silence.[28]

16 October

Fordyce's brigade at Mundell's farm was called at 2 a.m. in a pitch-dark and bitterly cold morning; they had then to wait unfed for an hour before moving off. The 91st were in the lead, then came the 74th and the 12th, followed by the levies and pack horses; once again the enemy's predilection for attacking the rear seems to have been overlooked. The brigade marched over the hill to the west where the mounted rebels had drilled the previous evening. The enemy was not to be surprised for Lieutenant King noticed a large fire burning ahead, signifying that their approach had been noticed.[29]

Somewhere near to the entrance to the Waterkloof, the brigade descended by a steep rocky pass. In the dim light of early dawn they were barely able to see the ground and the men slipped from rock to rock or slid on their backsides down the sheer, gravelly slopes. By sunrise the infantry had reached the ruins of Nel's farm, and there they halted to wait for the mules and pack horses. Lieutenant King had time to walk through Nel's derelict garden, which, it being spring, was full of vines, bananas, oranges, lemons, tangerines, pomegranates, as well as fig, peach and almond trees, their blossoms scenting the still morning air.

It had begun to drizzle when, at 6 a.m., the brigade turned eastwards and resumed its march. This was Lieutenant King's first visit to the Waterkloof and he found it a 'beautifully wooded valley, which was shut in by high mountains, half covered by the fleecy clouds resting on their bush-covered heights, the broad path, cut through a perfect grove of flowering bushes, followed the course of a winding, rocky burn up the centre of the glen'.[30]

As they marched, the rain gradually ceased and the clouds slowly lifted, revealing lofty krantzes rising from the dark bush above. When the sun broke through the clouds King felt as if he were on a road winding through a park in Scotland, expecting at every turn to come in sight of a mansion. Instead, the melancholy ruins of two more farmhouses were passed, their blackened heaps a sharp contrast to their blossom-filled orchards.

Many dead bodies of the enemy, who had been killed by the shelling two days before, were found on either side of the track close to the bush. Clouds of flies rose with a startling buzz from corpses which lay broiling in the hot sun, some on their faces in the long grass, others with legs drawn up and their swollen features exposed. King counted eighteen bodies near the road.[31]

Fordyce now deployed his brigade in an attempt to clear the insurgents out of the bush. The Port Elizabeth and Peddie Mfengu and the Beaufort West Levy were sent to scour the south side of the Waterkloof right up to the krantzes, while the Fort Beaufort Mfengu were sent to the northern slope. Two companies of the 91st were extended across the floor of the valley, advancing through the scattered bush in line with the levies up the mountainsides. The 12th and the 74th, together with the mounted forces, followed along the wagon track.

Many huts were found abandoned, with fires still burning in the centre of their mud floors. Half-ground coffee was found on flat grinding stones, proving that shop goods were still being obtained, but the remains of freshly chewed roots suggested that all was not well with their commissariat. The huts were set on fire and within a few minutes were roaring and crackling, their flames scorching the trees under which they had been built.[32]

The ascent from the valley to the Horseshoe was by the slip-path used the previous July. Private Scott found 'grate [sic] trees throwen [sic] in our path for a stumblainblock [sic] that the Kaffirs thought that it would [pro] long our time and they might get a better chance to fire at us'.[33] To cover the ascent, Fordyce ordered the Beaufort West Levy and some of the Mfengu to sweep round to the right of his column while the Fort Beaufort Mfengu were sent into the bush on the left. By 1.30 p.m. the 91st and all but one company of the 74th had emerged from the bush and were forming up in column on the Horseshoe, when the enemy fired a volley and then rushed in with assegais to attack the rear company of the 74th and, behind them, the 12th Regiment and the pack horses.

The suddenness of the attack caused the 12th, who were supposed to guard the rear, to panic and bolt out of the bush, past the 74th and into the open, leaving the Light Company of the 74th to bear the brunt of the attack. Private Alexander Leitch was killed immediately while Lance-Corporal Robert McAlister lay wounded on the ground, struggling with four Ngqika. Lieutenant John Gordon ran back to help him and succeeded in shooting one Ngqika and wounding another before he received support and the other two were driven off. McAlister's face was severely cut by assegais and his skull was so battered by blows by Ngqika women with knobkerries that little hope was held for his recovery.[34] He lived, however, but was intellectually incapacitated for the rest of his days. Meanwhile, the Light Company was in a dangerous position. The men had to take cover in old saw pits and behind trees, but were hemmed in by the enemy and could not get out. Somehow a message reached the general and a troop of the CMR under Captain Carey came to their rescue.[35]

At 8 a.m. that misty morning, after seeing the wagons with the wounded off to Post Retief, General Somerset and Lieutenant-Colonel Michel moved off with their brigades to the Horseshoe. They first headed south to the brow of Mundell's Krantz, which Baines found to be an immense cliff with a chasm in its centre and columns on either side, like the portal of some ruined castle. The voices of Fordyce's invisible Mfengu came up from the depths below, while rocks, playfully dislodged by Mfengu near him, were heard thundering and crashing through the bush long after they were lost to view. Here the brigades turned eastwards along the ridge overlooking the Waterkloof, marching parallel with Fordyce's brigade, which could be seen whenever the mist cleared. Some of the Mfengu entered the Waterkloof bush from above, destroying huts and bringing out about fifteen Ngqika women, who were made to carry the Mfengu plunder from their own households. One of the women, having lost her headgear and being ashamed to appear uncovered before strangers, had picked up a round powder-canister with its pink Hall & Bells label and was carrying it on her head.[36]

It was still misty when they reached the Horseshoe at noon but it cleared soon afterwards. The guns were then promptly turned onto some huts on the eastern promontory where one bold Ngqika was shouting defiance from a roof-top. The shells soon sent dust and splinters flying and drove him off. The 2nd Queen's, with a company of the 6th in support, then went forward and began the systematic destruction of all the huts.

Fordyce, on emerging from the bush, formed his brigade in line facing south, making them lie down behind whatever cover they could find. Two

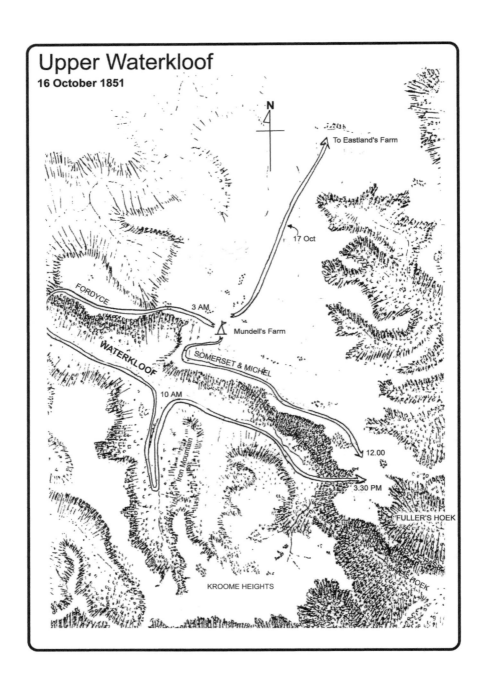

Upper Waterkloof
16 October 1851

N

To Eastland's Farm

17 Oct

FORDYCE

3 AM

Mundell's Farm

WATERKLOOF

SOMERSET & MICHEL

10 AM

Iron Mountain

12.00

3.30 PM

FULLER'S HOEK

HOEK

KROOME HEIGHTS

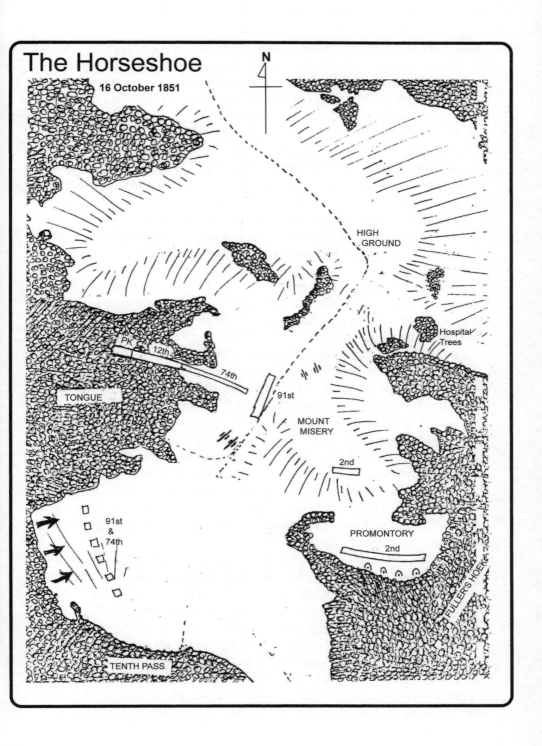

The Horseshoe

16 October 1851

N

HIGH GROUND

Hospital Trees

PK
12th
74th
91st

TONGUE

MOUNT MISERY

2nd

91st
&
74th

PROMONTORY

2nd

FULLER'S HOEK

TENTH PASS

companies of the 91st and No. 3 and the grenadiers of the 74th under Captain Bruce then advanced in skirmishing order towards some low rocks and bush on the southern point of the Horseshoe from which the enemy were delivering intense fire. The general had ordered two guns under Lieutenant Field to bear on the rocks and within a few minutes the enemy fire was silenced, but Baines saw the Ngqika dash out after each shell had exploded and gather up the the liberated balls. Fordyce, who was with the four companies, ordered Bruce to charge the enemy. Bruce drew a Bowie knife from his belt and then, with wild shouts, the men dashed in, regardless of the renewed musket fire, and put the enemy to flight.

McKay saw one man of the 91st in tears. Asking him what was wrong, the man replied that nothing was wrong, he was just overcome by the bravery of the grenadiers' charge: 'Who would not be proud', he said, 'to belong to that company?'

In contrast, McKay found one man from the 12th lying on his face. On turning him over to see where he had been shot, the man looked sideways at him and then stood up. He had lain down through fear. Reticently, McKay says, he 'reproved the man' and attributed the conduct of the 12th, charitably, to the fact that this was their maiden skirmish.[37]

Baines, who was sketching near the guns, found the scene before him dramatic. Troops on three sides of the Horseshoe were keeping up an incessant fire, which was being answered by the enemy from behind trees and rocks within the bush. The rattle of musketry was frequently swamped by the thunder of the guns and the dull boom of the shells. Wounded men were being carried on stretchers by their comrades up the centre of the Horseshoe towards the aid station in the area called the 'Hospital Trees' just below the high ground. The CMR were kept busy wherever the enemy appeared and were successful in dispersing them, although a few horses were lost; one stood wounded in the middle of the Horseshoe all afternoon, neither side thinking him worth the risk of bringing in.

By 2 p.m. the enemy's fire had quietened down and preparations were made to retire for the day. As the troops withdrew towards the north, companies of skirmishers were thrown out on either side as guards. As each company withdrew from the field, the rear skirmishers would then have to run to avoid the fire from the enemy warriors who had swiftly occupied the abandoned positions. The Mfengu formed the rear guard to ward off the fast-approaching Ngqika. The two lines kept up a spirited but ill-directed fire, the bullets striking up clouds of red dust many yards wide of their mark. At length the Ngqika became too numerous for the Mfengu, who turned and ran, hotly pursued by their enemy. The leading Ngqika had nearly caught up with the slowest of the Mfengu when Baines and Captain A.H.P. Stuart Wortley of the CMR fired at the Ngqika with their rifles. Baines used up his last two bullets and missed, as did Wortley, but by now – fortunately for the Mfengu – the Ngqika had given up the chase.[38]

Unexpectedly, as they marched away, the enemy opened fire from a narrow belt of bush to the left, just north of the Horseshoe. Skirmishers of the 74th were sent forward and sharp firing ensued from both sides. Lieutenant King was with the skirmishers when a large ball, with a mass of about thirty grams, struck the rock on which he stood and with a loud whirring sound flattened itself in a small crevice at his feet;[39] another ball severely wounded Private John Hickey, who died at Post Retief on 23 October. The 6th now came up in support of the skirmishers, allowing the 74th to charge the belt of bush, whereupon the enemy threw down their muskets and fled into its depths.

No sooner had the column re-formed than it came under fire from another belt of bush to the front. As the men approached it, one of the 12th was injured, four men of the 91st were severely wounded, Sergeant James Scott and Private Philip Fritzland of the levies were killed, and two others were wounded. This area of bush was then cleared, several of the enemy being killed. They were found to be Khoikhoi rebels in possession of double-barrelled service carbines; they were almost certainly deserters from the CMR, judging by the unusual accuracy of their fire.

Suddenly it was very quiet, with not an enemy to be seen. The bugle sounded the recall and the troops formed column on the open ground. They marched at 4 p.m. for their bivouac at Mundell's farm, the men bearing their dead and wounded on stretchers. John Burgess supported the body of his brother on the limber of one of the guns.[40]

Lieutenant-Colonel Michel, with two guns and the 2nd, 6th and CMR, formed the rear guard. They had not retired more than a kilometre when, from the very bush they had just left totally deserted, about twenty Khoikhoi emerged and fired half a dozen shots at them, which, however, fell a few hundred metres short. One of the guns was hastily unlimbered and a shell sent amongst the rebels, killing several and driving the rest into the bush.

Although exhausted from the day's work the men immediately did all they could to take care of their wounded and dying comrades. The hospital tent was pitched and single blankets were placed on the ground for beds; canteens or stones covered with handkerchiefs were used as pillows. The horses having been fed and picketed for the night, each man wearily rolled himself in his blanket and fell asleep.[41]

17 October

At five in the morning, while the mist was still thick on the ground, the dead were buried. Their bodies had been wrapped in their blankets and they were placed in graves dug a little below the bush where Norris lay. The service was read by the duty officer and afterwards large fires were made over the graves to disguise them from hyenas and grave-robbing Ngqika.

The mist still lay thick as they marched at 7 a.m. to new camping grounds. The absence of water on the Horseshoe was the reason for not camping there, and now even the stream at Mundell's was proving too small for all the troops, horses and cattle. After an eight-kilometre march northwards they formed camp at the edge of a detached strip of bush with a stream flowing below it, near the ruins of the homestead on Eastland's farm 'Kaal Plaats'. The skeleton of James Eastland, who was murdered there on 28 December 1850, was still lying where it had fallen. His remains were collected and buried in a grave dug in his own garden.

Supplies were scarce and there was little to eat except for some bad meat from Post Retief and a few starved cattle. After being three days without a change of clothing, Lieutenant King greatly enjoyed washing in the reed-lined stream, 'in spite of the tepid waters and the quantities of immense bull frogs which we surprised basking on the slimy reedy banks'.[42]

The casualties for the campaign were: Lieutenant Norris and six men killed; Captain Addison, Ensign Ricketts and twenty-three men wounded.[43]

Second October Campaign

The plan for the next stage of the campaign was for Somerset's 1st and Fordyce's 2nd brigades to march directly to the Horseshoe from their camp ground at Eastland's farm; some of the guns and all the cavalry were to take up their position on the high ground a little to the north-west of the Hospital Trees. The remaining guns were to shell Fuller's Hoek while Fordyce's brigade attacked the enemy all round the Horseshoe.

Michel's 3rd Brigade was to march from his Blinkwater camp and force its way up Arie's Hoek to join the general's forces on the Horseshoe.

Nesbitt's brigade would march from the Blinkwater camp through Schelm Kloof, then climb Wolf's Back Ridge and join up with the general.[44]

23 October

It was dark, cloudy, cold and misty as Somerset's and Fordyce's brigades left Eastland's farm at 4 a.m. to march south along the edge of the Blinkwater escarpment towards Mount Misery. At daybreak, the clouds lifted and a fine view was presented of small, bushy, mist-filled kloofs leading into the valley below, colourfully tinted in shades of pink and orange by the rays of the rising sun.[45]

Some enemy horses were seen on the edge of the bush where they had been left out to graze during the night and had been left too long. Mounted men of the brigade gave chase and captured the horses without anyone getting harmed by the musket shots being fired from the mist. On reaching the high ground, a group of Ngqika was seen on Wolf's Back Ridge. As their presence there might have been for the purpose of opposing Colonel Nesbitt's brigade, which was seen slowly making its way up Schelm Kloof, Somerset ordered the artillery to fire at them and after several shells had fallen they dispersed.[46]

More of the enemy were seen running across the Horseshoe towards the tongue of bush. The Light and No. 7 companies of the 74th, under Captain Walter Douglas P. Patton, were sent after them and, extending in skirmish order, the bush was approached with the Light Company leading and No. 7 forming the right flank. Sergeant McKay, with the Light Company, passed near a large, black greyhound, which barked furiously at him. He was tempted to shoot it but did not, on the advice of Lieutenant Gordon, who suggested that the dog's master would not be far away. Private Peter Gordon of No. 7 did shoot it – sure enough, moments later a second report was heard and Private Gordon fell dead.[47]

The two companies came under steady fire from the enemy, who were strongly posted behind a fold in the ground at the edge of the bush. The companies charged the bush, the enemy retreated and soon their swarthy forms, mingling with the deep shadows, were lost to the soldiers coming from the blinding sunlight. Turning left, the two companies emerged onto the open ground and Patton was now ordered to burn a group of huts further to the south and dislodge the enemy posted there, the rest of the 74th being held in reserve near derelict gardens. The two mule guns were in the meantime brought to a position behind the reserve and from there shelled the huts and surrounding bush.[48]

As the two 74th companies approached the huts, they were fired on, not from the front where the shells had done their deadly work, but from the bush to their left. Lieutenant King had the task of setting the huts in the open on fire and with six volunteers proceeded to do so. His task was not easy because the reeds were green and needed a great deal of heat to make them burn.[49] By the time half the huts were smouldering, the thick smoke was making matters very difficult for Patton and his men, who were trying to enter the bush. In addition to being under musket fire, the smoke, blown by a strong wind, was making it impossible to see anything of the enemy.

Upper Waterkloof
23 October 1851

N

Eastland's Farm
4 AM

Mundell's Farm

FORDYCE & SOMERSET

FORDYCE & SOMERSET

2 PM

9 AM

2 PM

SCHELM KLOOF

WOLFS BACK RIDGE

NESBITT

9 AM

FULLER'S HOEK

ARGYLL PASS

ARIE'S HOEK

MICHEL

KROOME HEIGHTS

One of Patton's men was killed and Private William Stewart was badly wounded in the thigh. Another man was on the point of firing when a ball hit the mechanism of his musket, locking the hammer at full cock and lacerating his fore-finger. The man went to the rear, where the doctor attended him, whereupon the man asked for another musket so that he could rejoin his comrades. Fordyce, though pleased with his willingness, ordered him to stay back.

Patton at this stage thought the task beyond the capability of his small force and ordered the 'retire' in spite of objections from both lieutenants Gordon and Charles Breton. At the gardens, an irate Fordyce ordered Patton to return to attack the huts again. It was on this return trip that Ensign Robert Lowe told Sergeant McKay to take a man's name for extra drill, as he had not responded to an order with alacrity. To McKay the notion of punishing 'Pat' Durden was, in view of all the hardships the men were suffering, absurd. It seemed to McKay that the order pushed Durden past his breaking point, for he gave Lowe a dirty look, muttered something which nobody caught and then ran ahead into the bush where the enemy fire was thickest. Durden was dead when they found him.[50]

The rest of the huts in the open were now set on fire and Patton seemed to have made some progress towards disposing of those in the bush, when his courage failed him once again. He sent for McKay, who found him crouching in a hole in the ground: a very undignified position, McKay thought, for an officer. A thoroughly disgruntled McKay was then ordered to run back to the gardens through enemy fire to ask for reinforcements. His conversation with Fordyce went something like this:

F.   Go back and tell Capt. Patton to continue attacking that position until I relieve him.
M.   There are many men killed and wounded, Sir.
F.   I don't care if the Captain and all his men were killed and wounded, they must hold their position.
M.   The ammunition is nearly expended.
F.   Let me see your pouch.

Luckily, McKay's pouch had only three rounds out of sixty left, so Fordyce sent two companies to assist Patton and ordered the artillery to renew their bombardment.[51]

Baines, who was with Lieutenant Campbell at the guns, saw one shell burst so exactly on target that the shadow of its smoke completely covered the group of Ngqika at whom it had been aimed.[52]

Colonel Michel's brigade, consisting of the 2nd Queen's, the 6th and the 91st, had left Blinkwater station early that morning. They took the difficult route through the dense bush of Arie's Hoek, going up the rocky gorge towards Tenth Pass, then, just before reaching the actual pass itself, they cut northwards and, under smart fire from the enemy, came out of the bush on the south side of the Horseshoe.

Lieutenant B. found the going bad enough without being fired on by Somerset's gun's as well: one shell had actually burst almost at the feet of the advancing skirmishers. It was not until their buglers had sounded the 'cease fire' for a considerable time that the shelling ceased.[53] By 9 a.m. the vanguard of Michel's brigade had, on Somerset's orders, advanced towards the huts where Patton was unhappily engaged. Just before the rear of Michel's brigade cleared the bush, however, it was attacked by the enemy. The 91st wheeled about and, after a sharp skirmish in which three of their men were wounded, drove the rebels back. The 91st remained behind to hold the bush between Tenth Pass and Argyll Pass while the rest of the brigade reinforced the four companies under Patton.

After two hours of continuous roaring of muskets and booming of guns, the enemy's forces were driven from all their positions around the Horseshoe and some were seen retreating over the open ground beyond Tenth Pass going towards the Kroome Range.[54]

The 60th (King's Royal Rifle Corps), under Lieutenant-Colonel Cosby Lewis Nesbitt, had only disembarked at East London on 3 October 1851.[55] They were now to experience their first encounter with the Ngqika in Southern Africa. Nesbitt was fortunate in having with him 150 men of the 45th Regiment. They were veterans, having been in South Africa since the 1846–7 War of the Axe, and had learned how to fight the Xhosa through bitter experience. He had, in addition, the support of the navy. There had been a great shortage of troops at the Cape in 1851 and the call had gone out to the navy for volunteers; a hundred seamen and marines had responded, and they formed part of Nesbitt's brigade under Lieutenant Harris, R.N.

Nesbitt marched his men from Blinkwater Post northwards along the Blinkwater River until he reached the eastern end of Wolf's Back Ridge. Here he swung to the west and entered Schelm Kloof. General Somerset states in his report that the Rifles were hotly engaged and moved up in skirmish order in fine style along the northern face of Wolf's Back Ridge, receiving the enemy's fire and driving them up the hill. Nesbitt joined Somerset on the high ground at 9 a.m., having captured fifty-nine head of cattle.[56] His losses were one marine, Private A. Scott, dangerously wounded (he died four days later) and one of the Rifles, Private James Owen of E Company, who was wounded in his left arm. Amputation being necessary, his arm was immediately taken off in the field.[57]

The Horseshoe
23 October 1851

A rebel Khoikhoi was captured rather unexpectedly. The man was handed over to the Mfengu to guard as a prisoner but these independent levies hanged him from a yellowwood tree and continued to practise throwing assegais at him long after he was dead.[58]

Towards noon, as more and more of the enemy retreated towards the Kroome Range, Somerset ordered the troops, who had been on the move since 4 a.m., to halt for breakfast. All the brigades united in the centre of the Horseshoe to eat a meal of biscuit and beef while fresh supplies of ammunition were issued to all regiments from the reserves on the pack mules.[59]

The two Highlanders, Privates Peter Gordon and Frederick Durden, were buried on the highest point of the high ground and stones were piled above their grave. Sergeant McKay was horrified the next day: 'The bodies of Gordon and others . . . were found disinterred, denuded of every vestige of clothing, and brutally disfigured.'[60]

After a halt of about two hours the brigades separated. Nesbitt's, having moved up in light order without blankets, returned to Blinkwater by the route they had come, their return being covered by the guns.[61] Captain Ayliff and his Port Elizabeth Mfengu went down into the Blinkwater Valley to waylay any cattle that the enemy might try to carry off. With the copious rains, many springs were flowing well enough to provide sufficient water and so Michel's brigade was ordered to form a standing bivouac on the Horseshoe. This was the first time it was to be occupied for a twenty-four-hour period and, although no one made much of it at the time, this was the way that the fastness was to be successfully held, by permanently blockading the enemy and cutting off their supplies of food and grazing.

Somerset and Fordyce returned with their brigades to Mundell's farm and on the way were fired on from a belt of bush on the Waterkloof side. While the main body continued its march, a flank patrol of the 74th and the CMR went to deal with the nuisance. The snipers turned out to be few in number and the only harm they did was to wound a couple of horses. As the shadows of the evening grew long, the brigades entered the lines of burnt-out fires on their old ground. Lieutenant King was feeling the effects of his exposure to the wet and cold and, in spite of great fatigue, was kept awake by the acute pains of rheumatism.[62]

24 October

During the night it began to rain again and then the rain turned to sleet, so it was a miserable collection of men who left their bivouac the next morning. As they marched towards Mount Misery, several large fires were seen on the Kroome Heights, on the south side of the Waterkloof, the smoke hanging low in the damp air. The tops of the mountains to the north were white with the snow that had fallen during the night and a breeze from the mountains blowing on their saturated uniforms made the men, even while marching, absolutely numb with cold.

On Mount Misery they found Michel's brigade even worse off. The chill wind had blown all night over the unprotected plain, which was now covered with snow. The trenches, which they had made for shelter before the rain came, had filled with water.

The Mfengu, although nearly naked, were seemingly unaffected by the cold. They had been amusing themselves by hunting around and had captured and killed a Khoikhoi, a spy they said. To celebrate the event and perhaps to keep themselves warm, they gathered in a circle and performed a war dance. Lieutenant King was an enthralled spectator.[63]

A consultation took place among the commanders as to the practicability of attacking in the prevailing weather, for at 11 a.m. the rain was still pouring down. Afterwards, Somerset sent everyone back to their bivouacs.

The Ngqika had visited the ground at Mundell's farm during the troops' absence and had had a feast. The branches and grass that the men had used for bedding had been dragged to the fires and there the discarded entrails of the oxen slaughtered the previous evening had been roasted. Not a scrap of flesh remained, even the cartilage and the softer portions of discarded bones had been gnawed by the Ngqika's powerful jaws. The ground itself, after the incessant rain and trampling of men, horses and cattle, had become a bog into which the men's boots sank and stuck. Gusts of wind sweeping down the shallow valley drove the rain into their faces and sent ashes from the spluttering fires swirling in all directions.[64]

Private William Stewart, who had been shot in the thigh the day before, died at Post Retief on 12 November. McKay blamed his death on the carelessness of the surgeon.[65]

The casualties for this campaign were three men killed and seven men wounded.[66]

Chapter 9

The Writing on the Wall

The Last October Campaign

The plan for the next stage of the campaign was for Fordyce's brigade to proceed round the western spur of the heights into the Waterkloof Valley and march up its length to attack the new position of the enemy on the Kroome Heights. Meanwhile, Michel's brigade would occupy the extent of bush between Fuller's Hoek and the Waterkloof.[1]

26 October
Somerset ordered the brigades to march although the incessant rain was still pouring down. Fordyce's brigade mustered without bugle call about 4 a.m., the men taking their places in silence. Lieutenant King particularly noticed the 'blazing fires casting a bright, ruddy light on the dripping ranks, standing motionless in the heavy rain in which the men had lain all night without a murmur'.[2]

Fordyce moved off at 5 a.m. and after an hour's march through long, sodden grass, descended by a steep, rocky path into the Waterkloof, near the entrance to Nel's farm. After re-forming their ranks the brigade, with the 12th in the lead, proceeded up the Waterkloof to Brown's farm. Here they turned right into the kloof leading to the south and presently came to a group of huts 'prettily situated' and almost hidden in the bush. The Ngqika occupants had escaped just in time and only one or two who were lurking in the bush were caught by the Mfengu. More were seen creeping on hands and knees through the bush on the hill opposite and mounted men were sent to head them off.

The brigade then slowly climbed up the side of the kloof along a steep, winding path. By the time it reached the top of the Kroome Range the rain had stopped, the sun was shining and everyone was unbearably hot, even though only a few hours before it had seemed to Lieutenant King that he could never be warm again.[3]

Upper Waterkloof
26 October 1851

N

FORDYCE
26th Oct
5 AM
Mundell's Farm

MUNDELL'S
KRANZ

WATERKLOOF

SOMERSET

Iron Mountain

MICHEL

SOMERSET

MICHEL

FORDYCE

KROOME HEIGHTS

Turning towards the east, the brigade came to a belt of bush on their left and Fordyce ordered the 74th's Light Company under Captain Patton to form a left flank as they marched through it. Predictably, Patton, moving a little too far from the column, soon lost his way. Torn by thorny bushes, tripping over creepers, unable to see the sun, the Light Company had not the slightest idea of where they were going. Sergeant McKay was contemptuous: instead of cheering on his men, Patton fell back into the middle of the company, where he spent his time lamenting the situation they were in and their plight should the enemy appear. Meanwhile Fordyce, who was furious at the loss of his flank protection, had the Light Company's 'call' and 'assembly' sounded repeatedly, and at last they were heard. Once more in the clear, Patton now ordered his company to march at 'attention', keep their dressing in the ranks, their heads up and their shoulders back. This the men refused to do and hooted at him. Patton reported their behaviour to Fordyce but he, knowing Patton and having heard what had happened from Lieutenant John Gordon and Sergeant McKay, took no action.[4]

The brigade, without having seen any concentration of the enemy, halted when they reached the shallow valley on the Kroome Heights, a place memorable for the 8 September fiasco.

At 7 a.m. that same morning, Baines's opinion was that the day would have been better spent warming himself in front of a fire. Yet here he was with the CMR on the way to Mount Misery, where he was glad to find that the Mfengu had lit several fires in the shelter of the Hospital Trees. Everyone crowded round the fires, including the artillery men, who had to be called back whenever their services were required.

From the Hospital Trees, Baines saw Michel's brigade approach the bush on the southern point of the Horseshoe and, at a signal, dash into it with defiant shouts. They succeeded in driving off the enemy and were soon busy destroying the huts which had again been rebuilt. A grenadier of the 6th Regiment was carried to the Hospital Trees dying from a bullet in his head fired by a Khoikhoi rebel.

The Ngqika were gathering on a krantz near Fordyce's brigade so the artillery men shot off a few shells with the longest fuses and the optimum elevation of the guns. The aim was good and they dispersed. The CMR, apparently with nothing to do, camped on a promontory near a spring which, as a result of the rains, was strong enough to water the horses.[5]

The 91st, on Somerset's orders, went through Tenth Pass and joined Fordyce's brigade. This augmented brigade then penetrated the Tenth Pass bush and scoured the southern slopes thoroughly. Shots were exchanged,

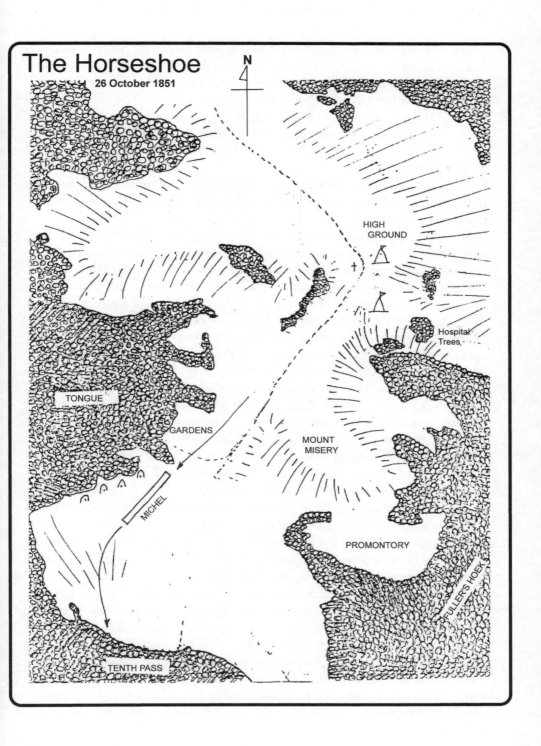

The Horseshoe
26 October 1851

N

HIGH
GROUND

Hospital
Trees

TONGUE

GARDENS

MICHEL

MOUNT
MISERY

PROMONTORY

FULLERS HOEK

TENTH PASS

killing a few of the enemy, and some horses were captured.[6] Simultaneously, Michel's brigade searched the northern slopes. After traversing the bush and encountering no more opposition, both brigades returned in a heavy shower of rain to their bivouacs, Fordyce's with the 91st to the shallow valley on the Kroome Heights, Michel's to Mount Misery. The general, with the CMR and the artillery, formed a separate camp below Michel's.[7]

27 October
Before dawn Fordyce's brigade entered Tenth Pass where, on his orders, a piper struck up 'Hey, Johnny Cope' to cheer on the men and let the enemy know that Highlanders were coming.

Near the top of Tenth Pass, on the Horseshoe side, many corpses of the enemy killed on 14 October were found, creating an intolerable stench. It was impossible to remove them and, as some lay right in the centre of the narrow track, the men had to pass by in single file. A little further on they found the clean-picked skeleton of a sergeant of the 12th who had also been killed that day. He was recognised by the fragments of his red coat, now torn to pieces and trampled in the dirt by hyenas. Just at the edge of the bush, in the open, more black corpses were found as well as the putrefying carcases of four horses; King was nearly ill and hurried to pass.

The brigade was now on the south-western edge of the Horseshoe, on the site of the principal enemy village. The ground was covered with the remains of burnt and levelled huts, native utensils, ornaments, burnt dogs and horses, hundreds of flattened bullets and fragments of exploded shells that had torn up the rocks around, with, here and there, the corpse of an Ngqika or Khoikhoi rebel. On the Horseshoe side of the huts he found a line of small stone breastworks made of loose rocks about one metre high and six metres long. They were almost invisible from a hundred metres away because of their similarity to the rocky ground on which they stood.[8]

The brigade halted long enough to give King time to examine the village, his interest being sufficiently aroused to endure the hot sun, which drove the men to shelter under blankets stretched on piled muskets.

At noon a mule wagon containing meal was sent over from headquarters, on the high ground. As they had eaten nothing since the previous evening, the food was greedily accepted. The meal was mixed with water in their mess tins and they were just trying to eat the 'porridge' when orders arrived for the brigade to support the 2nd Queen's, which was hotly engaged above the more southerly of the two krantzes overlooking Fuller's Hoek. Mess tins in hand and eating as they went, the brigade extended behind the Queen's and lay down amongst the loose rocks. The firing was heavy on both sides and stray

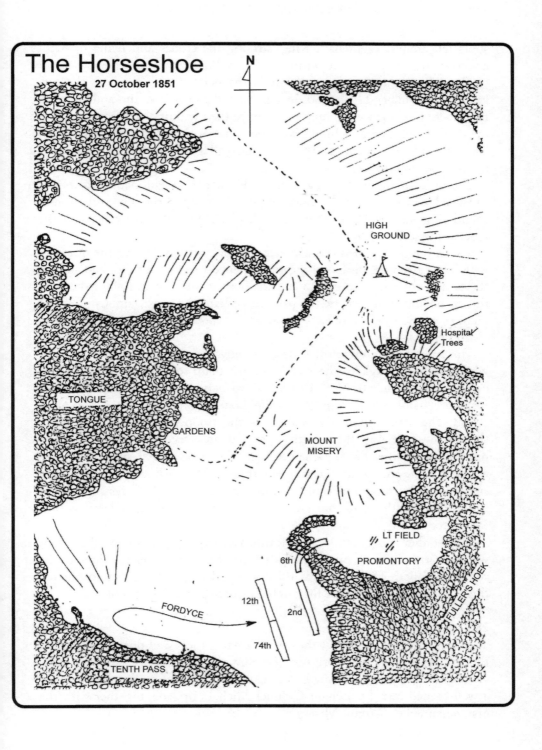

shots fell around Lieutenant King, striking the stones and flying off with angry whirrs. They lay there for more than an hour.[9]

The 6th now took up a position in the belt of bush dividing the two krantzes of Fuller's Hoek, and opened up a flanking fire. The 2nd Queen's, their faces begrimed with gunpowder, were then withdrawn, having lost one man killed and leaving behind a wounded quartermaster of the levies; he had been seized by the enemy and the mocking call 'Bring a stretcher' was heard, but no one could reach him.

The guns of the 2nd Brigade, under Lieutenant Field, had been moved to the edge of the northern krantz to rake the front of the one to the south; round shot and shell were hurled with precision whenever groups of the rebels were seen.

Two more guns joined those already on the northern krantz; the 6th were withdrawn from the bush and the guns opened fire, hurling shot and shell at the face of the southern krantz and the bush in front of it. Baines sketched this scene and from this sketch painted perhaps the most famous of all his pictures of the war, the several versions of *Attacking Maqoma's Stronghold in Fuller's Hoek*.[10]

The 2nd Queen's was now ordered to advance through the belt of bush while Fordyce's brigade advanced along the plain towards Fuller's Hoek. A cannon ball, ricocheting off a rock, passed between the 74th and the 12th, fortunately doing no harm as it went bounding along with a humming sound. The artillery fire was halted as the troops entered Fuller's Bush, the enemy receiving them with yells and an irregular volley. From the promontory, Baines heard loud cheers and the rattle of well-sustained fire as a line of white smoke advanced slowly through the bush and the flames and smoke from burning huts came up from the depths of the forest. Finally, as the troops withdrew, all four guns again opened fire on the enemy as they attempted to follow.

One soldier was killed in this skirmish. Many Ngqika, followed by their women carrying goods on their heads, were seen going over the ridge to the south of Fuller's Hoek towards the Kroome Range.[11] Somerset considered this trek to be evidence that they were evacuating the Waterkloof.

28 October
The next day, confident that they were leaving a job well done, the general, the artillery and Fordyce's brigade went down to Blinkwater Post. From there some of the officers, including Lieutenant King, went on to Fort Beaufort for a well-earned rest. Lieutenant-Colonel Michel's brigade, together with the 91st, remained on Mount Misery.[12]

The casualties for this stage of the October campaigns were one officer (Lieutenant Guirrea of an Mfengu levy) and three men killed and two men wounded.

The weather on the Kroome Heights remained very poor for the remaining days of October, Lieutenant B. remarking:

> The nights of the 28th and 29th, and the whole of the 30th, were very inclement with both the first and third brigades; frost, snow, hail, rain, and violent storm succeeding each other without intermission. All operations were consequently at a stand-still, and the troops had become so inefficient, through the continued prevalence of this severe weather, that it was decided to withdraw the troops to the Blinkwater station, at which a standing camp had been formed.[13]

The weather remained appalling, with continued torrents of rain preventing any further attacks. So bad, indeed, became the state of the camping ground at Blinkwater Post that the divisions were forced to return to Fort Beaufort on the 31st, where they 'occupied four large barrack-rooms'. A few of the men were fortunate enough to be issued with commissariat boots and trousers.

What was annoying to the general, however, was good news for the exhausted, hungry men, who were able to begin recovering their strength in this enforced hiatus. They stayed for three days, the thirteen officers of the 2nd Queen's sleeping in a billiard room, a few on the table and the rest on the floor, wrapped only in their patrol blankets. On 4 November they were off again to the Blinkwater camp, ready to launch yet another attack.[14]

Despatches from London

Earl Grey had arranged, in his despatch of 14 June 1851, for Sir Harry Smith to make use of one of the battalions of the 12th Regiment then serving at Mauritius. The governor had immediately sent a steamer to that island to bring back the reserve battalion of the 12th for service at the Cape.[15]

On 14 July, Earl Grey next wrote to Sir Harry Smith advising him that the home government had determined that a further injection of troops was necessary. Accordingly, the 2nd battalion of the 60th (King's Royal Rifle Corps) was already on its way to the Cape.[16] It would arrive on station in October. The 12th (The Prince of Wales's) Royal Regiment of Lancers also arrived in that month.[17] A summary of imperial troops on the frontier at mid-October, excluding artillery and engineers, was summarised thus:

	Officers	Men
12th Lancers	24	425
2nd Regiment	24	652
6th Regiment	23	654
12th Regiment	20	478
60th Rifles	25	651
73rd Regiment	24	633
74th Regiment	25	651
91st Regiment	21	651
Totals	186	4795

In addition, Colonel Cloete reported the total manpower of the CMR at that time as forty-two officers and 859 other ranks.[18] Grey had also announced the embarkation for the Cape of the 43rd (Monmouthshire) Regiment.[19]

Less encouraging were the Secretary's critical comments, which by now were becoming increasingly frequent. Major Warden, Resident in the Orange River Sovereignty, was a continuing target and it became clear that Grey was anxious to see the back of him.[20] Despite the heavy hints, Smith continued to praise Warden and defended him at every turn. Smith was also advised that the home government had determined to abandon the Orange River Sovereignty, an acquisition by Smith which they deeply regretted, and allow it to revert to the Boers.[21]

Closer to home, Grey was beginning to pierce the smokescreen created by Smith's half truths regarding the progress of the war. This was, in large measure, the result of statements made, for example, by Jack Bisset to a Parliamentary Select Committee sitting in London.[22] As well as Bisset, others called to give evidence to the committee included Sir Andries Stockenström,[23] Sir George Napier, Sir Peregrine Maitland[24] and the Rev. Henry Renton. Such external contributions led to the following:

> It is with great concern that I have received this intelligence, showing that much less progress than I hoped had been made towards the subjugation of the insurgent Kaffirs, and that they had succeeded in inflicting such severe injury on the colonists by their depredations.[25]

In his despatch of 14 November, the Secretary observed:

> It is with the deepest concern I have received this intelligence; by which it appears that there was, when you wrote, even less prospect than before of an immediate termination of the war; and that Her Majesty's forces have suf-

fered considerable loss in the conflicts which have taken place, without leading to any important advantage being gained over the enemy. I trust, however, that you may prove to have been right in the opinion you express in your despatch of the 8th of September last, as to the results you would be enabled to obtain by the reinforcements which had arrived, and those which you hourly expected, and which must long ere this have reached you.[26]

Both of the above despatches also mentioned Major Warden in somewhat disparaging terms and the last one approved of the governor's decision to send Messrs Hogge and Owen to the sovereignty to investigate matters more closely.

The governor made a spirited defence of his conduct of the war in his reply of 18 December 1851.[27] His argument was that the reinforcements that had been sent to him had not by then arrived, that he was still limited to those troops remaining to him after he had sent so many home and that two thousand levies had completed their term of service and wished to return to their homes in the Western Cape.

He need not have added that he faced a formidable opponent, of which a large number were Khoikhoi rebels previously trained in arms by the British as members of levies and the CMR. It seems that he numbered the insurgents at fifteen to twenty thousand, a considerable exaggeration. He noted that:

So long as the insurgents held together and acted in large bodies, they were defeated on forty-five different occasions, between the 24th of December and 21st of October. In these encounters twelve officers were killed and 18 wounded, 195 soldiers killed and 364 wounded, making a total of 589 casualties on our side; while the loss of the enemy was very severe, and he was spoiled of large herds of cattle. So soon as their prophet [Mlanjeni] told the Kafirs to rush into the colony in bands of 'wolves,' as he termed it, portions of the colonial frontier were ravaged, as I predicted would be the case if the population would not turn out; while certain traitorous traders were endeavouring to supply the insurgents with the munitions of war.[28]

He offered the view that it was quite natural for voices to be raised, asking the question, 'Why is this war not at once put an end to?' His answer was that previously he had not had the means to do so (despite his views to the contrary frequently expressed in earlier despatches) but the reinforcements soon arriving would rectify this limitation and would 'rescue the colony from its misery'.

Leopard of Fordyce

6 November

Sergeant McKay hated these 4 a.m. assemblies without bugles, the officers and NCOs moving about in the darkness cursing in undertones, every command demanding silence, the men nervous and excited, confusion everywhere. Then as the brigade marched from Eastland's farm towards Mount Misery, a heavy mist enveloped them, creating further confusion. It cleared at 7 a.m. just as the brigade reached the high ground overlooking the Horseshoe.[29]

To Captain Campbell, the scene at the Horseshoe was ominous: he had never seen so large a force of Ngqika and Khoikhoi gathering together from all directions. Colonel Fordyce, who had just heard that Sutton's men were moving up the Waterkloof, seemed to take very little notice of the enemy, so Campbell rode up to an aide-de-camp. Pointing to the horde, Campbell suggested that the edges of the bush should be shelled by their two guns before the troops entered. Fordyce, looking through his telescope, said Campbell was mistaken and that they were mostly women. 'We will soon find out what they are,' he continued, pointing to the Tongue, 'for I'm going in there with the "Elephants" (the name came from the badge of the 74th) to cover Sutton's advance.' And so he did.[30]

Campbell and his Mfengu were ordered to take possession of the krantz above Fuller's Hoek, presumably to prevent the enemy coming out and attacking the rear of the 74th. The 91st were posted up the slope behind him. The Khoikhoi rebels were just below the brow of the krantz, some not more than twenty paces away, and the Mfengu had to watch out, for they were good shots. Otherwise, it was monotonous work just sitting there and waiting. One Mfengu was eventually killed and three or four men in the 91st were wounded. Campbell could hear the sound of musketry from the direction of the Tongue and, faintly, the cheering of the 74th. Later he heard the rattle of an ambulance wagon and thought to himself that something serious must have happened. However, he had his own problems because his Mfengu suddenly bolted from sheer fright.

An Mfengu pointed a sniper out to Campbell, who took careful aim, waited until the rebel showed himself, and then fired. The man – who was dressed in the full uniform of the CMR, complete with sword – fell backwards over the edge of the krantz. Later still, the Mfengu, on hearing that one of their number had been shot, jumped up and all three hundred of them bolted again, and, of course, the officers had to follow. After a great deal of trouble the Mfengu were brought back and this time Campbell managed to keep them at their post until, to everyone's relief, the bugle sounded the 'retire'.[31]

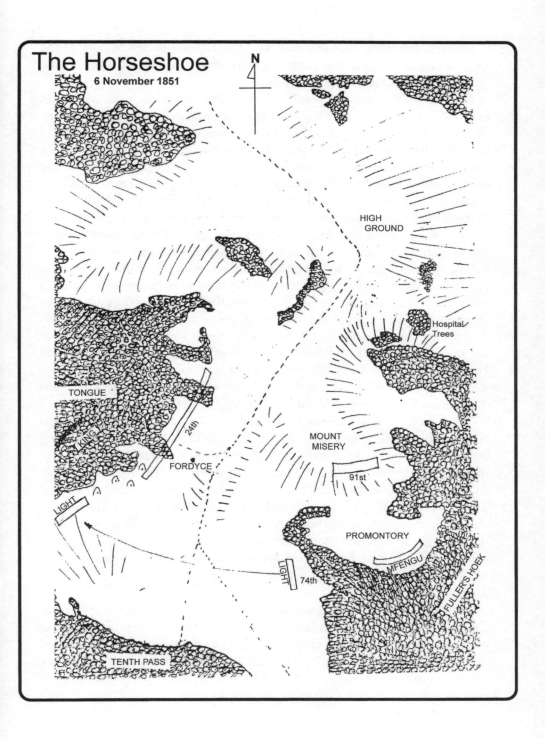

The Horseshoe
6 November 1851

N

HIGH GROUND

Hospital Trees

TONGUE

KING

24th

FORDYCE

MOUNT MISERY

91st

LIGHT

PROMONTORY

MFENGU

FULLERS HOEK

LIGHT

74th

TENTH PASS

Fordyce, extending four companies of the 74th supported by two of the 12th, advanced towards the Tongue and entered the belts of bush on the outskirts without much opposition.

The huts on the southern point had been rebuilt since their destruction on 23 October and Lieutenant King once again led volunteers to set them on fire. He succeeded in burning all the huts to the ground, as well as a large number of bullock hides stored for trading. King had a narrow escape from being shot by the sporadic fire from the bush: one ball whirred past his ears as he was kneeling down to blow on a bunch of lighted grass that he had stuck into the reed wall of a hut – the ball came so close that bits of the clay flew into his face.[32]

After burning the huts the skirmishers were ordered to go deeper into the Tongue, King's company being directed to turn the left flank of the enemy's position on a low krantz which was unapproachable from the front. Fordyce led the flanking movement in person and then, giving final orders, returned to the main body of his regiment to direct their movements into the bush from which the rebels were firing intermittently. He ordered the guns to take up positions nearer the enemy, which they did by advancing about four hundred metres down the slope. With his rifle over his right shoulder, Fordyce left the guns and walked down to the edge of the hollow which runs from Fuller's Hoek to the Tongue. Giving his rifle to an orderly, he shouted in his stentorian voice to Lieutenant Hirzel Carey's No. 2 Company, which was moving too far to its right. In the noise of the firing, even his voice could not be heard so he took off his cap and waved it. Just as he replaced his cap, a bullet hit him in the chest, passing right through his lungs. He staggered and fell. Colour Sergeant McDougal quickly came to his aid and lifted him up. Breathing with difficulty, Fordyce asked to be taken out of the heat of the sun, and called for the surgeon. The men carried him up the slope to the Hospital Trees where Dr Fraser was in attendance. Lieutenant-Colonel Yarborough was at Fordyce's side as his senses began to leave him. His last words were 'Yarborough, Yarborough: look after my Regiment.' Then, apparently without pain, 'one of the best, kindest and bravest men in the British army passed away!'[33] As a result of Fordyce's death, Maqoma was given the praise-name 'Leopard of Fordyce'.[34]

The 74th, momentarily confused by the loss of their leader, recovered as Captain Duff assumed command. Infuriated by the taunting of the rebels, who were mainly Khoikhoi, they charged the bush in front of them, driving the enemy deep into its recesses – though not without loss. Lieutenant Carey, a kinsman of Captain Carey of the CMR, fell dead from a shot through his body; Sergeant William Diamond and a private were also killed and seven men were wounded.

Colonel Yarborough, who now assumed command of the field, ordered the Light Company of the 74th under Lieutenant John Gordon to reinforce their comrades. This company, in which Sergeant McKay served, doubled across the Horseshoe from Fuller's Hoek to the southern point of the Horseshoe, receiving a shower of bullets on the way. Just before they entered the bush, a ball hit Gordon, passing through both thighs. As he fell to the ground, unable to rise, men ran to his aid, but he shouted to them to leave him and continue the charge. This they did, and immediately found themselves facing a totally unexpected hazard: right in front of them, just inside the bush, they came to a krantz about seven metres high, a continuation of the long krantz overlooking the Waterkloof. They could not descend and while they hesitated they were fired on by lurking rebels. All they could do was retreat into the open, where they took what cover they could on the stony ground – but they left McKay's friend, Sergeant Cairney, behind. He had been shot dead and lay with his legs dangling over the krantz. Private David Porteous, who had joined the 74th from a draft only a few days before, tried to rescue Cairney but was himself shot in the stomach. And so the Light Company lay, with the nearest man separated from the insurgents by only twenty paces.[35]

General Somerset had left Fort Beaufort early that morning with that part of his division which was under his immediate command: the ox artillery, a train of wagons and a Khoikhoi levy. After ponderously ascending the western escarpment of the Blinkwater Valley they turned south towards Mount Misery and, about 7 a.m., saw Colonel Sutton's cavalry in the direction of Bush Nek. No firing having been heard, Somerset assumed that the other brigades had not met with the enemy and proposed, in Baines's hearing, that on reaching the high ground they off-saddle and have breakfast. Then, in the afternoon they would move down through the various kloofs and if still no trace of the rebels could be found, the clearing of the Waterkloof would be confirmed.[36]

As he rode up to the crest of the high ground, Baines saw the 74th extend towards the Tongue and three or four men on stretchers being borne by their comrades to the rear. A number of men were grouped around the Hospital Trees and as the general came up, a sergeant went to him, touching his cap, and said: 'Our Colonel, Sir, is mortally wounded, and the regiment has so many disabled that we cannot bring them up.'[37]

The news hit the newcomers like a thunderbolt, changing the mood of relatively high spirits into that of the darkest gloom. Somerset was instantly galvanised into action. One of the guns that Fordyce had placed near the Tongue was brought back and ordered to fire into the deep recesses of that bush, a mule wagon was sent down for the wounded men, messages were sent to hurry on the arrival of the rest of his brigade and two companies of the 12th were sent to relieve the Light Company of the 74th. Sergeant McKay, with that company, saw that the 12th were reluctant to move. The Light Company's bugler sounded the 'advance' and the 'double' and they came a few hundred metres then halted. Shouting got them going again and at last they arrived, whereupon with a great 'hurrah' they dashed to the krantz. McKay wanted to recover Sergeant Cairney's body but it had been dragged over the edge and was nowhere to be seen. Saddened, they left the ground to the 12th.[38]

Lieutenant King and his company were in their assigned position over an extension of the krantz to the north of the Light Company. In the crevices of the krantz, which were ten metres high in places, they found several rebel caches containing axes, bullet-moulds, lead and the usual domestic articles.

About 11 a.m., some of King's men, lying flat on the large rocks and peering down into the deep forest, made signs to King and pointed below. Looking down he saw a group of Ngqika advancing along the bottom of the krantz:

> . . . creeping steadily through the undergrowth, perfectly naked and armed with assegais and guns. Stopping every few paces to listen and peer into the bush, their well-greased bodies glistened in the occasional gleams of sunshine that streamed down through the trees, and again moved on . . . preserving a noiselessness perfectly marvellous.[39]

King found it most exciting to watch them as he and his men crouched among the huge grey rocks, well camouflaged in their bush dress. The men slowly brought the muzzles of their muskets to bear and silently indicated to each other the whereabouts of the Ngqika. They waited for a 'fair shot' and then, at a signal, twenty muskets roared and the Ngqika met the death they had planned for others.

The general ordered King's position to be held so they remained there for some hours, the men smoking their pipes to ease the pangs of hunger. In spite of the occasional bullet fired by a skulking Ngqika or Khoikhoi, and the continuous roll of thunder as Somerset shelled the kloofs, King fell asleep.

Lieutenant-Colonel Michel and his brigade, which included the 2nd Queen's and the 6th regiments, were to have operated along the lower reaches of the Kroome Range, including Blakeway's and Arie's Hoek. They went only as far as Blakeway's farm, where they shelled the kloofs and met with no opposition.

Meanwhile, Lieutenant-Colonel Sutton had gone up the Waterkloof as far as Brown's farm and had then climbed out by a footpath just to the east of Mundell's Krantz, and he too saw nothing of the rebels.

At 3 p.m. the clouds again settled around Mount Misery and the mist became so heavy that all operations had to cease. The rebels was nowhere to be seen so the troops were called in and assembled in column in the open where they were ordered to bivouac for the night. Soon after dark the rain came, accompanied by a piercingly cold wind. The men made little walls of loose stones, or dug small trenches in the softer part of the ground, piling the earth around and placing large slabs of stone over the top for shelter but it was of no great help for, as if nature was giving expression to its wrath, a thunderstorm of great ferocity burst upon the Horseshoe.

Lieutenant King was depressed by the losses of the day and noticed that all the troops were going mournfully about their duties. The cries and groans of the wounded, which could be heard all over the camp, added to the gloom. To make matters even more depressing, the evening fires cast ghost-like shadows in the mist which lay around heavily after the storm.[40]

Sergeant McKay saw officers and men drawing together in groups, the subject discussed each time being the loss of Fordyce. The disciplinarian in him for once overlooked the negligent way the guards and pickets were paraded and the listlessness among the men.[41]

Baines visited Lieutenant Gordon and found him lying on a stretcher beneath the Hospital Trees. Other wounded men lay there too, surrounded by their comrades, whose tenderness in offering a mug of warm, weak tea or a blanket folded for a pillow contrasted strangely with their usual coarse behaviour. One fellow was delirious and, thinking himself still in the hands of the enemy, cried out continuously for help. Another rose up and staggered about, tearing the bandages from a wound in his side. Gordon recognised Baines and spoke cheerfully, but every now and then deep groans would interrupt his talk. Gordon said the man who shot him was so close that he could have grasped the barrel of the musket. 'By God, Baines, I never had such a spin-over in my life.' He asked probing questions about the pain of a broken leg which the artist had experienced. All Baines could do was to answer optimistically, hiding his fear that the lieutenant's wounds would become gangrenous. The doctors, when drawn aside and questioned about Gordon's chances, shook their heads in doubt. The ball had entered the outside of the right thigh and passing through it had then entered the inside of the left one, fracturing the bone close to the socket and leaving two badly lacerated wounds.

Three tents were brought up by ox wagon and set up near the Hospital Trees, two for the wounded and one for the dead. When Baines visited Gordon again that evening he found him lying in one of the wagons, attended by his friend Lieutenant Charles Breton of the 74th. Gordon was unable to speak coherently as he had been given opium by the doctors, so all they could do was to make him more comfortable. The oxen which had been tethered to the wheels of the wagon caused Gordon much pain by their continual movements, so they were moved to another wagon. Baines and Breton then left Gordon in the care of his faithful servant Patrick Stewart.[42]

Lieutenant King went to take a farewell look at the bodies of his late colonel, Lieutenant Carey and the other fallen men. They lay side by side, each corpse on the grass and covered with a blanket. Reverently uncovering their heads King gazed silently at each face. Fordyce's was as tranquil as though he were sleeping, except that his hands and uniform were covered in blood. Carey's features had changed: his once pleasant, friendly face, which had reflected his popular personality, now bore an angry snarl. The dead lay with fixed and rigid features, some with their eyes staring, others with their lower jaws hanging open. Slowly and silently King left the tent and returned to his fire.[43]

Sergeant McKay, with a corporal and six men, was placed on guard over the dead and wounded – it was a horrible assignment. No opiates had been given to Private Thomas Pinkerton and he died in agony with a clear mind, cursing every personal acquaintance, everyone that had been the cause of bringing him to this end – even his mother. Words of consolation were useless and he cursed and blasphemed until he ceased to breathe. Private Porteous, who had tried to retrieve his sergeant's body, had a ball through his entrails and the pain he bore was excruciating. McKay felt very sorry for him as he continually repeated 'Oh, Mother, oh, Mother', whereupon Dr Fraser – a man for whom McKay had little respect – would tell him to shut up as he was disturbing the others. McKay took the young man's hand and sat down beside him until, with a great sigh of agony and one last cry for his mother, he lapsed into unconsciousness.

A sad, tired and weary McKay crept into the tent where his dead commander and the other corpses lay. Placing his head on Fordyce's body, he fell asleep.[44]

7 November

Baines went to see Gordon, who had passed a restless night, dozing off with exhaustion and then waking up again with the pain. At about 7 a.m., the dead and wounded were loaded onto mule wagons to be taken to Post Retief. Gordon, who could not have stood the jolting, was carried on a stretcher for the whole twenty-five kilometres by men of his company. Baines walked beside him for a while, then had to take his leave as he had several painting commissions to fulfil. As Gordon had been lulled to sleep by the motion, Baines shook hands with Stewart and returned to the high ground.[45]

As the night had been foggy and wet, and a white frost now covered the ground, Somerset delayed the departure of his troops until 7 a.m., when the levies and Mfengu were sent off to the top of the krantzes overlooking Fuller's Hoek, with the 91st Regiment in support. The Beaufort West Levy and the Port Elizabeth Mfengu, with two companies of the 12th in support, were sent into the Tongue, while the guns under Captain Robinson and Lieutenant Field were ordered to shell the krantzes.[46]

Lieutenant-Colonel Michel's brigade had received orders the previous day to proceed up the Argyll Pass and join Somerset at the Horseshoe. As they emerged from the top of the pass they were received with a smart fire from the enemy, but they continued for two hundred metres, when they were ordered to lie down. Two companies of the 2nd Queen's and two of the 6th, as well as Mfengu, were sent back into the bush in order to keep the rebels in check. These skirmishers were immediately attacked and took some casualties but they held their ground. The rest of the brigade remained lying down while hostile shots, as well as some friendly ones, whizzed into and over them.

After twenty minutes, enemy fire came from the bush on the south-west side of the Horseshoe and the Mfengu and the Haddon Levy under Captain Stevenson were sent to suppress it. Lieutenant B. of the 2nd Queen's had never seen regular troops manoeuvre more steadily than these levies. They moved rapidly across the plain, extending as they went, and then plunged into the bush 'with a crash'. They succeeded in their objective, but some three or four of them had to be carried back to the rear.[47]

The Mfengu and the Beaufort West Levy who were in the Tongue met with some opposition as they drove their opponents deep into the bush. Captain Devenish of the Beaufort West Levy received a spent ball in the head. Looking pale from loss of blood, he recovered sufficiently to stagger back, assisted by two of his men who held him up by each arm.[48]

The rebels had by now disappeared so Somerset drew off his forces; then once again the Ngqika reappeared, but their fire was desultory. After a late breakfast, Michel's brigade, which had come without blankets or pack horses, began its return march back down Argyll Pass to Blinkwater Post. As they left, heavy rain and hail the size of musket balls drenched everyone and put out all the fires.

The troops shivered throughout the night, longing for morning to come, but the morning brought no change in the weather and so Somerset abandoned the whole operation.

Lieutenant King was in charge of the escort guarding the wounded on the way to Post Retief. He was struck by the contrast: the sad cortège moving against a background of the wide grassy plain glowing with gladiolus, amaranthus, aphelexis and a host of other beautiful flowers waving in the bright morning sun. The slopes of the Little Winterberg were covered with patches of scarlet gladioli which looked like red carpets spread out on the grass. All along the way the men gathered mushrooms and were soon laden with as many as they could carry.

Gordon suffered badly but he bore it with great fortitude, although his thirst was insatiable. Near the halfway point one of the poles of his stretcher broke but fortunately they had a spare stretcher. This was laid on the ground, the other was placed gently on it, the poles were withdrawn, and on they went.

The clouds had been gathering as they marched and seven kilometres from their destination it become as dark as indigo. Then, from behind Didima, lightning flashed, a terrific peal of thunder followed and there came such a downpour of hail and rain as King had never before seen. The hailstones were the size of walnuts and fell with such force that the horses became frantic, and within a minute everyone was soaked to the skin.

Before reaching Post Retief, the road became much rougher and the wounded yelled with agony as the unsprung wagon jolted over the stones. King himself rolled the larger loose stones out of the way and, seeing him do this, Private Thomas McColl jumped out of the wagon, his left arm in a bandage after the amputation of all the fingers, and helped King with his good hand for the rest of the way.

As they approached the post, a detachment of the 12th Regiment came out to meet them and help carry the wounded into the hospital, which was already half full of wounded men.[49]

King took a last look at Fordyce and Carey, who were laid out in the commissariat forage store, before the sergeant-major nailed down the rough deal coffins. As these were borne out, the funeral party, dripping wet and covered with mud, presented arms. With the pipers playing a Highland lament, the funeral party marched in slow time past the groups of men representing each regiment and went out through the south gate. A few hundred metres down the road south of the post they came to the place where the graves had been dug, close to those of other men who had died from wounds received during the October attacks.

Captain Duff read the service while the sound of thunder rolled among the mountains and black clouds threatened another downpour. Captain Carey stood by the grave-side of his brave young kinsman and, as the bodies were lowered into the graves and solemnly committed to the earth, everyone was visibly affected. Three times the reverberation of a hundred muskets joined

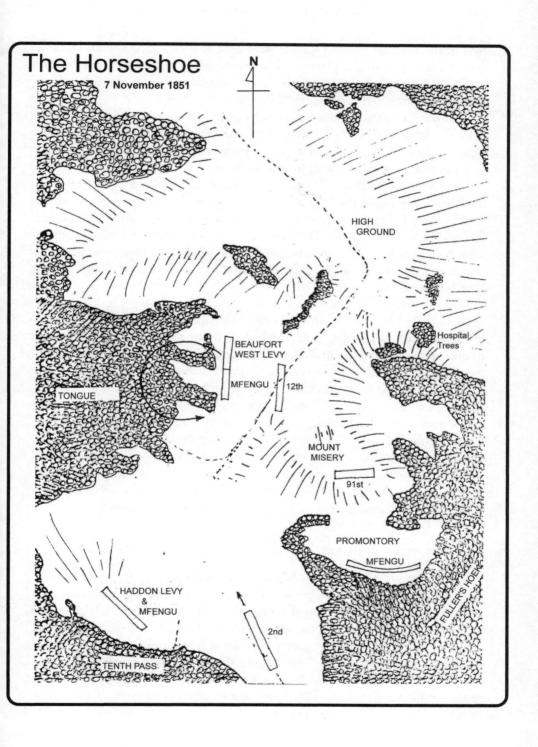

The Horseshoe
7 November 1851

N

HIGH GROUND

Hospital Trees

BEAUFORT WEST LEVY

MFENGU   12th

TONGUE

MOUNT MISERY

91st

PROMONTORY

MFENGU

HADDON LEVY & MFENGU

2nd

TENTH PASS

FULLER'S HOEK

that of the thunder as last honours were paid to the dead. As the final faint echoes died away in the distance, a hoarse word of command broke up the motionless group. One after another they stepped up to the grave-side for a last farewell look and then marched back to the fort in silence.

A miserable barrack room had been prepared for Gordon, and Lieutenant King placed all the blankets he could find on three straw mattresses to make him as comfortable as possible. Then, with a few words of cheer he left Gordon in the care of Stewart for the night.

King went to the hospital. The groans of the wounded were heart-rending and their suffering in the heat and cold was acute. Flies and maggots, which could not be kept from the wounds, added to their misery. King also visited Ensign Ricketts of the 91st. He lay alone in a small room and talked gaily of what he was going to do when he got out, though he had to stop regularly to cough and spit out blood. Blood bubbled out of the wound in his chest every time he breathed.

King saw Gordon for the last time the next morning. He helped the surgeon dress his wounds, arranged his bed, wiped his brow and moistened his lips. It was obvious that gangrene had set in. Ensign Ricketts was the first to die, having been in gradual decline for some time.[50] News of his death was purposely kept from Gordon, but the sound of the funeral volleys reached his ears and in a quiet voice he chided Stewart for not telling him. The next day an identical salute was fired over his own grave.[51]

For such a brief campaign, the casualties suffered were very heavy. Apart from the tragic loss of Colonel Fordyce, the 74th had lost Lieutenant Hirzel Carey, two sergeants and two privates. In addition, they had suffered the mortal wounding of Lieutenant John Gordon, Lance-Corporal James Thomson, and Privates Robert Irwin and David Porteous. Corporal James Wilson was also wounded, together with a further four privates.[52]

Invasion of the Transkei

In November 1851, Sir Harry Smith announced plans for an invasion of the Transkei.[53] The reasons given for such a move were the allegations of collusion of the paramount chief of the Xhosa, Sarhili of the Gcaleka, in the encouragement of the war; the concealment of stolen colonial cattle; and the harbouring of Rharhabe cattle well away from their own homesteads. It was even suggested that some of Sarhili's people had taken part in the rebellion in the colony.[54] These reasons, of course, were identical to those proposed by Sir Benjamin D'Urban for a similar invasion of Gcalekaland in 1835:

It may be in its proper place here to apprize your Lordship of my having, as early as the month of February, ascertained beyond all doubt, that Hintza (the chief of the country between the [Kei] and the Bashee and of the left bank of the latter river, and paramount chief of Caffreland,) had been, if not the original contriver and instigator of the combination among the chiefs of the savage tribes in western Caffreland against the colony, very early referred to and consulted by them therein; that he afforded them his countenance and advice; received into his territory the plundered herds and effects sent thither from the colony; permitted (if not directed) many of his own tribe to join in the invasion; and that, consequently, the bolder tribes in all their measures relied upon his support, and upon the ultimate refuge of his country in case of their failure.[55]

It is equally possible that Smith recalled the ease with which D'Urban and he had then overrun Gcalekaland (even though the paramount chief, Hintsa, had paid for the invasion with his life) and now needed a victory, any victory, to weigh against his lack of success in the Amathola and Kroome mountains. Mostert expressed the view that 'this expedition had more to do with his own temper and frustration than with military advantage.'[56]

With almost an embarrassment of troops now at his command, Smith made ample provision for the security of the colony during his foray across the Kei River. Lieutenant-Colonel Charles Cook Yarborough, commanding the 91st Regiment, assumed command at Fort Hare, having his own regiment and the 74th, together with 'such levies and foot and Fingoes as Major-General Somerset has organised in this district'. He was instructed to patrol the neighbourhood of Blinkwater and Fuller's Hoek. Lieutenant-Colonel James Maxwell Perceval, commanding the 12th Regiment, took command at Fort Brown on the Great Fish River, relieving Lieutenant-Colonel Eyre. Perceval's task was the security of the district of Albany, his line extending from Fort Brown to the mouth of the Fish River. Major Wilmot RA was to remain at Fort Peddie. The governor called this his 'colonial line of defence'. Thomas Stubbs found Perceval to be a 'thorough soldier and gentleman' and took a liking to him 'at first sight'.[57]

Despite the precautions taken by Smith to safeguard the colony during the absence of this huge force, the Kroome Heights had not been finally cleared and little had been effected in the Amatholas. The invasion was hardly more than a deflection from the principal effort to defeat, finally, the Ngqika and Khoikhoi rebels within the colony.

For the invasion, a force was to assemble on 2 December 1851 at the 'Umvani' mission station under the command of Major-General Henry Somerset, who was to raise as many burghers and Mfengu as he could in the meantime. These were to be men not required for the colonial defence previously arranged, and were also to include a column of four hundred levies from Shiloh under Captain Tylden, RE.

Lieutenant-Colonel Mackinnon was to meet at the rendezvous on 2 December with the following: 280 mounted men, 1,200 infantry and 277 Mfengu levies and guides. The contingent would also include thirty men of the Royal Artillery.

Troops were to carry with them three days' provisions and would be accompanied by a convoy of wagons with thirty days' rations for men and horses. There would also be a herd of slaughter cattle. These provisions were understood by General Somerset as being for the *whole* force under his command. No other wagons were to be taken by either column.[58]

In a later despatch, the governor advised Earl Grey that circumstances had compelled him to abandon his original plan of marching with one column from the Umvani mission station.[59] Instead he had decided upon three columns under General Somerset, Colonel Mackinnon and Lieutenant-Colonel Eyre. Eyre's column was to move directly to Butterworth in the Transkei on 1 December 1851, to ensure the safety of the missionaries and traders at that place. A second reason for this move was to divert Sarhili's attention from the north of his country.

Meanwhile, Somerset and Mackinnon had different tasks, Somerset being the military arm while Mackinnon played the diplomat. Somerset, equipped with guns, 150 CMR and three hundred Mfengu levies, was to march on 27 November to Shiloh, where he would collect Captain Tylden with his levies. The general's imperial infantry, being the 12th, 74th and 91st regiments, was to act as colonial defence on the Kei River border.

Colonel Mackinnon, with provisions for one month in a convoy of wagons, left for the Umvani on 29 November. Mackinnon was charged with recovering all stolen cattle, confiscating all Rharhabe cattle held by Sarhili in safekeeping and demanding ten thousand head of cattle from Sarhili for his perfidy. He was also to impose penalties upon the Gcaleka for damages and the theft of traders' property. Finally, he was to seek the surrender of Uithaalder and Hans Brander, two of the Khoikhoi rebel commanders.[60]

Eyre's column was, in effect, a flying column which was to reach Butterworth as quickly as possible. It consisted of 162 mounted men, 646 infantry and 147 levies and guides. When established in Butterworth, he was to make contact with the Gcaleka chief Maphasa and his son Boko, both of whom were expected to 'evince amity' towards the British, and ensure that their people were not harmed by the invasion force.[61]

It is difficult at this distance in time to determine exactly the routes taken by the various columns because the geographical names bear little relation to modern features. It also seems that the commanders had difficulty transmitting their reports, Somerset noting:

With reference to my despatch of the 29th ultimo, which was to have been forwarded by Toise's [Toyise's] people, and who, although they took the despatches, I have only this morning ascertained never proceeded at all, I again transmit my former despatch, and have now the honour to forward, for your Excellency's information, a detail of my operations from that date.[62]

Somerset marched to Shiloh, where he picked up Captain Tylden, then continued well to the north to what Somerset called 'Bolota Mountain'. The closest modern feature to this is Bolotwa. He then turned south to the Tsomo River, sending Tylden east to the Batshe (Bashee) River, then down its right (west) bank.

Colonel Eyre encountered some opposition when crossing the Kei River but, since the Gcaleka had few firearms, it was brushed aside. He then met more of the enemy as he climbed out of the river valley but again defeated them, this time by an outflanking movement. He then moved into camp to allow his footsore infantry to recover, while he rode on to Butterworth with his mounted men.

Having achieved his objective of safeguarding the traders and missionaries there, he should then have moved up to the junction of the Kei and Tsomo rivers. Instead, having in the meantime received intelligence of a very large herd of cattle some thirty kilometres to the east of Butterworth, he chose to ride out there in pursuit. His intelligence was incorrect and the number of cattle was much smaller than expected. Nevertheless, Eyre spent three days mopping them up and sending them in to Butterworth. He then went up to the Tsomo–Kei junction.[63]

Mackinnon arrived in Butterworth after Eyre's departure, then set out to the east, having received (perhaps the same) intelligence of large herds of cattle. He crossed the 'Nabagha' [Nqabara] River and shortly afterwards came upon Captain Tylden near the Batshe. Leaving Tylden to proceed down the Batshe, Mackinnon proceeded south down the Nqabara, where he found substantial numbers of cattle. He then turned round and again linked up with Tylden, sending both lots of cattle back to Butterworth under a small escort. He then turned north up the Batshe with Tylden for a while, finally returning to Butterworth on 3 January.

These operations continued in the northern part of the Transkei until mid-January. General Somerset and Colonel Mackinnon began their triumphant return to Fort Hare on 13 January with seven thousand cattle, while Eyre started back one day later. Somerset had thought that it might be best to leave

Eyre in possession of Butterworth but he was overruled by Smith, who needed Eyre's column for the forthcoming operations in the Amatholas.[64] In a repeat of history, Eyre brought back a contingent of Mfengu, seven thousand strong, who had also chosen this moment to leave their Gcaleka masters, relieving them at the same time of thirty thousand cattle. These Mfengu were to be the unwitting touchstone for the outbreak of the last frontier war in 1877–8.

The huge invasion exercise had lasted about six weeks, established the superiority of British forces over the Gcaleka people of the Transkei, and brought back a huge number of cattle, not to mention the jubilant Mfengu. However, there had been no contact with Sarhili and the coastal fringe of Gcalekaland remained undisturbed. It was a massive movement of manpower which gained little, while allowing the Ngqika and Khoikhoi rebels to re-occupy the areas in the Amatholas and Kroome which had been thought cleared.

Chapter 10

Harry Smith Learns his Fate

On 13 January 1852, Sir Harry Smith penned another of his optimistic despatches to Earl Grey, this time to emphasise the good work completed during the invasion of the Transkei.[1] Once again he sang the praises of every officer commanding troops, as well as the troops themselves. At the end of his encomium, and the repetition of the feats of arms so recently undertaken in Gcalekaland, the governor went on to outline his next step:

> Sandili, Macomo, and all the other chiefs must be beaten down by physical force never to rise again, and not be partially subdued through the medium of feudal authority. Now is the time, if I rightly understand your Lordship's instructions, to subdue, and for ever, these turbulent Gaikas; and my next step will be, the moment the men are somewhat refreshed, to fill the Amatolas with troops, and to carry on systematically that devastation, the horrid result of savage war, which will induce the people to submit to my terms, based alone on what is calculated to ensure the future peace and tranquility of the unoffending colonists.[2]

However, it was not until 6 February that he published a proclamation requiring all the burghers from the frontier districts between the ages of twenty and fifty to assemble, in order to 'expel the rebel Gaika tribes and the Khoikhoi rebels from the Water Kloof, Blinkwater, Fuller's Hoek, Kat River, and the whole of the Amatola mountains'. The men were to assemble according to the 'old commando system', except that they would receive rations from the commissariat, while providing their own 'arms, horses and appointments'.[3]

The Last Throw

Time, however, had now run out for Sir Harry Smith. On 1 March 1852, he received Earl Grey's letter telling him of his recall and replacement by Sir George Cathcart. Doubtless bitterly disappointed with the news, but ever the optimist, he saw a last opportunity to clear his military name in the short space of time allowed to him before the arrival of his successor. On 17 March, the fallen governor wrote a despatch to Grey setting out his actions since receiving the dismissal notice. They amounted to attacks on the Waterkloof area and a patrol through the Fish River bush. His call for burgher volunteers by means of a proclamation on 6 February had met with very limited success.

> I deeply regret, for the credit of the frontier inhabitants, to report that only 200 burghers from the district of Somerset, 200 from Cradock, and 33 from Graham's Town have responded to my command. They first objected to the volunteer system, which I offered to their loyalty. They then requested to be *commanded* to turn out. Their shuffling conduct is melancholy.[4]

Smith's hopes of ending the war were, however, doomed to failure. Sandile perhaps thought he might win more favourable terms from a new governor than from the old. He therefore maintained the status quo, at the same time ensuring that the old haunts of the Amathola Mountains, the Kroome, the Fish River bush and the Tyumie Valley were occupied by his Ngqika and the Khoikhoi rebels.

Nor had Maqoma remained idle. One of his sisters was the Great Wife of Quesha, chief of the Thembu, who lived in what is now the Queenstown district about 120 kilometres north of Fort Beaufort. Somehow Maqoma was able to persuade Quesha to join his rebellion. This was known to the authorities, for the following appeared in the *Grahamstown Journal*, although there was no mention of this incursion in Sir Harry Smith's official despatches to England: '. . . three captives state that Thembus, with their cattle, have been pouring into the Waterkloof for some time back to assist Maqoma; that they muster from 2000 to 3000 men, and are well supplied with ammunition.'[5]

Sir George Cathcart confirmed this fact in a summary of the state of the frontier on his arrival in April 1852, in which he noted: 'That obstinate and crafty chief [Maqoma] had associated with him the Tambook chief Quesha, with numerous followers . . .'[6]

Thembu in the Waterkloof

A division of troops was assembled at Haddon's farm, just to the west of the Waterkloof, under the command of Lieutenant-Colonel Yarborough. The force consisted of Yarborough's 91st, two companies of the 74th under now-Major Patton and one hundred CMR under Captain Richard Jennings Bramley.

A second division, under the immediate command of Major-General Somerset and consisting of a single howitzer and one hundred CMR under Captain Carey, kin to Lieutenant Carey of the 74th, lay at Adelaide, south of Yarborough.

The plan was for Colonel Yarborough to march with the infantry into the Waterkloof at midnight on 3 March and Captain Bramley with the CMR would start at 3 a.m. All the Thembu huts were to be destroyed and as many livestock as possible captured. The force would then withdraw towards Nel's farm at the mouth of the Waterkloof. General Somerset would follow at 4 a.m. with the howitzer and Captain Carey's squadron of the CMR; these were to be held in reserve at Nel's farm.

Silently, without bugle calls, Colonel Yarborough's men were roused from sleep at midnight on 3 March by orderly sergeants and assembled at the alarm posts outside their tents. The different duties of telling off the companies were carried out in whispers and, when all were present and ready, they moved off along the wagon road leading to the Waterkloof. The 74th knew the road, for they had marched along it on 14 July the year before under General Somerset and Colonel Fordyce. Thomas Baines had been with them then but he was now in Grahamstown fulfilling orders for paintings based on his sketches. He was to paint at least two rather implausible pictures from eyewitness accounts of this day's dramatic events.

4 March

An officer of the 91st, writing under the pseudonym 'Argyll', described how the chilly, moonlit night with a light mist hanging in the still air seemed to give the roadside objects a ghost-like appearance. There was no sound but the tramp, tramp of the troops, who marched without a word. There was none of the usual banter and facetiousness and it seemed to 'Argyll' as if the men were showing by their seriousness that they knew they were going to attempt with five hundred men what three thousand had failed to accomplish a few months before.

At 4 a.m., having reached Nel's farm, the column turned east up the Waterkloof Valley proper until, at the approach of dawn, a halt was called opposite Mundell's Krantz and the men were ordered to look to their arms. Argyll saw the veterans of the 91st placing cartridges into the home-made breast pockets of their jackets ready for quick firing, wiping the dew from their muskets, pouring fresh powder into the muzzles and renewing the percussion caps. Presently the grunt of horses and the squeak of leather was heard as Bramley's squadron of cavalry passed them and halted in front of the infantry. It was quiet as they finished their preparations, and the visibility increased

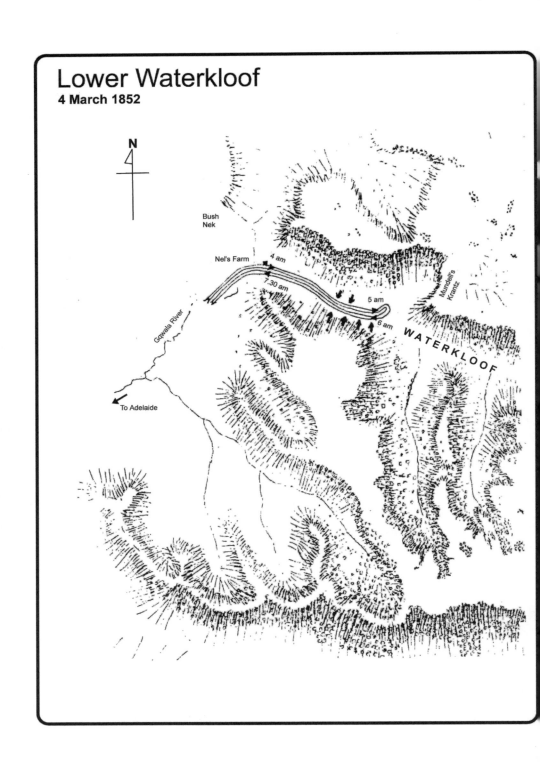

Lower Waterkloof
4 March 1852

N

Bush
Nek

Nel's Farm

4 am

7.30 am

5 am

6 am

Gqwala River

To Adelaide

Mundell's
Krantz

WATERKLOOF

rapidly as the mist, hanging round the tops of the headlands and krantzes, was dispelled by the approaching daylight. Across the tree-lined river they could see about 150 huts on the open ground at the foot of Mundell's Krantz. It was now 6 a.m.[7]

Suddenly a shrill cry startled the taut nerves of everyone in the column. The plangent yell came from a Thembu sentry, high up on a krantz, who had just caught sight of the troops. Although his men were not yet in the ideal position, Yarborough ordered the attack to begin at once. The cavalry dashed across the drift over the Waterkloof River and opened fire with their carbines as men, women and children ran from the huts towards the bush. Companies of the 91st followed at the double, extending in skirmish order as they came out into the open in hot pursuit of the Thembu. The huts were set alight and were soon enveloped in clouds of smoke and bursting flame. While the huts were being burnt, the CMR and other companies of the 91st were busily gathering livestock under intermittent musket fire and vicious counter-attacks by the enemy. As No. 1 Company was trying to drive off cattle and horses, the attackers came right in amongst them using every weapon they had – muskets, assegais, knobkerries and even hurling stones. Private Henry Currie was the first to fall, with a shot through the head. Colour Sergeant Robert Laing lagged behind while trying to bring in a horse which would not be led and he was captured alive in spite of all attempts by his company to save him.[8] Private Abbott, trying to snatch some goats for his own use, was set upon by three Thembu who knocked him down and took his musket. They were just going to finish him off when some of his comrades appeared and saved him.[9]

The Thembu sentry's cry had been taken up in succession by others and signal fires could be seen sending up their smoke from peak to peak, alerting the whole of the warlike population of the valley.

'Argyll' sensed that the column was in trouble: as far as the destruction of the village was concerned, the troops had arrived later than intended and very few of the enemy had been hurt, while their own camp was fifteen kilometres away. Yarborough had the bugler sound the 'assembly' and as the call echoed from krantz to krantz, groups of the 91st ceased burning and destroying and started to join up with the main body. The colonel, impatient at the tardiness of No. 1 Company, rode after them and was very nearly trapped himself.

While the wreaths of smoke were still pouring from the burning huts, masses of Thembu could be seen gathering on either side of the return road brandishing their assegais and muskets, leaping and whirling in circles, their bodies glistening with sweat, their red-painted faces hideous and demon-like as they worked themselves into a frantic state of fury in preparation for their attack.[10]

The 74th, all this time in support, was now ordered to take up positions on both sides of the drift to cover the withdrawal of the CMR and the 91st. Bramley was the first to cross over with the booty of a hundred cattle and forty horses.[11] The 74th skirmishers opened fire slowly and deliberately at the dancing warriors, covering the 91st now assembling on the near side of the river. The crashing tramp and roar of the war dance became louder and the musket fire of the 74th increased as the cavalry passed through on their way with the cattle. The 91st were almost in position, extending by companies in the 74th's rear, and the Thembu, in formidable numbers, were waiting impatiently for the signal to fall on the troops.

Just as the last company of the 91st crossed the stream and one of the 74th's companies began to retire, the storm broke. A Thembu chief standing on a rock high on the mountainside waved his assegai and, with a long loud cry, which rang clear above the rattle of musketry and the shouting, ordered his men to the attack. A dense black mass of warriors rose and, with wild shouts and yells, with volleys from their muskets and brandishing assegais and clubs, they threw themselves on the rear guard of the 74th Highlanders with the irresistibility of a tidal wave. Highlanders and Thembu mingled together in a fierce hand-to-hand struggle. More of them came raging down and No. 4 Company of the 91st was soon involved in the mêlée. Bayonets were doing their deadly work, musket butts were whirling in the air crushing skulls, knobkerries and assegais were clubbing and stabbing. Highlanders, redcoats and naked Thembu were all mixed together in a close and deadly struggle.[12]

As the soldiers were being steadily forced back before the onslaught, Yarborough came up with two more companies of the 91st. Calling on the men to fear nothing, he ordered bayonets to be fixed and then led the charge, driving the Thembu back and giving the 74th and the 91st's No 4 Company breathing space. The action now became more general, the retreat continuing as fast as the situation allowed. Musket fire became heavier until every man was engaged: skirmishers, supports and even the cavalry were firing as fast as they could load, the roar of musketry and the yells of the Thembu filling the Waterkloof with continuous echoes.

As they retreated, the troops were subjected to a cross fire from behind the rocks to the south and from the bushes on the banks of the river to the north. Long lines of warriors could be seen running with their weapons at the trail and their bodies stooped as they threaded their way between bushes to get ahead of the troops. The smoke of the fight lay dense and close amongst the men and the surrounding bush; it was a cloudy day without even a breeze and the air was stifling and suffocating. Every bush and rock seemed to shield an opponent and to belch forth flame and smoke, raking the harassed troops with dangerous precision. The 91st were old hands at bush-fighting and knew the tricks and moves of Xhosa warfare, knew the advantages of cover and, side by side with their comrades of the 74th, gave more than they received. There was no military order; every man had to fight for his life and there was confusion everywhere; it was an ideal situation for the attacking Thembu.

The losses among the troops were becoming heavier. Every minute, it seemed to 'Argyll', one of the men was hit and could be seen staggering down the valley towards the front of the column, which was still free from attack. Soon all the stretchers were filled with wounded, none of whom could be left behind for fear of their being tortured. Every now and then the bugles would sound the 'halt' in order to check the enemy and rest the men, for the further they retreated the more the enemy pressed on their rear, which had to be constantly relieved. The fighting was close and severe, the opposing parties not being more than a few paces from each other. Every time a halt was sounded, the enemy would rush in and then a series of desperate hand-to-hand combats would follow.

Colonel Yarborough rode coolly through the hottest fire. He seemed always to be where the fighting was heaviest and, although he was the only man mounted, he seemed to have a charmed life. 'Argyll' thought it lucky that Yarborough remained unharmed, for the confidence that the old soldiers of the 91st placed in him was so great that, had he fallen, not a man would have been saved.[13]

It took them an hour and a half to cover the four kilometres from Mundell's Krantz to Nel's farm, where the reserve under Somerset was supposed to have been waiting. But Somerset was late, as usual, and the rendezvous was deserted. The farmhouse was a small stone building about ten paces long by five broad; it was roofless but the walls were standing. The ruins of out-buildings lay scattered about, the whole being surrounded by a large orchard enclosed by a hedge. Yarborough decided to make a stand at the farm and, as the exhausted men arrived, he placed them in a defensive position behind the walls and hedge, the wounded being taken into the farmhouse. Amongst those who sheltered there was Major Walter Patton of the 74th.

Even here the Thembu were pressing hard on the rear of the column, almost entering the orchard with the retreating troops. Yarborough was still making his dispositions when a Xhosa, dressed in the uniform of the Kaffir Police, ran up to within twenty paces of him and, resting his musket on the fork of a tree, fired. The ball penetrated high up on Yarborough's thigh and he fell, badly wounded. A volley from the enemy now struck his horse in two places; it plunged fearfully and then, after galloping forward a few paces, it fell dead. The sight of the wounded horse caused confusion and the cry 'The colonel's hit' spread amongst the ranks. 'Argyll' considered that if the enemy had charged at that instant the day would have been lost. The men, however, rallied and, mindful of their wounded, fixed bayonets and charged the enemy, who immediately gave way before them.[14]

The colonel was carried to the rear by Captain Robert Middlemore and Sergeant-Major Grant, under a shower of bullets. In the confusion, most of the 91st and 74th had not received the order to make a stand at Nel's farm, so they had continued to retreat along the road towards Adelaide, carrying Yarborough with them. Only the wounded and stragglers, including Patton, remained behind in the house and orchard. The time was now about 7.30 a.m. The enemy closed around them, pouring in a continuous fire and Ensign Francis Hibbert of the 91st and several men fell badly wounded. Then, to everyone's consternation, it was found that ammunition was running low, there being only about five rounds left per man. Firing was halted and strict orders were given to fire only when there was no doubt about hitting the target. Strangely, the Thembu fire also diminished at this time. Perhaps they had decided to shut the troops in with the intention of storming the position that night. Stray shots were still exchanged, however, Captain Bramley of the CMR fell from one of these, pierced through his side.[15]

According to McKay – who, having gone on with the rest, must have heard it from the defenders – Major Patton was by this time in a pitiable state of fear as he declared they were all lost men. In despair, about 11 a.m. he offered a large sum of money to anyone who would go to the general to summon help. Private Peter Watson was the first to try but he was shot just as he emerged from the house and fell dead across the door sill. Then a trooper of the CMR made the attempt. He took hold of his horse, led it carefully and, stooping low, plunged his spurs in and dashed off. Musket fire was heard by those in the house and then silence.[16] Ensign Philip Philpot of the 74th also volunteered and he too was sent speeding on his way with a barrage of musket shots.[17]

The defenders waited. After an hour, a volley of musketry was heard and into the orchard galloped the unnamed CMR trooper with bags of cartridges hanging from his saddle bow. Shortly afterwards Ensign Philpot also returned unharmed, with more cartridges, but his horse had been shot through the back and it had fallen dead just outside the orchard. They both brought the news that the general was approaching with reinforcements.

They waited. After a while a few more cavalrymen came in with more ammunition and with orders to hold on to the position. At last, about 1 p.m., a distant rumbling sound was heard and the Thembu were seen moving away and taking up positions closer to the bush. The rumbling increased and then the defenders heard the bugle call, the cavalry 'charge'.

The defenders cheered as the right wing of Captain Carey's troop drove the enemy up the mountainside while the left wing galloped to the farmhouse, where they placed the wounded on spare horses and carried them back to safety.[18]

Later still that night McKay heard the adjutant, Lieutenant James Falconer, say to Patton: 'Have you heard the news? The *Birkenhead* has been lost.' To McKay the initial shock of this news was the loss of the men, there being a draft of the 74th on board; then came a deeper gloom, for the loss of Alexander Seton, Fordyce's replacement, meant that the 74th would have to continue in its abject state under Patton for many more months.[19]

The casualties inflicted by the attackers were heavy, giving an indication of the severity of the fighting. Three privates of the 91st, and one of the 74th, were killed. Sergeant Laing, first reported missing, was later found dead. The total number of wounded, from all units, was twenty-two men, including Yarborough, Hibbert and Bramley. For Major Patton the stress had unpleasant consequences: Reilly, his servant, told McKay that night that he had some nasty work to do on the captain's trews.[20]

A pertinent comment upon what Smith would describe as a 'smart affair' by Somerset appeared in the *Grahamstown Gazette*:

> . . . [Sir Harry Smith's] generous nature had been imposed upon by the incapacity of his second in command who has never yet conducted an extensive movement with ability. The Major-General [Somerset] possesses personal valour and at the head of a troop of Hottentot Cavalry works to admiration, but to manoeuvre an army is beyond his power. We hear very severe strictures passed upon him for having ordered Colonel Yarborough's force of a handful of Light Infantry and Cavalry right into the enemy's teeth, and not starting to their support as prearranged until four hours had elapsed, and then proceeded encumbered by a gun . . .[21]

Loss of the Birkenhead

HM troopship *Birkenhead* was on passage from Cork to the Cape.[22] She was carrying 488 officers and men in drafts to make up the numbers of the regiments then on active service at the Cape, together with a number of women and children.

Commodore Wyvill, commanding the Simon's Bay station, noted in his report dated 3 March 1852 that the *Birkenhead* had arrived there on 23

February. She was refuelled with 350 tons of coal, some provisions and horses for the officers. All the women and children, except for those going on to Algoa Bay, were put ashore. By the 25th, she was reported ready to sail and the captain of the ship, Mr Salmond, received government despatches for Sir Harry Smith and orders to proceed to Algoa Bay and East London. The ship sailed that same evening, with fine weather and a calm sea.

At 2.30 p.m. on 27 February, Dr William Culhane, assistant-surgeon of the *Birkenhead*, arrived at Simon's Bay by land and reported the ship lost at sea the previous day near Point Danger, and that two boats containing the only other survivors were at that moment at some distance from the land. The commodore at once despatched HMS *Castor* to the scene, with an extra twenty-five men in the steamer *Rhadamanthus* to act as additional boats' crews.

That evening, *Castor* fell in with the schooner *Lioness* which reported that she had on board the survivors from the boats, together with forty others plucked from the main topsail yard of the wreck, the only part of the *Birkenhead* remaining above the sea. The number of survivors was then counted as 116. *Rhadamanthus* towed *Lioness* into the anchorage and then left again to search for more survivors. Expeditions by land, and *Rhadamanthus* by sea, combed thirty kilometres of the shoreline, finding only those few who had landed during the previous day and night. *Rhadamanthus* returned with these on the morning of 1 March, adding a further 68 to those saved from the wreck. These included four military and two naval officers, all of whom had reached the shore by swimming or by clinging to pieces of the wreck. A further nine people had been able to reach the shore in the ship's gig, making a total of 193 survivors.

The last movements of the wrecked ship were re-constructed from reports of the surviving crew. A course was shaped from False Bay, keeping Cape Hanglip more than six kilometres on the port side. The man at the wheel was instructed not to allow the ship to move eastwards of the set course. There was a leadsman on the paddle box and lookouts were posted. The night was fine, with good visibility.

At 1.50 a.m., the leadsman reported soundings of twelve or thirteen fathoms to the officer of the watch, second captain Mr Davis. The ship was then sailing at about eight knots. Before the leadsman was able to make another cast, the ship struck an unmarked reef and he then found only seven fathoms on his side of the vessel. There were two fathoms under the bows and eleven under the stern.

Captain Salmond was roused from his bunk by the jolt of the ship's striking and, going quickly to the bridge, asked for the time and course. He was told it was a few minutes after 2 a.m. and that the course was SSE½E, the same course as laid in False Bay. The captain immediately ordered the engines stopped, the small bower anchor let go and the quarter boats to be lowered, to lie alongside the ship. He next ordered the paddle box boats to be got out. In doing so, the swell pulled them overboard and they were smashed into the hull. Military officers were asked to send men to the chain pumps, which was done immediately. When Captain Salmond was advised that there was water in the ship, he gave orders that the remaining seven women and thirteen children be put into a cutter in the charge of Mr Richards, the master's assistant.

Captain Salmond then gave the fatal order for the ship to go astern. While she was executing this manoeuvre, the rocks below 'bilged the side for several feet and [tore] open the bottom'. Water at once rushed into the hull, putting out the engine-room fires; the engineer and stokers immediately tried to make their way up to the deck.

The damage caused to the hull by the second grounding caused the *Birkenhead* to break in two, the section behind the main mast sinking straight away, leaving only the main topmast and topsail yard visible above the waves. The forward part of the hull went under a few minutes afterwards.

To this point, the three boats had remained by the ship but, with the sinking, all three left to go to the shore leaving those still in the water, and those clinging to the rigging, to their fate. The two cutters were found by *Lioness*, which took their survivors aboard. The gig landed at Port Durban with eight men and Dr Culhane.

The events described above were remarkable enough, but there was yet another which elevates this tragedy to a higher plane. In his statement, the senior surviving army officer, Captain Edward R. Wright of the 91st Regiment stated:

> Just before the vessel broke a second time, which was in about 20 minutes from first striking, the commander called out for all officers and men who could swim to jump overboard, and make for the boats. Lieut. Guardol was standing alongside of me by the poop rail at the time. We called out to the men not to go overboard to the boats, as we feared their being swamped, they being full of women and children (at least one of them we knew was);[23] very few men went, and the rest remained on the poop till that part sunk and then down we all went together. Every officer was on board the vessel when she sunk, except Mr. Richards, who was on board the cutter, and Dr. Culhane . . .[24]

This was the first recorded occasion at sea when the concept of 'women and children first' was embraced and it is to the very great credit of the officers and men who stood fast on the deck until what remained of the ship slid under the water. It was an act of great sacrifice and, indeed, of noble supererogation. The action of the officers and men to allow women and children first access to ships' boats came to be known as the 'Birkenhead Drill'.

Five officers and 122 other ranks were saved from the ship; ten officers and 353 other ranks were lost. Seven officers of the *Birkenhead*, including Captain Salmond, together with nearly eighty of his crew, went down with the ship.[25]

Harry Smith Intervenes

On 8 March, the governor issued instructions for a major attack on the Kroome Heights in a last effort to clear it of the Thembu and Maqoma's Ngqika.[26]

The troops to be used in the engagement were in three divisions under the overall command of Sir Harry Smith, a most unusual departure from previous actions. Smith was obviously determined to succeed on this occasion.

The right column under Lieutenant-Colonel Eyre was to consist of the 43rd and 73rd regiments, and two companies of the 74th, supplemented by European and African levies. He would also have four guns, and rockets, under Captain Faddy, RA. They would be based at the Blinkwater Post, where Sir Harry would also be located.

The centre column under Lieutenant-Colonel Michel, to be based at Blakeway's farm, would include the 6th Regiment, four companies of the 45th, and the 60th Rifles. These would be accompanied by Armstrong's Horse and African levies. Two guns would also accompany the column. These columns were to assemble on 9 March.

Lieutenant-Colonel Napier of the CMR was to command the left column, assembling at Haddon's farm, taking with him the 91st Regiment under Major David Forbes, four companies of the 74th, 150 CMR and 200 Mfengu levies. The burghers previously ordered to assemble in Smith's proclamation were instructed to join this column, together with another two guns. The column was to march on Nel's farm in the Waterkloof on 9 March.

A subsidiary force, under the command of Captain Bruce, consisted of a company of the 74th and about 150 burghers under Captain Tylden.

Smith's orders for the disposition of the columns can be determined as follows:

Colonel Eyre's column at Blinkwater Post was to direct its main efforts to dislodging the rebels from Fuller's Hoek, the ridge of which the enemy principally occupied, and where Maqoma's 'den' was said to be located.

Colonel Michel's column at Blakeway's was to ascend the high ridge by the route pursued by Colonel Fordyce in the former attack and would assail the bush around Tenth Pass.

Colonel Napier's column was ordered to assemble at Adelaide. It would then move by wagon road up the Waterkloof to its head and direct its infantry and the CMR to ascend the head of the kloof and join in the attack by Michel's column. Its mounted burghers were to patrol in order to cut off any dislodged fugitives who might try to cross from one kloof to another. They were to communicate with the mounted burghers under Captain Bruce, who were expected to move from Post Retief.

The troops would carry with them three days' bread and field rations. They might be able to supply themselves with slaughter cattle; but whether or not, they should not be withdrawn from any stronghold of which they might take possession.

The headquarters and Major-General Somerset would be established at Blinkwater.

10 March
Eyre's Column
At last the 73rd Regiment was given the opportunity to show its mettle in the Kroome. The rebels were well established in Fuller's Hoek and the column's approach route was always regarded as inaccessible, so Colonel Eyre sensibly had his guns drawn up at the foot of the Argyll Pass and from there Captain Faddy sent shells as well as rockets into and below the krantz reputed to hold Maqoma's den. After the bombardment, Eyre sent in eight small parties which carried everything before them without much opposition. One of the columns, under Captain Robert Parker Campbell of the 73rd Regiment, consisting of a company of the 73rd and two of the 43rd, succeeded in climbing right up Argyll Pass against some opposition and came out onto the Horseshoe. There the Ngqika were driven off, many huts were burnt and cultivated crops destroyed. Later the whole column ascended Argyll Pass and bivouacked for the night on the Horseshoe.[27]

Ensign Hugh Robinson of the 43rd Regiment wrote a series of letters to his family in England. His talents in sketching are matched by his vivid, amusing and sympathetic prose. The above account from Smith's bland report is brought to life as Robinson writes of his first experience in the Kroome:

On the morning of the 11th, we marched at day-break to attack the stronghold of Fuller's Hoek which we knew must be cleared, if our leader was not killed. The guns with three companies went up Argyll Pass; how the Horse Artillery

would have stared if they had seen the track those cannon went up! Some
companies went up the ridge to the right, their fate depending almost entirely
upon success elsewhere, while Colonel Eyre, with the main body went straight
through and scaled the hights [sic] above.

Then we saw what sort of 'bush' this really was. There were enormous
trees growing as thick as they could stand, through whose tops the sun never
penetrated, perpitual [sic] twilight; there they had grown uncared for from the
beginning of time: what one trod on was a mass of huge fallen logs rotting
and covered with a profuse and high vegetation, through which one might slip
suddenly into dark chasms, where one heard gurgling water, but saw nothing:
under the trees, and growing thick and woven round them, were huge bushes
of most virulent African thorns, whose stems only were visible, covered with
the most beautiful moss and lichen, the latter growing in long tufts like
women's hair, only longer, and the whole mass welded together by a woven
net of parasites, monkey-ropes twisted into every possible shape, coiled round
and round limbs of trees, forming arabesque patterns, reaching the ground and
springing up again, varying in thickness from a man's body to one's little finger,
imitating the rigging of a ship, huge snakes, or making cradles which swung
from tree to tree, sometimes invisible from masses of lichen. Through this we
had to cut away with axes, for a Caffre even could not have got thru' some of
these deeper places. There were some paths used by the Caffres, but they were
scarcely human, better known to them than to us, and probably the Totties were
in the tops of the trees ready to pick out the officers.

Meanwhile Captain Faddy was shelling away rather wildly apparently, but as
we afterwards found, with deadly effect. The Company to which I belonged was
with the guns the first day; we heard continual firing, occasional yells, and now
and then cheers, which we answered from the heights: they gradually worked
up and by six o'clock in the evening had emerged and crowned the precipice.[28]

Michel's Column

Leaving the camp at Blakeway's farm under a strong guard to look after
the wagons, this column climbed Wolf's Head Pass, having a great deal
of difficulty in getting the guns up. On reaching the Kroome Heights the
guns were posted on a hill overlooking the Waterkloof, whereupon the men
stripped off their blankets and other encumbrances and took to the Tenth
Pass bush in extended order. One regiment swept round towards Arie's Hoek
where Colonel Eyre was operating, while the remainder extended across the
pass from krantz to krantz and proceeded down the Waterkloof sweeping the
bush for Ngqika.

It was difficult and unproductive work; heavy firing was heard from the
direction of Fuller's Hoek, which was rightly assumed to be from Colonel
Eyre's guns. Lower down in the more open ground of the Waterkloof the

Upper Waterkloof
10 March 1852

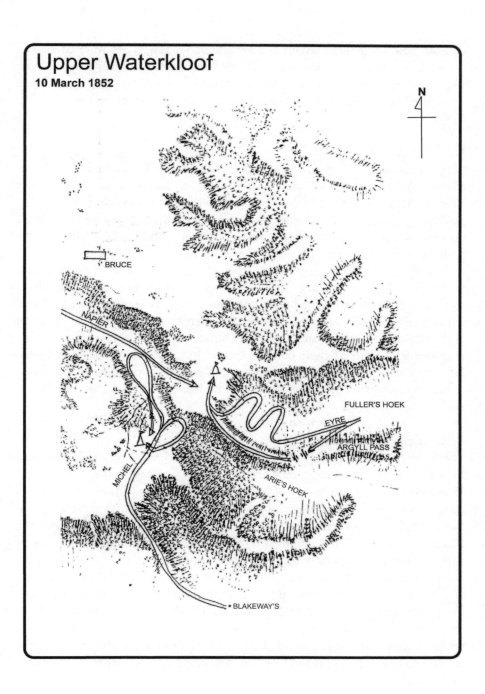

N

BRUCE

NAPIER

FULLER'S HOEK

EYRE

ARGYLL PASS

MICHEL

ARIE'S HOEK

BLAKEWAY'S

column saw some Xhosa who ran away when a few shots were fired. The column then turned back towards Tenth Pass and on the way several shots were fired at them from both flanks. After communicating with Colonel Eyre, the column crossed over to their guns, where they bivouacked for the night.

Napier's Column
Sergeant McKay was with this column as it left Haddon's farm for Mount Misery. At Nel's farm all were horrified to see the body of Private Peter Watson with his head and hands cut off and his trunk placed in a sitting position against a mud wall with his head lying on his outstretched legs. Their only consolation was the sight of many Thembu bodies, killed during the previous week's encounter.

In preparation for his arrival at the head of the Waterkloof, Napier had wisely placed the experienced 91st in the rear of his column. Sure enough, as soon as the 91st entered the bushy, winding path they were heavily attacked, with the loss of ten men wounded. The attackers were daring on this occasion and sustained the fight until, as the column reached the top of the valley, they saw men from Michel's column approaching, whereupon they fled deep into the bush.[29] McKay's sympathies were for the wounded men of the 91st – one was shot through the abdomen – who had to be carried all that day on stretchers, and the next day too.[30]

Bruce's Detachment
The Post Retief detachment had been reinforced by Captain Tylden and his burghers so, 160 strong, they arrived on the heights to the north of the Waterkloof just as the boom of guns started in Fuller's Hoek. As Napier's column advanced up the Waterkloof, Xhosa herd-boys drove their cattle up the steep, bush-covered sides with the intention of crossing over into the Blinkwater Valley. On reaching the plain, however, they got the shock of their young lives. Not only did they find soldiers in front of them but they were also being shot at accurately, for the burghers were excellent marksmen and Bruce's men were shooting well as a result of constant practice. The herd-boys hastily retreated, followed by the burghers, who captured many of their cattle. After this sharp lesson no herd-boy thereafter showed himself within a kilometre of the burghers, preferring to take his chances with the advancing skirmishers below; Captain Bruce had carried out his assignment most effectively.[31]

11 March
Eyre's Column

On this day, Eyre determined to locate and attack Maqoma's lair in Fuller's Hoek, a task which he superintended himself. The den was eventually discovered and overwhelmed, and several women were taken prisoner, including two of Maqoma's wives, one of them his Great Wife Noxlena, and his son Namba.[32]

Hugh Robinson described the action in a letter:

The second day was a repetition of the first, except that we went the other way, and in the morning the 74th (one company of them at least) with the Fingoes, came on a nest of Caffres chiefly women and children with all their valuables. The Fingoes, who make war on a common sense principle, saved the government the expense of rationing a large number of them. I cannot say I pity them; they are more cruel than the men, and always have the torturing of the prisoners, but their screams were very horrible.

I was on the top of a precipice when the massacre was going on 50 yards under my feet. The smoke rose up from the bush in clouds, and when we went down to the caverns, which were thought secret to all comers, we took all their treasures; there were leopard-skin karosses, quantities of skins embroidered with beads, snuffboxes made of tortoise shells, ivory rings for the arms, quantities of necklaces made of teeth, glass, etc. two very large saws (probably taken from white men) old muskets, pouches, bullets, tobacco, and a Cape Corps horse shoe pouch marked K57. Of these things I secured none, the skins being too lively to carry off, and the men snatched up the other things. Heaps of bodies were found, which had been killed by the shells the day before; around one fire were found eleven fighting Caffres killed dead by one shell. Certainly Artillery does save life wonderfully!

Colonel Eyre's division brought in 139 women and children, Maqoma's son and heir, Namba, among the latter. He is a most precocious young blackguard, and I wished the Fingoes had not overlooked him: I saw him upset a large pot of scalding soup on the body of another child. I made a sketch later of a small group of them including Maqoma's wife – wives rather for there were three of them. One of the women confessed to the torturing of the Bandmaster [Hartung] of the 74th Highlanders.

In the evening the Hon. Henry Wrottesley of the 43rd was shot in the thigh from out of a tree, on the edge of the Horseshoe where the Caffres had been singing a grand war song on the first day. The Tottie who killed him was picked off immediately, and fell to the ground.

Poor Wrottesley had to run 200 yards after he was wounded, for cover; he died shortly afterwards, from loss of blood. His body was taken to Blinkwater, and buried there. His funeral was attended by Sir Harry Smith (who knew how to behave to the son of a lord) and all his staff, a clergyman was sent for from Post Retief.[33]

There were other casualties: Captain Campbell of the 73rd had gone down Argyll Pass against stout resistance from the Ngqika; three other men of the 73rd were killed and one other wounded.[34]

Michel's and Napier's Columns

Both columns acting together went down into the Waterkloof, burning huts along the way. Nearing Iron Mountain they saw on its flat top a large body of rebels parading a number of cattle as if giving an open invitation to the troops to try their luck. It was considered impossible to attack Iron Mountain from the north so the force climbed the mountain from the east. There they found Michel's guns posted on the heights and the artillerymen busily throwing shells and rockets into the adjacent kloof wherever they saw the smoke of fires rising. As the climb had been steep and both men and horses were exhausted, it was decided to move back to the Kroome Heights for water and to spend the night there; the rebels on the Iron Mountain would be dealt with later. McKay thought it was a very fine gesture on the part of the 45th Regiment to help the 91st carry their wounded.[35]

12 March

On this day, the third of the operation, a temporary halt was called in order to obtain fresh supplies. Michel's column descended by Niland's Pass and on the way came across some human skulls. The doctor said they were those of Europeans and they were eagerly examined. Hartung's was not among them. Michel's column re-provisioned at Blakeway's farm, left their guns under guard there and returned to the Kroome Heights.

Two hundred more Boers from the districts of Somerset and Koonap arrived at Adelaide, and General Somerset was sent there by Sir Harry Smith to take command of them and of Napier's column.[36] Mule wagons were sent to Fort Beaufort bearing the ten wounded men of the 91st.

15 March

Eyre's Column

Maqoma's stronghold in Fuller's Hoek was again visited to show the rebels that Eyre was determined to expel them, although not a single Ngqika was to be seen. There was, however, gruesome evidence that they had suffered very heavily from the shelling of Eyre's four guns.

Michel's Column

Preparations were now complete for an attack on Iron Mountain. Michel moved down into the Waterkloof early and halted for breakfast with the red

17. Sir Harry Smith. (*Africana Museum, Johannesburg*)

18. Sir Harry Smith's house, King William's Town

19 The Boma Pass today

20. Christmas Day
Memorial, Woburn

21. Woburn Church

22. Fort Cox remains

23. Blakeway's farm

24. Wiggill's mill

25. The officers' mess, Post Retief

26. Fort Hare remains

27. The Upper Tyumie Valley

28. Fort Armstrong

29. The Kroome escarpment

30. The Upper Waterkloof

31. Mundell's Krantz

32. Fuller's Hoek

krantzes in view. The stronghold was a formidable one: high krantzes nearly surround the peak on three sides with only the south side free of them, it being joined to the Kroome Range by a long ridge. Michel tried to turn the position by a flank attack but in this he was unsuccessful as the ground was difficult, providing ample shelter for the rebels.

A direct assault from the front or north face therefore became necessary. Rockets were discharged into the krantzes and then the column advanced up the slope in extended order. Michel set a wonderful example: he snatched a rifle from one man and, shouting and cheering, led the 6th's charge up the mountainside. Near the top, however, the Ngqika met their advance with steady fire and the attack faltered.

Captain the Hon. Adrian Hope's company of the 60th Rifles fixed bayonets and, charging up the final slope, carried the mountain. Major William Fanshawe Bedford, with two other companies of the 60th Rifles, pursued the fugitives over rocks and krantzes, many cattle falling into his hands.[37] The whole attack, which had scarcely lasted an hour, resulted in the utter rout of the enemy and the capture of 560 head of cattle and seventy-five horses, some of the latter being very valuable animals.[38] The 60th's losses were one man killed and two wounded.[39] An anonymous correspondent who took part in the attack found several places where fourteen or fifteen of the rebels lay dead.[40]

Napier's Column

General Somerset and his column, suitably replenished and reinforced with two hundred burghers, left Adelaide marching north. They swung to the right before reaching the entrance to the Waterkloof and climbed the ridge to the grassy plain on top of the Kroome Range. Their task was to intercept any rebel attempts to escape from the Waterkloof into the bush to the south.

In the afternoon a number of Ngqika in possession of cattle were seen in a deep kloof. Somerset sent his mounted force of CMR and burghers, under Lieutenant-Colonel Napier, in pursuit. They succeeded in capturing 130 head of cattle and many horses; several of the rebels were killed and fifty women and children were made prisoners.

Sergeant McKay was in charge of the officers' baggage horses that day so he could only hear the musket fire as he climbed the ridge. When at last he reached the plain, however, he saw a horrifying sight: Ngqika women and children, who had been driven out of the bush, were being fired on by the burghers, around whose hats were written, in flaming letters, the word 'EXTERMINATION'. The fugitives were running to the British soldiers and clinging to their coats and legs to save themselves from the Boers' fury. These burghers shouted to McKay and those around him to shoot them down, but the soldiers refused to do so. McKay sympathised with the Boers, many of whom had had family members killed, but he felt it would set a bad precedent to return evil for evil.[41]

Cleaning Up

On 10 March, when Smith had launched his attack on the Kroome Heights, he had also initiated an attack on the Fish River bush by the large patrol under Lieutenant-Colonel Perceval, 12th Regiment, to which reference was made earlier. They first attacked the chief Stokwe of the Mbalu. There was a fierce engagement in which the 12th easily prevailed, the Mbalu being driven off and cattle and horses being captured.[42] Perceval then continued his campaign and was able to report to the governor that the Fish River bush had finally been cleared of rebels, taking a total of 350 cattle, many horses and goats, together with several stands of firearms, while at the same time inflicting heavy casualties on the Ngqika.[43] At the conclusion of the patrol, Perceval was ordered to Fort Cox.

General Somerset pursued the fleeing Ngqika along the upper reaches of the Kat River, where a number of horses were captured.[44] The two columns of Colonels Michel and Eyre joined Sir Harry at Blinkwater Post on 16 March and, two days later, Smith led them out towards the Tyumie Valley. On 21 March, both officers were ordered to take their columns into the Amatholas while Colonel Perceval, who had by this date reached Fort Cox, was ordered to penetrate the mountains from that direction. For four days, being joined by Perceval on the third day, the columns operated in a manner which Smith described as 'Colonel Eyre acting on the arc of a circle of which the operations of Colonel Michel and Colonel Perceval were the chord'. Colonel Michel stated:

> From my own observation I am enabled decidedly to say that the Gaika tribes generally have migrated from these their strongholds. With crops utterly destroyed, and with a spirit so broken that now two companies may traverse with safety where heretofore a large column was required, I deem the war in this quarter virtually concluded, although the faithlessness of seeming allies, and bands of marauding Hottentots, may yet for a time prevent the conclusion of a peace.

Colonel Eyre reported:

> We advanced through the Bomah Pass to the Quilli Quilli, thence through the Gulu Valley, ascending the heights, and back again through the Bomah Pass.

The result satisfied me that this part of the mountains was entirely abandoned. With the exception of three Kafirs whom I could see through my telescope, all 'treking' [sic] towards the Kabousie Neck, two or three women in the bush too old to 'trek', and two Kafirs near the Bomah Pass, there was not a living soul to be seen, while all the spoor indicated that the cattle had 'treked' towards the Kabousie during the rains that fell as we entered the mountains.

On 25 March, the governor moved his headquarters to Fort Cox, and quartered Colonel Michel and his column there. The next day, Smith returned to his headquarters at King William's Town, ordering Colonels Eyre and Perceval to scour the Pirie bush and the area around Murray's Krantz, long a hiding place for Ngqika rebels.

On 28 March, Smith received intelligence that the Ngqika were all heading east, collecting their large herds of cattle at the junctions of the Kei with the 'Doorn' and Thomas rivers.[45] Smith ordered Eyre to detach to Keiskamma Hoek while he himself moved, with the 12th Lancers, to the Kabousie Nek. Eyre marched at once and, arriving on 31 March, took the refugee Ngqika entirely by surprise. After some slight opposition, Eyre was able to capture 1,220 head of cattle, a number of horses and 'thousands' of goats. A detachment under Major Armstrong fell upon another herd nearby, and the total haul was 1,391 cattle.

In the meantime, the column under General Somerset had penetrated as far as the Windvogelberg, where he trapped a number of rebels trying to return to the Amatholas. They were driven back, and 1,500 head of cattle were taken.

On his arrival at King William's Town the governor learned that Chief Stokwe had applied to Phato to intecede in his [Stokwe's] favour.

There also occurred in March 1852 a quite bizarre incident when, or so it seemed, Sandile attempted to have Charles Brownlee, the Commissioner for the Ngqika, assassinated. The dates of the events are not entirely clear but it seems that Sandile was driven to this act by his state of mind as a result of the increasing difficulty of continuing the war. He commanded his warriors to kill Brownlee and, as proof of his death, to bring his head back.[46] In the meantime, Brownlee had taken part in some activity with Colonel Mackinnon, during which he had been wounded by an assegai in the thigh.[47]

Some days later, Brownlee's brother James, his clerk at Fort Cox, went out on a separate errand to recover some cattle stolen from King William's Town. The small party was surrounded by Ngqika and James was mortally wounded. Unaware that the dead man was not Charles Brownlee, the warriors decapitated James and took his head back to Sandile. The chief realised that the wrong man had been killed, saying, 'You should not have killed this man.'[48]

Smith's vigorous personal direction of the war in March 1852 proved more successful, particularly on the Kroome Heights, than most of his earlier efforts, despite the tragic losses of his troops. The last campaign certainly proved that the governor still retained his outstanding staff and tactical ability. A more negative consequence was a severe downturn in Smith's health.

Thus ended Sir Harry Smith's command at the Cape. In one of his last reports to the Colonial Secretary, Earl Grey, he found some personal satisfaction in being able to write:

> I pronounce these difficult and heretofore well-maintained positions of the enemy, viz., the Waterkloof, Blinkwater and Fuller's Hoek, to be now completely cleared.[49]

Up to the end, Sir Harry Smith, however, had still not understood the lesson that the artist Thomas Baines, no soldier, had learned on early acquaintance with engagements on the Kroome Heights:

> Every position, as it was abandoned by us, was occupied by the enemy, with a rapidity and boldness that spoke well for their courage, as well as judgement.[50]

However, nor did he know that the Whig government had also fallen and that Earl Grey, like Sir Harry himself, had been replaced.

Chapter 11

Changes

As a result of Sir Harry's earlier appeals for more troops, the 1st Battalion, Rifle Brigade, seven hundred strong, left Dover on HMS *Magaera* on 2 January 1852. The regiment was Harry Smith's own and he was colonel commandant of the 2nd Battalion.[1]

Only two hundred of the men were Cape veterans. The ship met with rough weather in the English Channel and had to put into Plymouth on the 5th for repairs, having twice caught fire. The ship hurriedly left Plymouth on 7 January, caught fire yet again in the Bay of Biscay, stopped at Madeira on the 24th, Sierra Leone on 6 February and arrived at Simon's Town on 24 March. The brigade rested at the Cape and finally arrived at Algoa Bay on 30 March with Lieutenant-Colonel George Buller in command of thirty-two officers, 665 men, twenty-three horses and a quantity of ordnance stores, ammunition and camp equipment.[2]

The New Governor

Lieutenant-General the Honourable George Cathcart also arrived at Cape Town on 30 March 1852 to assume his duties as governor of the Cape, high commissioner and commander-in-chief. Mostert described the new governor thus: 'The Governor, "a striking-looking man", tall and slender, always appeared in hip-length boots, which earned him the derisive name of 'Boots' Cathcart, and the sarcastic assumption that he slept in them. He would, Robinson said, "be a very fine soldier in the Low Countries".'[3]

In an unusual departure, but one which was not entirely unknown, a new lieutenant-governor, in the person of Lieutenant-General Henry Charles Darling, also arrived, just prior to Cathcart.[4] Both Cathcart and Darling were sworn into their respective offices on the last day of March.

The new governor also brought with him yet another senior soldier, Major-General Charles Yorke, who was to be his second-in-command on the frontier. Yorke had served with the 52nd Regiment in the Peninsular War and also at Waterloo.[5] Cathcart had expressed some concern that Somerset was senior to himself.[6] This concern could not have referred to his military rank because all three men, Cathcart, Yorke and Somerset, were promoted major-general on the same day: 11 November 1851.[7] It must, therefore, have referred to Cathcart's lack of experience in South African warfare.

It may be considered that Yorke's appointment was an implicit criticism of General Somerset, with so many informal reports of his venality and incompetence having reached England. This was not, it seems, the case. In 1850, Somerset had been advised that he was to be appointed to a post in India and had put his home Oatlands Park, close to Grahamstown, up for sale. The time for such a sale was not auspicious, with the result that a group of his friends joined together to purchase it from him, on the understanding that he was to remain in possession until his departure from the country.[8]

Cathcart left Cape Town for the frontier in HMS *Styx*, disembarking at East London on 8 April and arriving at King William's Town on the 9th. Lieutenant-Governor Darling remained behind in Cape Town to carry the administrative burden there, thus relieving the pressure on Cathcart to a considerable degree. The next day Cathcart met Sir Harry Smith, 'who devoted the whole of that day to the purpose of giving me every insight into the affairs of the colony generally, and more particularly to the Eastern Frontier'.[9] Smith left King William's Town at 3 a.m. on 11 April and looked a very sick man on his arrival at Cape Town on the 14th. He departed from South Africa, with his wife Juana, on 18 April, Captain King-Hall of the *Styx* noting that his condition had greatly improved, having thought the previous day that he might not reach England alive.[10]

Although little time had elapsed before the new governor began issuing orders to his senior officers, some of his decisions seem to have been eminently sensible. For example, the Ngqika had been required by Smith to cross the Kei River, having been expelled from the Ciskei. Cathcart therefore thought it a

> contradiction to place troops on the open country of the Kabousie to intercept them, and therefore I have recalled the cavalry detachment under the command of Major Tottenham of the 12th Lancers to King William's Town till further orders. They will be replaced when the Gaikas shall have been expelled, and the object may then be to prevent their return.[11]

On an equally refreshing note, he decided that not only should Colonel Eyre and his force remain at Keiskamma Hoek, but that he would 'cause a stone tower or blockhouse to be erected . . . which may suffice as a rallying point for a few men, , the fire of whose musketry might effectually protect those left in camp . . .'

Cathcart was also fully aware of the difficulties faced in the Kroome Heights:

> By all accounts which I have received there can be no doubt that the Kroome Range in which the Waterkloof is situated, and which is only about twelve miles from Fort Beaufort within the colony, is again occupied by Macomo and his followers, associated with rebel Hottentots; and it is likely that other desperate characters may seek for shelter in this stronghold, to the terror and annoyance of neighbouring farmers.[12]

He therefore proposed that further permanently manned posts, or 'castles' as he preferred to call them, be built, communicating with each other to form a mutually defensive area.

On 12 April, Cathcart published a proclamation addressed to 'the people who dwell between the Rivers Kei and Keiskamma'. He assured those who had remained loyal to the Queen that they would continue to enjoy the governor's friendship; among these he named Phato, Siwani, Toyise, Mqhayi and others of the Ndlambe. On the other hand, Sandile, Maqoma and all the Ngqika chiefs, including Siyolo of the Ndlambe, who had been parties to the rebellion, had committed a great crime and could not be forgiven. Although the governor wished for peace, these men must cross the Kei River 'and none of them will ever be suffered to return and live in peace in the country they occupied before the war.'[13]

It was not long, however, before he decided to begin his own campaigns on the Kroome Heights.

The Kroome Heights, April–May 1852

Two of these campaigns were carried out by the 60th Rifle Brigade under the command of Colonel George Buller. In the first, he took with him a quite modest force, consisting of three companies of his brigade, a few CMR, a small number of Mfengu and one six-pounder gun.[14]

29 April

The column fell in at 4 a.m. and was ordered to move forward to Mount Misery in silence. Captain Edward Arthur Somerset's company, with the gun, went round by a wagon track, while Captains Lord Alexander George Russell and Charles John Woodford, with Colonel Buller in command, marched via Mundell's farm along the northern ridge of the Waterkloof. An anonymous officer of the Rifle Brigade, here called Lieutenant R.,[15] accompanied the patrol. He found the going difficult in the dark over the rough and broken ground but eventually they reached the Horseshoe. There, an enemy village was seen in a position that would have been very familiar to Lieutenant King of the 74th – just south of the Tongue.

Captain Russell, extending his company, advanced steadily, with Woodford's company covering him, to a thicket within 150 metres of the main bush where the Ngqika had taken up a strong position. The Riflemen began firing with their modern weapons, which were far more accurate at this distance than the enemy's, although the latter, firing from behind rocks and under cover of the bush, maintained their ground very stubbornly. During this exchange, Lieutenant Arthur William Godfrey was wounded, the missile grazing the top of his forehead and carrying away the tip of his ear. Two privates were also wounded, though not seriously.[16] It was evident to Lieutenant R. that the Riflemen were not getting the best of it for, although they themselves were in the bush, the Ngqika were making more intelligent use of the cover behind rocks and tree trunks, frequently shifting their position.

Eventually Captain Edward Somerset arrived with his gun (the Somersets seem to have had a penchant for arriving late), although he also brought with him something even more vital: the news that a strong body of rebels was heading their way from another quarter. Colonel Buller immediately gave the order to retire out of the bush. Once in the open, a few shells were thrown into the enemy's position, while all the huts that could be found in the vicinity were burnt. Lieutenant R. felt that the day, though not outstanding in terms of results, had been an arduous one.[17]

During the march back, the Ngqika tagged behind but did not come within range and the column arrived back at Bear's farm at 2 p.m.[18] There, Colonel Buller addressed the men, thanking them for their steadiness and giving them that praise which, Lieutenant R. thought, could not be anything but gratifying to gallant men.

Little more than two weeks later, the second foray was made to the Kroome Heights, once again under the command of Colonel Buller. This time he took with him two guns of the Royal Artillery, and four companies of his own Rifle Brigade. There were no CMR or Mfengu with him on this occasion.

18 May[19]
Colonel Buller's force left Bear's farm before daylight with William Bear himself as a guide – at the rate of fifteen shillings a day plus forage for one horse. On arrival at the Horseshoe, near the scene of their engagement

of 29 April, some huts were burnt and three of the enemy's horses were captured while several musket shots were fired at the Rifle Brigade from the bush.

Suddenly, the rebels came out of the bush and made as if to attack in force. This menace was too much for Colonel Buller and he immediately ordered the 'retire' to be sounded. It took all Major Alfred Horsford's persuasion to have the order cancelled; he pointed out that it was 'ridiculous to retire until compelled to do so'. Reluctantly, Buller changed his mind, and the Riflemen were extended in skirmishing order to meet the onslaught, while the two guns opened fire at close range. The Ngqika, however, continued to advance in spite of their losses, until at last Buller could stand the strain no longer and once more ordered the brigade to retire. He also ordered the guns to be spiked, as there was no time to bring them away. The artillerymen, however, ignored the order and, while the Rifle Brigade retired, they continued firing. A mounted officer rode up to them with express orders from Colonel Buller, saying that if they did not spike their guns immediately, they would be court-martialled. The gunners still disobeyed the order and kept up a heavy accurate fire on the enemy, limbering and unlimbering time and time again in a fine, rear-guard action.[20] The Rifle Brigade, meanwhile, had retired by companies, each in turn facing the enemy and firing while the rest doubled to the rear. They were thus engaged for four hours and retired fighting over eight kilometres. During this harassment by the enemy three men of the Rifle Brigade were wounded. The artillerymen were not court-martialled.[21]

Abduction of a Spy

On 22 May 1852, an extraordinary event occurred which allows us a small window into the world of espionage at the Cape. The commissioner for the Ndlambe, John Maclean, reported to the chief commissioner, Colonel Mackinnon, that the chief Toyise, a cousin of the powerful Mhala of the Ndlambe, had been kidnapped by a group of Khoikhoi rebels under the command of Willem Uithaalder. These people, thirty mounted and twenty on foot, had surrounded his homestead in the early morning. When asked what they wanted, their leader had replied that he had come to apprehend Toyise as their enemy. They lined up the few people in the homestead and threatened to shoot them if they did not reveal Toyise's whereabouts. When they did so, the men went inside a hut and brought Toyise out, demanding a horse for the chief. When one was found, they rode off with him after stripping his wives naked, taking with them about sixty of the chief's cattle.[22]

Mostert gives a very good, if startling, explanation of this event:

The most valued [collaborator] was a chief named Toyise, a cousin of the
principal of the Ndlambe chiefs, Mhala, who became the fore-most spy among
his own people. Toyise even made special journeys among the Ngqika to obtain
information and went so far as to promise to capture Sandile. But although he
begged Maclean not to betray him as a collaborator, the Ngqika appear to have
been well informed about him . . .[23]

Toyise was then in his thirties and was described as an 'attractive' man.
Lieutenant Hugh Robinson said that he was the best-mannered Xhosa he
had met, a 'gentleman at first sight'. At the same time, he was applying himself as a spy with diligence and zest.[24]

It seems that Sandile desperately wanted to apprehend Toyise with the
intention of executing him. Uithaalder agreed to undertake his capture and
carried him off to a nearby village. Luck was to remain with Toyise because,
when Sandile's councillors and his half-brother Anta arrived, Uithaalder
refused to allow the execution without a full trial. Before Sandile himself could
arrive, the Khoikhoi had released their prisoner and allowed him to escape.[25]

George Cory was more circumspect in his telling of this story, remaining
silent on Toyise's intelligence operations.[26] Sir George Cathcart was, however,
less coy, noting that the chief had 'carried his loyalty [to Britain] beyond
that of the other T'slambies [Ndlambe] in the way of obtaining and giving
information . . .'[27]

The chief was well rewarded for his 'loyalty' to the Cape administration,
having been given a very large portion of land between the Amathola
Mountains and the Kei River. As a direct result of this incident, and the
odium in which he was then held by the Ngqika, it was felt that his safety
would be in jeopardy in such an exposed area and he was re-located to the
vicinity of Fort Murray, East London.[28]

Needless to say, Toyise resumed his clandestine operations as soon as he
deemed it safe to do so.

Major Hogge Departs

Commissioner Hogge had long enjoyed the confidence of Earl Grey but
when the latter was replaced as Secretary of State for the Colonies by Sir
John Pakington, Major Hogge fell out of the limelight. His (and Owen's)
influential communiqués from the Orange River Sovereignty had determined
the British government to resign its control over the territory. Now the
importance of their work was diminished.

William S. Hogge died in Bloemfontein on 9 June 1852, as the result of a fever brought about by long exposure to bad weather during his travels in the sovereignty and Basutoland.[29]

The ubiquitous Sergeant McKay wrote of his death as follows:

Major Hogg proved himself an active and zealous officer during the brief period of his career in this country, but unfortunately he died the following June. A recent writer in the *Friend of the Free State* newspaper, alluding to the military churchyard at Bloemfontein, says:– 'Next to this grave is that of Major Hogg, in life time of H.M. 7th Dragoon Guards, and an assistant commissioner charged to arrange with the inhabitants of this country (Free State now) for its future Government. He died here in the execution of his enormous responsibilities in the prime of life, aged forty. Here we have lying a man who shortly before his death left his father's palatial residence and aristocratic circle to die in this land (Sovereignty), at that time a semi-barbarous country – a curious, yet not uncommon vicissitude of life's phases.'[30]

With his passing, Owen too passes out of view and out of this history.

Cathcart's Preparations

Cathcart's consultations caused the governor to identify three difficult areas requiring special attention: the Amathola Mountains, the area north of the Amatholas between the Klip Plaats and Kei rivers, centred on the Windvogelberg, and finally the Fish River bush.[31]

After a further month of investigation, the governor put forward a draft proclamation for the formation of an armed mounted police force,[32] at the same time moving his headquarters from King William's Town to Fort Beaufort.[33]

On the same date, he set out his achievements and plans for bringing the war to an end.[34] He had visited both Colonel Eyre and Colonel Michel in the Amatholas, finding that they were able to keep the heavily forested area clear of Ngqika, except for about one-third of it in the north-west. It was here that he believed Sandile and his adherents were based.

The promised tower, called 'Castle Eyre', had been completed in Keiskamma Hoek. Cathcart was proud to give a full description of its features:

The tower which I have caused to be built in the centre of the Amatolas, on a most favourable site, is of stone found on the spot, rubble work, 15 feet square, and two stories high, with a flat roof to carry a gun; the cost will not exceed £300. The object is that for which church towers were originally, no doubt, intended in early stages of society . . . viz., a rallying point from whence a very few men, possessed of superior projectile weapons, might command a radius, within which the community, and even their cattle, might take shelter when suddenly beset by swarms of savages.[35]

He observed, somewhat acerbically, that had such a tower been built in the military villages, the massacres of Christmas 1850 would not have taken place. Cory noted: 'With a garrison of ten men, a musket fire could command a rayon of two to three hundred yards, while the gun on top would make itself felt at a distance of six hundred yards.'[36]

A similar tower had been ordered to be built on the Grahamstown road some nineteen kilometres from King William's Town and ten kilometres from Line Drift, near the source of the Tamacha River. This was later to be called Tamacha Post and was designed to keep Chief Siyolo under control prior to his ejection. A third was planned for Line Drift.

Cathcart posted what he called his second division, under the command of General Yorke, at King William's Town in British Kaffraria. Colonels Michel and Eyre formed his two columns, the former based at Fort Cox covering Mount MacDonald.

The first division, under General Somerset, remained at Fort Beaufort and '[required] much personal attention and support of the chief in command to bring into a satisfactory state'.[37] Somerset had troops at Bear's farm, Balfour, Post Retief, Blinkwater, the Mankazana River, Eland's Post and Haddon's farm. These posts surrounded the Kroome Heights and also controlled the area to their north.

Still another, smaller, column, under the command of Colonel Perceval, was based at the Fish River.

On 1 June, the governor posted a general order announcing the formation of his armed mounted police.[38] There was to be a unit in each of the districts of Albany, Somerset, Cradock, Albert and Victoria, all of which were adjacent to the frontier. Each unit was to be under the command of a commandant, with no more than 150 men in each. He also posted the rules and regulations for the force on the same date.[39]

In a letter to the Commanding Royal Engineer, Cathcart revealed plans for a further five of his 'castles'. These were to be located at Brown's farm in the centre of the Waterkloof, on 'the top of the hill which commands Waterkloof and Fuller's Hoek', at the Middle Drift, in the Lenea(?) Valley, and the fifth at the summit of Mount Macdonald.[40] In this memorandum the governor also ordered the repair of Fort White and foreshadowed a move of that post to a less exposed position.

During these preparations, attacks by rebels still continued. Just before dawn on 13 June five wagons left Fort Brown for Fort Beaufort. They had crossed the Fish River and were making their way up the steep Koonap Hill. Moving at a leisurely pace and in assumed security, they were suddenly brought to a standstill by volley fire from the bush on both sides of the road. The mules of the first wagon in the convoy were quickly killed, blocking the road to further progress, while the few soldiers also began to fall under fire. The total casualties here were seven men and one woman killed, with eleven more men wounded. Common sense dictated a retreat towards Fort Brown and the remaining wagons were turned round. By the time this was accomplished the draft oxen had been killed and the wagons had to be abandoned. Refuge for the people was found in a deserted house, the windows of which had already been bricked up and loopholes cut. The firing was heard at Fort Brown and assistance was quickly sent. The people were saved but it made no difference: the Khoikhoi rebels had looted the wagons and nothing remained.[41]

Murray's Krantz, June 1852

It was discovered that a large number of rebel Khoikhoi under Willem Uithaalder were located in the area of Murray's Krantz, in the western Amatholas. Two columns were ordered to converge on the area. The first, under Lieutenant-Colonel Michel, marched north from King William's Town while the second, under Lieutenant-Colonel Eyre, left from Keiskamma Hoek to march south.

On 20 June,[42] Colonel Eyre was in the vanguard of his column with only two companies of the 43rd Regiment under Captain the Honourable Percy Egerton Herbert, when he stumbled on the rebel camp. Without waiting for the remainder of his column to come up, Eyre took advantage of the confusion caused by his appearance and attacked the Khoikhoi, who had taken a position on the fringe of a wooded area.

He ordered one of the companies to extend into skirmishing order and advance on the trees while the second company was extended in its rear in support. The two companies then drove the rebels through the woodland to the edge of Murray's Krantz. A number of Khoikhoi were killed and more were literally thrown over the precipice, the remainder scrambling down to safety. Eyre's companies suffered only three men wounded. The rebel camp was burnt and a large number of firearms, including a number of Minié rifles, and ammunition were recovered.[43] Michel, 'from difficulties of the road and the darkness of night', arrived after the victory was won.

The Kroome Heights, July 1852

The governor decided that the time had now arrived for him to drive the Xhosa and Khoikhoi rebels out of the Waterkloof area. His Excellency left Government House, Fort Beaufort, for the front at noon on 6 July with his staff, a guard of the 12th Lancers and some Cape Mounted Riflemen. The governor, a correspondent noted, was wearing a 'wideawake' hat, was smoking a cigar and seemed in good health and spirits.[44]

The viceregal entourage proceeded to the ruins of Painter's farm, 'Yellowwood Trees', on the Gcuwa River, about five kilometres south of the escarpment of the Kroome Mountains. There they joined Nesbitt's column and together bivouacked for the night.

The troops to be engaged consisted of three columns, all under the command of General Cathcart. The first column, under the command of Colonel Buller, consisted of the Rifle Brigade and a small detachment of CMR. Buller was to march from Bear's farm.

Colonel Napier's second column consisted of three companies of his 91st Regiment, a detachment of CMR, a recently formed mounted unit called Lakeman's Corps and the Kat River Levy. He also took with him two guns, and began his march from Blinkwater Post.

The third column, under Colonel Nesbitt, included the 60th Rifles, the Fort Beaufort Mfengu Levy under Captain Peter Campbell and a detachment of engineers. This column also had two guns, and was to be accompanied by Cathcart and his headquarters. They would begin their march from Niland's farm south of the escarpment.[45]

A smaller detachment of fifty mounted burghers under Captain Bruce was to move down from Post Retief to intercept any movement of cattle or fugitives.[46]

7 July
Buller's Column
The Rifle Brigade camp at Bear's farm was struck and the tents and baggage were placed in the farmyard under the charge of Captain Woodford's company. The remaining companies paraded at midnight, the men carrying their coats and blankets and three days' rations, which they had been ordered to pre-cook. They marched off in the cold sleet of a winter morning down Bush Nek, past the entrance to the Waterkloof and climbed up the Kroome Range. They continued along the top of the range until 1 p.m. when, after being on the march for thirteen hours, they came to the head of Niland's Pass. There they halted to wait for the governor.[47]

Nesbitt's Column

As Cathcart climbed Niland's Pass with Nesbitt's column, he remarked on the complete absence of any sign of the enemy, in contrast to the resistance displayed on former occasions. On joining Buller's column, the force proceeded to the plateau and prepared their bivouac on the same ground on which the lunch of Fordyce's men had been interrupted previously, on 8 September. The two columns then went to the ridge overlooking the Waterkloof and from there sent shells and rockets into any places where Xhosa and Khoikhoi rebels might be lurking. They could not, however, see any homesteads, nor could they find any cattle tracks. After this display of force against an invisible and possibly non-existent enemy, the governor and two columns returned to the shallow valley to bivouac for the night.[48]

The only action that any of Buller's men saw that day was back at Bear's farm, where some Ngqika, rushing out of a nearby kloof, drove off seven of the Rifle Brigade's grazing oxen. Captain Woodford had his company stand to arms but reluctantly came to the decision that he could not leave the camp as the Ngqika appeared in numbers on the surrounding hills; instead, he sent the wagoners to re-capture the oxen. As these men approached, the Xhosa retired, leaving the oxen behind; then, seeing they were only wagoners and not real soldiers, the Xhosa returned and made off with their prizes.[49]

Napier's Column

Napier's men marched from Blinkwater Post at 3 a.m. and climbed up to the Horseshoe, probably by Wolf's Back Ridge, without firing a shot or seeing many of the rebels.[50] On the Horseshoe they came under attack from Xhosa and Khoikhoi, who not only fired at them from behind rocks and trees but had the audacity to come out into the open and attack. Napier had two guns with him and as soon as it was light enough, he ordered the gunners to shell them wherever they could be seen, causing severe losses.

These would have been all the known facts about Napier's fighting that day had it not been for the presence of Captain Lakeman and his corps of volunteers. Stephen Lakeman was the twenty-two-year-old son of a wealthy Englishman of Dutch descent, an ancestor having come over with William III. His great passion was for soldiering and he had already voluntarily sought and found active service in Hungary and with the French against the Arabs in Algeria. His one fault, if such it can be called, was that he was not a modest man, and claimed at every turn the acknowledgement that he thought was his due.

At his own expense, Lakeman had recruited eighty men, mostly ex-sailors, in Cape Town for his corps. He had dressed them in unorthodox but very

effective uniforms, the garments and helmet being of leather, and they were
armed with the latest Minié rifle. On arriving at Fort Beaufort, Lakeman,
with refreshing frankness, expressed his astonishment at the closeness of the
enemy: 'There they were in shoals, perfectly unmolested, only twelve miles
away from thousands of British troops; a badly armed, undisciplined throng
of naked savages braving with impunity, day after day, week after week, the
energies of the British Empire.'[51]

Now he was on the Horseshoe with orders to attack a group of Ngqika
in the wooded Tongue. With his men in skirmishing order he approached
the area obliquely from the north, trying to keep his men in line, for he
was conscious that the eyes of Colonel Napier, the old soldiers of the 91st
Regiment and many others were upon him. A shot from an enemy marksman
brought down his orderly David McIntyre, mortally wounded with a ball
through his chest, and the whole line stopped. With commendable quick
thinking Lakeman ran to the front and shouted: 'We shall all be shot if
we stay here in the open! To the bush, my lads! To the bush!' Whereupon
with shouts of 'Hurrah', which Lakeman thought did more to drown their
own fears than to frighten their antagonists, and amidst a rattling fire which
was more noisy than dangerous, they charged the bush. Once inside, they
kept up their cheering and firing and made such a hullabaloo that the
Ngqika fled. Lakeman was astonished at the calming effect the noise and its
reverberations had on his own nerves: instead of the spookiness of a silent
wood, the noise produced a sense of comradeship and togetherness. Charging
right through the Tongue they came out on the south side, surprised at not
meeting more resistance. Lakeman and his men then rejoined the main body
in a cool, collected manner; they were veterans now, and received the thanks
of Colonel Napier, conveyed by a staff officer, for their gallant and orderly
bearing.[52]

They sat down to breakfast and had hardly begun to eat when the same
staff officer came back and ordered Lakeman to dislodge the Ngqika from
some boulders overlooking the head of the Waterkloof. Lakeman thought
this rather unfair as many companies of the 91st and the Kat River Levy had
not moved since their climb from the Blinkwater and were, he was sure, eager
for an opportunity to distinguish themselves. He said nothing, however, but
gathered his men for the mission, which seemed to him to have little strategic
importance as the position neither threatened the enemy's stronghold nor
interfered with any movement to take it. Before reaching the boulders,
Lakeman split his force into two: one group for a flanking movement to the
left, he himself taking the other on a course that would approach the boulders
obliquely from the right.

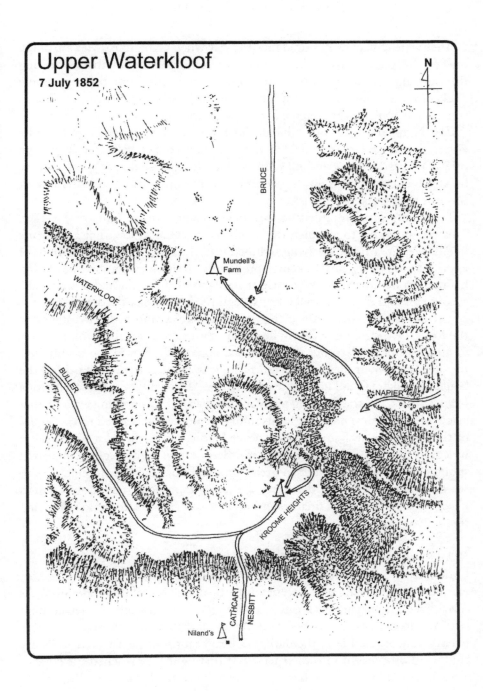

They were still a few hundred metres away when Captain Rowley's artillery opened fire, giving most of his men a sensation new to them, that of hearing the hurtling sound of shot coming over their heads from the rear. Some ducked, some stopped, others went on and, to Lakeman's distress, his line of skirmishers took on the shape of a zig-zag mob.

The Ngqika, on the other hand, did not seem very much frightened by either shot or shell. They fielded the shot like cricket balls, for they were prized as pestles for grinding corn, and as for the shells, as soon as they burst the enemy picked up the pieces and contemptuously threw them back towards the attackers.

Lakeman's most humiliating experience came from a Congreve rocket. This was intended to astonish the rebels but it came so low that Lakeman's line ducked in a ridiculously undignified way, the crouch bringing a shout of approval from the enemy. Lakeman profited from this humiliation by ordering his men to lie down properly, raise their sights to five hundred metres, take steady aim and fire. The volley left several of the Ngqika dead and sent the rest scurrying for cover. Advancing cautiously to within a short distance of the rocks, he ordered his men to lie down again to wait for the flanking party to attack from the left; but the latter had apparently moved too deeply into the bush and when they were heard firing it was not at the rebels behind the boulders. Lakeman did not know what to do – the enemy was too strong for a frontal attack and the flanking party sounded as if it was moving even further away. At this critical moment in his military career he was saved by the sound of the 'recall' far away in the rear; never before had he heard a sound more welcome. So they fell back in a most orderly manner, the Ngqika, however, spoiling it all by coming out in great numbers from behind the boulders to see them off and hooting derisively at their ignominious retreat. As a sop to his ego, Lakeman fired a final volley and at least had the satisfaction of seeing them dive for cover.[53]

Bruce's Detachment

Orders arrived for Captain Bruce to join the combined operation, his assignment once again being to intercept any cattle driven out of the Waterkloof. As it was necessary to gain his position at Mundell's farm unseen, the detachment left Post Retief two hours before daybreak and they had an uncomfortable twenty kilometres ride in the dark in a heavy storm of sleet which a bitterly cold wind drove right into their teeth. At first light they reached the edge of a small area of bush where they were able to lie concealed all day. With numb fingers, saddles and bridles were removed and the horses tethered to the trees. The rain and sleet eventually cleared up and, as the sun rose, many beautiful

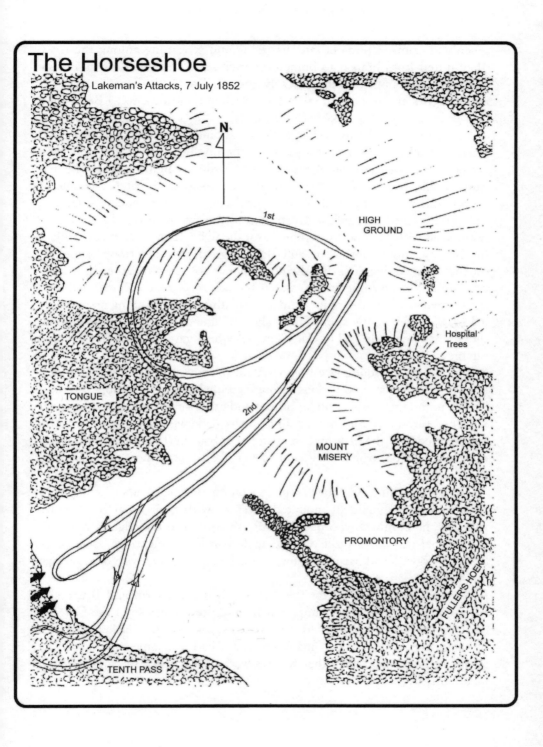

The Horseshoe

Lakeman's Attacks, 7 July 1852

N

1st

HIGH
GROUND

TONGUE

Hospital
Trees

2nd

MOUNT
MISERY

PROMONTORY

FULLERS HOEK

TENTH PASS

green and crimson birds began chattering and screaming among the trees. They flitted from branch to branch quite close to Captain King as if they knew he dared not fire at them. Only one small fire was allowed for all the coffee kettles and to prevent even that revealing their presence, a Boer stood over it dispersing the smoke with his hat.[54]

King could see a Thembu village about a kilometre away and with his usual interest watched it through his glass. At the first boom of artillery the men armed themselves and ran at top speed towards the fighting. Two Thembu came within five hundred metres of Bruce's position, to catch a couple of horses which the troops had failed to see. Being forced to remain concealed, the burghers had to watch in frustration as the two men raced back to the homestead with their booty to prepare for the fight. Then, as Napier's artillery fire became more continuous and Buller's green-jacketed troops appeared on the opposite heights, the Thembu women collected together in a large circle under a spreading tree to watch the action. King could distinctly see the women smoking their pipes and gesticulating, some standing up perfectly naked, the sleek ebony skin of their shapely figures shining in the sunlight, though most were draped in black karosses which gave the group an evil and satanic appearance.

It was a picturesque place they were in; the sun streamed down through trees completely covered by long, drooping bunches of lichen, horses' tethers looped round their hoary trunks, bridles and other gear hanging on the lower branches. Groups of burghers lay in an open glade while others crouched on the outer edge of the little area of bush peering at the Thembu and watching eagerly for cattle, which they could keep if captured. The cattle, however, never came.[55]

Towards evening, Colonel Napier's column was seen approaching and soon its advance guard of mounted Mfengu, with their usual zeal, fired a volley at the burghers who had incautiously moved to the edge of the bush to see what was going on. Everyone, including King, fell flat on their faces. Several burghers had narrow escapes, some being spattered with mud thrown up by bullets.

Napier's column halted for the night at Mundell's farm and Bruce and King visited them at their camp, which still bore the marks of the October occupation: picketing pins, old cattle enclosures and the blackened circles of camp fires around which many comrades had sat, some now dead. The graves of Norris and the other fellows were undisturbed, the grass waving luxuriantly over them.[56]

8 July

At daybreak General Cathcart, together with Buller's and Nesbitt's columns, crossed over Tenth Pass, leaving their guns at their bivouac under a guard. The pass was crossed without opposition; after joining up with Napier's column, a total of two thousand men then proceeded to attack the rebels. The Rifle Brigade with Mfengu and other levies scoured the Tongue and drove the Xhosa deep into the bush. Other regiments spent their time burning numerous huts around the Horseshoe while the artillery shelled homesteads in the kloofs below wherever they could be seen, and frightened everyone with their rockets.

Napier's column carried its attack to Mundell's Krantz where the 91st's skirmishers fired on the rebels sheltered behind rocks on the edge of the Waterkloof.[57] Lakeman, who had attacked some huts on the edge of the promontory at Mundell's Krantz, thought the whole thing rather a tame affair.[58] Lieutenant King, from his little patch of bush, could see the Ngqika firing on the 91st; they ran with wonderful agility and cunning from rock to rock, displaying a use of cover that thrilled his professional pride. In the afternoon, Napier's column again returned to bivouac at Mundell's farm.[59]

While these attacks were under way, General Cathcart toured the Horseshoe with Captain Jesse, RE, to find a site for a permanent post to command the Waterkloof. At noon Cathcart, with Buller's and Nesbitt's columns, re-crossed Tenth Pass to their bivouac. The crossing was made without opposition but numbers of the rebels were seen running towards the pass just as the Rifle Brigade entered it. Their leaders, however, arrived only in time to exchange a few shots with the rear guard of the 60th Rifles.

Lieutenant King had a miserable day. At daylight he mounted his shivering horse and, in a well-soaked saddle, rode stiff with cold to report to Colonel Napier for orders. His column was just falling in for the march to the Horseshoe when King was ordered to remain behind with fifteen men to ambush scavenging Xhosa, so he entered the Mfengu's old bush on the west side of the valley and there he waited. No sooner had the last section of Napier's column disappeared over the furthest ridge than the ground was covered with enormous vultures, black-and-white crows and secretary birds, the latter stalking within a few paces of where King lay hidden. After two hours of watching, lying in a ditch in wet clothes and on a bitterly cold day, King's zeal evaporated. With not a single rebel having appeared, and the lookout on top of the highest tree having seen nothing moving on the plain, King and his men came out of their hiding place – much to the astonishment of the birds – and rejoined their comrades in the little scrap of bush.[60]

The only casualty of the day was one man of the Rifle Brigade mortally wounded. To Lakeman, who happened to be nearby when the man was shot, it was a singular example of tenacity for life. The shot had gone through the Rifleman's head so all Lakeman could do was to prop him up on his pack and place his cap, with Lakeman's own handkerchief underneath, over his face. That evening Lakeman was at Post Retief, probably to attend the burial of his orderly David McIntyre, and there he found the Rifleman still alive – in spite of a hole in his head through which a ramrod could have been pushed. Incredibly, the man lived until the early hours of the morning.[61]

9 July

Daylight came to find the mountain ranges white with snow as far as the eye could see. The sleet turned to rain and the wind, piercing their wet clothing, was so intensely chilling that the men who had been lying in puddles all night were nearly helpless. Cathcart suspended all operations and ordered the troops, except for the 91st and Lakeman's Corps, to return to their permanent camps until the weather improved.

During the next few days Lakeman set to work building a stone-walled enclosure near where he had first entered the Tongue, as a defence against night attacks. The position was well chosen: it had a good view all round, it was near the only reliable supply of water on Mount Misery and there were plenty of stones for construction in its immediate vicinity. With the men spurred on by the cold, the barricade was soon high enough to shelter the men from the wind and to resist a major attack.[62] It was promptly dubbed Lakeman's Fort although Lakeman himself named it Fort McIntyre after his late orderly – in spite of his brash exterior it would seem that he did have a sentimental streak.

As he was free from official constraints, Lakeman decided on a form of harassment that was simple and effective – night attacks. His argument was that at night the black man's dread of the dark reduced his mobility while the dark increased the white man's chance of moving about unnoticed. It would appear that he assumed the role that the Rifle Brigade had overlooked: the commando. These night attacks proved very effective in discouraging the enemy from grazing their cattle at night and so, as there is little cattle feed in the bush, hastened the day when they would have to leave the Waterkloof to avoid starvation.[63]

14 July

The weather having improved, General Cathcart returned to Mount Misery with all his available troops: Buller's, Napier's and Nesbitt's. All bivouacked there for the night except for the 60th, which camped at Eastland's farm. The Rifle Brigade finally left their camping ground at Bear's farm and moved to Mount Misery along the northern edge of the Waterkloof. General Cathcart joined the forces there and selected the sites for two redoubts, which he considered all that was necessary to secure a permanent camp. Cathcart had written to the Colonial Secretary on 21 June enclosing a memorandum that he had sent to the Commanding Royal Engineer on 12 June:

> My object being to retain possession of the country gained, what I want is to have established in the right place a defensible nucleus adapted for a large or small force in which ten men, perfectly safe themselves, may command a radius of two or three hundred yards by the fire of musketry and six hundred metres with a gun, so that within that area a large camp may be covered and protected during the absence of the force on patrol.[64]

15 July

Within about a week all the troops had returned to their camps, with the exception of the Rifle Brigade and Lakeman's Corps, the former helping Captain Jesse, RE, build the two redoubts, which were both on the high ground about a hundred metres apart. The reason for two being built was that no single site could overlook both Fuller's Hoek and the Waterkloof. In fact, both chosen sites have splendid views of Schelm Kloof, but neither looks into the Waterkloof and their view of Fuller's Hoek is at best distinctly poor. The more northerly of the two was named Fort Fordyce and the other Fort Jesse, although this name does not seem to have survived long.

Lakeman was not impressed with either. He pointed out to Captain Jesse that the forts could not be defended without firing into one another – that the enemy could camp between the two and defy either to fire a shot. Jesse's reply was that he had taken this into consideration and had decided that the enemy did not have sufficient sense to discover this weakness in his plan.[65] It was entirely irrelevant: neither of these two forts ever fired a shot in anger.

24 July

The men of the Rifle Brigade were probably delighted, after weeks of fort-building, to receive orders to march with the 60th Rifles and the levies at 4.30 a.m. for action against the Ngqika at Mundell's Krantz. It was daybreak as they approached within range of the cliffs and Lieutenant Stuart Wortley, seeing some Xhosa with cattle, galloped forward with his detachment of CMR. Falling upon them, he killed two men and captured twelve oxen and four horses. Colonel Buller next ordered the howitzers into position to fire on rebel concentrations but they were unable to do so because the Mfengu were too eager to advance in search of cattle. Major William Fanshawe Bedford, commanding the 60th Rifles and one company of the Rifle Brigade, advanced directly on the krantz while Major Horsford of the Rifle Brigade posted his companies so that they protected the 60th's flank, which was exposed to the Waterkloof bush. Several shells were fired into the Waterkloof bush to which the Xhosa had fled and from where they kept up a smart fire, wounding several men. Sergeant Green had a narrow escape, the ball passing behind his ball bag and bending the brasses of his waist belt.

John Fisher, a private in the Rifle Brigade, wrote a short but engaging account of his experiences in the Waterkloof many years later. He enlisted in 1850 at the age of seventeen and appears to have been an outstanding recruit for he was made 'chosen man' after nine months and acting corporal after fifteen. Fisher was with the company of the Rifle Brigade that joined the 60th under Major Bedford in its attack on Mundell's Krantz:

> We took them by surprise as they were not expecting us. We soon got up a good row with them, but we soon scattered them after killing a great number of them. We burnt their huts and destroyed a great deal of ammunition and fire arms in the huts, the artillery playing with them from the top. We were then ordered to make a feint retreat from the bush to draw them out. It had the desired effect and after leading them far enough we turned upon them, big guns and all, when they soon found out their mistake, we completely routed them in a short time.

According to Buller, when the troops were retiring to Fort Fordyce the Ngqika came out in considerable numbers and fired a great deal of ammunition, but many fell from the fire of the artillery and troops, and the Xhosa subsequently acted with greater caution.

Lakeman saw the withdrawal differently. He had gone to sleep that morning after one of his night patrols and had been awakened in the afternoon by the sound of guns. On looking out he saw the 60th engaged with the rebels about halfway back from Mundell's Krantz. As they appeared to be hard pressed, Lakeman ordered his men to follow and went to the 60th's assistance, gathering up some of the men who were retreating. When he had a force sufficient to give an impetus to the movement he went at the Xhosa with a rattling cheer and pursued them almost to Mundell's Krantz.

Now his difficulties began, however, for in his enthusiasm he had become separated from any supporting troops. Holding his position as best he could, Lakeman sent his sergeant, Herridge, back to ask for assistance, and after a long delay Herridge came back with the reply from Colonel Nesbitt, whom he had found at breakfast, that Lakeman must return the best way he could.[66]

They did manage to get back but it had been a close thing, for as soon as they started to retire, the Ngqika came out of the Waterkloof bush to cut them off. Lakeman drove them back into the bush only to find more of them out in the open on his other flank. Here the Minié rifle did a fine job of deterring them. And so, struggling on both flanks alternately, they at last got to an outcrop of rocks. Here they halted until one of Lakeman's lieutenants arrived with the rest of his men and with this reinforcement they eventually reached camp.

Lakeman did not conceal his opinion of Nesbitt's conduct and seems to have had the support of some of the regular officers. He wrote a report to headquarters that stated matters as he saw them. He received a reply from Colonel Cloete, quartermaster-general: 'Having submitted your report of the 29th inst., I am directed to convey to you His Excellency's satisfaction with the constant activity and military energy you have displayed since you have been engaged in the operations in the vicinity of the Waterkloof.' Lakeman had to be satisfied with this response.

Lieutenant King, who did not take part in this attack, was at Post Retief when the wounded arrived, escorted by a detachment of the Rifle Brigade under Lieutenant the Honourable Leicester Curzon. One Rifleman was dangerously wounded, one sergeant slightly and one man of the CMR, Colonel Buller's orderly, was wounded in the face and neck, though not dangerously. To King, Post Retief now bore the appearance of a large military hospital: the sloping barrack square on a warm day saw men with bandaged heads, with arms in slings and others hobbling on crutches; two poor fellows were each minus a leg.

During this month of July 1852, General Somerset also finally said farewell to his troops and left the field to prepare for his departure to India. He would no longer influence military affairs on the frontier, as he had done since his arrival in June 1818 as a humble captain.

Chapter 12

The Peace

The amity which previously existed between the Ngqika under Sandile and the Khoikhoi rebels under Uithaalder was beginning to unravel. This may have had its origins in the abduction of Toyise by Uithaalder under orders from Sandile, and his subsequent unauthorised release by the Khoikhoi. The fact that Sandile later denied that he had anything to do with the abduction would not have helped the situation. It seems, however, that while neither party sought peace, each was now determined to pursue its own path to victory.

Take No Prisoners

Evidence suggests that the British chose to intensify the pressure on Sandile by embracing a 'take no prisoners' policy towards the end of the war, as well as adopting a brutality unusual in them. One can only assume that this was a reaction to the many instances of murder and torture on the part of the Khoikhoi and Ngqika, many of which have been recounted earlier, and the frustration felt by the senior officers at their inability to defeat the rebels.

The policy seems to have become more pervasive following the influx of new regimental commanders about the same time as the Honourable George Cathcart arrived to take command. It is also clear from the evidence that Colonel Eyre was the most ruthless of them all. The substantiation for these atrocities is scattered throughout the source material, and is sometimes given a humorous, if macabre, touch. A case in point is that of Captain Lakeman's bath.

It seems that Lakeman took a large copper vat with him on campaign for the purpose of taking what he called a 'matutinal tubbing'. One morning his servant told him that he was unable to bathe that day. Earlier, Dr Robert Alexander, a surgeon of the 60th Regiment, had asked some of Lakeman's men to acquire a few African skulls of both sexes, a task, they assured him, that was easily accomplished.

One morning they brought back to camp about two dozen heads of various ages. As these were not supposed to be in a presentable state for the doctor's acceptance, the next night they turned my vat into a caldron [sic] for the removal of superfluous flesh. And there these men sat, gravely smoking their pipes during the live-long night, and stirring round and round the heads in that seething boiler, as though they were cooking black-apple dumplings.[1]

One might suppose that this compensated for the occasion when two Winterberg settlers were killed and their heads sent to Mlanjeni.[2] We have already seen that James Brownlee's head was sent to Sandile. King himself was not entirely immune to such impulses. He relates how, during a particular patrol in the Kroome, the party's horses dislodged the skulls and bones of dead Ngqika on a steep slope.

A fine specimen of a Kaffir head, I took the liberty of putting into my saddle-bag, and afterwards brought home with me to Scotland, where it has been much admired by phrenologists for its fine development.[3]

With regard to the policy of 'take no prisoners', this is evinced by Thomas Stubbs, who had found Lieutenant-Colonel Perceval to be 'a thorough soldier and gentleman, very quiet and unassuming'. Now, however,

I found [my men] had taken a prisoner (Hottentot). It appeared one of the men had levelled his gun when one of the other men struck his gun up and made the fellow prisoner. I told him as he had taken him he must take charge of him and consider himself disgraced by taking a prisoner as he knew it was against orders. He said he thought [that] as Colonel Perceval was there it would not do to shoot him. The Colonel then told him they were not to neglect their duty on his account.[4]

There seems to be no doubt that at least some of the orders pertaining to the murder of prisoners came from Eyre himself, on one occasion telling his subordinates: 'There is to be no quarter. All that were taken were to be hanged at the two gateways.'[5]

Cathcart's Transkei Invasion

Not long after his arrival at the frontier, General Cathcart had written a letter to Sarhili, the paramount chief of the Xhosa and chief of the Gcaleka in the Transkei.[6] The governor made it clear that he still regarded the chief as his enemy because he had failed to pay the fine imposed upon him by Sir Harry Smith. He now gave Sarhili one month, from the date of the chief's receiving the letter, to pay the fine in full and also to 'do [his] best to put an end to this war'. Failure to do so would require the governor to 'immediately let loose upon your country numerous commandos . . . to eat you up'.

Cathcart also made it clear that Sandile and his people must cross the Kei out of the colony and British Kaffraria 'and they never more will be allowed to live in peace on this side.'

In preparation for this new invasion and to provide the 'commandoes', Cathcart issued a proclamation for the assembly of colonists to defend their farms and their country.[7] In this proclamation, the governor invited the settlers 'to join [him] on the Umvani River near Bram Neck, midway between Shiloh and the White Kei River on 6 August'. The reason for choosing this location for his start-point was that Sarhili's Great Place was close to the White Kei, just to the north of its confluence with the Black Kei.

In a subsequent circular to his civil commissioners, Cathcart gave two reasons for his invasion of Gcalekaland. These were, first, that he wished 'to test the power and the willingness of the colonists to come forward in their own cause'; and second, were the settlers to come forward, it would demonstrate to Sarhili that there was a power independent of the imperial troops 'sufficient to chastise him should he again be guilty of aiding or abetting in hostilities against the colony'.[8]

In the six weeks prior to his arrival, he had built up a huge base near Whittlesea which he stuffed with supplies. Accordingly, on 6 August 1852, Cathcart arrived at the rendezvous on the Umvani River, bringing with him his headquarters and Colonel Napier's column from Fort Beaufort. He was joined there by Colonel Michel's column from King William's Town.[9]

The number of burghers who also arrived was somewhat disappointing: he was well-satisfied with those from some districts, and had sympathy for the excuses of others for non-attendance, but 'in others again I am disappointed in the favourable opinion I would have wished to have formed of them.' Nonetheless, his cavalry ranks were swelled to more than one thousand men.

His first task was to find a suitable location for this huge force, close to wood and water. During the next three days, he caused a large 'bushed and stockaded square enclosure' to be built under the directions of Captain Tylden, RE, about ten kilometres to the east, near the source of the Bolotwa River.

The route followed by the 60th Rifles was probably that followed by all the troops. After spending the night near Shiloh, the regiment marched only thirteen kilometres on 5 August, bivouacking overnight near the Klaas Smits River. On the 6th, they marched a further thirty-two kilometres, when they reached the Umvani River. They had an easy march of another thirteen kilometres on the 7th, arriving at the base camp on the Bolotwa River.[10]

On the evening of 9 August, two messengers arrived at the camp from Sarhili. The governor chose not to see them personally but they were interviewed by Rev. John Ayliff, his acting-secretary and interpreter. The purport of the chief's message was to enquire as to the reason for the presence of the governor and his troops. Cathcart responded that he had previously sent a message to Sarhili demanding payment of the fine imposed by Sir Harry Smith, and that the chief had returned the message unanswered. Two months had now passed and 'the Great Chief [had] now come to take the fine and as much more cattle as will pay for the trouble of [his] coming . . .' The messengers then asked Cathcart to remain where he was until Sarhili had collected the cattle to pay the fine – to which the governor demanded that the chief surrender himself, at which point he would halt the troops. The messengers replied that, while Sarhili would pay the fine, he would not surrender.[11]

The invasion proper began on 10 August, when the force marched to the Black Kei River, a distance of some sixteen kilometres, which they crossed at a shallow drift. Cathcart left one company each of the 6th and 91st, together with a detachment of the CMR and some auxiliary troops, under the command of Captain John Campbell Cahill of the 91st, to guard the camp. The main force bivouacked that night on the left bank of the White Kei River, at a place called Sabella.[12] At this point they must have been very close to Sarhili's Great Place.

On the morning of the 11th, two columns moved out, an hour apart, in the direction of John Crouch's abandoned trading station,[13] which was to be their base. From there, one column under Colonel Michel was to operate in the direction of Butterworth while the other, under Colonel Napier, was to move towards the confluence of the Kei and Tsomo rivers. Both commanders were to gather cattle but not burn homesteads, this being thought by Cathcart to be unnecessary.

Again leaving a small force, under Major Horsford, Rifle Brigade, to consolidate and guard the camp, Cathcart marched his remaining troops some twenty kilometres to the east before again camping for the night.

That day the Gcaleka put the grassland around the column to the torch in an attempt to limit their supply of forage. In the evening, a large force of Gcaleka, some of them mounted, were seen assembled on a hill at some distance.

On the morning of 12 August, Cathcart took four companies of the 6th Regiment, with all the burghers and irregulars, and fell upon Sarhili's Great Place, located about twelve kilometres from his camp. The village was deserted and some of the burghers and Mfengu under Captain Peter Campbell put it to the torch. Campbell complained that his only 'trophy was a tiger's [leopard's] tail stuck onto a little kerrie'.[14] The governor then returned to his camp to await the reports of Michel and Napier before deciding on his next step.[15]

In this same despatch, Cathcart mentions quite casually that he had received, and accepted, the resignation of Colonel Mackinnon as Chief Commissioner of British Kaffraria, who was with him on this expedition.

On 15 August Colonel Michel reported that he had been able to capture only about six or seven hundred cattle, with a few sheep and a couple of horses. There were large herds to be seen but they were too far away for the Mfengu to reach them. He had returned to his camp at Crouch's station to await further orders.[16] Pending Napier's report, Cathcart ordered Michel to withdraw to the Sabolela Drift camp and await further orders.

When Colonel Napier reported on 20 August, he said that he had captured six thousand cattle, as well as many other animals.[17] By this time, the total cattle taken by all the forces had reached nearly ten thousand head and the governor decided that he would close the campaign. He left Colonel Mackinnon in command at the Bolotwa camp and proceeded with his staff and cavalry escort to King William's Town, arriving there on 24 August.[18]

Mackinnon arranged the distribution of the cattle taken from the Gcaleka and then sent the imperial troops back to their stations. On 21 August, the burghers rode off, and the Mfengu scampered away, each taking with them the cattle with which they had been rewarded as their 'prize money'.[19]

Cathcart's return required that he now refocus his attention on matters in British Kaffraria and, accordingly, he noted in his despatch: 'The next object of military importance was [to be] the final expulsion of the lawless bands of Kafirs, Tambookies, and Hottentots from the Waterkloof and other fastnesses comprised within the Kroome range of mountains.'[20]

On Tuesday 7 September 1852, Major-General Henry Somerset, accompanied by his wife and family, left the eastern frontier for the last time, sailing on HMS *Styx* for Simon's Bay, to take passage to India.[21] On board the same vessel, and bound for England, was Colonel George Mackinnon, his resignation as chief commissioner for British Kaffraria having finally been effected. His place was taken by John Maclean, a very different personality.[22]

The Last Kroome Assault, September 1852

On 10 September 1852, Colonel Cloete had issued a memorandum of movements to commence on the following Wednesday, 15 September.[23] It required the assembly of four major columns, under the overall command of General Cathcart.

Colonel Napier would have four guns of the Royal Artillery, five companies of the 91st regiment under Major David Forbes, a detachment of the CMR and the Kat River Levy. This column was 'to act from the high open ground north of the Waterkloof'.

Colonel Nesbitt was to take two howitzers of the Royal Artillery, six companies of the 60th Rifles under Major William Fanshawe Bedford, Lakeman's Corps and two companies of Mfengu, and occupy a position at Fort Fordyce between the Waterkloof and Fuller's Hoek.

Colonel Eyre would have three Royal Artillery rocket tubes, the 73rd Regiment under Major Frederick George Augustus Pinckney and a company of the 74th Regiment under Lieutenant William Ross King. His auxiliaries would be the Graaff-Reinet Mounted Levy under Lieutenant Huswell, Armstrong's Horse, the Fort Beaufort Mfengu under Captain Peter Campbell, the Alice Mfengu under Captain Hoare, a European Corps under Captain Stevenson and Captain Ainslie's Mankazana Mfengu.

Eyre would ascend the Kroome escarpment from Niland's farm via Niland's Pass and 'assail the south scarp of the Waterkloof'. To assist in this task, Nesbitt was to assign Lakeman and some of the Mfengu to go down into the Waterkloof to co-operate with Eyre's column. Eyre would then join the Rifle Brigade at Brown's farm and together they would clear the valley of the enemy.

A fourth column, under Major Alfred Horsford, would consist of the Rifle Brigade, one company of Mfengu and a detachment of the CMR. This column would move from Nel's farm into the Waterkloof as far as Brown's farm, there to co-operate with Eyre's column.

A smaller force, under Captain Bruce, was to move down from Post Retief to Mundell's farm, to operate as required.

All these parties were to march in sufficient time to arrive at their destinations by 6 a.m. on Wednesday, 15 September. The troops were to march with three days' supplies.

15 September
Nesbitt's Column
In obedience to orders, this column played a static role, preventing the enemy escaping across the line between the Kroome Heights and Forts Fordyce and Jesse, including Tenth Pass.

Stephen Lakeman had been allowed, 'if opportunity offers', to go down into the Waterkloof to co-operate with Colonel Eyre, and he made sure that the opportunity came.

Lakeman started off the evening before, knowing the way to Brown's farm

very well from his earlier night excursions. His only opposition was from a
group of rebel Khoikhoi, who were recognised by the use they made of the
bugle, and they were chased until they took refuge up the Iron Mountain. It
was now day-break and Lakeman waited there for Colonel Eyre's column to
come down from the Kroome escarpment. Whilst he was waiting – not one
of Lakeman's strong points anyway – Lakeman gradually convinced himself
that his 'position was growing serious'; the rebel Khoikhoi had crept down
the mountainside and, from disagreeably close by, had opened up a galling
fire on his position. Then again, if by some mischance Colonel Eyre did not
appear, he, by his inaction, was increasing the boldness of the enemy and
making his eventual retreat more difficult. He waited until 10 a.m. and then
decided that the only way out of his dilemma was to take the rebel position
with his own corps, and to do so immediately.

It was harder than he thought. The day was hot, his men were hungry, the
mountain was steep and the rebels were tenacious. While charging, a shot
came so close to Lakeman's head that he ducked, an act which shamed him so
much that he pretended to have stumbled. Scrambling up, he received another
shot just over the eyebrows which blew his helmet off and left him bareheaded
before the jeering Khoikhoi. In those days there was a great fear of sunstroke
so Lakeman took off his coat and placed it over his head, Red Riding-Hood
fashion. Amidst the laughter and cheers of the men, he continued leading the
charge and drove the rebels out of their position, some running further up the
mountainside. The position turned out to be the 'Blacksmith's Shop', where
rebel CMR armourers repaired the enemy's firelocks. The men also found
some food and were sitting down to a meal when they heard the sound of
musket fire and saw Colonel Eyre's forces on the heights to their left. Hurriedly finishing breakfast, the prisoners were gathered together and, carrying
anvil, hammers, bellows and tongs, they marched back to headquarters on the
Horseshoe. Lakeman found Cathcart grilling a chop over a fire at the end of
a ramrod. He laid the trophies of his victory at the general's feet while Colonel Cloete gravely wrote down his report. Lakeman's Corps then returned to
their quarters, receiving congratulations from all around.[24]

Horsford's Column
The Rifle Brigade had made themselves comfortable at Nel's farm near
the entrance to the Waterkloof. They had built a 'fort' there, consisting
of a rectangular stone wall one hundred metres square with an abattis of
chopped-down mimosa bushes which Private John Fisher thought provided
very good protection on account of their 'very long and sharp thorns'.[25]
Inside the wall they built two redoubts, one of stone and the other of earth,

Upper Waterkloof
15 September 1852

N

WATERKLOOF

HORSFORD

BRUCE

NAPIER

LAKEMAN   FORDYCE

ARIE'S BUSH

NESBITT

EYRE

Mount Misbelief/Misbelief Mountain

Niland's
Farm

and put up the hospital and commissariat marquees together with the officers' tents.[26]

On the 14th, leaving fifty of the least-fit men to guard their fort, Horsford marched at 3 a.m. in silence for Brown's farm, four kilometres away. He expected to receive a warm reception as he moved up the Waterkloof but no resistance was offered. On the way they destroyed several huts, killed a few Thembu, captured some horses and took many prisoners, chiefly women and children. The Rifle Brigade reached Brown's farm at daylight on the 15th, according to both Fisher and Cope,[27] thus confirming the suspicion that Lakeman had jumped the gun in his craving for action when he said that he had waited until 10 a.m.

Eyre's Column

King was on leave in Fort Beaufort while the operation was being planned and there to his joy he was given command of the one 74th company attached to Eyre's column. He had only recently been gazetted captain.[28]

Captain Peter Campbell of the Fort Beaufort Fingo Levy nearly missed taking part. His previous service had earned the respect of General Cathcart who now asked him to assemble another Mfengu levy, promising him a guinea (twenty-one shillings) a day plus feed for his horse. But Colonel Cloete, the QMG, balked at paying so much and reduced it to fifteen shillings so Campbell sent in his resignation and rode off home. What Cathcart said to Cloete on hearing this is not recorded, but Campbell's promised pay was restored the next morning, whereupon he and his Mfengu joined Colonel Eyre's camp at Niland's farm.[29]

For Captain King it was one of those pitch-black, foggy nights, when a hand could scarcely be seen in front of one's face, that the column groped its way out of camp. Colonel Eyre was leading with an advance guard of mounted men and two Boers as guides. Niland's Pass brought back poign-ant memories for King, especially when daylight revealed skulls and scattered bones near the top of the pass, and he knew that there must have been many more lower down where the fighting on 8 September, now over a year ago, had been hottest. After a stiff climb, halting frequently to catch their breath, they reached the summit, which was enveloped in a thick, cold mist. The men were coughing violently, a sure sign of the effect that the hardship and expo-sure was having on their lungs.[30]

On the open ground the regimental adjutant, Lieutenant Frederick Reeve, fell back and got into conversation with Captain Campbell, informing him that they were going to the Iron Mountain. Campbell, who knew the country well, having patrolled it in 1846 and having hunted there since, pointed out that the path they were taking was the wrong one as it led to the old saw pits, far to the east of Iron Mountain. Reeve galloped off with this intelligence and Campbell was soon summoned by the colonel who, having halted the column and sent for the two unfortunate guides, questioned Campbell closely as to his knowledge of the country. The guides were treated to a clear exposition of their worth and a threatened hanging, whereupon the colonel turned to Campbell and asked him if there was a short cut. Campbell sensibly replied that he did not know that, though he did know there was intervening bush. This answer did not please the colonel, who muttered something about Campbell not knowing much about the country and ordered the advance guard to 'right shoulder forward and advance', he himself leading the way on horseback. This rather shut Campbell up and he was sorry that he had volunteered any information about the route. He was aware that Colonel Eyre was a man of very strong will and would insist that there had to be a short cut, so he waited. Eyre had not gone many yards before he found himself entangled in tall brambles impossible to penetrate. If Eyre had a temper, and all the indications are that he had, he must have turned purple as he retreated and led the column, now an hour late, back to the path indicated by Campbell.[31]

While they moved along the plain towards the Iron Mountain the mist became so thick that the column had to halt until the sun rose and burnt the mist off. King realised that all chance of a surprise attack had evaporated with the mist, for about four hundred of the rebels were seen running on the narrow peninsular ridge leading to the Iron Mountain, with the obvious intention of taking possession of its towering krantzes.[32]

The column followed as quickly as possible but was held up by a section of the ridge that was so narrow and bushy that there was barely enough room for two men to walk abreast. There followed a long, gradual ascent which was negotiated without opposition until at last the plateau on top of the Iron Mountain was reached. The enemy fired half a dozen shots from the krantzes, the balls whistling harmlessly overhead, and then fled to the bush below by paths which King thought were so precipitous and narrow that they were practicable only to Ngqika and baboons. The enemy left behind two women, and several horses which were captured.[33]

As the soldiers spread about the mountain top looking here, there and everywhere, as soldiers will, Campbell saw one fellow seized by the leg and pulled towards what proved to be a cave. The man screamed and several men got hold of him and pulled him out. It turned out that there was an Ngqika inside the cave who had seized him but, fortunately for the soldier, the Ngqika could not hold him and use his assegai at the same time. In the scuffle, the soldier had dropped his bayonet in the cave and the men were trying to get it for him but could not, for as soon as they tried to reach it they were jabbed with an assegai. Campbell was watching when one of his men, a Thembu named William, volunteered to get the bayonet. He posted himself at the mouth of the cave and with his own assegai fought a harmless duel with the man inside, neither being able to hurt the other until eventually he managed to hook the bayonet out. The question now arose as to what to do with the Ngqika and it was decided to burn him out. A hundred willing hands collected a large quantity of wood which was piled on the rocks at the entrance to the cave and set alight. Campbell never found out what the fire did to the inmate for orders came for them to move on.[34]

Eyre was determined that none of the Ngqika should escape so he sent small parties back along the narrow ridge to descend both sides of Iron Mountain as quickly as possible to intercept their flight. Captain Wyndham Edmund Bewes, with the Grenadier Company of the 73rd and King's company of the 74th, went down into the eastern kloof by a path so smooth and steep that only the greatest care prevented them following the loose stones that bounded down into the depths below. The ammunition and pack horses slid down on their haunches and the rocket troop had the greatest difficulty keeping the heavy apparatus off the horses' necks. The eastern party scoured the bush and, although some of the rebels did succeed in dispersing and hiding in the thickest parts of the thorny bush and thus making their escape, many were killed. Half a dozen rebel Khoikhoi, CMR deserters, were also killed in the attack and their bodies were hung from the nearest trees as an example to others who might pass that way.[35]

The western party consisted of two companies of the 73rd, the mounted levies and all the Mfengu, under the command of Major Pinckney. Campbell thought this another example of the colonel's stubbornness – instead of taking a nice easy footpath down to the Waterkloof, he was determined that they should go down the side of the mountain where there was no path and where the horses suffered a good deal. Campbell was ordered to use his Mfengu to scour the kloof, the colonel telling him that he would breakfast in the Waterkloof and that Campbell could find him by the smoke of his camp fire. It was rough going: the bush was dense and in some places so thick that they could not skirmish at all but had to walk in single file. Campbell saw that the Ngqika was really suffering from hunger; fifteen were killed for they were in such an emaciated state that they could not get away from his men. He also captured a number of horses before getting into the more open bush and there he was able to put his men into order and skirmish down towards the camp.[36]

The colonel himself, with the remaining companies of the 73rd, captured seventy-one women and twenty children hiding among the recesses in the rocks, as well as a large quantity of assegais, muskets and native ornaments.

As the 73rd approached Brown's farm they met the Rifle Brigade for the first time, whom they had not seen since fighting together in the 1846 war. The 73rd sent up a ringing cheer which was heartily returned by the Green Jackets and then the 91st on the heights to the north took it up until the whole Waterkloof echoed with their cries. As if in celebration of the meeting, the whole valley from end to end was wreathed in smoke from numerous burning huts as a result of the work of the 60th and 91st.[37]

Campbell delivered his report to Colonel Eyre, who was gracious enough to say that he had never seen better skirmishing in his life. The quality of his leadership can be discerned.[38]

After two hours' rest the combined forces under Colonel Eyre moved up the Waterkloof.[39] Some of the rebels were seen assembling on a ridge on the south side, so two companies of the Rifle Brigade, those of Captain Charles John Woodford and Captain Edward Arthur Somerset, and the Grenadier Company of the 73rd, all under Major Horsford, were sent to clear them. The colonel's orders were to go up slowly and keep their wind until they were fired on and then to give a cheer and rush on to the top. On a ledge about halfway up and hidden from below by trees, a village was found, which was set on fire, the smoke from the burning huts proving to be a great nuisance as the men continued climbing.

On reaching the top, firing commenced and they charged as instructed, amidst cheers from the 91st on the opposite ridge, but the rebels, as usual, just disappeared into the adjoining bush. Second Lieutenant Henry Gore Lindsay and four Riflemen chased them, rather too eagerly, far into the bush and lost their way. They wandered about for some time before hearing the bugle and so getting their bearings.[40]

The three companies bivouacked for the night in the small area of bush on the peninsular ridge leading to the Iron Mountain. According to Private Fisher they were nearly all dead with fatigue; he himself could scarcely move as they had been marching through the bush and up and down mountains for sixteen hours continuously.[41]

Colonel Eyre had also sent the cavalry and some of the Mfengu up the heights to the south and west of Iron Mountain in order to intercept any stragglers who might try to escape in that direction. The remainder of his column had been ordered to continue on their way up the Waterkloof, where, on reaching Arie's Bush, they climbed up by the slip-path while the 91st and 60th Rifles covered their ascent. On the Horseshoe they turned south and went through Tenth Pass, which King found to be lined by the 60th Rifles. Here, instead of being treated, as before, to volleys of enemy bullets, they were now presented with cigars and brandy-and-water.

After a short march – though one which seemed to King to be long and weary – they reached their bivouac on a bleak and bare ridge after dark. The ground was so rocky that nearly all the pegs of their patrol tents were broken without succeeding in getting them pitched.[42]

16 September

Colonel Eyre ordered his force to be divided into four columns. They were to start at daylight and repeat the operations of the previous day. Captain Robert Campbell of the 73rd, with two companies of the Rifle Brigade and one of the 73rd, went down the Waterkloof from the Kroome Heights. Major Horsford, also with two companies of the Rifle Brigade and one of the 73rd, again assailed the Iron Mountain itself.[43] There they found a cave and, having seen a Ngqika enter, the mouth was blocked with large boulders. Other boulders were playfully rolled down the mountainside where they cleared great swathes of bush before them.

Colonel Eyre, with one company of the 73rd, King's company of the 74th and a body of Mfengu, proceeded along the Kroome Heights towards Nel's farm, searching the various kloofs that ran into the Waterkloof on the way, and throwing rockets into inaccessible places where the nimble enemy might have hidden.

On reaching the 'fort' at Nel's farm at 10 a.m., Colonel Eyre, with his staff and escort, rode off to his force's rendezvous at Brown's farm, leaving his column to halt for breakfast. The pack horses had been sent to Brown's farm by another route so King and the other officers had nothing to eat until Captain Jesse, RE, the commander of the fort, brought out a loaf, a cold leg of mutton and a bottle of wine – absolute luxuries for ravenous men.

The column then marched up the Waterkloof and King was again struck by its appearance. It was spring and the valley was as fragrant as it was beautiful; the boerboon, covered with thick clusters of crimson blossoms, were conspicuous above all other flowers. Monkeys abounded in the larger trees.

They arrived at Brown's farm at the same time as a party of Mfengu brought a despatch from the general, who was on the Horseshoe directing the whole movement. The order was to prepare to assail Blakeway's Kloof and Arie's Hoek the next day. Soon a long line was seen ascending the Waterkloof: redcoats, Green Jackets, Highlanders, rocket artillery, mounted levies, Mfengu, Ngqika prisoners and, bringing up the rear, the pack horses.[44]

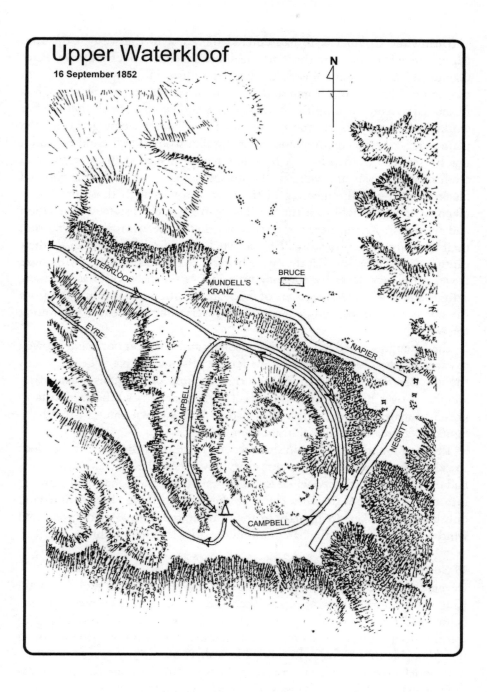

Upper Waterkloof
16 September 1852

N

WATERKLOOF

EYRE

MUNDELL'S KRANZ

BRUCE

NAPIER

CAMPBELL

NESBITT

CAMPBELL

Meanwhile Colonel Eyre had entered the kloof to the west of the Iron Mountain where he sent the Fort Beaufort Mfengu under Captain Peter Campbell up the mountainside to scour the bush. High up at the foot of the krantz, sharp firing began and wreaths of smoke traced their progress in the dark trees, enabling the soldiers below to keep pace with them. After working their way to the top of the kloof, the Mfengu emerged onto the plain driving before them about thirty Ngqika women and children and a few horses. The women had their woolly hair entwined with the claws and teeth of wild beasts and wore finely dressed karosses which had been dyed black. King found the meeting of the new prisoners with those previously taken an affecting sight to witness. All were in a wretched state of emaciation and weakness, having nearly starved on a diet of beans, roots and berries; their arms and legs were more like black sticks than limbs. King excused their capture on the grounds that they were being saved from starvation. Moreover, it was a military necessity, for they were just as much enemies as the men, acting as sentries, spies, procurers of food, ammunition and information from the towns and camps, and generally doing everything they could to prolong the war.

The Mfengu wanted to kill all the prisoners and sulked at not being allowed to carry out their idea of warfare. One female prisoner, unable to keep up with the rest, was shot dead by an Mfengu right in front of King, his horse nearly stumbling over her body. It required all King's and other officers' efforts to prevent further cruelty; in fact they had to knock down some of the 'half-tamed savages' and forcibly restrain them.[45]

The men found the climb up the steep, rocky slope at the head of the kloof so exhausting that they had to rest every few paces. The officers' patrol tents had only just been pitched when torrential rain descended, the water running into the tents before trenches could be dug around them. The men, having only a single blanket, sat all night by their fires in the storm. An intensely cold wind which swept over the bare mountain made sleep impossible.[46]

17 September

Reveille sounded at 4 a.m. and after a more or less sleepless night Captain King was glad to be moving again. The wind and sleet were even colder than before and the mountain tops all around were white with snow. Trying to warm himself in front of a fire, he scorched his clothes on one side while on the other side they clung to his body like a sheet of ice.[47]

Colonel Eyre moved his forces along the top of the Kroome Range towards their objective, Blakeway's Kloof and Arie's Hoek. At the head of Wolf's Head Pass, they met the 60th Rifles guarding the edge of the bush, the men half

Upper Waterkloof
17 September 1852

N

BRUCE
MUNDELL'S KRANZ
WATERKLOOF
NAPIER
NESBITT
EYRE
ARIE'S HOEK
CAMPBELL
Andrews's Farm ■
Niland's Farm ■
■ Blakeway's Farm

frozen and envying the column on the move. From here King could also see the artillery of Nesbitt's column shelling the bush around Tenth Pass. After Eyre's column had fired rockets into Blakeway's Kloof, Captain Campbell was sent with his Fort Beaufort Mfengu down a rudimentary path into its depth. The cavalry were left on the heights to be used by Colonel Nesbitt.

The remainder of the force, which included King's company, descended Wolf's Head Pass but no sign of the enemy was seen all the way down to Blakeway's farm where they halted. Captain King found the sun thankfully hot, and he admired the almond and peach trees in the deserted garden, covered with pink blossoms. Here, too, they met a group of the CMR under Captain Carey who had arrived only a few minutes before with two hundred sheep which they had captured in the kloof.[48]

After resting an hour, Eyre's column marched across Blakeway's Kloof and over Blakeway's Ridge into Arie's Hoek. Colonel Eyre split his forces into small groups in order to scour the kloof right from its base up to the heights occupied by the 60th Rifles. The dense bush in the kloof was penetrated in ten directions across and lengthwise.[49]

Captain King was with the group ordered to climb up Blakeway's Ridge. The path at times became so narrow that even in single file the whole group had to halt every twenty paces to allow the men in front to move on; their pace was regulated by bugles sounding the 'halt' and the 'advance' from the front to the rear by companies. Further up they came to a cluster of burnt-out rebel fires, the ground all round being covered with the residue of chewed root. King heard firing ahead and in due course came across a recently killed Ngqika lying in the bush. A little later he saw the corpse of a rebel Khoikhoi deserter hanging from a tree, with a bullet hole in his forehead and the blood trickling down his face and dropping on to his bare toes. As soon as King's group reached the ridge they turned and descended into Arie's Hoek again by another more difficult and steeper route, down which man and horse sometimes slid twenty or thirty paces at a time. At the bottom, a large Xhosa village was set on fire and some horses captured. The group then turned and, now under the colonel himself, climbed to the head of the kloof again through a dense, dark tangled bush.

The various groups of Eyre's column were directed by bugle, with company and regimental calls, and the 'advance', 'retire', 'right' and 'left incline' being ordered by the colonel, who had a bugler from each regiment at his side. It was in this fashion that the movements of a thousand men in different groups in an immense bush were controlled unseen.[50]

It was exhausting work searching through the bush and the order to move out at sunset and bivouac down the kloof where the ground was more open was very welcome: King had been on his feet for thirteen hours. Eyre's column had killed thirty-six of the rebels, taken 168 prisoners and captured forty-one horses and a few cattle.[51]

Private Fisher had also had a hard day. His group had come across a cave which had been used by the rebels as a hospital. The dead and living were all heaped together and he could scarcely go near for the stench. Nevertheless, they separated the living from the dead – some were badly wounded – and buried the latter. On arriving at his bivouac, Fisher found that captured cattle had been slaughtered and served out, which was very acceptable. This was his third day from camp and his ration of meat had spoiled on the first day in his mess tin, as it had been closed up in the sweltering sun.[52]

18 September

Heavy rain, as well as the depletion of supplies and the negligible resistance of the enemy, caused General Cathcart to cease operations. The Rifle Brigade was dispersed on the 19th: four companies were posted to Brown's farm, one to the top of Mundell's Krantz and one remained at Nel's farm. The men were employed in building stone bastions, making roads and occasionally going on patrols, rarely meeting any Ngqika or Khoikhoi rebels.[53]

Captain King and his company marched round the spurs of the Kroome Range to their little camp at Niland's farm, which they reached at noon. He was wet through, but delighted once more at the opportunity to enjoy the luxury of a tent.[54]

Years later, all Captain Peter Campbell remembered of his activities was that they patrolled and re-patrolled the Waterkloof, seldom meeting with any opposition. The high command thought that the rebels had now been finally cleared out and for once he was inclined to agree with them.[55]

On 12 October 1852, Cathcart was pleased to be able to add an extra paragraph to his despatch to Sir John Pakington:

> In my last military despatch . . . I reported the clearance of the Waterkloof, and the means I had taken for its occupation and security. I am happy to say that the measures have been attended with the successful result that I anticipated, and that the Kroome district is now entirely abandoned and deserted by the enemy, and I hope forever.[56]

From mid-November until late December 1852, Cathcart was sufficiently diverted to engage in a short punitive expedition against the Basotho chief Mshweshwe. On 20 December, Mshweshwe having failed to deliver the number of cattle demanded by Cathcart, the British troops stormed the table-topped mountain Thaba Bosiu, the chief's stronghold. Colonel Eyre succeeded in reaching the top but Colonel Napier had less success, being driven off to nearby Platberg.[57]

The total casualties during these operations were given officially as fifty-three: one officer killed, four non-commissioned officers and thirty-three privates; two officers wounded, four non-commissioned officers and nine privates.[58]

The next day, Cathcart received a placatory message from Mshweshe begging him to consider the cattle he had taken to be sufficient and asking for peace between them. On 23 December, the governor published a proclamation which declared peace had once again been established between the Queen and the chief Mshweshwe.[59]

Surrender of the Chiefs

During the months October and November 1852, Colonel Eyre was very active in patrolling the whole of the Amathola fastness while General Yorke concentrated on the Fish River bush. It was becoming increasingly clear that the Ngqika were being driven over the Kei River, although some of their leaders, including Sandile and Maqoma, remained at large. Similarly, the Khoikhoi rebels had been so shattered that only small roaming bands remained, although they continued to raid remote farms and travellers.

On 6 October 1852, Cathcart attended a meeting of the Ndlambe chiefs, who had held so loyally to their agreement to support the British cause. He thanked them for their loyalty but stressed that they must not give succour to any of the rebel chiefs, nor give them any aid whatsoever. In particular, he singled out Xaimpi for mention, stating:

> If I find him in any one of your countries, and that you have not done your best to give him up to justice, I shall be sorry for it; but I must treat the chief who harbours him and all his people as I have done the Gaikas; for that bad man went as a friend in the villages on the Chumie, and treacherously led on his men to murder his friends.[60]

In 1857, Xaimpi was finally arrested but his prosecution for the attack on Auckland was abandoned because, on 2 March 1853, Governor Cathcart had issued a proclamation bestowing a general pardon on the Ngqika people, including Xaimpi. The powers of the proclamation did not, however, extend beyond the borders of the colony, and did not thus include British Kaffraria. Thus, any Ngqika who entered, and was apprehended in, the colony was liable to prosecution for any crimes committed there. Unfortunately, because

Xaimpi had remained in British Kaffraria during the massacre at Auckland, he was unable to be prosecuted for the murder of the villagers.

On 9 October, Siyolo of the Mdushane presented himself to John Maclean. He wished to surrender himself but his followers stuck so closely to him that Maclean had to resort to a ploy to separate him from them. He called Siyolo into his dressing room and then brought in some of his own men, at which point Siyolo was hustled away. Maclean told him that he could guarantee his life but that he must remain in custody.[61]

In a statement translated by George Shepstone, the son of Theophilus Shepstone, Siyolo stated:

> I have come to surrender myself and [my] followers before the Chief Commissioner. I am tired of the war. I joined 'Sandilli' in the rebellion, thinking that it would only last for a short time. I see now that war is no small thing. I have come to crave for mercy to Maclean. I see I have done wrong.
>
> My followers have but a few arms; many of them lost their guns during this war. I sent to the officer commanding at the 'Tamacha' post to cease sending patrols into my country, as I was talking to the Government about peace. 'Conway' sent to me to come in and surrender at the 'Tamacha'. I declined doing so, as I said I did not know any one at that place.[62]

The chief was sent to Grahamstown where he was held in the same cell in the Drosdty where Maqoma had been confined in 1847.[63] On 11 November, he was tried by court martial on charges of rebellion and sedition, found guilty and sentenced to death. This was immediately commuted to imprisonment for life and Siyolo was sent in the *Styx* to Cape Town and confined in the town prison.[64]

This news galvanised Sarhili to appreciate his own situation and in the same month of October he sent the first instalment of 122 head of cattle as part payment of Sir Harry Smith's fine, promising to send more. He was as good as his word and a further donative of more than five hundred head was sent in February 1853. He then pleaded that the total of more than 750 head should suffice to satisfy the fine, taking into account the number of cattle taken by the governor in his recent Transkei expedition.

Cathcart was anxious to come to an agreement with the paramount chief and waived the balance of the fine. However, he set out conditions under which a peace might be concluded with Sarhili. These included recognition that the Kei River was the western boundary of his country; he must restrain and punish all who disturbed the peace in the lands allotted to the Thembu; he must be responsible for the security of the lives and property of British subjects who, with his permission, settled in his country; and finally, he must restore any stolen property driven into his country. This latter clearly referred to cattle.[65]

Sarhili agreed to these terms and on 14 February 1853, Cathcart published a proclamation declaring that amity had been restored with the Gcaleka chief, subject to the same conditions, which were incorporated into the proclamation.[66]

It was not long before Sandile, and even Maqoma, were compelled to follow suit and cross the Kei River. From there, and being unwilling to appeal directly to Maclean, Sandile enquired of Phato of the Gqunukhwebe if he would act as intermediary in peace negotiations.[67] Phato agreed and soon Cathcart heard of the overture and welcomed it.[68]

A message was conveyed to Sandile that the governor was prepared to pardon him and Maqoma, but that the Ngqika would never be allowed to live in the Amathola Mountains again, their land being forfeit to the Crown. Instead, they were to be settled on the land immediately to the east of the Amatholas. Sandile was to be held responsible for the good conduct of his people and also for the security of the great north road and the safety of the property of those who travelled on it. Sandile agreed to these terms and a proclamation announcing the final peace with the Ngqika was published on 2 March 1853.[69]

The problem with the Khoikhoi rebels remained. However, their leaders subsequently deserted them and fled across the Kei River – and kept going. Leaderless, they now consisted of small parties of outlaws who were gradually hunted down and either killed or taken into custody. Cathcart's 'castles' performed their duty well and kept the peace as well as it had ever been kept.[70]

Epilogue

The War of Mlanjeni, the eighth and greatest Xhosa war, was over. It remains only to recount the fates which were to befall the principal players in our story.

The Xhosa

The Cattle Killing 1856–1857

In September 1853, a ship arrived in Mossell Bay bearing perhaps the greatest scourge ever to visit the shores of South Africa. It was a disease which affected only cattle and had already devastated the herds of Europe. It began with a dry cough and developed into a fatal infection of the lungs which was given the name 'lungsickness'.[1] Government regulations failed to stop its spread across the colony. By March 1854 it had reached Uitenhage, a year later it was to be found in King William's Town and it broke out in the Transkei in January 1856. Cattle losses were enormous, especially among the Xhosa, and in such times of severe stress, they again turned to a mystical solution.[2]

In June 1856, Charles Brownlee brought the news of the emergence of a new sage.[3] Her name was Nongqawuse and she was the niece of Mhlakaza, a baptised member of the Methodist Church. Mhlakaza's homestead was on the Gxara River. Running just north of Kei Mouth the Gxara barely deserved the appellation 'river': it is more a stream, fed by a spring, and runs for little more than twenty kilometres before it joins the sea. In times of drought, there remained only a few deep pools, much of the stream having dried up.

One day, the fifteen-year-old Nongqawuse and her younger friend, Mhlakaza's sister-in-law Nombanda, were in the fields frightening off birds from the crops when they saw two men in a nearby bush. They told her that she was to spread the word that they were the spirits of men long dead and asked that all the Xhosa people kill their cattle, plant no more gardens and renounce witchcraft. This would prepare the way for the rising of the dead, who would help drive out the white men and usher in the new world which would emerge. Cattle would also appear to replace those killed, or which had died from lungsickness.[4]

At first, their words were ignored but, with the encouragement of Mhlakaza, they were eventually taken up by those living in the area, and then spread more widely until the paramount chief Sarhili himself came to believe the prophecies. Over the coming weeks and months, the message spread rapidly through the Gcaleka people and thousands of cattle were killed, in part because they thought that the new disease was going to kill their cattle anyway, so what did they have to lose? Mhlakaza announced that the resurrection of the 'new people' would take place on 16 August 1856. That date came and went, the non-appearance of the 'new people' being blamed upon those Gcaleka who had failed to kill all their cattle, or who had planted crops. The date of the new millennium was changed to 11 December, to be heralded by a full moon. The night proved to be wet and misty, so no one could see if the moon was full or not.

Soon the belief had spread across the Kei to the Rharhabe and the Gqunukhwebe. Brownlee constantly criss-crossed Ngqika country trying to dissuade them from what he knew would be a disaster. Sir George Grey, the new governor, on the other hand, saw the catastrophe as an opportunity to undermine the authority of the chiefs further, an ambition which he cherished.

By the end of 1856 some forty thousand cattle had been destroyed and their rotting carcases were spread across the countryside. No crops were planted and the people were beginning to starve.

Thousands of Gcaleka gathered at Butterworth, and early in January 1857 Sarhili and a large group of his councillors went down to the Gxara to meet Mhlakaza and Nongqawuse. They were not to be found. They had left a message saying that the spirits had left as a result of the disbelief of the Gcaleka chiefs and Sarhili should return to the Gxara if the next full moon, due on 10 January, were to rise blood-red. If not, then they should look to the February full moon. There was no change to the colour of the January full moon.

There was yet another great meeting of the Gcaleka at Butterworth, after which Sarhili announced that he would go down to the Gxara once more. On 8 February Mhlakaza announced that all remaining cattle were to be killed within eight days, after which the sun would rise blood-red, then set, and after the ensuing darkness a great storm would erupt, following which the supernatural events would take place. By this time Sarhili entertained grave doubts about the event but gave instructions for the killing of all remaining cattle except for one cow and one goat. The Xhosa carried out his instructions, killing their remaining animals and digging grain pits for the new era that they thought was approaching.

The eight days came and went and still no supernatural events occurred: no dead heroes or cattle arose. Hope springs eternal and it took some time for realisation of the truth to sink in. In the meantime, many lost their lives, the aged and infirm being carried off first. Among them was Mhlakaza, although Nongqawuse survived. She fled to Pondoland and was arrested there in 1858. She too was tried and sent to Robben Island but was eventually permitted to return to live near Grahamstown, where she died in 1898.[5]

Peires asserts that in the two years of the Cattle Killing, the black population of British Kaffraria fell from 105,000 to 37,500. The low point was reached at the end of 1858 when the population fell to 25,900. In that same period, the white population increased from a mere 949 to 5,388. 'While this did not exactly equalise the racial mixture . . . to the extent that Grey had hoped, it did increase the white population from less than 1% to a healthy 12.5%.'[6]

The number of dead must have been at least as high among the Gcaleka. Survivors strong enough to do so flocked into the colony in search of work, leading to the fragmentation of a hitherto stable society, while the remainder endured appalling conditions. It was perhaps the worst catastrophe ever to befall the normally happy-go-lucky Xhosa.

The effects of the Cattle Killing were devastating and it is not surprising that, despite their animosity towards the colony and its authorities, they were in no position to consider another war. Indeed, it was to be twenty-five years after the end of the War of Mlanjeni before they could again do so.

Loss of Land

As seems inevitably to be the case, the end of a war usually signalled that the Xhosa were about to lose land, and the end of Mlanjeni's War was no different. As indicated earlier, the Ngqika were required give up their land in the Amathola Mountains, being re-located to land 'between the Kei and the great north road to the Windvogelberg, and bounded to the north by the Thomas River and to the south by Mhala's country'. The Amathola Mountains were proclaimed a Crown Reserve, but were soon thrown open to habitation by white settlers and, horror of horrors, to the Mfengu.

The rebel Thembu were also dealt with severely, even though Maphasa had been killed in the later fighting. Their lands on the west bank of the Kei River were confiscated and made the district of Queenstown, being then thrown open to white settlement. The Thembu were forced to the east bank, an area then labelled 'Emigrant Tembu' on many contemporary maps.

The Chiefs

Maqoma

Maqoma was another victim of the Cattle Killing, although not directly. Its impact caused him to lapse back to his alcohol dependence and, in a fit of anger, probably while under its influence, he assaulted a magistrate in the street. He also applied for a pass to pursue a woman whom he had seized as a concubine when she fled into the Amatholas. The pass was denied but, in August 1857, Maqoma pursued her anyway, was arrested and taken to Grahamstown, where he was allowed a pint of wine a day in his cell.

Governor Grey wanted to bring Maqoma to heel in order to undermine the authority of the Xhosa chiefs further. The lieutenant-governor, John Maclean, was not satisfied that the pass offence would be sufficient to deal with Maqoma effectively and dredged up the murder of an informer named Vusani by a gang of Maqoma's followers in July 1857.

On 17 November, Maqoma and nine others were charged with the murder of Vusani and receiving stolen property. Their defence was left to the accused themselves and Maqoma declared that he had only ordered Vusani's cattle to be confiscated as a fine, denying all other charges. On the following day, three of the nine men were found guilty of the murder and the remainder guilty of the robbery. Maqoma was found guilty of inciting the robbery and receiving stolen property, and was sentenced to transportation for life. When the sentences were confirmed, Grey reduced the transportation sentences to twenty years with hard labour, although Maqoma, now in old age, was excused the latter. In December, Maqoma found himself first in Cape Town gaol and then on Robben Island.[7]

Throughout the decade of the 1860s, the Xhosa chiefs who had been transported to Robben Island were brought back one by one, although Governor Wodehouse did not allow Maqoma, Siyolo and Xhoxho to return until 1869. Maqoma again established his household surreptitiously in the Waterkloof but one night in November 1871 his homestead was surrounded and he was arrested. He was taken to Fort Beaufort where, without trial, he was again bundled off to Robben Island, to spend the rest of his days in idle contemplation. Maqoma, possessing perhaps the greatest military mind of all the Xhosa leaders, died alone on 9 September 1873. He was, notes Mostert, about as old as the century.[8]

A postscript to this tragic tale is that, in May 1978, what were alleged to be Maqoma's remains were exhumed and brought back to the apartheid Nationalist government's black homeland of Ciskei, where they were interred on 13 August with great ceremony in what was then called Hero's Acre atop the Ntaba kaNdoda.[9] The place is now neglected and dilapidated, surrounded by the concrete skeletons of buildings that were once erected to honour great Xhosa men. No other heroes were brought to be interred there and his untended grave remains, isolated and alone.

Sandile

We have already noted that Charles Brownlee and Sandile had virtually grown up together. It is no surprise, therefore, that the commissioner had a great deal of influence over the Ngqika chief and there is clear evidence of this during the Cattle Killing period.

> Mr. Brownlee had to content himself with going among his own people. This he did week after week, coming home on Saturday to be off again on Monday. This he did to strengthen by his presence and advice those who resisted the delusion, and to hold back the timid and the wavering, among whom were Sandile, his turbulent half brother Dondas, and many others who waited on his word. Mr. Brownlee's object was if possible to prevent the Gaikas from obeying the prophet at all, and if this failed, to retard the destruction of cattle and so avert unity of action with the Gcalekas.[10]

When the sage had issued her instructions that all cattle were to be killed within eight days, Brownlee was extremely anxious and his wife feared for his safety, there being many evilly disposed who 'believed his influence kept Sandile from obeying the prophet'.[11]

A few days after the expiry of Nongqawuse's eight days, Sandile appeared sullen and withdrawn. When questioned, he told Brownlee that he wished to move his Great Place to its original location. That night, in pouring rain, he fled with his wives and children, having first killed his cattle.

When pressed for his reasons later, he said that Maqoma had sent him a message to say that he had seen 'two councillors who had died seven years before, who had told him to send and warn Sandile to rise from the dust and save himself'.[12]

On 20 October 1857, Brownlee wrote:

> From the Butterworth drift to the Thomas River all the country for fifteen miles on either side of the Kei is now uninhabited, with the exception of a kraal here and there containing a few individuals who cannot long continue to drag out the miserable existence they now lead. My tour on the Kei was shortened by the failure of provisions caused by sharing with the people I found by the way.[13]

Sandile survived the Cattle Killing but many of his people did not. He was to die in the last Xhosa War, on 29 May 1878, killed during a skirmish between his people and some Mfengu levies. Milton avers that Sandile had abandoned his dependence on alcohol during the last few months of his life.[14]

Sarhili

Sarhili was later involved in the Ninth Frontier War and was heavily defeated in the battle of Kentani on 7 February 1878, after which the chief went into hiding in a remote area of the Transkei. He made several enquiries as to the terms to be imposed on his surrender but they came to nothing. Despite the declaration that the war was over and an amnesty declared for all rebels except their leaders, the hunt for Sarhili went on.

A special patrol was sent out specifically to hunt him down, including a mounted section of the 1/24th Regiment, under the command of Lieutenant Teignmouth Melvill. It narrowly failed to capture him. According to a report of 18 July, 'Kreli and his followers were found in the forest and followed until sundown; three prisoners were taken but Kreli escaped and from this date until the 23rd August, no traces of him could be found, although constant patrols were made, night and day, into Bomvanaland as well as Gcalekaland.'[15]

Sarhili crossed the Mbashe River, passing through Bomvanaland into the country of the Mpondo. There he took refuge with the chief Gwadiso, despite the fact that Moni, the paramount chief, had already accepted British rule in the previous January. The Pondo chief Nqwiliso reported his presence and Sarhili narrowly avoided capture.

He remained in Pondoland for about a year, after which he re-crossed the Mthatha River and took up residence on the Bomvana side of the Mbashe. In 1881, he was offered a free and unconditional pardon, with residence near his old homestead of Holela, but he refused. He continued to ask to be allowed to return to his country; however, the government had concerns about his potential influence. In 1883, he was pardoned and allowed to settle in the Mbashe valley. He was subsequently offered permanent habitation in three locations, including Qolora, provided that he accept British rule and its laws and regulations. The old chief was now backed into a corner and finally acquiesced. He died in 1893 at the age of eighty-three.[16]

Mlanjeni

The seer's influence quickly waned with the passage of time and the direction of the war. Cory recorded his passing: 'Umlanjeni having, long before this, sunk into insignificance and held in contempt by those for whom he pretended to be able to do great things, died and was buried on 28 August, 1853.'[17]

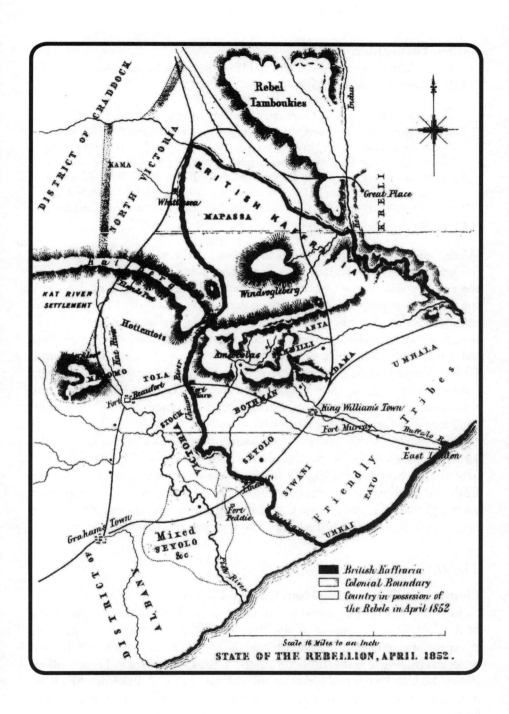

STATE OF THE REBELLION, APRIL 1852.

Scale 16 Miles to an Inch

British Kaffraria
Colonial Boundary
Country in possession of
the Rebels in April 1852

Willem Uithaalder

Of all the African antagonists, Uithaalder alone died by his own hand. His last days were recorded by Milton:

> Uithaalder found refuge in Gcalekaland. A traveller encountered him in 1865, doing odd jobs about a trading store and found him a quiet, reserved, respectful individual, grateful for the tip he received. Soon after this he crept into King William's Town one Sunday and heard John Brownlee preaching. The next day he rode out of the town until he came to some Xhosa huts. There he asked for water and after drinking it went outside. The inhabitants heard 'a wrestling noise' and, going out, found that Uithaalder had thrust a knife into his [own] throat and lay dead on the ground.[18]

When studied closely, the Xhosa lost none of the wars they fought with the white people, at least not in a military sense. Relentless harassment; the ruthless killing of women and children and the murdering of prisoners; starvation through destruction of their gardens; some or all of these resulted in the Xhosa seeking an end to the fighting, but they never gave up the notion that, one day, they should recover their lost lands. The Eighth Frontier War did not really end in their surrender but rather in something in the nature of a temporary truce. A parallel might be the games children play when, crossing their fingers, they might claim 'barley'. It would merely require the metaphorical uncrossing of Xhosa fingers to renew the fighting when conditions for their possible victory improved.

The veracity of this statement is demonstrated when one considers the intervals between the wars. The shortest interval was only three years – between the Seventh and Eighth – the longest was fifteen years, between the Fifth and Sixth wars. The average between all the wars from 1811 to 1850 was a mere eight years. However, the Cattle Killing was to prevent the Xhosa from fighting another war with the colony for a quarter of a century.

The British

Lieutenant-General the Hon. George Cathcart

In July 1853, General Cathcart was honoured by the Queen with the award of the Knight Commander of the Bath (KCB). In May 1854, the peppery governor was appointed adjutant-general to the force which the British were assembling for the invasion of the Crimea with their French allies. Before he left, he penned a document addressed to Colonel John Maclean, in which he set out his views on how the frontier, and its peoples, were to be managed.[19]

Shorn of his extensive powers and superiority, set in quite a different place, and in a very different role, this is how the ex-governor was perceived:

> The Hon. Sir George Cathcart was at sixty the youngest of them all, apart from the Duke of Cambridge. He had been bought a cornetcy in the Life Guards when he was fifteen by his father, General Earl Cathcart, at that time Ambassador at St. Petersburg; and by a succession of purchases and exchanges found himself a lieutenant-colonel in the 7th Hussars in 1826. He had not distinguished himself since; but he was granted a 'dormant commission' by the Government, which provided for his succession to the command of the army in the event of the death of the Commander-in-Chief in the Field. Touchy, inexperienced, stubborn and tactless, he was an unfortunate choice.[20]

There was no reference to his time in South Africa, where he was clearly perceived as not having greatly distinguished himself.

On 13 September 1854, the British and French armada carrying the invading army lay off the beach at Calamita Bay in the Crimea. During that day, the troops landed on the beach, without food and without tents. It began to rain in the afternoon and continued for the rest of the day. The sodden troops sat helplessly on the sand, not knowing what might happen to them next.

Less than two months later, on 5 November, Sir George Cathcart lay dead on the field of Inkerman.

> In the meanwhile, Lieutenant-General, the Honourable Sir George Cathcart, with a few companies of the 68th Regiment, considering that he might make a strong impression by descending into the valley, and taking the enemy in flank, moved rapidly forward, but finding the heights above him in full occupation of the Russians, he suddenly discovered that he was entangled with a superior force, and while attempting to withdraw his men, he received a mortal wound, shortly previously to which Brigadier-General Torrens, when leading the 68th, was likewise severely wounded.[21]

His famous last words are said to have been: 'We are in a mess. We must try the bayonet.'[22]

Sir Harry Smith

Harry Smith did not survive much longer than Cathcart. He was not offered further active service and remained in England commanding various military districts. On 20 June 1854 he was promoted to the rank of lieutenant-general, since his rank at the Cape was only local to the country. He retired from the army on 30 September 1859 and his health continued to fail from that point on.

Sir Harry Smith died of heart failure on 20 October 1860 at the age of seventy-three. He was buried at the New Cemetery in Whittlesea. At the Cape, his name was by then nearly forgotten. There is an insightful paragraph which might almost be his epitaph, at least for his time in South Africa:

> In his posturing, his play-acting before the Xhosa, and in the rashness of his assurances and promises to the settlers late in 1850 Smith only succeeded in making himself look foolish, as many contemporaries, among them Stockenström, Berkeley, Napier, Fairbairn, Godlonton, Dyason and Brownlee, saw only too clearly.[23]

His devoted wife Juana died on 10 October 1872 and was buried in the same place.

Notes

Acknowledgements

1   Susan Newton-King, 'The Labour Market of the Cape Colony, 1807–1828', in Shula Marks and Anthony Atmore (eds), *Economy and Society in Pre-Industrial South Africa*, London: Longman, 1980, p. 201, n. 4.

Introduction

1   Noël Mostert, *Frontiers: The Epic of South Africa's Creation and the Tragedy of the Xhosa People*, London: Jonathan Cape, 1992, p. 1077.

2   See B. Le Cordeur and C. Saunders, *The War of the Axe, 1847*, Johannesburg: Brenthurst Press, 1981.

3   This matter is covered in depth by J.B. Peires, *The Dead Will Arise: Nongqawuse and the Great Cattle-Killing Movement of 1856-7*, Jeppestown: Jonathan Ball, 2003.

4   Eric A. Walker (ed.), *The Cambridge History of the British Empire, Vol. VIII: South Africa, Rhodesia and the High Commission Territories*, London: Cambridge University Press, 1963, p. 369.

5   During the War of the Axe, for example, the governor, Sir Henry Pottinger, could not exercise a military command because of a continuing relationship with the East India Company. Lieutenant-General Sir George Berkeley therefore acted his as commander-in-chief.

6   BPP 124: Return of the white and coloured population of the Cape of Good Hope, 1852.

7   The title 'Prime Minister' does not constitutionally exist in Britain, even today. The official title of the office holder is 'First Lord of the Treasury'. See www.parliament.uk/.

8   John Sweetman, *War and Administration: The Significance of the Crimean War for the British Army*, Edinburgh: Scottish Academic Press, 1984, p. 12.

Chapter 1

1   Walker, p. 21.

2   Walker, pp. 26ff.

3   The Nguni languages use affixes to indicate various parts of speech. The prefix 'ama' in this context indicates a plural definite article meaning 'the'. Such affixes will not be further used to avoid confusion, but note the form of the modern words Amathola and Amalinde, both of which will occur later.

4   Walker, pp. 33ff.

5   Walker, p. 45.

6   J.B. Peires, *The House of Phalo: A History of the Xhosa People in the Days of their Independence*, Berkeley: University of California Press, 1981, pp. 29, 46.

7   Donald Moodie (ed.), *The Record, or a Series of Official Papers Relative to the Condition and Treatment of the Native Tribes of South Africa*, reprinted by A.A. Balkema: Cape Town, 1960, Part 1, p. 9: extract from van Riebeeck's journal.

8   Moodie, p. 280: instructions to van Riebeeck to permit discharge of employees for the purpose of establishing their own farms.

9   Peires, *The House of Phalo*, pp. 46–7.

10 George McCall Theal, *Records of the Cape Colony*, Vol. I, Cape Town: Government of the Cape Colony, 1897, *passim*.

11 Mostert, pp. 291ff.

12 Mostert, p. 323.

13 For a very detailed account of the early history of the Cape, under the Dutch and British administrations, see Mostert. For a more summary review of the individual frontier wars, see John Milton, *Edges of War: A History of Frontier Wars 1702–1878*, Kenwyn: Juta & Co. Ltd, 1983.

14 Mostert, pp. 446–51.

15 Mostert, pp. 427ff.

16 F. Herbst and D. Kopke, 'Site of the Battle of Amalinde', *Military History Journal*, Vol. 13, No. 5, June 2006.

17 Timothy Stapleton, *Maqoma: Xhosa Resistance to Colonial Advance 1798–1873*, Johannesburg: Jonathan Ball, 1994, p. 30.

18 Mostert, pp. 473ff.

19 Milton, p. 69.

20 Mostert, pp. 490–1.

21 Mostert, pp. 506–7.

22 Quoted in Mostert, p. 533. Mostert cites the quotation as coming from Charles Brownlee, *Reminiscences of Kaffir Life and History*, Lovedale: Lovedale Mission Press, 1896, p. 20, but it was not found in my own copy.

23 Mostert, p. 533.

24 A.L. Harington, *Sir Harry Smith: Bungling Hero*, Cape Town: Tafelberg Publishers, 1980, p. 3.

25 Later in the year, the corps was re-named the 95th Regiment and in 1816 became the famous Rifle Brigade.

26 Dorothy E. Rivett-Carnac, *Hawk's Eye*, Cape Town: Howard Timmins, 1966, p. 68.

27 The *mfecane* refers to the scattering of the people of southern Natal by constant warfare. This has been blamed on King Shaka of the Zulu, but this view has been challenged recently. See, for example, Dan Wylie, *Myth of Iron: Shaka in History*, Scottsville: University of KwaZulu-Natal, 2006, chapter 13.

28 The Gqunukhwebe were a people of Gonaqua Khoikhoi origin who, as a result

of giving great assistance to the Xhosa in earlier days, were admitted to the Xhosa hierarchy and were from then on treated as Xhosa.

29 Milton, p. 241.

30 Mostert, p. 826.

31 Johannes Meintjes, *Sandile: The Fall of the Xhosa Nation*, Cape Town: T.V. Bulpin, 1971, p. 115.

32 Mostert, p. 990.

33 BPP 912, Enclosure 5 in No. 17, pp. 60–1: Sir Henry Pottinger to Sir George Berkeley, 24 March 1847.

34 Sir George E. Cory, *The Rise of South Africa: A History of the Origin of South African Colonial Development towards the East from the Earliest Times to 1857*, Vol. V, London: Longmans, Green, 1930, p. 15. This is an apparent contradiction of Mostert's assertion that the rations *were* stopped. Cf. Mostert, p. 919.

35 Mostert, p. 914.

36 BPP 912, Enclosure 4 in No. 13, p. 45: Pottinger to Berkeley, 8 March 1847.

37 Pottinger could not take the office of commander-in-chief, as most other governors did, because he was still officially a 'servant' of the East India Company.

38 BPP 912, Enclosure 2 in No. 17, p. 59: Sir George Berkeley to Sir Henry Pottinger, 23 March 1847.

39 Emphasis in the original.

40 Cory, p. 15.

41 Harington, p. 88.

42 Quoted in Harington, p. 92.

43 Harington, p. 92.

44 MS 6806, Cory Library: Extract of a letter from Sir John Wylde, Chief Justice, Cape Town, to Sir Benjamin D'Urban, 24 January 1848. Smith's Letters Patent finally arrived in May 1848.

45 Harington, p. 94.

Chapter 2

1 'I rise again with greater splendour'. Coincidentally, this was the motto of the Cape Mounted Rifles.

2 Smith's activities in India are well described in chapter V of Harington.

3 Pottinger was granted the title 'High Commissioner' to give him an additional salary after he had complained that the income from the post of governor was inadequate. See Le Cordeur and Saunders, p. 20.

4 BPP 457: Letters Patent of the 15th December 1847, appointing Sir Harry Smith governor of the Cape of Good Hope, and the instructions therewith given, p. 3.

5 Mostert, p. 658.

6 John Jarvis Bisset, *Sport and War: Or Recollections of Fighting and Hunting in South Africa from the Years 1834 to 1867*, London: John Murray, 1875, pp. 124–7.

7 Brownlee, p. 311.

8   MS 6806, Cory Library: Extract of a letter from Sir John Wylde, Chief Justice, Cape Town, to Sir Benjamin D'Urban, 24 January 1848: Menzies was a judge at the Cape and John Montagu was Colonial Secretary.

9   The Letters Patent finally arrived on 2 May 1848, following which he was properly sworn in.

10   Smith to Grey, 4 December 1847, cited in Le Cordeur and Saunders, p. 258.

11   T.J. Lucas, *Camp Life and Sport in South Africa: Experiences of Kaffir Warfare with the Cape Mounted Rifles*, London: Chapman & Hall, 1878; reprinted in Johannesburg: Africana Book Society Ltd, 1975, p. 51.

12   The diary of Captain William King-Hall can be found in L. King-Hall, (ed), *Sea Saga*, London: Victor Gollancz, 1935.

13   Harriet Ward, *The Cape and the Kaffirs: A Diary of Five Years' Residence in Kaffirland*, London: Henry G. Bohn, 1851, p. 214.

14   Ward, p. 214.

15   S.E.K. Mqhayi, *Abantu Besizwe*, ed. and trans. J. Opland, Johannesburg: Wits University Press, 2009, p. 362.

16   Mostert, p. 931.

17   Rev. George Brown, *Personal Adventure in South Africa*, London: James Blackwood, 1855, p. 203.

18   Ward, p. 215.

19   Ward, p. 215.

20   BPP 969, Enclosure 1 in No. 6, p. 22: 17 December 1847.

21   BPP 969, Enclosure 5 in No. 7, pp. 27–8: 23 December 1847.

22   BPP 969, No. 10, pp. 31–2: Smith to Earl Grey, 1 January 1848.

23   Meintjes, p. 209. Theal says that Brownlee's appointment 'had not the slightest effect on a single Kaffir' because of his already close relationship to the Ngqika, being 'regarded almost as one of them'. See G.M. Theal, *History of South Africa from 1795 to 1872*, Vol. III, London: George Allen & Unwin, 1927, p. 93 and note.

24   BPP 969, No. 6, p. 21: Smith to Grey, 18 December 1847.

25   BPP 969, Enclosure 1 in No. 6, p. 22: Proclamation of 17 December 1847.

26   Named for Smith's birthplace of Whittlesey in England.

27   BPP 969, No. 7, pp. 24–5: Smith to Earl Grey, 23 December 1847.

28   Mostert, p. 931.

29   *Eastern Province Herald*, 4 January 1851.

30   BPP 969, Enclosure 1 in No. 7, pp. 25–6: 23 December 1847.

31   BPP 969, Enclosure 2 in No. 7, p. 26: 24 December 1847.

32   Cory, pp. 129–30.

33   See http://genforum.genealogy.com/southafrica/messages/5517.html.

34   *London Gazette*, 26 December 1851.

35   BPP 969, Enclosure 6 in No. 7, p. 28: 24 December 1847.

36   BPP 912, No. 13, pp. 35–6: Pottinger to Grey, 13 March 1847. See also Enclosures 5 and 6 to the same despatch.

37   Cory, pp. 132–3.

38   BPP 969, Enclosure 2 in No. 18, pp. 53–4: Government Notice dated 1 January 1848.
39   BPP 969, No. 10, p. 32: Smith to Grey, 1 January 1848.
40   BPP 969, Enclosure 1 in No. 18, pp. 49–50: Smith to Grey, 7 December 1848.
41   Cory, p. 110.
42   BPP 969, Enclosure in No. 22, p. 57: Smith to Grey, 14 January 1848.
43   BPP 969, No. 24, p. 58: Smith to Grey, 15 February 1848.
44   BPP 969, Enclosure 3 in No. 26, p. 63: Smith to Grey, 3 February 1848.
45   The force consisted of four companies of CMR, two guns and two companies each from the 45th, 91st and the Rifle Brigade.
46   Convicts who had earned their Ticket of Leave were treated almost as free men and were not chained or directly supervised. They were able to take paid work and their employer was their supervisor.
47   BPP 1138, No. 12, pp. 152–3: Grey to Smith, 30 November 1849.
48   Cf. BPP 969, No. 6, p. 21; Enclosure 6 in No. 7, p. 29; No. 25, p. 59.
49   BPP 969, No. 32, p. 70: Smith to Grey, 18 March 1848.
50   Paradoxically, prior to 1856 officers were members of the Royal Engineers and their men belonged to the Royal Sappers and Miners; see Richard Holmes, *Redcoat: The British Soldier in the Age of the Horse and Musket*, London: HarperCollins, 2001, p. 130.
51   Other regiments were also named but their numbers were very small, being largely the repatriation of the sick and wounded.
52   BPP 969, No. 32, p. 71: Smith to Grey, 18 March 1848.
53   Fort Murray was close to Mount Coke, just outside King William's Town.
54   BPP 1334, Sub-enclosure 1 in Enclosure in No. 4, p. 17: John Maclean to Colonel Mackinnon, 26 August 1850.
55   BPP 1334, Enclosure in No. 2, p. 15: Mackinnon to Smith, 30 September 1850.
56   Peires, *The Dead Will Arise*, p. 23.
57   BPP 1334, No. 7, p. 28: Smith to Grey, 21 October 1850; No. 9, p. 38: Smith to Grey, 31 October 1850. The proclamation deposing Sandile was published in Enclosure 5 to this despatch, dated 30 October 1850.
58   BPP 1334, Enclosure 1 in No. 14, p. 59: Mackinnon to Smith, 2 December 1850.
59   Mackinnon to Somerset, Public Notice, 5 December 1850.
60   BPP 1334, Enclosure 6 in No. 15: 14 December 1850, p. 69, Resolution sent to Sir Harry Smith by farmers in the East Somerset district.
61   BPP 1334, Enclosure 4 in No. 15, pp. 68ff.
62   Quoted by Joseph Lehmann, *Remember you Are an Englishman: A Biography of Sir Harry Smith*, London: Jonathan Cape, 1977, p. 280.
63   BPP 1334, Enclosure 5 in No. 15, p. 69: Proclamation of Suthu's elevation to Chief of the Ngqika.
64   BPP 635, p. 385: evidence of Rev. H. Renton to Parliamentary Select Committee.

Chapter 3

1 This is a fictitious outburst conceived by Mapham, but one which may come very close to the truth.

2 The force consisted of 244 men of the 6th Regiment, 77 men of the 73rd Regiment and 174 Cape Mounted Rifles. There were also 92 Kaffir Police. See BPP 1334, footnote to Enclosure 1 in No. 16, p. 73: Mackinnon to Smith, 24 December 1850.

3 Mostert states that there was a company of the Rifle Brigade among the British troops at the Boma Pass but this could not be so: the 1st Battalion had left the Cape for England on 12 July 1850. Cf. Mostert, p. 1017 and Sir William H. Cope, *History of the Rifle Brigade*, London: Chatto & Windus, 1877, p. 267.

4 This is attested by the evidence of Rev. H. Renton to a Parliamentary Select Committee. See BPP 635, p. 386.

5 Bisset, pp. 131ff.

6 Bisset, p. 133.

7 Bisset and Lucas both spell the doctor's name as 'Stewart' but its correct spelling is shown in Hart, *New Annual Army List for 1851*, London: John Murray, 1852, p. 259.

8 Lucas spells the seer's name as 'Mlangeni'.

9 Lucas, pp. 173–4.

10 Much of what follows is found in Lieutenant Armytage's detailed account, in Cory, pp. 306–10.

11 Africana Collection, Weinstein family, Pretoria: Letters of Colour-Sergeant Thomas Golding, 6th Regiment and Cape Mounted Rifles.

12 Bisset, pp. 134ff.

13 Bisset, p. 136.

14 Lucas, pp. 174–5.

15 Strangely, there is no mention of a medical officer named Fraser, either with the CMR or the two infantry regiments, in Hart's *New Annual Army List* for either 1851 or 1853. One might surmise that this person was a civilian doctor attached to the CMR, a not uncommon practice.

16 Bisset, pp. 138–9.

17 Bisset, p. 142.

18 Lucas, pp. 175–6.

19 Lieutenant Baillie had been killed, together with his twenty-eight-man patrol, in the war of 1835.

20 Lucas, pp. 178ff. Mackinnon, in his official report of the return from Keiskamma Hoek, reported the number as a 'sergeant and 14 rank and file'. See BPP 1334, Enclosure 2 in No. 16, p. 73: Mackinnon to Smith, 25 December 1850. Sergeant Golding added a civilian to the count.

21 Lucas described the features of the fort thus: 'Fort White, the scene of our next encampment, is built in the usual wattle-and-daub style of the country, and is a collection of little irregular hovels, inclosed by a mud wall, formidable against Kaffirs, but utterly indefensible against a disciplined foe. As it is only just large

enough to hold its garrison, about a hundred men, the patrols encamp on the ground outside the walls.' See Lucas, p. 159.

22   Brownlee, p. 321. Brownlee here recounts the story of Xhoxho, Sandile's half-brother, being with Smith on that day. The governor asked Xhoxho if he had heard any firing earlier and the chief replied that he heard one or two shots. In fact, Xhoxho had been at the pass during the engagement and had hurried to Fort Cox at the governor's command only after he had returned to his homestead after the battle.

23   Lieutenant Armytage in Cory, p. 309.

24   The many letters of Ensign Hugh Robinson are in the Howard-Vyse family's ownership in the United Kingdom. There are poor-quality microfilm copies of the letters at the National Army Museum, Chelsea and the Cory Library of the Rhodes University, Grahamstown, South Africa. Robinson was commissioned as ensign by purchase in the 43rd Regiment on 14 December 1849. He was subsequently commissioned lieutenant, without purchase, on 6 July 1852. (See *London Gazette*, 14 December 1849 and 6 July 1852.)

25   Colonel J.C. Gawler, 'British Troops and Savage Warfare, with Special Reference to the Kafir Wars', *Royal United Services Institute Journal*, Vol. 17, 1874, pp. 922-39.

26   Cory, p. 128.

27   This account was given to Captain Stevenson by a government employee named Henry McCabe, who stayed on in Juanasburg. See PR 1478, Cory Library, an article by the only survivor of the Woburn attack, Captain Stevenson, entitled 'A Terrible Christmas Day', in the *Alice Times/Seymour and Peddie Gazette*, 16 December and 23 December 1920.

28   R. Godlonton and E. Irving, *A Narrative of the Kafir War of 1850-51-52*, Cape Town: Struik, 1962, p. 57. Their names were given as W. Maher, J. Fee and J. Murphy.

29   PR 1478, Cory Library: 'A Terrible Christmas Day'.

30   PR 1478, Cory Library: 'A Terrible Christmas Day'.

31   Brown, pp. 53-4.

32   This, and all of the following quotations are taken from MS779, Cory Library: P.B. Blanckenberg, 'The Treachery at Auckland'.

33   Rev. John Ayliff, letter to the *Grahamstown Journal*, 18 January 1851.

34   Cory, p. 320.

35   Cory, pp. 320-1.

36   Cory, p. 321.

37   The source of what follows is provided by Bisset, pp. 150-9.

38   Mostert, p. 1079, gives the date of this attack as 3 January but Bisset is quite clear as to the date: two days after their arrival on 25 December.

39   Bisset, p. 152.

40   Bisset, pp. 152-5.

Chapter 4

1   BPP 1334, No. 16, p. 72: Smith to Grey, 26 December 1850.

2   Siyolo (sometimes spelled Seyolo) was the second son of Mdushane and a grandson of Ndlambe.

3   BPP 1352, Enclosure 5 in No. 9, p. 123: Reports on capture and burning of Line Drift Post, 28 December 1850.

4   BPP 1352, Enclosure 5 in No. 9, p. 123: Report of Commissariat Officer J. Wilson, 28 December 1850.

5   BPP 1352, Enclosure 2 in No. 8, p. 15: Somerset to Colonial Secretary, 1 January 1851.

6   BPP 1334, No. 17, p. 75: Smith to Grey, 7 January 1851.

7   Isaiah Staples, *A Narrative of the Eighth Frontier War of 1851–1853*, ed. J. de Villiers, Pretoria: State Library, 1974, pp. 11–12.

8   Staples, pp. 12–13.

9   Staples, p. 13.

10   The editor of Staples's account identifies Bear as Mr. W. de Beer: Staples, p. 14, n. 22.

11   Staples, pp. 14ff.

12   Staples, p. 16.

13   Staples, pp. 18–19.

14   Staples, p. 18.

15   Sarah Ralph, 'Diary', *Martello Magazine*, Fort Beaufort Museum, 25 December 1850.

16   Sarah Ralph, 'Diary', 4 January 1851.

17   Colonel Henry Somerset was promoted by Sir Harry Smith to the local rank of major-general by a general order dated 2 January 1851. See BPP 1334, Enclosure 3 in No. 17, p. 77 and WO 1/447: Wellington to Grey, 10 May 1851.

18   Lucas, pp. 63–4.

19   Lucas, p. 67.

20   Sarah Ralph, 'Diary', 28 December 1850.

21   Sarah Ralph, 'Diary', 29 December 1850.

22   Sarah Ralph, 'Diary', 30 December 1850.

23   Captain William Wynne, letter to the *Grahamstown Journal*, 18 January 1851.

24   Sarah Ralph, 'Diary', 30 December 1850.

25   Sarah Ralph, 'Diary', 3 January 1851.

26   Sarah Ralph, 'Diary', 3 January 1851.

27   Sarah Ralph, 'Diary', 3 January 1851.

28   Sarah Ralph, 'Diary', 4 January 1851.

29   Sarah Ralph, 'Diary', 3 January 1851.

30   Sarah Ralph, 'Diary', 4 January 1851.

31   'Pa' was Robert Godlonton, the editor of the *Grahamstown Journal*.

32   Matilda Booth, letter to the *Grahamstown Journal*, 14 January 1851.

33   Sarah Ralph, 'Diary', 4 January 1851, p. 3.

34 Peter S. Campbell, *Reminiscences of the Kafir Wars*, Walthamstow: Duck Bros, n.d., p. 41.
35 Campbell, pp. 42–3; Sarah Ralph, 'Diary', 6 January 1851.
36 Sarah Ralph, 'Diary', 6 January 1851.

Chapter 5
1 Stoep: a porch or steps at the door of a house.
2 Mr Mewett, letter to the *Grahamstown Journal*, 18 January 1851.
3 William Wynne, letter to the *Grahamstown Journal*, 18 January 1851.
4 Sarah Ralph, 'Diary', 7 January 1851.
5 William Wynne, letter to the *Grahamstown Journal*, 18 January 1851.
6 Mr Mewett, letter to the *Grahamstown Journal*, 18 January 1851.
7 Sarah Ralph, 'Diary', 7 January 1851.
8 Sarah Ralph, 'Diary', 7 January 1851.
9 Lt-Col. Sutton, letter to the *Grahamstown Journal*, 14 January 1851.
10 Sarah Ralph, 'Diary', 7 January 1851.
11 Sarah Ralph, 'Diary', 7 January 1851.
12 Sarah Ralph, 'Diary', 7 January 1851.
13 Rev. J. Ayliff, letter to the *Grahamstown Journal*, 18 January 1851.
14 William Wynne, letter to the *Grahamstown Journal*, 18 January 1851.
15 Sarah Ralph, 'Diary', 7 January 1851.
16 Mr Mewett, letter to the *Grahamstown Journal*, 18 January 1851.
17 BPP 1334, Enclosure 1 in No. 18, pp. 80–1: General Order, dated 10 January, 1851. The emphasis is the author's.
18 BPP 1334, No. 18, p. 8: Smith to Grey, 10 January 1851.
19 Mostert, p. 1084.
20 Mostert, p. 1084.
21 BPP 1380, Enclosure in No. 3, p. 5: Wienand to Somerset, 31 January 1851.
22 BPP 1352, No. 9, p. 119: Montagu to Grey, 11 January 1851.
23 BPP, 1380, Enclosure 3 in No. 6, pp. 10–11: Tylden to Somerset, 3 February 1851.
24 Milton, p. 197.
25 Cory, pp. 345ff.
26 BPP 1380, Enclosure 1 in No. 7, p. 21: Proclamation dated 22 February 1851.
27 Cory, p. 371.
28 Cory, pp. 371ff.
29 Sarah Ralph, 'Diary', 17 January 1851.
30 Staples, p. 19. Staples says there were four men, and the editor suggests that the fourth was Staples himself.
31 Staples states that the forty horsemen returned with the four from Post Retief. Staples, p. 20.
32 Staples, p. 24.
33 Staples, p. 24.
34 Staples, p. 25.

35   Staples, p. 26, editor's note 42: 'Smith's camp must have been on the farm 'Hartebeestfontein', owned by John Joseph Smith.' Smith was then aged seventy-two.

36   John Wesley Wiggill was the eldest son of Eli Wiggill, and was born in 1832.

37   Most of what follows is taken from Staples, pp. 27–30.

38   A riem is a narrow length of leather used for reins or harness.

39   Susannah Wiggill, née Bentley, died 29 March 1869.

40   I. Mitford-Barberton, *Comdt. Holden Bowker*, Cape Town: Human & Rousseau, 1970, p. 169. According to Bowker, the cornet's name was Sweetman.

41   J. Kenneth Larson, *History of the Genealogy of the Talbots, Sweetnams and Wiggills*, Cory Library, pamphlet box 253, pp. 39–40.

Chapter 6

1   Mitford-Barberton, p. 170.

2   BPP 424, Enclosure 1 in No. 2, p. 9: Somerset to Smith, 24 February 1851.

3   The Lushington Valley lay between the military village of Woburn in the Tyumie Valley and Seymour, to the north-west.

4   BPP 424, Enclosure 2 in No. 1, p. 7: Extract from Commandant Walter Currie's Journal, published in the *Grahamstown Journal*, 25 February 1851. See also BPP 424, Enclosure 2 in No. 1, p. 7.

5   Mr R. Sparks, letter to the *Grahamstown Journal*, 23 February 1851. See also BPP 424, Enclosure 2 in No. 1, p. 8.

6   'Graaff-Reinet Englishman', letter to the *Grahamstown Journal*, 8 March 1851.

7   Staples, pp. 31–2.

8   Commandant Walter Currie, letter to the *Grahamstown Journal*, 25 February 1851.

9   Staples, p. 32.

10   Staples, p. 33.

11   Mitford-Barberton, p. 170.

12   Commandant Walter Currie, letter to the *Grahamstown Journal*, 25 February 1851.

13   Staples, p. 34.

14   Somerset says 2 a.m. See BPP 424, Enclosure 1 in No. 2, p. 9: Somerset to Smith, 24 February 1851.

15   BPP 424, Enclosure 1 in No. 2, p. 9: Somerset to Smith, 24 February 1851.

16   This seems unlikely, in view of his actions in the taking of Fort Armstrong earlier. It is more likely that he saw the writing on the wall and was placing himself in the best position for the aftermath.

17   Major Charles Somerset was the brother of Henry Somerset.

18   'Another Hand with Somerset', letter to *Grahamstown Journal*, 23 February 1851. See also BPP 424, Enclosure 2 in No. 1, p. 8.

19   Staples, p. 35.

20   The interior of the tower at Fort Armstrong was badly damaged during the battle for its recovery. A complete example of such a tower interior may be seen at Fort Brown, in the South African Police compound.

21 John Wiggill in Larson, p. 42.

22 Winston S. Churchill, speech at the Mansion House, 10 November 1942.

23 Smith was at this time still confined at Fort Cox and must, therefore, have been enabled to send the text of this despatch to Somerset at Fort Hare.

24 BPP 1380, No. 1, p. 1: Smith to Grey, 27 January 1851.

25 BPP 1352, Enclosure 2 in No. 10, p. 127: Somerset to Major Burnaby, Grahamstown, 23 January 1851.

26 BPP 1380, Enclosure 1 in No. 2, p. 8: Mackinnon to Smith, 1 February 1851.

27 BPP 1380, Enclosure 1 in No. 5, p. 14: Cloete to Smith, 18 February 1851.

28 See, for example, BPP 1334, Enclosure 5 in No. 17, p. 79: Notice dated 31 December 1850; BPP 1352, Enclosure 7 in No. 9, p. 124: Circular letter from Montagu to Civil Commissioners, 4 January 1851; BPP 1380, p. 9: Proclamation dated 3 February 1851.

29 BPP 424, No. 5, p. 21: Smith to Grey, 17 March 1851.

30 BPP 424, Enclosure 1 in No. 5, pp. 23ff.: Proceedings of Court of Enquiry.

31 BPP 424, No. 5, pp. 21ff: Smith to Grey, 17 March 1851.

32 BPP 1352, No. 10, pp. 139ff.: Grey to Smith, 8 March 1851.

33 BPP 424, No.1, p. 57: Grey to Smith, 13 May 1851.

34 TNA, WO 1/447, No. 4088 Cape: Wellington to Grey, 10 May 1851.

35 TNA, WO 1/447, No. 4421 Cape: Wellington to Grey, 22 May 1851.

36 BPP 1428, No. 2, p. 16: Smith to Grey, 6 May 1851. The regiment arrived at Port Elizabeth on 16 May 1851.

37 James McKay, *Reminiscences of the Last Kaffir War*, Cape Town: Struik, 1970, p. 6.

38 McKay, p. 13.

39 The Duke of Cambridge subsequently became Commander-in-Chief of the British Army.

40 McKay, p. 30.

41 These patrols, and Mackinnon's sortie, are reported in BPP 1428, Enclosures 1 and 2 in No. 4, pp. 2–23.

42 Sir Stephen Lakeman, *What I Saw in Kaffirland: The Kaffir War 1850–53*, London: William Blackwood, 1880, p. 80.

43 The sjambok is a leather whip used in South Africa. It is traditionally made from an adult hippopotamus or rhinoceros hide.

44 William Ross King, *Campaigning in Kaffirland: Or Scenes and Adventures in the Kaffir War of 1851–1852.*, London: Saunders & Otley, 1883, p. 264.

45 W.A. Maxwell and R.T. McGeogh, *The Reminiscences of Thomas Stubbs*, Cape Town: A.A. Balkema, 1978, p. 155.

46 Mostert, pp. 1111–12.

47 King, p. 269.

48 Reports of these movements are to be found in BPP 1428, enclosures to No. 5, pp. 26ff.

49 BPP 1428, Enclosure 3 in No. 5, pp. 31–2: Somerset's report.

50 Maxwell and McGeogh, pp. 41–2. William was made of stern stuff: he learned to shoot a pistol left-handed and was back in action by mid-1852.

51   BPP 1428, Enclosure 2 in No. 7, p. 47: Somerset to Smith, 3 June 1851.

52   BPP 1428, Enclosure 4 in No. 7, p. 48: Somerset to Cloete, 6 June 1851.

53   Maxwell and McGeogh, p. 42.

54   BPP 1428, Enclosure 9 in No. 7, p. 52: Smith to Mackinnon, 4 June 1851.

55   Lt C.H. Bell, 'The Eighth Kaffir War', *Africana Notes & News*, Vol. IV, No. 4, September 1947. Bell was Somerset's field adjutant during this patrol.

56   BPP 1428, Enclosure 1 in No. 9, pp. 62–4: Somerset to Smith; Bell, 'The Eighth Kaffir War'.

57   BPP 1428, Enclosures 2 and 3 in No. 9, pp. 65ff.: Mackinnon to Smith, 1 July 1851; Michel to Mackinnon, 1 July 1851.

58   BPP 1428, Enclosure 5 in No. 9, p. 68: Cooper to Mackinnon, 1 July 1851.

59   Capt. P.H. Dalbiac, *History of the 45th: 1st Nottinghamshire Regiment*, London: Swan Sonnenschein, 1902, p. 200.

60   BPP 1428, Enclosure 6 in No. 9, p. 79: Government Notice, 1 July 1851.

61   BPP 1380, Enclosure 3 in No. 5, p. 15: Smith to Pine, 26 December 1850.

62   Shepstone had begun his career as an interpreter, coincidentally with Harry Smith during D'Urban's invasion of the Transkei in 1835. (Smith was godfather to Shepstone's eldest son Henrique, born in 1840.) At this time, Shepstone was 'diplomatic agent to the natives' under Lieutenant-Governor Sir Benjamin Pine. See R.E. Gordon, *Shepstone: The Role of the Family in the History of South Africa, 1820–1900*, Cape Town: A.A. Balkema, 1968, *passim*.

63   BPP 1380, Enclosure 4 in No. 5, pp. 15–16: Pine to Smith, 17 January 1851.

64   BPP 1428, No. 8, p. 55: Smith to Grey, 17 June 1851.

65   BPP 424, No. 2, pp. 57ff: Grey to Smith, 13 May 1851.

66   Harington, p. 200.

67   Oliver Ransford, *The Great Trek*, London: John Murray, 1972, p. 197.

68   Cory, Chapter 3, *passim*.

69   Private letter from Pottinger to Earl Grey, 23 February 1847, quoted in Le Cordeur and Saunders, p. 29. Emphasis is in the original.

70   Cory, pp. 132–3.

71   BPP 424, Enclosure 2 in No. 9, pp. 44–5: Major Donovan to Lieutenant-Colonel Cloete, Deputy Quartermaster-General, 29 March 1851.

72   Harington, p. 199.

73   Cf. Walker, p. 352.

Chapter 7

1   BPP 1428, Enclosure 1 in No. 15, pp. 86–7: Somerset to Cloete, 20 July 1851.

2   What is here called the Gqwala is now the Kaalhoek River.

3   Thomas Baines, *Journal of Residence in Africa*, Vol. II, ed. R.F. Kennedy, Cape Town: Van Riebeeck Society, 1961, p. 196.

4   McKay, pp. 66–73

5   Unless otherwise indicated, what follows is drawn from Baines, pp. 196–212.

6   Baines obviously owned the new Minié rifle, the rifling of which imparted great spin to the special bullet and improved its range and accuracy.

7 BPP 424, No. 4, pp. 62–3: Grey to Smith, 11 June 1851.

8 BPP 1428, Enclosure in No. 27, p. 163: Owen to Montagu, 11 August 1851.

9 BPP 1428, Enclosure 1 in No. 28, p. 164: Hogge Memorandum, 29 September 1851.

10 BPP 1428, Enclosure 2 in No. 28, p. 164: Smith to Hogge, 29 September 1851.

11 BPP 1428, No. 22, p. 122: Smith to Grey, 3 September 1851.

12 BPP 1428, Enclosure No. 19, p. 109: Smith to Grey, 16 August 1851.

13 BPP 1428, No. 20, p. 110: Smith to Grey, 20 August 1851.

14 BPP 1428, Enclosure 3 in No. 24, pp. 142–3: Report of Major Burns, 4 September 1851.

15 Thola was a member of the Dange clan and a brother of Bhotomane.

16 BPP 1428, Enclosure 3 in No. 24, p. 143: Report of Major Burns, 1 September 1851.

17 McKay, p. 121

18 BPP 1428, Enclosure 5 in No. 26, p. 158: Instructions to Colonel Mackinnon, 5 September 1851.

19 BPP 1428, Enclosure 5 in No. 26, pp. 159–60: Colonel Mackinnon's report, 17 September 1851. Much of what follows is taken from this report.

20 BPP 1428, Enclosure 5 in No. 26, p. 159: Colonel Mackinnon's report, 17 September 1851.

21 BPP 1428, Enclosure 5 in No. 26, p. 160: Colonel Mackinnon's report, 17 September 1851.

22 BPP 1428, Enclosure 5 in No. 26, p. 161: Casualty report.

23 McKay, p. 93.

24 King, pp. 84–5.

25 McKay, p. 94. He names the bandmaster as 'Hartong'. Cf. King, p. 87.

26 King, pp. 85ff.

27 McKay, pp. 94–5.

28 McKay, p. 95.

29 King, p. 87.

30 King, pp. 87ff.

31 King, p. 89.

32 McKay, p. 97.

33 McKay, pp. 99–100.

34 BPP 1428, Enclosure 5 in No. 26, pp. 155ff.: Fordyce to Somerset, report, 9 September 1851.

35 King, p. 90.

36 McKay, p. 99.

37 McKay, pp. 104–5.

38 McKay, p. 99.

39 King, pp. 90–1.

40 McKay, p. 101.

41 McKay, p. 105.

42 King, pp. 91–2.

43 BPP 1428, Enclosure 5 in No. 26, p. 137: Return of killed and wounded, 8 September 1851.
44 McKay, pp. 106–9.
45 BPP 1428, Enclosure 5 in No. 26, p. 155: Somerset to Cloete, 11 September 1851.

Chapter 8
1 BPP 1428, p. 182: State of Troops in Fordyce's column.
2 McKay, pp. 221–2.
3 BPP 1428, p. 181: Fordyce report, 15 October 1851.
4 BPP 1428, p. 181: Fordyce report, 15 October 1851.
5 King, p. 104.
6 Baines, pp. 227–8.
7 Baines, p. 228.
8 'One of the Ragged Brigade', 'Operations in the Waterkloof', *United Service Magazine*, Part I, April, 1852, p. 586. Neville Mapham avoided the use of the author's cumbersome nom-de-plume by using the name 'Lieutenant B.' and I have followed the same convention.
9 King, p. 104.
10 BPP 1428, Enclosure 1 in No. 31, p. 180: Précis of General Somerset, 17 October 1851.
11 King, p. 105.
12 King, pp. 105–6.
13 BPP 1428, p. 181: Fordyce report, 15 October 1851.
14 King, p. 107.
15 BPP 1428, Enclosure 1 in No. 31, p. 180: Précis of General Somerset, 17 October 1851.
16 BPP 1428, Enclosure 1 in No. 31, p. 180: Précis of General Somerset, 17 October 1851.
17 King, p. 107.
18 Baines, p. 231.
19 Baines, pp. 231–2.
20 King, pp. 107–8.
21 King, p. 108.
22 Baines, p. 232.
23 King, p. 109. Carey's mention in despatches is in BPP 1428, Enclosure in No. 31, p. 180.
24 'One of the Ragged Brigade', 'Operations in the Waterkloof', p. 588.
25 Baines, p. 233.
26 King, p. 110.
27 Baines, p. 233.
28 King, pp. 110–11.
29 King, p. 111.
30 King, p. 111.
31 King, p. 112.

32 King, pp. 113–14.
33 'Diary of No. 1366 Private Thomas Scott' of the 12th Regiment, *Suffolk Regimental Gazette.*
34 McKay, p. 138.
35 King, p. 115.
36 Baines, p. 234.
37 McKay, pp. 137–8.
38 Baines, p. 235.
39 King, p. 116.
40 McKay, p. 139.
41 King, p. 118.
42 King, pp. 118–19.
43 BPP 1428, Enclosure 1 in No. 32, p. 191: Return of killed and wounded.
44 BPP 1428, Enclosure 1 in No. 32, pp. 188–9: Somerset's report, 28 October 1851.
45 Baines, p. 237.
46 King, pp. 127–8.
47 McKay, p. 145.
48 McKay, p. 148.
49 King, p. 128.
50 McKay, pp. 148–9.
51 McKay, pp. 149–50.
52 Baines, p. 238.
53 'One of the Ragged Brigade, 'p. 589.
54 King, pp. 128–9.
55 Anon., 'The Records of the 2nd Battalion, King's Royal Rifle Corps', Museum of the Royal Green Jackets, p. 24.
56 BPP 1428, Enclosure 1 in No. 32, pp. 188–9: Somerset's report, 28 October 1851.
57 'Records of 2nd Battalion', p. 25; King, p. 129.
58 McKay, p. 152.
59 King, p. 129.
60 McKay, p. 151.
61 BPP 1428, Enclosure 1 in No. 32, pp. 188–9: Somerset's report, 28 October 1851.
62 King, pp. 129–30.
63 King, p. 131.
64 King, pp. 130–1; Baines, p. 240.
65 McKay, p. 149.
66 BPP 1428, Enclosure 1 in No. 32, p. 191: Casualty report, 28 October 1851.

Chapter 9

1 BPP 1428, Enclosure 1 in No. 32, pp. 188–9: Somerset's report, 28 October 1851.
2 King, p. 132.
3 King, pp. 132ff.
4 McKay, pp. 140ff.
5 Baines, pp. 240–1.

6   BPP 1428, Enclosure 1 in No. 32, pp. 188–9: Somerset's report, 28 October 1851.
7   'One of the Ragged Brigade', p. 590.
8   King, pp. 133ff.
9   King, pp. 135–6.
10 Baines, pp. 241–2.
11 Baines, pp. 242–3.
12 BPP 1428, Enclosure 1 in No. 32, pp. 188–9: Somerset's report, 28 October 1851.
13 'One of the Ragged Brigade', p. 591.
14 'One of the Ragged Brigade', p. 591.
15 BPP 1428, Enclosure No. 19, p. 109: Smith to Grey, 16 August 1851.
16 BPP 1428, No. 3, p. 239: Grey to Smith, 14 July 1851.
17 BPP 1428, Enclosure 2 in No. 30, pp. 166ff.
18 BPP 1428, Enclosure 10 in No. 30, p. 178: Colonel Cloete, 16 October 1851.
19 BPP 1428, No. 8, pp. 241–2: Grey to Smith, 15 September 1851.
20 See, for example, BPP 1428, No. 8 of 15 September 1851, p. 241 and No. 13 of 14 November 1841, p. 245
21 BPP 1428, No 11, p. 244: Grey to Smith, 21 October 1851.
22 BPP 635: Report from the Select Committee on the Kaffir Tribes, August 1851.
23 Sir Andries Stockenström had enjoyed a long period of public service in the colony, beginning at the age of sixteen, when he had acted as interpreter to Lieutenant-Colonel Richard Collins in 1808. He had last served as Lieutenant-Governor on the frontier from 1836 to 1839. During much of his service Stockenström had been a determined critic of Henry Somerset.
24 Both men had served as governor at the Cape, Napier in the years 1838–44 and Maitland between 1844 and 1847.
25 BPP 1635, No. 11, p. 244: Grey to Smith, 21 October 1851.
26 BPP 1635, No. 13, pp. 245–6: Grey to Smith, 14 November 1851.
27 BPP 1635, No. 37, pp. 219–20: Smith to Grey, 18 December 1851.
28 BPP 1635, No. 37, p. 220: Smith to Grey, 18 December 1851.
29 McKay, p. 162.
30 Campbell, p. 48.
31 Campbell, pp. 48–9.
32 King, pp. 144–5.
33 McKay, pp. 163–4.
34 Stapleton, p. 144.
35 McKay, pp. 164ff.
36 BPP 1428, pp. 203–4: Report of General Somerset, 9 November 1851.
37 Baines, p. 245.
38 McKay, p. 167.
39 King, p. 148.
40 King, p. 149.
41 McKay, p. 168.
42 Baines, p. 247.

43 King, p. 150.
44 McKay, p. 170.
45 Baines, p, 247.
46 BPP 1428, pp. 203–4: Report of General Somerset, 9 November 1851.
47 'One of the Ragged Brigade', pp. 592–3.
48 Baines, p. 249; McKay, p. 171. Devenish later died of his wound.
49 King, pp. 151ff.
50 Ricketts died on 8 November 1851 and was interred next to Colonel Fordyce. See G.L.J. Goff, *Historical Records of the 91st Argyllshire Highlanders*, London: Richard Bentley, 1891, p. 183.
51 King, pp. 154–5.
52 BPP 1428, p. 205: Return of casualties, 18 November 1852.
53 BPP 1428, No. 34, p. 202: Smith to Grey, 19 November 1851, and Enclosure 3 in No. 34, pp. 205ff: General Arrangement of Movement, dated 14 November 1851.
54 BPP 1428, Enclosure in No. 38, p. 226: Instructions to General Somerset, 28 November 1851.
55 BPP 279, No. 3, p. 15: D'Urban to Earl of Aberdeen, 19 June 1835.
56 Mostert, p. 1127.
57 Maxwell and McGeogh, p. 169.
58 BPP 1428, Enclosure 3 in No. 34, pp. 205–6: General Arrangement of Movement, 14 November 1851.
59 BPP 1428, No. 38, pp. 221ff.: Smith to Grey, 20 December 1851.
60 BPP 1428, Enclosure 6 in No. 38, p. 227: Instructions to Mackinnon, 28 November 1851.
61 BPP 1428, Enclosure 6 in No. 38, pp. 227–8: Instructions to Eyre, 28 November 1851.
62 BPP 1635, Enclosure 5 in No. 1, p. 10: Somerset to Smith, 4 January 1852.
63 BPP 1635, Enclosure 2 in No. 1, pp. 6ff.: Eyre's reports, 14 and 21 December 1851.
64 Harington, p. 213.

Chapter 10

1 BPP 1635, No. 1, pp. 1ff.: Smith to Grey, 13 January 1852.
2 BPP 1635, No. 1, p. 3: Smith to Grey, 13 January 1852
3 BPP 1635, Enclosure 9 in No. 6, p. 32: Proclamation of 6 February 1852.
4 BPP 1635, No. 10, pp. 62ff.: Smith to Grey, 17 March 1852.
5 *Grahamstown Journal*, 17 February 1852.
6 Sir George Cathcart, *Correspondence of Lieutenant-General the Hon. Sir George Cathcart KCB Relative to Military Operations in Kaffraria . . .*, New York: Negro Universities Press, 1969, Report to the Secretary of State for the Colonies, 11 February 1853, p. 8.
7 'Argyll', 'Action at Nell's [sic] Farm; An Incident of Kaffir War', *United Service Magazine*, November 1861, Pt III, pp. 407ff.
8 McKay, p. 211.

9   'Argyll', p. 410.
10 Based on a description in 'Argyll', p. 411.
11 'Argyll', pp. 410–11.
12 'Argyll', p. 411.
13 'Argyll', pp. 412–13.
14 'Argyll', p. 413.
15 'Argyll', p. 414.
16 McKay, pp. 212ff.
17 'Argyll', p. 414.
18 McKay, p. 213.
19 Patton had been promoted to major on 27 February 1852. See Hart, *New Annual Army List for 1853*.
20 McKay, p. 213.
21 *Grahamstown Journal*, 13 March 1852.
22 The material for this section is taken from BPP 426: Court Martials on the loss of the ship *Birkenhead*, June 1852.
23 It is said that this order was given by Major Alexander Seton of the 74th Regiment, who subsequently lost his own life.
24 BPP 426: statement of Captain Edward R. Wright, 91st Regiment, 1 March 1852, p. 28f.
25 The precise number of crew lost is not known because the muster books were lost in the wreck. Army records of losses were more exact because records of the drafts were kept at the depots, thus the names of the soldiers lost are known.
26 BPP 1635, Enclosure 2 in No. 10, p. 68: Smith's Orders, 8 March 1852.
27 BPP 1635, No. 10, p. 63: Smith to Grey, 17 March 1852.
28 Howard-Vyse Papers, Letter of Lieutenant Hugh Robinson, 16 March 1852.
29 BPP 1635, No. 10, p. 64: Smith to Grey, 17 March 1852.
30 McKay, p. 221.
31 King, pp. 213–14.
32 BPP 1635, No. 10, p. 64: Smith to Grey, 17 March 1852.
33 Letter of Lieutenant Hugh Robinson, 16 March 1852.
34 BPP 1635, No. 10, p. 64: Smith to Grey, 17 March 1852.
35 McKay, p. 221.
36 BPP 1635, No. 10, p. 64: Smith to Grey, 17 March 1852.
37 King, pp. 216–17.
38 BPP 1635, No. 10, p. 65: Smith to Grey, 17 March 1852.
39 'Records of the 2nd Battalion', p. 27.
40 *Grahamstown Journal*, 27 March 1852.
41 McKay, pp. 218–19.
42 BPP 1635, No. 10, p. 65: Smith to Grey, 17 March 1852.
43 BPP 1635, No. 11, p. 69: Smith to Grey, 7 April 1852.
44 Unless otherwise indicated, the material which follows is drawn from BPP 1635, No. 11, pp. 68ff.: Smith to Grey, 7 April 1852.

45 The 'Doorn' River cannot now be specifically identified although the junction of the Thomas and Kei rivers is well known.

46 Meintjes, pp. 209–10.

47 Brownlee, p. 5.

48 Brownlee, p. 6.

49 BPP 1635, No. 11, p. 64: Smith to Grey, 7 April 1852.

50 Baines, p. 232.

Chapter 11

1 Hart, *New Annual Army List for 1851*, London: John Murray, 1851.

2 Cope, pp. 269–70.

3 Mostert, p. 1150. The 'Robinson' to whom he refers is Ensign Hugh Robinson, who was somewhat scathing about Cathcart in his letters home.

4 Cathcart, p. 2.

5 Hart, *New Annual Army List for 1853*, London: John Murray, 1853.

6 Cathcart, p. 1: Cathcart to the Duke of Wellington, 9 January 1852.

7 Hart, *New Annual Army List for 1853*, p. 16.

8 Rivett-Carnac, p. 159.

9 BPP 1635, No. 14, p. 83: Cathcart to Grey, 20 April 1852.

10 King-Hall, pp. 191ff.

11 BPP 1635, No. 14, p. 84: Cathcart to Grey, 20 April 1852.

12 BPP 1635, No. 14, p. 85: Cathcart to Grey, 20 April 1852.

13 BPP 1635, Enclosure 2 in No. 14, p. 87: Proclamation dated 12 April 1852.

14 Cope, p. 274.

15 Lieutenant R., letter to the *Grahamstown Journal*, 8 May 1852. The writer may have been Lieutenant John Ross, the only lieutenant in the Rifle Brigade with that surname initial.

16 Cope, p. 275.

17 Lieutenant R., letter to the *Grahamstown Journal*, 8 May 1852.

18 Cope, p. 275.

19 Mapham dates this engagement to 17 May but the 18th is confirmed in a record by the quartermaster-general, Colonel Cloete, in BPP 1635, Enclosure in No. 23, p. 119: Summary of Reports, 20 May 1852.

20 The above narrative concerning Buller and the artillery is found only in McKay, pp. 239ff. Since McKay was not present, his account may not reflect the truth of what took place.

21 Cope, p. 276.

22 BPP 1635, Enclosure 1 in No. 25: Eye-witness report, 22 May 1852.

23 Mostert, pp. 1004–5.

24 Mostert, p. 1151.

25 Mostert, pp. 1151–2.

26 Cory, pp. 457ff.

27 Cathcart, p. 26.

28 Cathcart, p. 26.

29 Cory, p. 461.
30 McKay, p. 153.
31 BPP 1635, No. 15, pp. 90ff.: Cathcart to Grey, 20 April 1852.
32 BPP 1635, Enclosure in No. 20, p. 106: Memorandum on armed mounted police, 20 May 1852.
33 BPP 1635, No. 20, pp. 103ff.: Cathcart to Pakington, 20 May 1852.
34 BPP 1635, No. 22, pp. 116ff.: Cathcart to Pakington, 20 May 1852.
35 BPP 1635, No. 22, p. 117.
36 Cory, p. 453.
37 BPP 1635, No. 22, p. 117: Cathcart to Secretary of State, 20 May 1852.
38 BPP 1635, Enclosure 1 in No. 24, pp. 121–2: General Order dated 1 June 1852.
39 BPP 1635, Enclosure 2 in No. 24, pp. 122–3: General Order dated 1 June 1852
40 BPP 1635, Enclosure 2 in No. 26, pp. 133ff: Cathcart to Commanding Royal Engineer, 12 June 1851.
41 Cory, pp. 458–9.
42 Cory erroneously gives the date of this engagement as 20 July and not 20 June (Cory, p. 459.)
43 BPP 1635, Enclosure 1 in No. 31, p. 152: General Order dated 27 June 1852. This general order also confirms the date as 20 June.
44 *Grahamstown Journal*, 10 July 1852.
45 BPP 1635, Enclosure 2 in No. 31, p. 152: General Order dated 12 July 1852.
46 King, p. 241.
47 Cope, p. 279.
48 King, p. 242.
49 Cope, p. 279.
50 Lakeman, p. 53.
51 Lakeman, p. 52.
52 Lakeman, pp. 53ff.
53 Lakeman, pp. 55ff.
54 King, p. 242.
55 King, p. 243.
56 King, pp. 243–4.
57 BPP 1635, Enclosure 2 in No. 31, p. 152: General Order dated 12 July 1852.
58 Lakeman, p. 63.
59 King, pp. 245–6.
60 King, p. 245.
61 Lakeman, pp. 64–7.
62 Lakeman, pp. 59, 61.
63 Lakeman, pp. 61–2.
64 BPP 1635, Enclosure 2 in No. 26, pp. 133ff.: Cathcart to Commanding Royal Engineer, 12 June 1851.
65 Lakeman, pp. 61–2.
66 Lakeman, p. 69.

Chapter 12

1   Lakeman, pp. 94–5.
2   King, p. 119.
3   King, p. 271.
4   Maxwell and McGeogh, p. 169.
5   Quoted in Peires, *The Dead Will Arise*, p. 50.
6   BPP 1635, Enclosure 1 in No. 21, p. 110: Cathcart to Sarhili, 14 May 1852.
7   BPP 1635, Enclosure in No. 29, pp. 144–5: Proclamation dated 1 July 1852.
8   BPP 1635, Enclosure in No. 32, pp. 156–7: circular to commissioners, 20 July 1852.
9   BPP 1635, No. 36, pp. 163–4: Cathcart to Pakington, 15 August 1852.
10 Cope, p. 282.
11 BPP 1635, Enclosure 1 in No. 36, p. 165: Minute of conversation with Sarhili's messengers, 9 August 1852.
12 Cope, pp. 282ff. Cathcart called this place the Sabolela Drift.
13 John Crouch was a trader in the Eastern Cape and Transkei for many years. It is also rumoured that he was a government spy.
14 Campbell, pp. 65–6.
15 BPP 1635, No. 36, pp. 163–4: Cathcart to Pakington, 15 August 1852.
16 BPP 1635, Enclosure 2 in No. 38, p. 170: Michel, report, 15 July [sic] 1852.
17 BPP 1635, Enclosure 5 in No. 38, p. 171: Napier, report, 20 August 1852.
18 BPP 1635, No. 38, pp. 167ff.: Cathcart to Pakington, 20 September 1852.
19 Cory, p. 463.
20 BPP 1635, No. 38, p. 167: Cathcart to Pakington, 20 September 1852.
21 Rivett-Carnac, p. 163.
22 Mostert, p. 1156.
23 BPP 1635, Enclosure 7 in No. 38, pp. 171–2: Memorandum of Movements, 10 September 1852.
24 Lakeman, pp. 80–3.
25 Major Hugh Pearse, Journal of Pte John Fisher in 'The Kaffir and Basuto Campaigns of 1852 and 1853', *Rifle Brigade Chronicle*, 1934. (First published in *United Service Magazine*, 1898.)
26 BPP 1635, No. 38, p. 168: Cathcart to Pakington, 20 September 1852.
27 Cope, p. 286.
28 King, p. 260.
29 Campbell, p. 54.
30 King, p. 261.
31 Campbell, pp. 58–9.
32 King, p. 261.
33 King, p. 262.
34 Campbell, pp. 60ff.
35 King, pp. 262–3.
36 Campbell, p. 61.
37 Cope, p. 286.
38 Campbell, p. 61.

39 King, p. 263.
40 Cope, pp. 286–7.
41 Pearse, p. 230.
42 King, p. 263.
43 BPP 1635, Enclosure 8 in No. 38, pp. 172–3: Eyre's report, 18 September 1852.
44 King, pp. 264–5.
45 King, pp. 265ff.
46 King, p. 267.
47 King, p. 268.
48 King, p. 268.
49 BPP 1635, Enclosure 8 in No. 38, p. 173: Eyre's report, 18 September 1852.
50 King, pp. 268–9.
51 King, p. 270.
52 Pearse, p. 231.
53 Cope, p. 288.
54 King, p. 270.
55 Campbell, p. 61.
56 BPP 1635, No. 40, p. 175: Cathcart to Pakington, 12 October 1852.
57 Details of the operations will be found in BPP 1635, Enclosure 1 in No. 48, pp. 205ff. See also Cathcart, pp. 169ff.: Cathcart to Pakington, 18 January 1853.
58 Cory, pp. 476–82.
59 BPP 1635, Enclosure 1 in No. 48, pp. 205ff.
60 BPP 1635, Enclosure 1 in No. 41, pp. 180–1: Meeting with Ndlambe chiefs, 6 October 1852.
61 BPP 1635, Enclosure 1 in No. 41, p. 181: Arrest of Siyolo, 9 October 1852.
62 BPP 1635, Enclosure 3 in No. 41, p. 182: Siyolo's statement of surrender.
63 The 'Drosdty' was the office of the Landdrost. The one in Grahamstown still exists and serves, in part, as an entrance to Rhodes University.
64 BPP 1635, Enclosure 5 in No. 44, p. 197: Announcement of Siyolo's court martial and conviction.
65 Cory, pp. 466–7.
66 BPP 1635, Enclosure 1 in No. 53, p. 231: Proclamation of peace with Sarhili, 14 February 1853.
67 BPP 1635, Enclosure 2 in No. 53, p. 232: Message from Sandile.
68 Cathcart, p. 262: Letter from Maclean to Cathcart, 13 February 1853.
69 Cathcart, pp. 265–6: Proclamation of Sandile's pardon.
70 Cory, p. 468.

Epilogue

1 The disease is now recognised as Contagious Bovine Pleuropneumonia (CBPP) and is caused by Mycoplasma mycoides SC. It was brought to South Africa by means of infected bulls imported from Holland in 1853. The disease is spread by direct droplet infection, especially at watering places and in cattle enclosures.

See *Contagious Bovine Pleuropneumonia (Lungsickness)*, Pretoria: National Department of Agriculture, Directorate Animal Health, 1996.

2 Peires, *The Dead Will Arise*, pp. 93–4.

3 Brownlee, pp. 138–9: letter to Colonel John Maclean, chief commissioner, 28 June 1856.

4 Peires, *The Dead Will Arise*, pp. 99–100. Charles Brownlee thought that she was a ventriloquist: Brownlee, p. 135.

5 Peires, *The Dead Will Arise, passim*.

6 Peires, *The Dead Will Arise*, p. 347.

7 Brownlee, p. 165.

8 Mostert, p. 1241.

9 There is no evidence that the grave thus disturbed was that of Maqoma, the identification of the Robben Island site being made by a traditional Xhosa seer.

10 Brownlee, p. 143.

11 Brownlee, p. 145.

12 Brownlee, p. 146.

13 Brownlee, p. 150.

14 Milton, p. 272.

15 Regimental Museum, Royal Welsh, Brecon, Accession No. BCRM1959.46: *Records of the 1st Battalion 24th Regiment, The Kaffir War 1877–78*, 12 and 18 July 1878.

16 Mostert, p. 1254.

17 Cory, p. 471. Cory was not strictly accurate with his date, which is recorded as Mlanjeni's date of burial in BPP 1969, No. 5: Cathcart to the Duke of Newcastle, 13 September 1853, p. 14.

18 Milton, p. 220.

19 Cathcart, pp. 385–6.

20 Christopher Hibbert, *The Destruction of Lord Raglan: A Tragedy of the Crimean War*, London: Longman & Co., 1984, p. 14.

21 Extract from report of the battle of Inkerman, *London Gazette*, 22 November 1854.

22 Holmes, p. 344.

23 Harington, p. 227.

A Note on Sources

It might perhaps be helpful to give an overview of the principal source of contemporary information used in this work. I refer to those mysterious archives known as the British Parliamentary Papers, or, more properly, sessional papers of the House of Commons.

Sessional papers, often referred to as 'Blue Books' from the colour of their covers, were primarily published for the benefit of Members of Parliament, providing information on matters of policy and administration, and 'ordered by the House to be printed'. They fall into three categories:

1. Bills – drafts of legislation, to be reviewed through various parliamentary stages. If the Bill passed through these stages, it became an Act of Parliament.
2. House Papers – documents resulting from the work of the House and its committees.
3. Command Papers – government papers (from ministers) conveying information or decisions that the government wished to draw to the attention of the House, presented 'by Command of Her Majesty'.

We are concerned here only with the second and third of these categories.

As the parliamentary papers evolved, each of these categories acquired its own unique numerical sequence. Prior to this, from the beginning of the nineteenth century, when papers first began to be bound into sessional volumes, all papers consisted of a single, numbered series, with a new sequence beginning with each session from 1801. The convention adopted here is to show the numbers of house papers in parentheses, thus (424), while command papers are shown in square brackets, thus [1335]. Note too that command papers, which began with a numerical identifier, soon took a series of prefixes, viz., 'C', 'Cmd', etc.

These papers provided an astonishing wealth of detail on the most seemingly trivial matters and the almost unimaginable volume of material thus published exceeded seven thousand volumes for the nineteenth century alone. Nowhere in the world, including the Parliament itself, were all these volumes available in one place. Further, each volume contained very varied material, which made coherent research in them almost impossible.

This was the situation until the decision was made to commit the editors of the Irish University Press to comb through five thousand volumes of the papers (thereby excluding debates) and group the material chronologically by subject matter, with the intention of publishing the most significant of them. Thus came about the Irish

University Press (IUP) publication *British Parliamentary Papers 1800 to 1900*, an enormous archive of more than one thousand volumes, each averaging some seven hundred pages. Each volume contains one or more individual, numbered papers, depending upon their size.

One of these subject categories is 'Colonies' and this includes seventy volumes of material relating to Africa. (Note that Australia is covered in thirty-four volumes and Canada in thirty-three, together still less than the African group.) Those papers relating to the Cape of Good Hope are to be found in volumes 9 to 27. I have been fortunate to locate all the African volumes of this huge undertaking in the bowels of the Library of New South Wales in Sydney, whose staff were ever helpful.

I have chosen to identify references to the papers in the endnotes by citing the paper number, and then their content, rather than only the IUP volume and page, e.g. BPP 424, Enclosure 1 in No. 2, p. 9: Somerset to Smith, 24 February 1851. I trust that this method will enable the reader to locate the quoted material more easily than otherwise.

Bibliography

I. Unpublished Documents
A. The National Archives (TNA), London
Colonial Office papers
CO 879/1/8: Earl Grey to Sir Harry Smith, 13 May 1851, re. Martial Law.
CO 879/1/12: Kafir War.
CO 879/1/13: Copies of confidential letters relating to the formation of two separate colonies within the Cape.

War Office papers
WO 1/447: War Department In-Letters: 3. Colonial Office: Military In-letters: b. Cape of Good Hope: Departmental and Miscellaneous, 1851.

B. Cory Library, Rhodes University, Grahamstown, South Africa
MS779: Blanckenberg, P.B., 'The Treachery at Auckland'.
MS 6806: Extract of a letter from Sir John Wylde, Chief Justice, Cape Town, to Sir Benjamin D'Urban, 24 January 1848.
PR 1478: Captain Stevenson, 'A Terrible Christmas Day', extracts from *Alice Times/ Seymour and Peddie Gazette*, 16 December and 23 December 1920.
Larson, J. Kenneth, History of the Genealogy of the Talbots, Sweetnams and Wiggills, Cory Library, pamphlet box 253.

C. Royal Green Jackets (Rifles) Museum, Winchester, UK
Anon., The Records of 2nd Battalion, King's Royal Rifle Corps.

D. Regimental Museum, Royal Welsh, Brecon, UK.
Accession No. BCRM11959.46, 'Records of the 1st Battalion 24th Regiment: The Kaffir War 1877–78'.

II. Official Publications, British Parliamentary Papers
(279): Cape of Good Hope; Caffre War and Death of Hintza, May 1836.
[786]: Correspondence with the Governor of the Cape of Good Hope relative to the state of the Kaffir Tribes on the Eastern Frontier of the Colony, February 1847.
(457): Copies of the Letters Patent of the 15th day of December 1847, appointing Sir Harry Smith governor of the Cape of Good Hope, and the instructions therewith given.

[912]: Correspondence with the Governor of the Cape of Good Hope relative to the state of the Kaffir Tribes on the Eastern Frontier of the Colony (in continuation of papers presented in February 1847), February 1848.

[969]: Correspondence with the Governor of the Cape of Good Hope relative to the state of the Kaffir Tribes on the Eastern Frontier of the Colony (in continuation of papers presented in February 1848), July 1848.

(217): Transportation – Convicts: Transportation (Cape of Good Hope), 4 April 1849.

[1056]: Correspondence with the Governor of the Cape of Good Hope relative to the state of the Kaffir Tribes on the Eastern Frontier of the Colony (in continuation of papers presented in July 1848), May 1849.

[1059]: Natal: Correspondence relative to the establishment of the Settlement of Natal and the recent rebellion of the Boers (in continuation of papers presented July 1848), 3 May 1849.

[1138]: Despatches relative to the reception of Convicts at the Cape of Good Hope, 31 January, 1850.

[1288]: Correspondence with the Governor of the Cape of Good Hope relative to the state of the Kaffir Tribes on the Eastern Frontier of the Colony (in continuation of papers presented 3 May 1849), 14 August 1850.

[1334]: Correspondence with the Governor of the Cape of Good Hope relative to the state of the Kaffir Tribes and the Recent Outbreak on the Eastern Frontier of the Colony (in continuation of papers presented 14 August 1850), 20 March 1851.

[1352]: Letters from John Montagu, Esq., Colonial Secretary, to B. Hawes, Esq., M.P., Under Secretary of State; Despatches from the Right Hon. Earl Grey, Secretary of State, 20 March 1851.

[1380]: Correspondence with the Governor of the Cape of Good Hope relative to the State of the Kaffir Tribes and the Recent Outbreak on the Eastern Frontier (in continuation of papers presented 20 March 1851), 2 May 1851.

(424): Correspondence with the Governor of the Cape of Good Hope relative to the State of the Kaffir Tribes after the Recent Outbreak on the Eastern Frontier of the Colony (in continuation of papers presented 20 March and 2 May, 1851), June 1851.

(635): Report from the Select Committee on the Kafir Tribes; together with the proceedings of the committee, minutes of evidence, appendix, and index, 2 August 1851.

[1428]: Correspondence with the Governor of the Cape of Good Hope relative to the state of the Kaffir Tribes and the Recent Outbreak on the Eastern Frontier of the Colony (in continuation of papers presented 20 March, 2 May, June 1851), 3 February 1852.

[1635]: Correspondence with the Governor of the Cape of Good Hope relative to the state of the Kafir tribes, and to the recent outbreak on the eastern frontier of the colony (in continuation of papers presented 20 March, 2 May, June 1851, 3 February 1852), 31 May 1853.

(124): Return of the white and coloured population of the Colony of the Cape of Good Hope, in the several Districts of the Eastern and Western Divisions, and also of British Kaffraria, according to the latest Returns received at the Colonial Office, 27 February 1852.

(89): South Africa. Further returns of the number of Her Majesty's troops who have been employed in South Africa, in each year since 1843:– and, of the general abstract of the expenditure by Great Britain on account of South Africa, for each year since 1843 (similar to part of Parliamentary Papers, nos 224 and 239, of session 1849), 20 February 1852.

(426): Court Martials on the loss of ship *Birkenhead*, 3 June 1852.

(258): Troops, &c. (South Africa). Returns of the number of Her Majesty's troops who have been employed in South Africa, in each year since 1849–50:– and, of the general abstract of the expenditure by Great Britain on account of South Africa, for the year 1850–51 (in continuation of Parliamentary Paper, no. 683, of session 1851, and no. 89, of session 1852), 18 March 1853.

III. Newspapers

London Gazette, 1851.
Alice Times/Seymour and Peddie Gazette, 1920.
Grahamstown Journal, 1850–2, 1920.
Eastern Province Herald, 1850.

IV. Books and Compilations

Baines, Thomas, *Journal of Residence in Africa*, Vol. II, ed. R.F. Kennedy, Cape Town: Van Riebeeck Society, 1961.

Bisset, John Jarvis, *Sport and War: Or Recollections of Fighting and Hunting in South Africa from the Years 1834 to 1867*, London: John Murray, 1875.

Brown, Rev. George, *Personal Adventure in South Africa*, London: James Blackwood, 1855.

Brownlee, Charles Pacalt, *Reminiscences of Kaffir Life and History*, Lovedale: Lovedale Mission Press, 1896.

Campbell, Peter S., *Reminiscences of the Kaffir Wars*, Walthamstow: Duck Bros, n.d.

Cathcart, Sir George, *Correspondence of Lieutenant-General the Hon. Sir George Cathcart KCB Relative to Military Operations in Kaffraria . . .*, New York: Negro Universities Press, 1969; originally published London: John Murray, 1856.

Coetzee, C.G., *The Unfortified Military Villages of Sir Harry Smith, 1848–1850*, Cape Town: Westby Nunn, 2010.

Cope, Sir William H., *History of the Rifle Brigade*, London: Chatto & Windus, 1877.

Cory, Sir George E., *The Rise of South Africa: A History of the Origin of South African Colonial Development towards the East from the Earliest Times to 1857*, Vol. V, London: Longmans, Green, 1930.

Dalbiac, Capt. P.H., *History of the 45th: 1st Nottinghamshire Regiment*, London: Swan Sonnenschein, 1902.

De Kok, W.J. (ed.), *Dictionary of South African Biography*, Vol. II, Cape Town: Human Sciences Research Council, 1977.

Duminy, A.H., et al. (eds), *The Reminiscences of Richard Paver*, Cape Town: A.A. Balkema, 1979.

Ex-CMR, *With the Cape Mounted Rifles: Four Years' Service*, London: Richard Bentley & Son, 1881.

Godlonton, R. and Irving, E., *A Narrative of the Kafir War of 1850–51–52*, Cape Town: Struik, 1962.

Goff, G.L.J., *Historical Records of the 91st Argyllshire Highlanders*, London: Richard Bentley, 1891.

Gordon, R.E., *Shepstone: The Role of the Family in the History of South Africa, 1820–1900*, Cape Town: A.A. Balkema, 1968.

Harington, A.L., *Sir Harry Smith: Bungling Hero*, Cape Town: Tafelberg Publishers, 1980.

Hart, Major H.G., *New Annual Army List for 1851*, London: John Murray, 1851.

—— *New Annual Army List for 1853*, London: John Murray, 1853.

Hibbert, Christopher, *The Destruction of Lord Raglan: A Tragedy of the Crimean War*, London: Longman & Co., 1984.

Holmes, Richard, *Redcoat: The British Soldier in the Age of the Horse and Musket*, London: Harper Collins, 2001.

Hook, D.B., *With Sword and Statute: On the Cape of Good Hope Frontier*, Cape Town: J.C. Juta, 1905.

King, William Ross, *Campaigning in Kaffirland: Or Scenes and Adventures in the Kaffir War of 1851–1852*, London: Sauders & Otley, 1883.

King-Hall, L. (ed.), *Sea Saga, Being the Naval Diaries of Four Generations of the King-Hall Family*, London: Gollanz, 1935.

Lakeman, Sir Stephen, *What I Saw in Kaffirland: The Kaffir War 1850–53*, London: William Blackwood & Son, 1880.

Le Cordeur, Basil and Saunders, Christopher, *The War of the Axe, 1847*, Johannesburg: Brenthurst Press, 1981.

Lehmann, Joseph, *Remember you Are an Englishman: A Biography of Sir Harry Smith*, London: Jonathan Cape, 1977.

Levinge, Sir Richard George Augustus, *Historical Records of the Forty-Third Regiment, Monmouthshire Light Infantry*, London: Clowes & Sons, 1868.

Lucas, T.J., *Camp Life and Sport in South Africa: Experiences of Kaffir Warfare with the Cape Mounted Rifles*, London: Chapman & Hall, 1878; reprinted by Africana Book Society Ltd, Johannesburg 1975.

McKay, James, *Reminiscences of the Last Kaffir War*, Cape Town: Struik, 1970.

Marks, Shula and Atmore, Anthony (eds), *Economy and Society in Pre-Industrial South Africa*, London: Longman, 1980.

Maxwell, W.A. and McGeogh, R.T., *The Reminiscences of Thomas Stubbs*, Cape Town: A.A. Balkema, 1978.

Meintjes, Johannes, *Sandile: The Fall of the Xhosa Nation*, Cape Town: T.V. Bulpin, 1971.

Milton, John, *Edges of War: A History of Frontier Wars 1702–1878*, Kenwyn: Juta & Co. Ltd, 1983.

Mitford-Barberton, I., *Comdt. Holden Bowker*, Cape Town: Human & Rousseau, 1970.

Moodie, Donald (ed.), *The Record, Or a Series of Official Papers Relative to the Condition and Treatment of the Native Tribes of South Africa*, Cape Town: A.A. Balkema, 1960.

Moore-Smith, G.C. (ed.), *The Autobiography of Lieut.-General Sir Harry Smith*, London: John Murray, 1902.

Mostert, Noël, *Frontiers: The Epic of South Africa's Creation and the Tragedy of the Xhosa People*, London: Jonathan Cape, 1992.

Mqhayi, S.E.K., *Abantu Besizwe*, ed. and trans. J. Opland, Johannesburg: Wits University Press, 2009.

Peires, J.B., *The House of Phalo: A History of the Xhosa People in the Days of their Independence*, Berkeley: University of California Press, 1981.

——*The Dead Will Arise: Nongqawuse and the Great Cattle-Killing Movement of 1856–7*, Jeppestown: Jonathan Ball, 2003.

Ransford, Oliver, *The Great Trek*, London: John Murray, 1972.

Rivett-Carnac, Dorothy E., *Hawk's Eye*, Cape Town: Howard Timmins, 1966.

Staples, Isaiah, *A Narrative of the Eighth Frontier War of 1851–1853*, ed. J. de Villiers, Pretoria: State Library, 1974.

Stapleton, Timothy, *Maqoma: Xhosa Resistance to Colonial Advance, 1798–1873*, Johannesburg: Jonathan Ball, 1994.

Sweetman, John, *War and Administration: The Significance of the Crimean War for the British Army*, Edinburgh: Scottish Academic Press, 1984.

Taylor, A.J.P., *War by Time-Table*, London: McDonald & Co., 1969.

Theal, G.M., *History of South Africa from 1795 to 1872*, Vol. III, London: Allen & Unwin, 1919.

—— *Records of the Cape Colony from February 1793 to December 1796*, Vol. I, Cape Town: Government of the Cape Colony, 1897.

Walker, Eric A. (ed.), *The Cambridge History of the British Empire. Vol. VIII: South Africa, Rhodesia and the High Commission Territories*, London: Cambridge University Press, 1963.

Ward, Harriet, *The Cape and the Kaffirs: A Diary of Five Years' Residence in Kaffirland*, London: Henry G. Bohn, 1851.

V. Journal and Other Articles

'Argyll', 'Action at Nell's Farm: An Incident of Kaffir War', *United Service Magazine*, Part III, November 1861.

Baker, Marian, 'Grog and Black Raw Beef', *Military History Journal*, Vol. 14, No. 4, December 2008.

Bell, Lt C.H., 'The Eighth Kaffir War', *Africana Notes & News*, Vol. IV, No. 4, September 1947.

'Diary of No. 1366 Pte Thomas Scott, XIIth Regiment 1839–1869: Kaffir War 1851–1853', *Suffolk Regimental Gazette*, April–July 1814.

Gawler, Col. J.C., 'British Troops and Savage Warfare, with Special Reference to the Kafir Wars', *Royal United Services Institute Journal*, Vol. 17, 1874.

Harington, Andrew L., 'Sir Harry Smith', *Journal of the South African Military History Society*, Vol. 3, No. 1, June 1974.

Herbst, J. and Kopke, D., 'Site of the Battle of Amalinde', *Military History Journal*, Vol. 13, No. 5, June 2006.

Henderson, Robert, 'Loading and Firing British Muskets during the Crimean War 1854–56', www.military heritage.com, accessed 22 January 2010.

'The Journal of Lt-Col. John Scott', *Journal of the South African Military History Society*, Vol. 1, No. 5, December 1969.

Kirk, Tony, 'Progress and Decline in the Kat River Settlement, 1829-1854', *Journal of African History*, Vol. 14, 1974.

Malherbe, V.C., 'The Khoekhoe soldier at the Cape of Good Hope; Life and Times in the Cape Regiment c. 1806 to 1870', *Journal of the South African Military History Society*, Vol. 12, No. 4, December 2002.

Napier, Colonel, 'The Present Kaffir War', *United Service Magazine*, Part II, July 1851.

'One of the Ragged Brigade', 'Operations in the Waterkloof', *United Service Magazine*, Part I, April 1852.

Pearse, Major Hugh, Journal of Pte John Fisher in 'The Kaffir and Basuto Campaigns of 1852 and 1853', *Rifle Brigade Chronicle*, 1934. (First published in *United Service Magazine*, 1898.)

Ralph, Sarah, 'Diary', *Martello Magazine*, Fort Beaufort Museum, Nos 3–6 inclusive.

Saks, D.Y., 'A Forgotten Battle of the Frontier Wars', *Journal of the South African Military History Society*, Vol. 9, No. 4, December 1993.

Saks, David, 'Hunting Maqoma', *Military History Journal*, Vol. 13, No. 4, December 2005.

Index